*Advance Praise for*

ON SETTLER COLONIALISM IN CANADA: LANDS & PEOPLES

"This pathbreaking volume exposes unsettling truths at the heart of Canadian settler colonialism in a broader global context of imperialism and genocide. Through a decolonial lens of Indigenous resistance and resurgence, essays investigate how settler colonial identities rooted in historical myths of empire, racial superiority, and multiculturalism adapt over time to perpetuate structural and relational violence against Indigenous peoples and territorial lands. A thought-provoking and insightful 'must read' for all those seeking reconciliation based on truth, justice, and accountability."
—**PAULETTE REGAN**, author of *Unsettling the Settler Within* and former research director for the Truth and Reconciliation Commission of Canada

"Groundbreaking in the depth and scope of its engagement with all aspects of the structuring principle of settler colonialism, this volume is essential reading for Canadians. A major contribution to the literature."
—**ROBERTA RICE**, Professor and Department Head of Political Science, University of Calgary, and series editor of *Global Indigenous Issues*

"This book holds many complicated truths about the inequality of the colonial experience, about implicit and explicit violence, and unceasing pragmatic resistances. The authors bring together multiple perspectives and stories, and they explore hard-edged questions for Indigenous, Black, Chinese, French Canadian, settlers, and of course, mixed peoples. Some of the issues are the lethal Starlight Tours, Indigenous women's challenges, denialism, TRC strategies, and most importantly, they ask: Where do we go from here?"
—**VAL NAPOLEON**, Professor and Law Foundation Chair of Indigenous Justice and Governance, University of Victoria

# On Settler Colonialism in Canada

## Lands & Peoples

EDITED BY

David B. A. MacDonald
& Emily Grafton

*Afterword by* Jeremy Patzer

Printed and bound in Canada. The text of this book is printed on 100% post-consumer recycled paper with earth-friendly vegetable-based inks.

Cover art: "Glacial Erratic" by David Garneau, 2020, 58.5 x 58.5 cm, acrylic on canvas.
Cover design: Evan Marnoch
Page design and layout: John van der Woude, JVDW Designs
Copyeditor: Rachel Ironstone
Proofreader: Ryan Perks
Indexer: Patricia Furdek

**Library and Archives Canada Cataloguing in Publication**

Title: On settler colonialism in Canada : lands and peoples / edited by David B. A. MacDonald & Emily Grafton ; afterword by Jeremy Patzer.
Names: MacDonald, David Bruce, editor | Grafton, Emily (Emily Katherine), editor.
Description: Includes bibliographical references and index.
Identifiers: Canadiana (print) 20250158116 | Canadiana (ebook) 20250158248 | ISBN 9781779400659 (hardcover) | ISBN 9781779400642 (softcover) | ISBN 9781779400666 (EPUB) | ISBN 9781779400673 (PDF)
Subjects: LCSH: Settler colonialism—Canada. | LCSH: Canada—Ethnic relations. | LCSH: Canada—Race relations.
Classification: LCC FC104 .O564 2025 | DDC 971.004—dc23

10 9 8 7 6 5 4 3 2 1

University of Regina Press, University of Regina
Regina, Saskatchewan, Canada, S4S 0A2
TEL: (306) 585-4758 FAX: (306) 585-4699
WEB: www.uofrpress.ca

We acknowledge the support of the Canada Council for the Arts for our publishing program. We acknowledge the financial support of the Government of Canada. / Nous reconnaissons l'appui financier du gouvernement du Canada. This publication was made possible with support from Creative Saskatchewan's Book Publishing Production Grant Program.

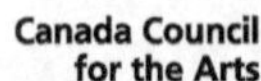

# Contents

PART FOUR
## Asserting Indigenous Knowledges in Settler Colonial Canada

# Acknowledgements

We have been working on this book for several years and are grateful for the help, advice, and support of many people. This book project was supported by a SSHRC Connection Grant in Fall 2022, which helped bring together numerous contributors to the University of Regina, First Nations University of Canada, and the mâmawêyatitân centre. A series of gatherings, in person and virtual, were held and culminated in this book and a second one nearing publication.

Specifically, we would like to thank kēhtē-ayak Alma Poitras, a chapter contributor to the second book, for thoughtfully opening and closing the 2022 gatherings in a good way. Thank you to Desmond McAllister for your passionate and inspirational steel pan performance. A very special thank you to Dr. Jérôme Melançon, book contributor and co-applicant to the SSHRC grant, who provided valuable support for the planning and facilitation of these gatherings. We also extend a thank-you to Solomon Ratt for allowing us to reprint some of his excellent and compelling poetry.

Our thanks to Karen Clark, Elsa Johnston, and Rachel Stapleton at University of Regina Press, their production team, and to our three anonymous reviewers. Everyone helped to make this book stronger and more focused.

We also express deep gratitude to the research assistants who have helped us stay on track over these years, navigating the Covid-19 pandemic (and its many viral waves), meeting funding deadlines and reporting, communicating with contributors, planning and facilitating our 2022 gatherings, and staying on top of chapter collection and organization: Ibukun Fasunhan, Alyssa Parker, and Hannah Tait of University of Regina; and Clare McKendry and Lauren Fillier of University of Guelph.

• • •

**David B. A. MacDonald**: My work is funded by two SSHRC Insight Grants, 430413 and 430855, and I thank the University of Guelph for their support. Also, much of this was written while I was a visiting fellow at the Auckland Law School, hosted by Te Puna Rangahau o te Wai Ariki / Aotearoa Centre for Indigenous Peoples and the Law in New Zealand, and later as an honorary academic in Politics and International Relations, Faculty of Arts, University of Auckland. I would like to thank my wife, Dana, and son, Gulliver, for their love and support—thanks, family! I was raised in Regina, and when coming back to my hometown, I stayed with my parents and sister, who have always taken an interest in this work: thank you, Mom (Olive), Dad (Bruce), and Rachel. My mom travelled from Barrackpore, Trinidad, to Regina in 1964. She was descended from Indian indentured labourers and spent her childhood in the rural south of Trinidad before studying at Luther College in Regina, where she obtained her BA degree. Mom was always interested in Indigenous Peoples and issues, took a keen interest in the work of the Truth and Reconciliation Commission, and really enjoyed coming to our conference dinner in 2022 and meeting many of the contributors. I dedicate my work on this book to her, commemorating her passing in June 2023.

**Emily Grafton**: I thank my parents, Wayne and Jonine, for my early childhood in Winnipeg's inner city, an experience that made me curious and passionate about the politics of Canada. I am especially indebted to my father's stories of our Métis ancestors, the Lafrenières, and this expansive family. I married into the Smith family, my invitation to Treaty 4 where I now reside. This move brought the ever-evolving and expanding gift of family, and I am most grateful to my husband, Matt, and children, Sebastian and Elliotte. Above all, I dedicate this book to my children in my ever-optimistic hopes for the Canada they will grow up in.

# Contributor Biographies

**Malissa Bryan** is a Black queer intersectional feminist researcher and scholar with a background in work, gender, race, and education studies. Malissa is a passionate equity, diversity, and inclusion specialist and advocate who supports individuals and organizations in adopting anti-oppressive practices. Malissa is the founder and CEO of the Rainbow Diversity Institute, a consulting firm that focuses on increasing awareness and support for EDI initiatives and training. Malissa also sits on the University of Guelph's Presidential Advisory Committee on Anti-Racism and is a co-lead of the Sexual and Gender Diversity cluster at the Live Work Well Research Centre. Malissa's MA thesis focused on racialized collectives in predominantly white institutions, examining the experiences of Black students and Black collectives in these spaces. Malissa is currently completing a PhD in sociology focusing on race, Black and Caribbean mothers, education, and work-life balance.

**James Daschuk** is a settler scholar living as a guest in Treaty 4 territory for almost thirty years. He is an associate professor in the Faculty of Kinesiology and Health Studies at the University of Regina. Jim has a PhD in Canadian History from the University of Manitoba. His research experience includes the fields of medicine, climate change, and population health. He is currently a researcher with SPHERU (Saskatchewan Population Health and Evaluation Research Unit). His book *Clearing the Plains: Disease, Politics of Starvation, and the Loss of Aboriginal Life* (University of Regina Press, 2013) won five Saskatchewan Book Awards and three prizes from the Canadian Historical Association, including the Governor General's Award for Scholarly Achievement in 2014.

**Karine R. Duhamel** is of Anishinaabe and mixed European ancestry, and is an off-reserve status member of Opwaaganisiniing (Red Rock Indian Band). Her education includes an MA and PhD in History from the University of Manitoba. She has worked in legal research, in museum curation, and in elementary and post-secondary education. She served as director of research for Canada's historic National Inquiry into Missing and Murdered Indigenous Women and Girls, and as chair of the MMIWG2S+ National Action Plan Data Working Group, which produced the MMIWG2S+ Data Strategy. Currently, Karine is the director of Indigenous strategy for SSHRC. She is also a member of the Project Advisory Council for Debwewin: The Oakville Truth Project (Oakville, Ontario), a member of the Iswewak Awetowak Nipocawin (Women Leading Knowledge) Advisory Council (Winnipeg, Manitoba), and works to support the Treaty Relations Commission of Manitoba as a frequently requested speaker on the spirit and intent of treaty relationships.

**Bernie Farber** has focused a career spanning more than three decades on human rights, diversity, and countering antisemitism and extremism. Recognized and called upon as an expert in human and civil rights, he is one of the few in the field to be accepted by Canadian courts as an expert in hate crime, white supremacy, and extremism. His efforts have been documented in numerous Canadian human rights publications, books, films, newspapers, and magazines, and in academic publications. He has successfully run large NGOs and foundations such as Canadian Jewish Congress, the Paloma Foundation, and the Mosaic Institute. Originally from Ottawa, Ontario, he is a published author and writes for various Canadian newspapers and other publications. He is the founding chair of the Canadian Anti-Hate Network and a past chair of Community Living Toronto's Rights and Ethics Committee. He is a former member of the federal government's expert advisory group on online safety.

**Emily Grafton** (Métis Nation) has a PhD in Native Studies from the University of Manitoba (Winnipeg). She worked for several years in differing orders of government, including the Manitoba Legislative Assembly, Assembly of Manitoba Chiefs, and City of Regina. In addition, Emily has held leadership roles related to Indigenous Peoples and decolonial movements, including as the research-curator of Indigenous content at the Canadian Museum for Human Rights (Winnipeg, Manitoba); executive lead, Indigenization; and later the Indigenous research lead at University of Regina. She is currently an associate professor of Politics and International Studies at the University of Regina, where her work concerns settler colonialism, reconciliation, Indigenous research practices, and feminist theories. Emily is a faculty advisor for the Saskatchewan Electoral Parity Project and board member for the Canadian Political Science Association (CPSA). She has a forthcoming book with Fernwood Publishing entitled *Divided Power: How Federalism Undermines Reconciliation*.

**Joyce Green** is a professor emerita of Political Science (retired) at the University of Regina. She is the editor of the first two editions of *Making Space for Indigenous Feminism* (2007, 2017) and of *Indivisible: Indigenous Human Rights* (2014) through Fernwood Publishing. She currently lives in ʔa·kiskaqǂi ʔit—"where two trails meet on the prairie" (known in English as Cranbrook, BC), in ʔamakʔis Ktunaxa—the unceded and stolen territory of the Ktunaxa Nation. She is a citizen of the Ktunaxa Nation and a member of Yaq̓it ʔa·knuqǂiʔit (Tobacco Plains Indian Band). Dr. Green is of English, Ktunaxa, and Cree-Scots Métis ancestry.

**Fazeela Jiwa** has writing published in anthologies as well as magazines such as *This*, *Ricepaper*, *Understorey*, *filling Station*, *Plenitude*, and *TOPIA*. She is an acquisitions and development editor with Fernwood Publishing and received the Tom Fairley Award for Editorial Excellence from Editors Canada in 2023. She is frequently invited to participate in events about writing and editing such as those curated by the Festival of Literary Diversity, the Writers' Union of Canada, the Social Sciences and Humanities Research Council of Canada, and the Association of Canadian Publishers.

**Peter Kulchyski** is a professor in the Department of Indigenous Studies at the University of Manitoba in Winnipeg. He has published extensively on northern Indigenous history, law, politics, and culture in Canada. Among his books are *Like the Sound of a Drum: Aboriginal Cultural Politics in Denendeh and Nunavut* (University of Manitoba Press, 2005) and *Report of an Inquiry Into an Injustice: Begade Shutagot'ine and the Sahtu Treaty* (University of Manitoba Press, 2018). His forthcoming book with Henry Heller, *Mode of Production: The Final Horizon of Practice and Theory*, takes a theoretical approach to a variety of issues, including those pertaining to Indigenous cultural politics.

**Chris Lindgren** is an Anishinaabe father from Tootinaowaziibeeng Treaty Reserve 292, which is located on Valley River 63A Reserve in Manitoba. Chris is a Sixties Scoop survivor born in Rossburn, Manitoba, in 1966 and adopted out to a family in Minnesota in 1971. Chris reconnected with his birth family when he was a young adult. Chris has been a long-haul transport driver for twenty-eight years and is currently collaborating on a documentary about his brother, Neil Stonechild, and the Starlight Tours.

**David Bruce Amichand MacDonald** is an Indo-Trinidadian and Scottish settler-academic from Treaty 4 territory, Saskatchewan, and is descended from Girmitiyas (indentured labourers). He is professor of Political Science at the University of Guelph and an honorary academic at the University of Auckland. He was previously a faculty member at the University of Otago and École Supérieure de Commerce de Paris. He shares a SSHRC Insight Grant on Indigenous self-determination with co-researcher Sheryl Lightfoot. He has authored numerous books, academic articles, and book chapters on Indigenous-settler relations, comparative genocide studies, and comparative foreign policy in CANZUS states. His publications include *The Sleeping Giant Awakens: Genocide, Indian Residential Schools, and the Challenge of Conciliation* (University of Toronto Press, 2019) and the co-edited *Populism and World Politics: Exploring Inter- and Transnational Dimensions* (Palgrave, 2019). He has a PhD in International Relations from the London School of Economics.

**Rebecca Major** is an associate professor and Northern Governance research chair at Yukon University, specializing in Indigenous Governance. She is a Métis and Mi'kmaq academic, with a background that also includes settler ancestries. Rebecca holds a PhD in Public Policy from the University of Saskatchewan and has expertise in Indigenous Public Policy and institutional change. She has worked as a policy analyst at the Métis Nation–Saskatchewan (MN-S) and served at the local and provincial levels of the MN-S, focusing on supporting Métis community members. She also taught for nearly a decade at NORTEP (Northern Teacher Education Program) for the University of Saskatchewan before spending six years at the University of Windsor Political Science Department. Rebecca's background in academic research and engagement with Métis communities enhances her expertise and capacity to contribute to advocacy efforts.

**Desmond McAllister** is a pannist hailing from Regina, Saskatchewan. He draws much of his talent from his rich and diverse cultural background—specifically that of his mother's birthplace, Trinidad and Tobago, where the steel pan was invented. He plays a mix of calypso, soca, chutney, reggae, R&B, and pop music—and he's always willing to expand his repertoire. Desmond is also the director, arranger, and founder of Regina's Pacesetters Steel Orchestra.

**Jérôme Melancon** is a professor of Philosophy at the University of Regina. He has recently published journal articles on colonization, racialization, intercultural relationships, social and economic positions, and the role of francophones, all in relation to settler colonialism in Canada. He is the co-editor of two journal issues of the *Cahiers franco-canadiens de l'Ouest* on marginalization, privilege, and Indigenization within francophone communities. He is also the author of the book *La politique dans l'adversité: Merleau-Ponty aux marges de la philosophie* (Métispresses, 2018) and has edited four journal issues or books on the philosopher Maurice Merleau-Ponty. His current research includes a focus on anti-colonial thought and movements, as well as on the Indian residential school system in Canada and on the ideas and history of the Catholic Church in relation to these residential schools.

**Liam Midzain-Gobin** is an assistant professor in the Department of Political Science at Brock University. A settler scholar, his research focuses on the ongoing reproduction of settler colonialism as well as Indigenous governance and decolonization. He is author of *Settler Colonial Sovereignty: Visions of Improvement and Indigenous Erasure* (2025) and his work has also been published in *Millennium*, *Security Dialogue*, *Borderlands*, and elsewhere. He also serves as associate editor at *Critical Studies on Security*.

**Ajay Parasram** is a transnational multigenerational by-product of the British Empire, with roots in South Asia, the southern Caribbean, and the settler cities of Vancouver, Ottawa, and Halifax. He is an associate professor of Colonialism, Postcolonialism, and Development in the Departments of International Development Studies and History at Dalhousie University, Kjipuktuk (Halifax, Nova Scotia). Ajay's research surrounds questions of the colonial present, the many ways through which historical colonial encounters and entanglements continue to limit freedom and decolonization. He has recently focused on structural white supremacy, pluriversal sovereignty, and the ethical and political requirements of decolonization. He is the author of *Pluriversal Sovereignty and the State: Imperial Encounters in Sri Lanka* (Manchester University Press, 2023) and co-author (with Alex Khasnabish) of *Frequently Asked White Questions* (Fernwood Publishing, 2022). Find him online at ajayparasram.com.

**Jeremy Patzer** is an associate professor in Sociology and Criminology at the University of Manitoba. From his maternal side of the family, he is Indigenous from the West Interlake region of Manitoba (Métis and Saulteaux/Anishinaabe). His research interests lie in Indigenous Rights (particularly in settler state courts), the forms of legal-political resolution and repair employed by settler states in the wake of colonial dispossession, as well as the sociology of law and contemporary theory. He is currently developing a research project bridging (socio)legal and political scholarship on Indigenous Rights, seeking to study the perspectives of Indigenous Rights advocates, leaders, and claimants in Commonwealth settler states as they perceive and navigate the relative opportunities, obstacles, and strategies for advancing Indigenous Rights through the adjacent fields of law and politics.

**Solomon Ratt** has been a professor of Cree language and literature at the First Nations University of Canada for over thirty years. His work has been essential to keeping the Cree language alive in Saskatchewan and across Canada. Solomon is from the community of Stanley Mission in Northern Saskatchewan, and although he was sent to the Indian residential school in Prince Albert as a child, he managed to keep his Cree fluency into adulthood. Solomon has written and published many textbooks for teaching the Cree language, such as *mâci-nêhiyawêwin / Beginning Cree*, and several books of Cree stories, in addition to translation. His 2023 memoir, *kâ-pî-isi-kiskisiyân / The Way I Remember*, was published by University of Regina Press. In 2024, he was appointed a Member of the Order of Canada. To view more visit *www.creeliteracy.org*.

**Len Rudner** is a former director of community relations and outreach for the Centre for Israel and Jewish Affairs, and a former regional director for Canadian Jewish Congress. He has spoken at international and domestic conferences focusing on Holocaust education, antisemitism, and the balance of hate speech and freedom of speech. He is qualified as an expert witness in criminal proceedings relating to hate crimes. Len sits on the advisory committee of the Canadian Anti-Hate Network and is a former member of the Ontario Anti-Racism Directorate. *We Resist: Defending the Common Good in Hostile Times*, a collection of essays to which Len has contributed, was published by McGill-Queen's University Press in the summer of 2020. He is a recipient of the Queen's Diamond Jubilee Medal for community service.

**Paul Simard Smith** is a citizen of the Métis Nation–Saskatchewan and was born and raised in Regina, Saskatchewan. His Métis family comes from Meadow Lake, Saskatchewan, with roots in the Qu'Appelle Valley and in the Saint François Xavier (White Horse Plain) community of the Red River in Manitoba. He is currently an assistant professor in the Department of Philosophy and Classics at the University of Regina. His general areas of research specialization are in Epistemology and Metaphysics, as well as Social and Political Philosophy, especially the Philosophy of Law. He is actively involved in several research projects that draw on concepts found within theoretical and normative areas of analytical philosophy to help shed light on the injustices involved within colonial political orders and to envision more ethical and just political relationships between Indigenous nations and states.

**Michelle Stewart** is a professor at the University of Regina who focuses on racialized practices in the justice and child welfare systems. As project lead for the Integrated Justice Program, Michelle works with a team writing specialized court reports meant to address the over-representation of Indigenous Peoples in the justice system. Michelle identifies as being neurodiverse and was raised as a settler. Michelle is an applied community-based scholar and forensic social scientist. Michelle places equity and collaboration at the centre of their projects and uses evidence-based practices and intersectional analysis to address the ongoing impacts of settler colonialism and structural inequality.

**Angie Wong** is a second-generation Chinese person born in Canada and a first-generation scholar of the humanities. She teaches Asian Canadian Histories and Settler Colonial, Social Justice, Gender, and Postcolonial

Theory. Angie is an adjunct assistant professor in Community Health Sciences at the University of Calgary and senior consultant on Indigenous health at Alberta Health Services.

**Andrew Woolford** is professor of Sociology and Criminology at the University of Manitoba, an emeritus member of the Royal Society of Canada College, and former president of the International Association of Genocide Scholars. He is author of *This Benevolent Experiment: Indigenous Boarding Schools, Genocide, and Redress in Canada and the United States* (University of Manitoba Press, 2015) and *Between Justice and Certainty: Treaty Making in British Columbia* (UBC Press, 2005), as well as co-author of *The Politics of Restorative Justice: A Critical Introduction* (Fernwood Publishing, 2019) and *Informal Reckonings: Conflict Resolution in Mediation, Restorative Justice and Reparations* (Routledge, 2005). He is co-editor of *Did You See Us?: Reunion, Remembrance, and Reclamation at an Urban Indian Residential School* (University of Manitoba Press, 2021), *Canada and Colonial Genocide* (Routledge, 2017), *The Idea of a Human Rights Museum* (University of Manitoba Press, 2015), and *Colonial Genocide in Indigenous North America* (Duke University Press, 2014). He has worked on two community-based research projects with residential school Survivors: Embodying Empathy and Remembering Assiniboia. He has recently initiated a project on human and more-than-human relations within genocidal processes under the title "Genocide with Nature."

INTRODUCTION

# Critical Engagements with Canadian Settler Colonialism

## *Colonization, Land Theft, Gender Violence, Imperialism, and Genocide*

David B. A. MacDonald and Emily Grafton

WELCOME TO OUR BOOK ON INDIGENOUS-SETTLER relations in settler colonial Canada. Our main research focus is to explore, from a range of critical perspectives, how contemporary society in Canada can come to terms with the problems inherent to settler colonialism: ongoing processes of colonization, gender violence, land theft, genocide, the suppression of Indigenous voices and institutions, and the destruction of our lands, waters, plants, and animals, with which we are interdependent. Both editors are political scientists, one Métis (Emily) and the other Indo-Trinidadian and Scottish mixed race (David). Our expertise as well as our own life journeys and perspectives inform how we have structured and presented this book and the one to follow. Our two books are coming out at different times; each is a stand-alone volume, but we have designed them to be complementary. This book, coinciding with the tenth anniversary of the Truth and Reconciliation Commission of Canada's *Final Report* (2015), is rooted primarily in Canada's past and present, laying the basis for understanding many aspects of Indigenous-settler relations today. We recall the words of former Truth and Reconciliation Commission chair, the late Justice Murray Sinclair (Anishinaabe, Peguis

First Nation): "The truth will set you free, but first it will piss you off."[1] This book and the truths it offers will address some of the key problems of settler colonialism in Canada, including the ongoing dispossession of Indigenous Peoples, and it should, if successful, help you understand why change needs to take place in our country.

This book showcases a range of contributors who represent the diversity of our country, featuring perspectives from Indigenous Peoples; Black, mixed-race, and other racialized peoples; queer people; and white European-descended settlers. While many settlers were raised with the narrative that Canada was a kind, generous, and peaceful place to live, this has not been the lived experience of many Indigenous Peoples. Indeed, settlers have been taught to buy into what feminist critical race scholar Sherene Razack terms a "fantasy" view of national history, insofar as settler Canadians tend to disavow notions of conquest, invasion, and genocide in favour of myths of peaceful settlement.[2] This doesn't mean we cannot be optimistic and work towards change. However, it does mean we need to be realistic, and can join nêhiyaw political scientist Kiera Ladner in concluding that "reconciliation is not a great big hug." Instead, it "requires settler society to acknowledge and accept some really uncomfortable truths about how they acquired their privileges. It requires settler society to cede the privilege it has denied Indigenous Peoples."[3]

It is fair to say that we and our contributors may make some readers uncomfortable (maybe even unsettled), but this is an important part of learning to appreciate the distinct truths of living in a country that consciously divides by its colonizing structures. At least historically there have been fundamental perceptive differences between many Indigenous Peoples and settler Canadians about how the country was founded and why. There are also marked differences in opinion about how benign the country is and how universal and acceptable are its institutions. Ladner has noted, "For Indigenous Peoples, the story of Canada is one of myth, magic, deceit, occupation, and genocide. For Canadians, the story is one of discovery, lawful acquisition, and the establishment of peace, order, and good governance."[4]

Our second book, scheduled for release in early 2026, offers some insights for progressive change, ways that we might form solidarities and relationalities. It will explore in some detail issues like the return of stolen Indigenous Land, settlers working to promote treaty relationships, solidarity between white settlers and Indigenous Peoples, solidarities between Indigenous, Black, and other racialized peoples, and some ways that Indigenous Peoples can promote self-determination. Our second book will also highlight Indigenous laws, cultures, and understandings of self-determination. Both books were written during the era of Justin Trudeau's federal liberal government and went through final edits during his resignation and the federal election in early 2025. We are now in a new era with Mark Carney's minority liberal government and a growing economic and political challenge from south of the Canadian border.

## Indigenous Peoples and Settler Colonialism

We now turn to definitions and discussion of the key terms we will use in this volume, followed by an outline of the four sections of our book, as well as summaries of our contributor chapters and their foci. Currently, Indigenous nations are in 40 percent of the world's countries, constituting about 476 million people or 5 percent of the global population.[5] While Indigenous Peoples have been systematically marginalized in settler states, they have organized collectively to promote their inherent rights, domestically, across borders, and internationally through regional organizations and the United Nations. The United Nations Declaration on the Rights of Indigenous Peoples (adopted by the UN in 2007 and incorporated into federal Canadian law in 2021) was the result of many decades of deliberation, negotiation, and consensus decision-making, laying out a minimum standard of Indigenous Rights. Indigenous Peoples have in many cases been subjected to genocidal actions by colonizing states, which means their populations suffered dramatic demographic losses, have been alienated from the majority of their ancestral lands and waters, and may have lost key aspects of their languages, spiritual practices, governance structures, and other indicia of group identity. Forcible transfer out of the group through residential schooling or the removal of children by child welfare agencies has reduced knowledge of Indigenous identities amongst some Indigenous Peoples.[6]

How can we define who is Indigenous? Definitions are contested, but we can make a general claim that all Indigenous Peoples have long-standing practices for defining themselves and setting parameters for inclusion through citizenship rules or various kinship practices. However, due in large part to a long and complex history and the continued realities of colonization, many Indigenous Peoples do not seek an official legal definition, because creating strict criteria can exclude some people from consideration. This is especially so in a climate where many governments want to avoid recognizing Indigenous Peoples, seeing their existence as a challenge to state sovereignty.[7] Nevertheless, there are definitions we can use as a shorthand to help us better understand. The United Nations (in 1981) identified Indigenous Peoples by such attributes as maintaining a "historical continuity with pre-invasion and pre-colonial societies that developed on their territories," and "consider[ing] themselves distinct from other sectors of the societies now prevailing on those territories, or parts of them." They are further identified as being non-dominant, seeking to "preserve, develop and transmit to future generations their ancestral territories, and their ethnic identity, as the basis of their continued existence as peoples, in accordance with their own cultural patterns, social institutions and legal system."[8]

In the case of Canada and other settler colonial states, we can also say that Indigenous Peoples are subject to specific modes of political, legal, social, economic, and territorial domination derived from Europe. Instead of Indigenous self-determination and autonomy (which Indigenous Peoples had before and, in many ways, still practise since colonization), settlers as the numerical majority are largely in control of the state, its intuitions, and its norms. This control has important implications for Indigenous identities. Part of settler state control is the power to define who is and who is not Indigenous within Canadian territory. Indeed, the Canadian state, according to the *Constitution Act, 1982*, recognizes three classifications of "Aboriginal" peoples: First Nations, Inuit, and Métis. Within the First Nations category, the state has divided Indigenous Peoples into those with "status" and those without. Numbers of Indigenous Peoples are growing due to higher birth rates and an increase in self-identification.[9] The 2021 census indicates that there are 1,807,250 Indigenous Peoples in Canada, including 1,048,405 First Nations, 624,220 Métis, and 70,545 Inuit. All of these population numbers have grown considerably since the last census in 2016 (on average by 9.4 percent versus 5.3 percent growth for all non-Indigenous populations). This is about 5 percent of the overall Canadian population. Indigenous Peoples are and have always been diverse, with over seventy Indigenous languages, more than six hundred First Nations, a number of groups as part of the Métis Nation, and Inuit peoples divided into four regions and approximately fifty communities, the majority living in their homeland:

Inuit Nunangat.[10] Many Indigenous Peoples also live in urban centres across Canada. Inuit, First Nations, and Métis have differing homelands, linguistics, cultural practices, and specific ways of knowing; while we often discuss Indigenous Peoples in Canada in juxtaposition to settler populations, within these groups are innumerable distinctions, and these are not homogenous nations.

The largest group of Indigenous Peoples are First Nations with treaty status, those with recognized membership in one of the 630 First Nations located on one or more of the 3,394 reserves located within the territory of what is now Canada. Having status means in most cases being subject to the *Indian Act*, a political instrument that has reduced the political power and numbers of Indigenous Peoples by dividing them into bands and imposing on them a settler colonial administrative and political structure.[11] As a tool of colonial control, the *Indian Act* has denied status to some First Nations people through regulatory mechanisms. These mechanisms are in flux and, briefly, have included past state practices such as attending post-secondary education, moving off-reserve, or when women marry people who do not have Indian status; in these scenarios, many have lost their status under the *Indian Act*. Today, some have been able to restore this status, but many First Nations people live in Canada as non-status and are not recognized with Aboriginal status or its corresponding benefits. Inuit and Métis Peoples can be understood differently as they do not have Indian status and are not subject to the *Indian Act*, though they are understood as Indian under the *British North America Act, 1867*. Inuit have been understood as such since the landmark legal case *Re:Eskimo* (1939) and the Métis since the case *R. v. Daniels* (2016).

As individual contributors note, Indigenous Peoples in Canada have been marginalized because of the continued colonization of their territories and bodies. While 7.7 percent of all children in Canada are Indigenous, Indigenous children make up 53.8 percent of all kids in foster care. There are gaps in education, which are especially pronounced at the university level, where non-Indigenous Peoples are twice as likely to have a university degree or higher.[12] For adults, there is a gross overrepresentation of Indigenous Peoples in prisons (relying on 2018 statistics). In federal institutions, 28 percent of inmates are Indigenous men, though they represent only 4.1 percent of the total population. For Indigenous women, it is worse at 40 percent incarcerated, while representing only 4 percent of women in Canada.[13]

Disparities in determinants of health between Indigenous Peoples and settlers have long been tracked, with Indigenous women being particularly at risk. The TRC identified eleven key areas where disparities were most acute, including lower life expectancy, poorer access to medical and mental health care services, and higher rates of poverty, unemployment, addiction, suicide, poor housing, and food insecurity.[14] As the medical journal *The Lancet* concluded, these problems result from settler state policies and practices: "Indigenous Peoples face systemic issues, including racism, discrimination, and bias within institutions (eg, hospitals and health-care facilities) related to this historical context, which have not stopped after the closure of the last residential school."[15]

## Being Trauma Informed and Genocide Aware

This book is trauma informed, meaning that we deliberately foreground the intergenerational legacies of settler colonial violence on Indigenous Peoples, laws, lands, waters, and communities. Our work is also genocide aware, in that we recognize that genocide against Indigenous Peoples has taken place in the creation and maintenance of Canada as a settler state. Both the editors have been members of the Canadian Political Science Association Reconciliation Committee, which has recognized at least fourteen instances of genocide in Canada. We do not believe the state is a neutral or benign actor, and we bring this perspective into the book. Furthermore, this book is written in the shadow of many conflicts around the world, including the Russian invasion of Ukraine, the ongoing violence and death in Gaza, repressive misogynist rule in Afghanistan under the Taliban, and further conflicts in Sudan, Yemen, Ethiopia, the Sahel, Haiti, and Burma/Myanmar, amongst other places.[16]

At the same time, we emphatically do not see Indigenous Peoples as primarily victims. We heed the injunction of Eve Tuck (Unangax̂, St. Paul Island) to avoid "damage-centered research" and "deficit models," which see Indigenous Peoples as "broken" and Indigenous communities as "sites of disinvestment and dispossession."[17] Instead, she calls for research that centres the strength, "survivance," and self-determination of Indigenous Peoples within a context of colonialism, occupation, and genocide.[18] Kanien'kehá:ka anthropologist Audra Simpson has rightly critiqued a tendency to present Indigenous Peoples as "injured claimant[s]... whose 'prior' is suffering, rather than sovereignty, or the injustice of stolen land

and stolen selves."[19] The point here is that while it is accurate in some ways to use terms such as *victim* and *survivor*, Indigenous Peoples "are also nationals of Indigenous political orders."[20]

The larger context of this book is ongoing genocide, which is a theme volume co-editor David develops in his chapter. The term *genocide* was coined in 1944 by Raphaël Lemkin, who described it as "a coordinated plan of different actions aiming at the destruction of the essential foundations of the life of national groups, with the aim of annihilating the groups themselves."[21] The 1948 United Nations Convention on the Prevention and Punishment of the Crime of Genocide, which flowed from Lemkin's efforts, defines genocide as follows:

> Any of the following acts committed with intent to destroy, in whole or in part, a national, ethnical, racial or religious group, as such:
> (a) Killing members of the group;
> (b) Causing serious bodily or mental harm to members of the group;
> (c) Deliberately inflicting on the group conditions of life calculated to bring about its physical destruction in whole or in part;
> (d) Imposing measures intended to prevent births within the group;
> (e) Forcibly transferring children of the group to another group.

The TRC concluded in its 2015 *Final Report* that Canada was guilty of cultural genocide in the operation and maintenance of the Indian residential schools (1880s to the 1990s). This was a type of genocide that involved coercive forms of assimilation:

> For over a century, the central goals of Canada's Aboriginal policy were to eliminate Aboriginal governments; ignore Aboriginal rights; terminate the Treaties; and, through a process of assimilation, cause Aboriginal peoples to cease to exist as distinct legal, social, cultural, religious, and racial entities in Canada.[22]

From 2016 to 2019, the National Inquiry into Missing and Murdered Indigenous Women and Girls carried out hearings throughout Canada, documenting the violence of the settler state, especially against Indigenous women and girls, who are twelve times more likely to go missing or be killed than other women in Canada.[23] In 2019, they highlighted a "race-based genocide of Indigenous Peoples, including First Nations, Inuit and Métis, which especially targets women, girls, and 2SLGBTQQIA people."[24] Genocide as defined by the UN Convention was eventually recognized by Canadian Parliament in late 2022. Specifically, a non-binding motion was passed in the House of Commons recognizing that Article 2e of the UN Convention had been violated when Indigenous children were forcibly transferred to Indian residential schools. Some have also suggested that the Sixties Scoop can be seen as genocide. From the 1930s and '40s, thousands of Indigenous children were taken from their parents and sent for adoption or to foster homes, the majority to white homes. At the Scoop's height, one in four status First Nations children were removed from their parents.[25]

## Settler States and Settlers

Settler states are not defined in international law, but social scientists identify these as states where the majority of the population are descended from those who colonized and settled territories originally inhabited and controlled by Indigenous Peoples. Processes of settlement were often violent, with European colonizers primarily focused on asserting control of territory so that lands and waters—indeed anything that could be commodified as "natural resources"—were claimed by the state.[26] Patrick Wolfe has referred to a "logic of elimination" as a key aspect of settler colonialism, where Indigenous societies are dissolved, to be replaced by "a new colonial society on the expropriated land base."[27]

Yes, settler states are often democratic, but the voting power of the settler majority can be used to actively suppress Indigenous Peoples and their institutions.[28] Bear in mind that the rules of the game and the institutions wherein those rules apply were established by settlers after they had dismantled—but did not destroy—Indigenous forms of government and law and had taken most Indigenous Lands and waters. Robert Jago (Kwantlen First Nation and Nooksack) highlights a constant problem, the overriding of Indigenous Rights by settlers: "With their majority, their control over our lands and resources seems natural and is granted democratic cover. With their pursuit of the greatest good for the greatest number, so-called democracy ensures this works against us."[29]

How can one best define who is a settler? We share Métis writer and lawyer Chelsea Vowel's suggestion to understand *settler* as a "relational term," signifying those who engage in the "deliberate physical occupation of land as a method of asserting ownership over land and resources."[30] Settlers, as Stó:lō scholar Dylan Robinson observes, can also be defined as those who bear "intergenerational responsibility" for "intergenerational perpetration."[31] This can help us understand that whether settlers are newly arrived in Canada, have no European ancestry, or can trace their ancestry within Canada back many generations, settler choices right now are embedded within settler colonial structures that determine whether we are contributing to ongoing problems of colonization or working to roll back and alleviate those problems.

At the same time, we need to be careful about generalizing. Aaron Mills (Waabishki Ma'iingan, Baatwetang) reminds us that settlers and Indigenous Peoples are not simply one thing or another, existing in a binary relationship. Many people have Indigenous and settler ancestry and identify with one or both groups. The key issue for Mills is not so much a label but rather what view of reality we adopt, whether it be a settler view of the earth as property and commodity, or an "earth-centred Anishinaabe view of treaty constitutionalism," which can frame a role for settlers within Indigenous legal traditions instead of those derived from Europe.[32]

## A Triangular Understanding of the Settler State and Society

Certainly, the playing field for those living in the Western settler state is not level. Lorenzo Veracini has identified a triangular relationship between white settlers, Indigenous Peoples, and racialized people, including Black people.[33] Settler states have historically pursued policies of othering Indigenous Peoples while also historically restricting the entry of non-Europeans. This creates a system run by European settlers where other groups of people are largely excluded from political power and from the ability to influence how political institutions and national identity are shaped. As Veracini puts it: "Settlers are *founders* of political orders and carry their sovereignty with them." He differentiates these from migrants, who "can be seen as *appellants* facing a political order that is already constituted." Certainly, he notes that migrants can be "individually co-opted within settler colonial political regimes," but contrary to European settlers, they do not enjoy the same presumed inherent rights and sense of sovereign entitlement.[34]

The role of non-Europeans as settlers in Canada is contested, and there is arguably no one-size-fits-all model. Many people of colour have been marginalized and for much of the early history of Canada were barred entry based on racist immigration laws. This feeling of not fully belonging is all the more salient for Black Canadians, who continue to be the target of carding, police shootings, and other egregious racist policies.[35] The term *arrivant* has often been used for Black people to make the point that millions of Africans were enslaved and brought to what are now the Americas against their will. The ancestors of many Black people did not choose to come to "Canada" or the "Americas" and consequently may have a different relationship to the state. Certainly, of course, others did make the choice and left Africa or elsewhere in the twentieth century and after.

Arguably, people of colour can and do express solidarities with Indigenous Peoples and can share some experiences of settler racism, and yet, people of colour may echo settler stereotypes of Indigenous Peoples as part of their journey to integrate into what they understand as mainstream Canada. Melissa Phung notes, for example, that "assimilated people of colour can produce similar settler colonial narratives in order to emplace their settler belonging on Indigenous lands."[36] For Bonita Lawrence and Enakshi Dua, racialized people must recognize that while they may experience structural racism, they nevertheless maintain "colonial relationships" with Indigenous Peoples. This is not to position racialized groups and white settlers as equals but to understand that everyone has choices and responsibilities and that the parameters of choice are often the result of unequal structures wherein people are differentially embedded. Racialized peoples, then, despite darker pigmented skin tones and colonial histories, "live on land that is appropriated and contested."[37] These definitions and discussions will be useful to keep in mind. In what follows, we will briefly sketch out the contributions in our book, which we have divided into four thematic sections.

Section 1 is entitled "Considering Violence and Genocide in the Canadian Settler State" and focuses on institutions of settler colonialism and their inbuilt violence towards Indigenous Peoples, which can at times be genocidal. The first chapter, by Karine Duhamel (Anishinaabe-Métis), begins with an exploration of the public framing of transitory discourse around Indigenous women, girls, and 2SLGBTQQIA+ people, whose very presence is seen as temporary and fleeting, tacitly excusing the violence against them that results. Karine is strongly critical of the deficit-based approach to understanding violence as a product of personal choice. Drawing on testimonies of those who offered their truths before the National Inquiry into Missing and Murdered Indigenous Women and Girls, Karine (who was research director of the inquiry) signals the importance of understanding violence as a crisis that is centuries in the making, with intergenerational root causes: colonial structures, ideas, and norms. Karine emphatically states that we must fully reject the normalization of violence. She calls for a fundamental shift, and a social reflexivity that acknowledges the importance of intergenerational trauma and the ways in which it has normalized violence. This shift must work to mobilize crisis as critique, rather than to reaffirm current approaches and policies towards violence.

Following this is a chapter by James Daschuk, which opens evocatively by discussing the hanging of eight Indigenous men in North Battleford in 1885, a shockingly violent and public crime by the state. This was used to demonstrate Canada's power, while reducing the agency and power of Indigenous nations in what is now Saskatchewan. James ably documents ways that genocide was committed against Indigenous Peoples through overt violence, starvation, discriminatory laws, forcible transfer into residential schools, and other means. He debunks myths of peaceful settlement and a just society, noting how the weight of these crimes continues "to fuel trauma from generation to generation."

Next, book co-editor David B. A. MacDonald engages with the contradiction that while Canada may be one of the world's most genocide-aware countries, the state has an extremely poor legacy of actually initiating concrete policies to stop ongoing genocide against Indigenous Peoples. His chapter explores several types of genocide in Canadian history before tracing out the long road towards genocide recognition through the work of Indigenous activists and scholars, the TRC, the NIMMIWG, and the 2022 motion through Parliament. He argues that the current federal government has at best engaged in a patchwork of reconciliation reforms, often pursuing an agenda that is more focused on a neo-colonial neoliberal agenda.

This section also features a chapter by Malissa Bryan, who puts into conversation Black Canadian voices with white settlers, Indigenous Peoples, and racialized people. She articulates Black arrivant experiences as being distinct from those of racialized settlers and promotes forms of solidarity with Indigenous Peoples against white patriarchy and dominance. Malissa notes important commonalities between Black and Indigenous Peoples in terms of criminalization, violence, and general disdain. Signally, the extraction of Indigenous Peoples' lands in collaboration with the exploitation of Black labour and the criminalization of Black bodies creates an ideal environment for potential Black and Indigenous solidarity and resistance.

We conclude this section with Angie Wong's rich historical analysis of early Chinese arrivants in settler colonial Canada. Angie explores the almost insurmountable obstacles for Chinese people seeking to immigrate to Canada, focusing on gender as a key variable for analysis. She highlights the hardships faced by early Chinese immigrants, offering critical analysis of poetry and other works written inside interment centres and other carceral locations. Gender is a key focus, as the *Chinese Immigration Acts* of the early twentieth century allowed only Chinese men in, excluding women, and thus socially engineered the interactions held between white settlers and early arrivants.

The second section of our book is entitled "Logics of Empire, Colonialism, and Unsettlement." We start with a chapter by Liam Midzain-Gobin, which delves into issues of mixed race and positionality and deals with linkages between multiculturalism, empire, and colonization. Liam offers an important contextualization of Canada as part of British imperial networks and a larger project of "possessive white supremacy." He also looks at the concept of Brown implicatedness in settler colonialism. Canada has become less white, but in many respects just as colonizing. This chapter suggests different possible trajectories for Brown settlers. One option can be to uphold and entrench white possessiveness, or one can act as "co-conspirators alongside Indigenous Peoples to interrupt settler colonialism and build a decolonial future."

We then turn to "A Contribution to Periodizing Settler Colonial History in Canada," in which Peter Kulchyski offers an innovative way to understand settler colonialism as a structure of dominance through periodizing settler colonial Canadian history. Peter suggests that traditional concepts of colonial dominance have been conceptualized by spatial difference, in that Indigenous Peoples, colonizers, and settlers are understood to occupy differing geographical locations. Peter offers a new periodization of settler colonial history influenced by French theorist Jean-Paul Sartre's "progressive-regressive" method.

In the third chapter of this section, Ajay Parasram focuses on white supremacy and how people of colour can be complicit and internalize white domination and norms in their quest to fit into a settler colonial order. Intergenerational forms of surviving and resisting white supremacy can include the normalization of many aspects of white settler society. This enables a thin and fragile sense of cultural distinctiveness within the dominant white settler state structure. Ajay is interested in understanding how the intergenerational and transnational experiences we carry may inadvertently fuel systemic white supremacy and further the ongoing colonization of Indigenous Peoples. What he calls "imperial refraction" makes South Asian people "desirable" in the context of multicultural settler colonial nationalism. He problematizes the concept of the "model minority," which places the burden of integration and accommodation squarely on the newcomer to conform and show gratitude to the white settler order.

In his contribution, Andrew Woolford explores how settler identities are fashioned from, and quite often against, the more-than-human world. His specific focus is on settler relationships with water—indeed, how settlers became settlers by taking from and working against water. Andrew effectively draws on his childhood memories of learning about water individually, and he contrasts this with Anishinaabe collective identity formation processes that take place alongside and with water. A central part of this chapter is exploring how Indian residential schools sought to destroy Anishinaabe relationships with nibi (or waters) and assimilate Indigenous Peoples to settler water regimes, which promoted an artificial separation between people and water. He calls for settlers to unsettle themselves by rediscovering a "liquid symbiogenesis," recognizing the vibrancy of water and its multiple roles in what it means to be human.

Our third section, entitled "Settler Colonial Society—Relating, Reckoning, and Unreconciliation," features five contributions. In their powerful chapter, Chris Lindgren (Saulteaux First Nation, Neil Stonechild's brother and a Sixties Scoop survivor) and settler scholar Michelle Stewart engage in dialogue and discussion rooted in their own positionalities. Their focus is the legacy of the infamous Starlight Tours—a form of racialized policing that targeted Indigenous Peoples and resulted in freezing deaths in Canada. This chapter offers searing detail and discussion concerning the freezing death of seventeen-year-old Neil Stonechild in 1990. Taken from his Indigenous mother and adopted by a white family, Chris later reconnected with his family, and in this chapter he engages with his brother Neil's death and the Starlight Tours through the lens of his lived experiences. Michelle acknowledges her white privilege and has worked on issues related to systemic racism and racialized policing. Fundamentally, this conversation is about settler colonialism. Agreement does not erase distinction, social location, fragility, and settler colonialism.

Next, Fazeela Jiwa introduces the idea of identity as displacement and movement rather than settlement, drawing from her family history within South Asian communities, where peoples moved around within the British Empire. Displacement, rather than settlement, becomes a key to identity as it has led to estrangement from what it meant to have place-based, linguistic, and religious-focused identities.

Based on a deep engagement with his own French-Canadian background, Jérôme Melançon analyzes settler colonialism through minority francophone communities in the next chapter. Jérôme argues that French Canadians have experiences of being conquered by the British but are also colonizers in their own right. He critically dissects the purportedly pro-Indigenous and even quasi-Indigenizing claims of some French Canadians and looks at a series of myths that have been spread over many centuries. These include the belief that French people were gentler to Indigenous Peoples relative to British colonizers, creating a borderless and inclusive relationship characterized by métissage and a francophone move to innocence. These myths serve a colonizing function towards newcomers, who are subjected to (sometimes racist) processes of assimilation into French language, culture, and religion, what we could call "francisation."

The next contribution is a short reflection by mixed-race Indo-Trinidadian and white settler Desmond McAllister, who focuses on the complexity of mixed-race identities and the challenges of not being white and mainstream in 1970s and '80s Regina, a settler colonial environment marked by white supremacy and widespread racism. An important aspect of this engagement is the key role of music in building friendships and alliances within and outside of one's own community.

Finally, Bernie Farber and Len Rudner offer two perspectives on Jewish Canadian identity and the role of witnessing, standing up, and recognizing Indigenous genocide. The authors are in dialogue and share similarities but also differences in their earlier lack of knowledge about settler colonialism. They trace their changes in mentality and discuss how Jewish Canadians and other settlers must do more to prevent further genocide, noting powerfully that since "the genocide against Indigenous Peoples in

Canada has not yet come to an end, then as settlers we have a responsibility to be upstanders rather than perpetrators or bystanders."

In our final section, "Asserting Indigenous Knowledges in Settler Colonial Canada," we open with two poems by Cree language and literature professor (and IRS survivor) Solomon Ratt: "Stolen Childhood" and "asastîwa—They pile up." The first chapter of this section is Joyce Green's "Being and Knowing Home," which offers a detailed focus on Indigenous Rights and relationality in settler colonial Canada. This heartfelt and deeply moving chapter explores the genocidal implications of settler colonialism on the unceded, ancestral, stolen, and occupied ʔamakʔis Ktunaxa territory of the Ktunaxa people. Joyce currently lives in ʔa·kiskaqǂiʔit—"where two trails meet on the prairie" (known in English as Cranbrook, BC), in ʔamakʔis Ktunaxa—the unceded and stolen territory of the Ktunaxa Nation. She is a citizen of the Ktunaxa Nation and a member of Yaq̓it ʔa·knuqǂiʔit (Tobacco Plains Indian Band), and is of English, Ktunaxa, and Cree-Scots Métis ancestry. Joyce calls strongly for change and recounts her journey to reconnect with her Ktunaxa culture, language, and history. She highlights challenges for many Indigenous Peoples: "Living as an authentic person in the conditions of political and personal contradiction and complexity is, for me, a life work still in progress."

In the next chapter, Métis scholar Rebecca Major offers a focus on violence by the settler state and its institutions against Indigenous Peoples, with a crucial focus on Indigenous women. Rebecca critiques the routine associations of Canada with politeness and kindness, and she focuses on the many aspects of Canadian life we are not supposed to talk about. These include the ways in which Indigenous Peoples are targeted with medical abuse and neglect (and the overtly gendered bias against women and girls herein), the biased use of "wellness checks" on Indigenous Peoples, the racist policing of the RCMP, forced sterilizations, and "birthing alerts" that can often lead to the removal of Indigenous children from their mothers.

Following this, Métis scholar Paul Simard Smith deploys Canada's own constitutional standards to unpack and reveal the hypocrisy of the settler state. He uses Canada's constitutional order as a lens through which to see if the country satisfies its own standards of legitimacy. For Canada's constitutional order to be legitimate according to its own standards, it is necessary for the state's fundamental laws, policies, and institutions to be justified from the perspective of Indigenous legal traditions. However, this is not the case, rendering Canada's constitutional order illegitimate from Indigenous perspectives.

In the final chapter of this section, Métis scholar and volume co-editor Emily Grafton provides an overview of Indigenous Rights and how these continue to exist but have also not been upheld by the Canadian state. Exercising these rights, she argues, is fundamental to resisting colonization. She makes the crucial point that settler colonial states are premised on the erasure of Indigenous Peoples, and we can see the mechanics of erasure through various economic, political, and social modes. The rights of Indigenous Peoples can be misperceived by settlers as jeopardizing the settler state and its settler citizenry and, therefore, are a political sphere that the state attempts to minimize. Yet, the state does recognize various Indigenous Rights, such as inherent rights based on specific relationships with lands, distinct languages and cultures, and long-standing governance and social structures and practices. Emily also outlines Indigenous Peoples' rights in settler Canada as codified by the state, whilst, throughout Canada's history, the state has sought to assimilate Indigenous Peoples and circumvent their rights.

Finally, Métis and Saulteaux/Anishinaabe scholar Jeremy Patzer provides a thoughtful and reflective afterword, noting the distinct and critical paths the authors follow in this volume. Jeremy concludes with the view that the richness of the volume "is testament to the richness of the contemporary critical scholarly engagement with settler colonialism, be this through the burgeoning fields of Indigenous studies and settler colonial studies or from scholars in traditional disciplines who share space and common cause with these." As editors, we sincerely hope that this volume offers thought-provoking, innovative, and diverse reflections on the history and current state of Indigenous-settler relations in settler colonial Canada and encourages you to not only find out more but to act to promote a better future.

## Notes

1 Kennedy, "Q and A: Murray Sinclair."
2 Razack, "Introduction," 2.
3 Ladner, "150 Years and Waiting," chap. 10.
4 Ladner, "Take 35," 279.
5 United Nations, "Indigenous Peoples."
6 MacDonald, *The Sleeping Giant Awakens*.

7 Chen, "Indigenous Rights."
8 Castellino, "International Law and Self-Determination," 33–34.
9 Galloway, Bascaramurty, and Maki, "Census 2016."
10 Statistics Canada, "Indigenous Population."
11 Palmater, *Beyond Blood*, 166–167.
12 Statistics Canada, "National Indigenous History Month 2023."
13 Government of Canada, "Overrepresentation of Indigenous People."
14 Toth, "Indigenous Healthcare in Canada."
15 Durand-Moreau, Lafontaine, and Ward, "Work and Health Challenges."
16 International Crisis Group, "10 Conflicts to Watch in 2024."
17 Tuck, "Suspending Damage," 409, 412.
18 Tuck, "Suspending Damage," 415, 422.
19 Simpson, "Sovereignty, Sympathy, and Indigeneity," 76.
20 Simpson, "Sovereignty, Sympathy, and Indigeneity," 83–84.
21 Lemkin, *Axis Rule in Occupied Europe*, 27–28.
22 Truth and Reconciliation Commission, *Canada's Residential Schools*, 3–4.
23 National Inquiry into Missing and Murdered Indigenous Women and Girls [NIMMIWG], *Reclaiming Power and Place*, 52–53.
24 NIMMIWG, *A Legal Analysis of Genocide*, 1.
25 Episkenew, *Taking Back our Spirits*, 67; Liebenberg and Ungar, *Resilience in Action*, 296.
26 Glenn, "Settler Colonialism as Structure."
27 Wolfe, "Settler Colonialism."
28 Bauder and Mueller, "Westphalian vs. Indigenous Sovereignty," 5–7.
29 Jago, "Their Country, Our Land."
30 Vowel, *Indigenous Writes*, 16.
31 Robinson, "Intergenerational Sense," 63.
32 Mills, "What Is a Treaty?," 210.
33 Veracini, *Settler Colonialism*, 14.
34 Veracini, *Settler Colonialism*, 3.
35 Cole, *The Skin We're In*.
36 Phung, "Are People of Colour Settlers Too?," 294.
37 Lawrence and Dua, "Decolonizing Anti-Racism," 120–143, 134.

## Sources

"10 Conflicts to Watch in 2024," International Crisis Group, January 1, 2024, https://www.crisisgroup.org/global/10-conflicts-watch-2024#sudan.

"Indigenous Peoples at the United Nations," United Nations Department of Economic and Social Affairs, 2021, https://www.un.org/development/desa/indigenouspeoples/about-us.html.

"Indigenous population continues to grow and is much younger than the non-Indigenous population, although the pace of growth has slowed," *Statistics Canada*, September 21, 2022, https://www150.statcan.gc.ca/n1/daily-quotidien/220921/dq220921a-eng.htm?indid=32990-1&indgeo=0.

"National Indigenous History Month 2023 ... by the numbers," *Statistics Canada*, last modified June 2, 2023, https://www.statcan.gc.ca/en/dai/smr08/2023/smr08_273.

"Overrepresentation of Indigenous People in the Canadian Criminal Justice System," Government of Canada, January 20, 2023, https://www.justice.gc.ca/eng/rp-pr/jr/oip-cjs/p3.html.

*A legal analysis of genocide: Supplementary report of the National Inquiry into Missing and Murdered Indigenous Women and Girls*, National Inquiry into Missing and Murdered Indigenous Women and Girls, 2019, 1.

Bauder, Harald, and Mueller, Rebecca. "Westphalian Vs. Indigenous Sovereignty," *Geopolitics* 26, no. 3 (2021): 5–7.

Castellino, Joshua. "International Law and Self-Determination," in *Self-Determination and Secession in International Law*, eds. C. Walter et al. (Oxford University Press, 2014), 33–34.

Chen, Cher Weixia. "Indigenous Rights in International Law," *Oxford University Press* (2017), https://oxfordre.com/internatinoalstudies/view/10.1093/acrefore/978-190846626.001.00001/acrefore-97801990846626-e-77.

Cole, Desmond. *The Skin We're In: A Year of Black Resistance and Power* (Doubleday Canada, 2020).

Durand-Moreau, Quentin, et al. "Work and health challenges of Indigenous people in Canada" *The Lancet* 10, no. 8, (2022), https://doi.org/10.1016/S2214-109X(22)00203-0.

Episkenew, Jo-Ann. *Taking back our Spirits: Indigenous Literature, Public Policy and Healing* (University of Manitoba Press, 2009), 67; Linda Liebenberg and Michael Ungar, *Resilience in Action* (University of Toronto Press, 2010), 296.

Galloway, Gloria, and Bascaramurty, Dakshana. "Census 2016," *Globe and Mail*, 25 October, 2017, https://beta.theglobeandmail.com/news/national/census-2016-highlights-diversity-housing-indigenous/article36711216/?ref=http://www.theglobeandmail.com.

Glenn, Evelyn Nakano. "Settler Colonialism as Structure," *Sociology of Race and Ethnicity* 1, no. 1 (2015): 54–74.

Jago, Robert. "Their Country, Our Land: Why Indigenous peoples have a problem with #Canada150," January 2, 2017, https://mediaindigena.com/their-country-our-land-why-indigenous-peoples-have-a-problem-with-canada150/.

Kennedy, Mark. "Q and A: Murray Sinclair on how residential schools taught aboriginal children they were 'heathens,'" *Ottawa Citizen*, September 26, 2014, https://ottawacitizen.com/news/politics/q-and-a-murray-sinclair-on-how-residential-schools-taught-aboriginal-children-they-were-heathens.

Ladner, Kiera. "150 Years and Waiting Will Canada Become an Honourable Nation?" in *Surviving Canada: Indigenous Peoples Celebrate 150 Years of Betrayal*, eds. Kiera Ladner and Myra Tait (Arbeiter Ring, 2017) chap. 10. Kindle.

Ladner, Kiera. "Take 35: Reconciling Constitutional Orders," in ed. A.M. Timpson, *First Nations, First Thoughts: The Impact of Indigenous Thought in Canada* (University of British Columbia Press, 2009), 279.

Lawrence, Bonita, and Dua, Enakshi. "Decolonizing Anti-Racism," *Social Justice* 32, no. 4 (2005): 120–143, 134.

Lemkin, Raphael. *Axis Rule in Occupied Europe: Laws of* (Carnegie Endowment for International Peace, 1944), 27–28.

MacDonald, David B. A. *The Sleeping Giant Awakens* (University of Toronto Press, 2019).

Mills, Aaron. "What is a Treaty: On Contract and Mutual Aid," in *The Right Relationship: Reimagining the Implementation of Historical Treaties*, eds. John Borrows and Michael Coyle (University of Toronto Press, 2017), 210.

Palmater, Pamela D. *Beyond Blood: Rethinking Indigenous Identity* (University of British Columbia Press, 2011), 166–67.

Phung, Melissa, "Are People of Colour Settlers Too?" in *Speaking My Truth*, eds. Shelagh Rogers, Mike DeGagné, Jonathan Dewar and Glen Lowry (Aboriginal Healing Foundation, 2013), 294.

Razack, Sherene. "Introduction: When Place Becomes Race" in *Race, Space, and the Law: Unmapping a White Settler Society*, ed. Sherene Razack (Between the Lines, 2002), 2.

*Reclaiming Power and Place: The Final Report of the National Inquiry into Missing and Murdered Indigenous Women and Girls*. National Inquiry into Missing and Murdered Indigenous Women and Girls, 2019, Web Archive. https://www.loc.gov/item/lcwaN0028038/, 52–53.

Regan, Paulette. *Unsettling the Settler within: Indian Residential Schools, Truth Telling, and Reconciliation in Canada*. Vancouver: UBC Press, 2010.

Robinson, Dylan. "Intergenerational Sense, Intergenerational Responsibility," in *Arts of Engagement*, eds. Dylan Robinson and Keavy Martin (Wilfred Laurier University Press, 2016), 63.

Simpson, Audra. "Sovereignty, Sympathy, and Indigeneity," in *Ethnographies of US Empire*, eds. C. McGranahan and J.F. Collins (Duke University Press, 2018), 76.

Toth, Katalina. "Indigenous Healthcare in Canada," *Harvard International Review*, March 4, 2022, https://hir.harvard.edu/indigenous-healthcare-in-canada/.

Truth and Reconciliation Commission of Canada, *Canada's Residential Schools: The History, Part 1 Origins to 1939* (McGill-Queen's University Press Montreal, 2015), 3–4.

Tuck, Eve. "Suspending Damage: A Letter to Communities," *Harvard Educational Review* 7, no. 3 (2009): 409; 412.

Veracini, Lorenzo. *Settler Colonialism: A Theoretical Overview* (Palgrave, 2010), 14.

Vowel, Chelsea. *Indigenous Writes: A Guide to First Nations, Métis & Inuit Issues in Canada* (Highwater Press, 2016), 16.

Wolfe, Patrick. "Settler colonialism and the elimination of the native," *Journal of Genocide Research* 8, no. 4 (2006): 387–409, https://doi.org/10.1080/14623520601056240.

PART ONE

# Considering Violence and Genocide in the Canadian Settler State

# "I Feel Like My Spirit Knows Violence"

## *Interrogating the Language of Temporality and Crisis for Missing and Murdered Indigenous Women, Girls, and 2SLGBTQQIA+ People*

Karine R. Duhamel

### Introduction

On December 8, 2015, the newly formed Liberal government, under Prime Minister Justin Trudeau, announced the initiation of a national public inquiry on the issue of missing and murdered Indigenous women and girls. In August of 2016, the Government of Canada announced the Terms of Reference, including its mandate, and the appointment of Commissioners Marion Buller, Qajaq Robinson, Marilyn Poitras, Michèle Audette, and Brian Eyolfson.

The product of decades of advocacy by family members and survivors as well as a Call to Action from the 2015 Truth and Reconciliation Commission of Canada, the NIMMIWG was in its construction, mandate, and output a historic undertaking. Comprised of fourteen concurrent inquiries independent from government—one in each province and territory, alongside one federal inquiry—those who worked within it had less than three years to investigate the broadest mandate ever provided to an inquiry in Canada—the roots of the crisis of missing and murdered Indigenous women, girls, and 2SLGBTQQIA+ people.

More than 2,380 people participated in the National Inquiry into Missing and Murdered Indigenous Women and Girls, some in more ways than one. Experiences and recommendations were shared by 486 family members and survivors of violence at fourteen community hearings. Over 270 family members and survivors shared their stories with us in 147 private, or in-camera, sessions. Almost 750 people shared through statement gathering, and 819 people created artistic expressions to become part of the National Inquiry's Legacy Archive. Another 84 expert witnesses, Elders and Knowledge Keepers, frontline workers, and officials provided testimony in nine Knowledge Keeper, Expert, and Institutional Hearings. In addition, guided dialogues with First Nations, Métis, Inuit, and 2SLGBTQQIA+ people brought together those with lived experience, alongside frontline service providers and other experts, to discuss practical solutions for change. In June 2019, the National Inquiry released its *Final Report* based on the thousands of testimonies and expressions of family members, survivors of violence, Elders, Knowledge Keepers, academic and institutional experts, and frontline service providers.

As the director of research for the National Inquiry from 2018 to the end of its mandate, I worked closely with family members and survivors of violence to produce the *Final Report*, anchored in the testimony of the nearly three thousand people who shared their stories with us. In so many ways, the *Final Report* represents the collective voice of Indigenous women and 2SLGBTQQIA+ people pushing back against many of the assumptions that continue to generate violence and perpetuate harm. More specifically, the way that the language of crisis operates in the context of this violence, and the characterization of Indigenous bodies as weakened or transitory within the crisis, obscure the ways in which governments and institutions implement change.

This chapter will first explore the public framing of the nature of the transitory discourse around Indigenous women, girls, and 2SLGBTQQIA+ people that characterizes their very presence as temporary and fleeting, and the particular framing of violence against them that results. The translation of harmful transitory frames of reference for Indigenous women, girls, and 2SLGBTQQIA+ people, as individuals perpetually in transition, promotes a deficit-based approach to understanding violence as a product of personal choice, absent of colonial structure and historical context. Then, drawing on testimonies of those who offered their truths before the NIMMWG, this chapter will document the importance of understanding violence as a crisis that is centuries in the making, through an intergenerational lens, so that its root causes—colonial structures, ideas, and norms that still prevail—can be exposed and addressed. In doing so, it reinterrogates the usefulness of the framework of crisis in understanding and moving to action.

## The Uses of Crisis

The idea of *crisis* as a framework for understanding society has a long history in European modernity, and crisis became, in the second half of the eighteenth century, a "structural signature" of Western modernity.[1] Its classical Greek roots and modern-day usage signal both an objective condition *and* a subjective judgment that can work to shape "a constative description of an objective state"[2] that can serve to animate or validate repressive state action and, in Canada's case, inaction, with reference to a particularly constituted reality.

By definition, a crisis is a temporary situation, a turning point, an emotionally significant event signalling emotional distress, an unstable or crucial time or state of affairs. Crises involve events, as Hannes Zacher and Cort Rudolph argue, that "can be characterized by several forms of 'un-ness'—they are unexpected, unscheduled, unimaginable, unprecedented, uncertain, undesirable, unpleasant and often unmanageable."[3] As a period within which there is an urgent threat to either core values or life-sustaining functions, crisis is a time of both discontinuity and change that includes threat, uncertainty, and urgency.[4] This uncertainty, which therefore necessitates action, serves as a further justification for intervention. Crisis is thus inherently temporal and transitory, an "in-between" time where intervention is often justified.

As people typically framed through the lens of crisis, the colonial spaces in which Indigenous Peoples appear are also characterized as transitory. This characterization places Indigenous Peoples collectively as temporary presences, fated either to assimilate or to disappear.[5]

The translation of harmful transitory frames of reference for Indigenous women, girls, and 2SLGBTQQIA+ people, as individuals perpetually in transitory crisis-scapes, promotes a deficit-based approach to understanding violence as a product of personal choice, absent of colonial structure and historical context. As applied to Indigenous Peoples, the notion of Indigenous Peoples as "transitory" in nature has bolstered the rhetoric around the temporality of the crisis of violence, with important effects. Indigenous women, girls, and 2SLGBTQQIA+ people have long been seen—or imagined—through a colonial gaze. This gaze is a structure of representation that functions as a mode of intervention in and of itself, as well as providing important pretext for other forms of practical colonial intervention. This is both a historic and a contemporary phenomenon, and how society has both seen and characterized groups of people has come to form what Marita Sturken has characterized as our cultural memory—"the memory landscape that we inhabit," which is "a complex mix of narrative, displacement, shared testimony, popular culture, rumour, fantasy, and collective desire."[6]

In Canada, cultural "memory" around Indigenous Peoples, and more specifically around Indigenous women, girls, and 2SLGBTQQIA+ people, has operated in a way that has harmed and targeted them. Drawing on the idea of Indigenous women, girls, and 2SLGBTQQIA+ people—and by extension, of our communities—as both transitory and in crisis is not accidental. Rather, these narratives are foundational elements in the logic of settler colonialism[7] that seeks to replace what is temporary with something different and that assumes its own victory in the end.

In Canada, and in reference to both action and inaction on the issue of violence against Indigenous women, girls, and 2SLGBTQQIA+ people, insights related to crisis as animating repressive tactics within the context of a particular time and space certainly carry some weight. Crisis has worked to legitimize state action and inaction; to constitute Indigenous women, girls, and 2SLGBTQQIA+ people as inherently vulnerable; and to fuel racism, discrimination, and "trauma-porn," eclipsing the strength embedded in Indigenous knowledge systems and communities. In its presential form, "crisis" has also worked to refocus dialogue towards the current situation, rather than inviting a broader understanding of the enduring structures of settler colonialism that animate potential solutions to addressing violence.

Characterized throughout the *Final Report* as a crisis, a tragedy, and, more recently, in the context of the Covid-19 pandemic, a "shadow pandemic"[8] unto itself, the rates of violence against all women, but against Indigenous women, girls, and 2SLGBTQQIA+ people in Canada specifically, are indeed an issue in urgent need of solutions. According to data from the 2018 Survey of Safety in Public and Private Spaces (SSPPS), more than six in ten (63 percent) Indigenous women have experienced physical or sexual assault in their lifetime. Significantly, Indigenous women (11 percent) were almost six times more likely than non-Indigenous women (2.3 percent) to have ever been under the legal responsibility of the government, and about eight in ten (81 percent) Indigenous women who were ever under the legal responsibility of the government have experienced lifetime violent victimization.[9] Studies further show that, despite these statistics, a large proportion of violent crime is not reported to authorities, such as the police,[10] and that for Indigenous women the issue of reporting is largely impacted by the mistrust in police and criminal justice systems that are based in a colonial order. As family members and survivors documented as part of the National Inquiry, thousands of victims remain unidentified in those statistics.

These rates of violence are most certainly catastrophic, constituting a crisis in urgent need of attention. And yet, while the language of crisis has helped to increase the profile of this issue in Canadian society and internationally, so, too, has it had impacts in the ways in which violence, and the solutions to confront violence, have been understood. More specifically, the language of crisis has limited the ability of Canadians, including policy-makers, to understand the true depth of the root causes presented in the National Inquiry's *Final Report*, especially in terms of intergenerational and multigenerational trauma, and, subsequently, the urgent need for transformative change that presents a direct challenge to how the issue has been addressed so far. In addition, the tendency to characterize the failure to move beyond the temporal characterization of crisis has led to the implementation of solutions that fail to confront and address the complex entanglement of past and present and that may dismiss the much broader impacts of colonization that persist today.

## The Transitory Colonial Spaces of Indigenous Women, Girls, and 2SLGBTQQIA+ People

Canadian society's creation of narrative and memory with reference to Indigenous Peoples has been remarkably consistent over its history. This is a common occurrence in many societies deemed by those not subject to such oppression as *postcolonial*—in other words, settler societies that acknowledge that colonization occurred, but that dispute the ongoing manifestations of it in practice and in policy on the colonized.[11] It is part of the logic and the structure of genocide—the belief by settlers that we were always destined to disappear.

This dimension of cultural memory has a long history in what would become Canada, in part because of its usefulness in the settler colonial project. In the 1850s, Paul Kane, an Irish-Canadian painter, decided to make an artistic record of the Indian because he believed him to be disappearing.[12] Kane's 1859 book, *Wanderings of an Artist among the Indians of North America*, vividly predicted the following: "Their tribes, not long since still masters of a whole world, are disappearing rapidly, driven back and destroyed by the inroads of the white race. Their future is inevitable.... The Indians are doomed; their fate will be that of so many primitive races now gone."[13] A short time later, in the 1900s, Emily Carr, a Canadian artist, undertook the project of recording through paint totem poles, house fronts, and village scenes. As she wrote, "Only a few more years and they will be gone forever, into silent nothingness, and I would gather my collections together before they are forever past."[14]

Finally, Duncan Campbell Scott, deputy superintendent of the Department of Indian Affairs from 1913 to 1932, also published nine volumes of poetry from 1893 to 1947. The primary architect of many of Canada's most destructive policies related to First Nations people, Scott's work often centred around the collapse and death both of Indigenous cultures and of the people themselves. One of his most famous pieces, "The Onondaga Madonna," describes an Indigenous mother as a member of a "weird and waning race," essentializing her as a relic of a strange past and doomed to disappear.[15] Scott's work, alongside the work of many others, revealed the remarkably stable preoccupation with the "vanishing Indian," as both a prediction and a wish, by settler colonials who reflected the structure they inhabited—one in which Indigenous histories, lands, and bodies would be overwritten by settler ones as a point of inevitability.

However, these myths served as much of a purpose as they did provide a prediction. As a kind of manifest destiny, they reflected the true scope of the settler colonial project. As Patrick Wolfe wrote in 2006, and many have expanded upon since then, the settler colonial "logic of elimination" destroys to replace.[16] Where colonizers sought to create a new nation in North America, they first set out to destroy the old ones that were already here. As Wolfe maintains, "Settler colonizers come to stay: invasion is a structure, not an event."[17] The negation of the strength and power of Indigenous ways of living, governance, educational, and other institutions was part and parcel of this work, which focused on highlighting the ways in which these institutions were transitory and Indigenous

Peoples themselves were in crisis. In short, this kind of logic allowed for Indigenous Peoples to be characterized as doomed because they were maladapted for the modern age. Indeed, as noted by Audra Simpson (Kahnawà:ke, Mohawk Nation), the colonial state requires the death and disappearance of Indigenous women in order to secure its sovereignty, in what she terms "a sovereign death drive."[18]

While the discourse has indeed changed, the many themes so prevalent in the myth of the "vanishing Indian" find their way into contemporary public discourse around Indigenous Peoples. For instance, in recent years, public discourse on Indigenous issues in Canada has largely drawn its rhetoric and raison d'être from the processes and products of reparative justice mechanisms, regarded by many as decisive authorities on these issues. Many of these have also characterized Indigenous Peoples within a transitory frame, emphasizing the inevitability of the colonial project. As an example, the Davies Commission Inquiry into the Death of Frank Paul (2007–2011) was an inquiry under Commissioner William H. Davies QC, a retired justice of the British Columbia Supreme Court (BCSC), Canada, whose final report was submitted in May 2011.

Paul, a forty-seven-year-old Mi'kmaq man from New Brunswick, died of hypothermia in the early hours of December 6, 1998. In the testimony, the inquiry heard that Sgt. Russell Sanderson did not believe Paul was intoxicated, even though the officers who picked him up for being drunk in a public place said he smelled of rice wine. On Sanderson's orders, Paul was removed from the drunk tank and left in an alley in another part of the city. A video shown at the inquiry revealed Paul was dragged out of the facility soaking wet and apparently unconscious, and he subsequently died from exposure. In the report, Davies consistently noted Paul's vulnerability as an Indigenous person. As Sherene Razack has argued of the Frank Paul inquiry: "as the frame for how we are invited to consider the death of Frank Paul, vulnerability restricts the extent to which anyone can be culpable; it is a condition connected to colonialism but not to colonizers."[19]

In another example, Ricardo Wesley and James Goodwin, both First Nations men in their twenties, burned to death on January 8, 2006, while being held at the Kashechewan First Nation police detachment, near James Bay, in Northern Ontario. The men, who were locked in cells, died after a fire started in the building that housed the jail. As Carmela Murdocca argues, an analysis of testimony in the inquiry related to their deaths and in others reveals a discursive narrative pattern emerging of "inevitable death," wherein Indigenous lives—and deaths—are understood on a settler colonial arc that "traverses catastrophe and disaster [and] follows from the present to the imminent to the enduring—and finally, to the inevitable."[20]

The frameworks of inevitable demise and vulnerability are also applied in other contexts, too, towards Indigenous women specifically. For instance, Project KARE, an RCMP task force launched in Alberta in 2003, encouraged women engaged in "high-risk lifestyles" to submit fingerprints, hair samples, and photos to aid in their identification in the case of their death.[21]

Assumptions around "inevitable death" also abound in traditional news media when dealing with the issue of violence against Indigenous women, girls, and 2SLGBTQQIA+ people. News media both report on, and continue to be, in their own right, relevant actors in a public discursive space, signalling what is important, and what is not.[22] As noted in the National Inquiry's *Final Report*, the content and framing of Indigenous victims in the media differs from stories devoted to non-Indigenous victims. For instance, in a case study of news media representation of missing and murdered Indigenous women compared with the representation of missing and murdered white women, researcher Kristen Gilchrist found that media highlighted the non-Indigenous women's personalities, families, ambitions, and hobbies but provided scant detail, in contrast, on the lives of Indigenous victims, which were in fact rather similar.[23] A separate study, focused on representation of Indigenous victims from 2006 to 2009, highlighted two dominant narratives emerging from news media coverage, including that of the "vermin-victim," which portrays Indigenous sex workers as dirty and as a nuisance to Canadian society and a second narrative of victim-blaming Indigenous women who are engaged in what have been characterized as "high-risk" lifestyles.[24]

As this example demonstrates, often, content related to Indigenous women, girls, and 2SLGBTQQIA+ people and the way in which it is framed are "both persuasive and analytical tools; they are heuristics, or mental shortcuts, that allow complex issues and ideas to be understood. Media frames can explicitly and implicitly shape attitudes and opinions based on what is included in the frame and how it is understood."[25] These tools have played a key role in perpetuating the idea that Indigenous Peoples themselves are both transitory and perpetually in crisis. Indigenous women, girls, and 2SLGBTQQIA+ people—by virtue of their existence, it seems—are "vulnerable." Within a transitory frame, then, the stories indicate that different solutions are needed. For instance, the victimization of sex workers might be solved by cracking down on sex work or by moving sex work away from highly visible spaces and further underground, in a way that may increasingly compromise safety and may not help sex workers. The dehumanization that accompanies the idea of human beings as disposable then becomes a key component of a transitory framework—one in which Indigenous women are here only temporarily and will therefore eventually disappear.

Throughout all of the testimony provided to the National Inquiry through its Truth Gathering Process, witnesses consistently pointed to the characterizing of Indigenous Peoples as transitory, in crisis, and inherently vulnerable as a cause for further violence, one with a long-lasting impact. Witnesses also pushed back, however. Where institutions claimed witnesses' loved ones were vulnerable, witnesses insisted their loved ones were targeted. As Dr. Barry Lavallee explained in his testimony before the Inquiry,

> Indigenous women are not vulnerable, Indigenous women are targeted in secular society for violence. There's a very big difference to [being] vulnerable. To be vulnerable in medicine means that if I irradiate your body and you have no cells, you are vulnerable to an infection. But, to be vulnerable to murder because of your colour, and your positionality and just being Indigenous is targeting. It is an active form of oppression of Indigenous women.[26]

While historical examples such as dispossession from land, the residential school system, and the Sixties Scoop have been acknowledged publicly by governments and state institutions as targeting Indigenous Peoples, contemporary systems have not been accorded the same level of critical insight. Of particular note, child welfare—which targets Indigenous children especially—was referenced many times as an example of this kind of violent impact. Notably, an analysis of eight existing reports on child welfare systems spanning from 1994 to 2015 addresses the need to improve child and family services for Indigenous Peoples with approximately twenty-eight recommendations, noting that apprehended children are more vulnerable to sexual abuse and exploitation while they are in care and are more likely to suffer negative mental health impacts, extending to suicide.[27]

Another example, within the context of child welfare, is the birth alert system—suspended since the release of the *Final Report* in several provinces.

According to the Province of Manitoba, "Birth alerts notify hospitals and other Child and Family Services (CFS) agencies of the need for further assessment before a newborn is discharged to the care of a parent who has been assessed as 'high risk.'" However, those individuals considered to be "high risk" are, more often than not, Indigenous and may be flagged as high risk simply for having aged out of care themselves, often many years later. Women who enter the hospital to give birth would not have been directly informed of the existing alert, meaning that they would find out in hospital and not be able to do anything to stop the apprehension. While Manitoba ended the birth alert system officially in 2020, advocates claim that it still operates under other mechanisms.[28] As reported by CBC News, Manitoba had a 65 percent decrease in the number of newborns taken into care since birth alerts ended; however, the downturn was much less pronounced in babies twelve months and younger—only 32 percent. Further, as of 2023, over two years after the end of the birth alert system officially, 91 percent of the 8,990 children in care were Indigenous—approximately the same number as prior to the ending of birth alerts.

The near constant threat of violence—real or discursive—and the way that it impacts trust in institutions also has important implications that can, and do, affect how people access services. In many cases, the testimonies offered by those who shared their stories spoke to the feeling of being a "walking target," resulting in a failure to seek help when needed. As a woman known in the report only as "Kohkom" explained, "I've been in survival mode since I was a little girl, watching my back, watching goings on. Because I've seen my aunties, my cousins, my female cousins brutalized by police. And, growing up as a First Nation woman in this city, in this province, in this country—we're walking with targets on our backs."[29] As Rebecca Moore, a member of the National Family Advisory Circle for the National Inquiry, explained, "It is not only Indigenous women who are living 'at-risk' lifestyles or are on the streets who are being targeted, it is Indigenous women as a whole. Because non-Indigenous society benefits from settler-colonialism."[30]

In an interesting exercise, Josie Nepinak, director of the Awo Taan Healing Lodge, compared the measurements on an assessment tool of perceived danger widely used by anti-violence services in Canada among Indigenous women, immigrant women, and settler Canadians who use their services. She found that, when comparing the level of perceived danger in the same situation, Indigenous women did not perceive themselves to be in as much danger as did immigrant or settler Canadian women.[31] For

Nepinak, this is telling: the results suggest that the assessment tool does not "speak to the lived experiences of Indigenous women. It does not take colonization, the paternalistic policy, the oppression, residential school experiences, the... child welfare experiences."[32] In considering these histories, and as researchers Sarah Hunt, a member of the Kwakwaka'wakw Nation, and Cindy Holmes assert, we should not be surprised that "the rhythm of today... is made possible through the historic and ongoing processes and ideologies of colonialism."[33]

## Disentangling Past and Present

Moving beyond a limited approach to violence that anchors solutions in transitory and crisis-based analyses means the ability to more fully confront genocide in Canada today. As we wrote in the *Final Report*,

> The violence the National Inquiry heard amounts to a race-based genocide of Indigenous Peoples, including First Nations, Inuit and Métis, which especially targets women, girls, and 2SLGBTQQIA people. This genocide has been empowered by colonial structures, evidenced notably by the *Indian Act*, the Sixties Scoop, residential schools and breaches of human and Indigenous rights, leading directly to the current increased rates of violence, death, and suicide in Indigenous populations.[34]

No matter where the victim was located or who they were, every single story provided to the National Inquiry mobilized a much longer history of implications within systems that target Indigenous Peoples and that generate collective, and ongoing, trauma.

In recent years, Indigenous researchers have adapted the concept of "trauma" to recognize its collective dimensions, as linked to colonial structures and events. For instance, Lakota social worker Maria Yellow Horse Brave Heart's development of the concept of "historical trauma" refers to the "cumulative emotional and psychological wounding over the lifespan and across generations, emanating from massive group trauma."[35] Brave Heart's related concept of "historical trauma response" reframes things like substance use, addiction, or suicidal thoughts as understandable responses to the trauma of colonial violence rather than as personal failings. As Dr. Amy Bombay noted in her testimony to the National Inquiry, concepts such as these "emphasize the cumulative effects that were transferred across generations, and that it [trauma] interacts with contemporary stressors and aspects of colonization like racism."[36]

Like many of the witnesses who shared their stories of lost loved ones, Cee-Jai J. talked about her sister, Norma, who went missing from Vancouver's Downtown Eastside on September 28, 1992, and was found deceased a few days later. Twenty-five years later, to the day of her sister's death, Cee-Jai's daughter Shayla J. died after a car accident on September 28, 2017, when police took her home rather than to a hospital. As in the lives of so many of the other families and support people who shared their truths, the violent act that took the life of their loved one was only one of many incidents of violence in their lives based in colonial structures of layered indifference. Like many of the witnesses, Cee-Jai experienced repeated acts of physical, sexual, and psychological violence throughout her entire life. Violence predated it as well, as colonial experiences and structures impacted her family members, who then themselves became perpetrators. Including witnessing her father stab her mother when she was very young, witnessing her mother being physically beaten and abused by men as a young girl, her own subjection to repeated sexual and physical abuse and neglect in various foster homes, and the sexual assault and physical violence she experienced as a teenager and adult, violence permeates Cee-Jai's life story. Her relationships reflect a truth that is unfortunately not uncommon. She shared, "I feel like my spirit knows violence."[37]

For many witnesses, the cumulative effects of intergenerational trauma were both mental and physical, but they also impacted the cohesion of the family or community. For example, as Carol B. explained, "I really feel that the intergenerational trauma brought on by the residential schools has really impacted our families in a negative way. How can you possibly learn to love and value yourself when you're told consistently—daily, that you're of no value. And that we need to take the Indian out of you. How could you value or love yourself? And how could you expect to love and value your children?" Speaking of her mother, Carol noted, "And so for me, it was really important that I speak on my mother's behalf because if she were alive today, we would have a loving relationship. Or she would love me the best... way that she knows how, given the circumstances that she had to grow up in."[38]

In addition, as reported by many who addressed the issue, the normalization of this kind of violence translated into a kind of feeling of hopeless predetermination—a cyclical process by which witnesses described wanting to break the cycle but not having the supports to do so. As Audrey Siegl noted, "For all the little girls who grow up witnessing the violence, for the girls the violence is normalized for the way it was normalized for us. You know... what's normal for me should never be normal for another human being."[39]

For many of those who spoke about experiences of violence in their own lives or the lives of their loved ones before the National Inquiry, acknowledging and naming the historical forces that shaped the disappearances or deaths of Indigenous women, girls, and 2SLGBTQQIA+ people in distinct ways were an important part of revealing the root causes of the crisis and of defining the scope of the crisis as much greater than assumed. They were also a way to move away from victim-blaming, removing the important structural blinders that may complicate efforts to effect transformational societal change. Colonial systems are, as witnesses shared, remarkably consistent—contributing to intergenerational trauma that continues to perpetuate violence. As family members and survivors have insisted, the intergenerational context in which colonial violence occurs means that, in Indigenous communities, and for Indigenous women, girls, and 2SLGBTQIA+ people, violence is lived differently, with necessary implications for the solutions that we apply.

## Difference Matters

These differences matter. For Indigenous women, girls, and 2SLGBTQQIA+ people, the intergenerational nature of violence and the need for individual and community healing are often overlooked in public policy solutions given the limited nature through which governments typically fund what has been marginalized, silenced, and masked as vulnerability but is actually structural oppression. As Bombay maintains, "without that understanding, people have a tendency to blame Aboriginal peoples for their social and health inequities and resist policies addressing them."[40]

Witnesses appearing before the National Inquiry, including experts whose research focuses on intergenerational trauma, consistently noted the need for greater investment to address intergenerational trauma through support for culture, as a protective factor from experiencing or perpetrating violence, and the tendency for governments to ignore investments in culture as an "extra" or add-on rather than as fundamental to safety and wellness. Public policy investments—or lack thereof—seem to reflect as much. For instance, in the 2021 Canadian federal budget, the government pledged in excess of $18 billion over the next five years to "improve the quality of life and create new opportunities for people living in Indigenous communities."[41] In addition to earlier investments in new shelters and transition housing for First Nations, Inuit, and Métis people across the country, including on reserve, in the North, and in urban areas,[42] the focus of the investments is on tackling violence through housing and other current challenges to safety. However, the absence of devoted funding for healing through cultural support for family members and survivors (absent a small investment of support for wellbeing[43]) means that the importance and centrality of intergenerational trauma as a driver for violence itself has not as of yet been incorporated well into public policy solutions.

Shifting the discursive framework of public policy requires more than investment. Indeed, it means engaging in the necessary work to dislodge the transitory spatial and temporal frames that inform the discourse around Indigenous communities, families, and individuals. These harmful discourses are deficit-based: they work to pathologize Indigenous Peoples and communities in crisis, drawing attention to what is going wrong. Instead, they should be pointing the way to enduring solutions that mobilize solutions that have existed and still exist in Indigenous languages, worldviews, and cultures. In her presentation to the National Inquiry, Knowledge Keeper Mavis Windsor (a member of the Heiltsuk Nation of Bella Bella, British Columbia, and the social development director of her community) delivered a clear message many times over the course of the Truth Gathering Process: "We are the legacy. Despite the trauma our communities continue to live through, we are capable of addressing the violence against women in our communities. The solution is within us—within our communities."[44]

## Reconceptualizing the Uses of Crisis

Despite its pitfalls and limitations, the concept of crisis can still be useful within the context of the crisis of missing and murdered Indigenous women, girls, and 2SLGBTQQIA+ people. As Boletsi, Houwen, and Minnaard suggest, rethinking critique and its relation to crisis, as a reflection of both their shared etymological roots and the relationship between reflection or critique in a time of crisis, can be a useful diagnostic tool.[45] In particular, a critical analysis of "critique" and "crisis" prompts us to think about how we might rearrange, create configuration, and ultimately move away "from the illness and from diagnosis as judgment of failure" in an approach that "stresses the creative, transformative, future-oriented, hopeful potential of critique and crisis, or, indeed, of crisis *as* critique."[46] An increased social reflexivity may indeed invite a reconsideration of what has failed to address the crisis of violence against Indigenous women, girls, and 2SLGBTQQIA+ people and thus engender new solutions. As Boletsi, Houwen, and Minnaard argue, "mobilizing our critical and creative diagnostic impulses is essential for recognizing and seizing those moments as occasions for social and historical change, even when the odds seem to be against that."[47] This is such a moment.

Within the context of the National Inquiry, all who shared their knowledge demonstrate the idea of crisis as critique and the importance of a social reflexivity centred in Indigenous histories and ways of knowing. More specifically, and in an important departure from the harmful narratives presented in this chapter that may serve to constitute a cultural *counter-memory*, witnesses emphasized the importance of understanding the heart of the work—the idea that our women, girls, and 2SLGBTQQIA+ people are sacred—and of using this knowledge to identify the gifts that exist, in communities, to confront violence. The idea of the sacred, in the context of the *Final Report*, is not ungrounded. Rather, as countless testimonies identified, the traditional and contemporary roles of women and 2SLGBTQQIA+ people in their families and communities "as teachers, leaders, healers, providers and protectors were and remain indispensable parts of the equation to generating solutions for the crisis of missing and murdered Indigenous women and girls."[48] These roles operate in a balance with those of men, drawing attention to the importance of balance in undertaking roles and responsibilities that promote community safety and wellbeing. As those sharing their truths emphasized, when we honour our own gifts and the gifts in others, we are recognizing the sacred in all of us.[49]

The National Inquiry's *Final Report* anchors the path ahead not in a focus on what has occurred but within the solutions to address violence that exist in community and that recognize these gifts and responsibilities. As Dawnis Kennedy, whose traditional name is Minnawaanigogiizhigok, expressed, "You know, I think that if women were taking up their role, we wouldn't be worried about protecting women. We'd just be watching the women do their work protecting life."[50]

As a critique of the crisis itself, the report also demonstrates how the failure to value Indigenous expertise and a deficit-based understanding of Indigenous women, girls, and 2SLGBTQQIA+ people undermine the necessary work ahead. Indigenous women, girls, and 2SLGBTQQIA+ people gifted the National Inquiry with countless truths that make clear that they are powerful, caring, and resourceful leaders, teachers, healers, providers, and protectors, and that they must be supported to ultimately improve safety. As Audrey S. noted, "A lot of people say we 'protest'... I protest nothing. I protect. Big difference. What I stand for is as important as... what stands against me."[51] Embracing the reclamation of power and place, led by Indigenous women and 2SLGBTQQIA+ people, is not one option—it is, as we heard, the only choice. As the testimonies presented in the *Final Report* emphasize, ultimately, conceptualizing the crisis as critique can lead policy-makers in a different direction—one based on supporting the reclamation of power and place, as the *Final Report*'s title denotes.

## Conclusion

This chapter has argued that the discourse around the transitory space of crisis—and of Indigenous women, girls, and 2SLGBTQQIA+ people's bodies within it as inherently vulnerable and doomed to extinction—has concrete implications for the ways in which violence is understood, or misunderstood, by public policy-makers. Notably, a failure to consider the importance of intergenerational trauma, and to invest in its treatment through a transformation of services, policies, and legislation, serves to further target Indigenous women, girls, and 2SLGBTQQIA+ people. These omissions have important consequences.

As this chapter has argued, transitory spatial and temporal frames, rooted in historical colonial processes and still manifest today, serve to limit necessary supports for cultural reconnection and healing and deny safety for Indigenous women, girls, and 2SLGBTQQIA+ people. Through these frames, the normalization of violence becomes yet another way in which Indigenous women, girls, and 2SLGBTQQIA+ people are targeted, and narratives around this as an inevitable fact make it easier for those who choose to commit violence to do so, without fear of detection, prosecution, or penalty.

While many have acknowledged colonialism as a "dark legacy" of Canada, fewer have acknowledged the way in which the deficient characterization of Indigenous women and Two-Spirit people persists, albeit in somewhat modified form, today. There is also a lack of acknowledgement of the way in which these enduring characterizations have influenced state policy and action—or, perhaps more accurately, inaction—in terms of addressing the root causes of violence. While the language of crisis can be useful—it can signal an important state of affairs, the need for change, or the need to substantially alter an approach—it cannot and should not be used to continue to minimize the actions necessary to achieve social transformation and to support the fundamental human and Indigenous Rights of Indigenous Peoples.

The failure of current state-led approaches to remediating these issues points to a fundamentally flawed logic in the way that the issue itself has been constructed. Addressing violence against Indigenous women, girls, and 2SLGBTQQIA+ people requires, therefore, a fundamental shift and a social reflexivity that acknowledges the importance of intergenerational trauma and the way in which it has normalized violence. This shift must work to mobilize crisis as critique rather than to reaffirm current approaches and policies towards violence.



## Notes

1 Koselleck and Richter, "Crisis," 359.
2 Boletsi, Houwen, and Minnaard, *Languages of Resistance*, 3.
3 Zacher and Rudolph, "Researching Employee Experiences," 7.
4 Rosenthal, Boin, and Comfort, "The Changing World of Crises and Crisis Management," 5–27.
5 See, for instance, Razack, "Memorializing Colonial Power"; Murdocca, "'A Matter of Time'"; Eberts, "Being an Indigenous Woman"; and Cowlishaw, "Disappointing Indigenous People."
6 Sturken, "The Remembering of Forgetting," 106.
7 In 1999, Patrick Wolfe's *Settler Colonialism and the Transformation of Anthropology* launched a major reconsideration in academic circles about the role of settlement in colonization. See Wolfe, "Settler Colonialism."
8 BC Association of Aboriginal Friendship Centres with Battered Women's Support Services, *The Road to Safety*.
9 Heidinger, "Violent Victimization."
10 Cotter, "Criminal Victimization in Canada, 2019." See also Perreault, "Criminal Victimization in Canada, 2014."
11 Tuhiwai Smith, *Decolonizing Methodologies*, 48.
12 Francis, *The Imaginary Indian*, 16.
13 Kane, *Wanderings of an Artist*, quoted in Francis, *The Imaginary Indian*, 23.

14 Carr quoted in Francis, *The Imaginary Indian*, 31.
15 Scott, "The Onondaga Madonna."
16 Wolfe, *Settler Colonialism*, 387. See also Kauanui, "'A Structure, Not an Event.'"
17 Wolfe, *Settler Colonialism*, 387.
18 Simpson, "The State Is a Man." See also Simpson, "The Chiefs Two Bodies."
19 Razack, "Memorializing Colonial Power," 913.
20 Murdocca, "A Matter of Time," 13.
21 Eberts, "Being an Indigenous Woman," 69–102.
22 The impact of these public sources of information remains significant, despite the rise of social media. For instance, a September 2022 Maru Public Opinion survey found that of 1,517 Canadian adults who were polled and who check the news daily, 45 percent said they get their updates from an evening TV newscast or late broadcast. This was followed by a newspaper website (29 percent), a TV news website (29 percent), a TV station dedicated to business news and information (29 percent), social media sites like Facebook or Instagram (26 percent), and radio news broadcasts (24 percent). See CityNews Staff, "Majority of Canadians Get Their News."
23 Gilchrist, "'Newsworthy' Victims?"
24 Corbett, "No News Isn't Always Good News."
25 National Inquiry into Missing and Murdered Indigenous Women and Girls [NIMMIWG], *Reclaiming Power and Place*, 387.
26 NIMMIWG, *Reclaiming Power and Place*, 125.
27 NIMMIWG, *Reclaiming Power and Place*, 427.
28 See "Institutionalized since Birth: Child Welfare Agencies and Birth Alert Systems," in NIMMIWG, *Reclaiming Power and Place*, 364–369.
29 NIMMIWG, *Reclaiming Power and Place*, 56.
30 NIMMIWG, *Reclaiming Power and Place*, 30.
31 NIMMIWG, *Reclaiming Power and Place*, 582.
32 NIMMIWG, *Reclaiming Power and Place*, 582.
33 NIMMIWG, *Reclaiming Power and Place*, 312–313.
34 NIMMIWG, *Reclaiming Power and Place*, 50.
35 Brave Heart, "The Historical Trauma Response," 7.
36 NIMMIWG, *Reclaiming Power and Place*, 112.
37 NIMMIWG, *Reclaiming Power and Place*, 504.
38 NIMMIWG, *Reclaiming Power and Place*, 335.
39 NIMMIWG, *Reclaiming Power and Place*, 147.
40 NIMMIWG, *Reclaiming Power and Place*, 112.
41 Black, "Federal Budget 2021."
42 Crown-Indigenous Relations and Northern Affairs Canada, "New Investments to Continue."
43 This amounts to $12.5 million over six years for the Support for the Wellbeing of Families and Survivors of Missing and Murdered Indigenous Women, Girls and 2SLGBTQQIA+ People Contribution Program.
44 NIMMIWG, *Reclaiming Power and Place*, 93.
45 Boletsi, Houwen, and Minnaard, eds., *Languages of Resistance*, 7.

46 Boletsi, Houwen, and Minnaard, eds., *Languages of Resistance*, 8.
47 Boletsi, Houwen, and Minnaard, eds., *Languages of Resistance*, 9.
48 NIMMIWG, *Reclaiming Power and Place*, 74.
49 NIMMIWG, *Reclaiming Power and Place*, 41.
50 NIMMIWG, *Reclaiming Power and Place*, 173.
51 NIMMIWG, *Reclaiming Power and Place*, 38.

## Sources

BC Association of Aboriginal Friendship Centres with Battered Women's Support Services. *The Road to Safety: Indigenous Survivors in BC Speak Out against Intimate Partner Violence during the COVID-19 Pandemic* (2022). https://www.bwss.org/wp-content/uploads/Road-to-Safety-final-web.pdf.

Black, Kerry. "Federal Budget 2021: $18 Billion Is a Step Towards Closing Gaps Between Indigenous and Non-Indigenous Communities." *The Conversation*, April 20, 2021. https://theconversation.com/federal-budget-2021-18-billion-is-a-step-towards-closing-gaps-between-indigenous-and-non-indigenous-communities-159104.

Boletsi, Maria, Janna Houwen, and Liesbeth Minnaard, eds. *Languages of Resistance, Transformation, and Futurity in Mediterranean Crisis-Scapes: From Crisis to Critique*. Palgrave Macmillan, 2020.

Brave Heart, Maria Yellow Horse. "The Historical Trauma Response among Natives and Its Relationship with Substance Abuse: A Lakota Illustration." *Journal of Psychoactive Drugs* 35, no. 1 (2003): 7–13. https://doi.org/10.1080/02791072.2003.10399988.

CityNews Staff. "Majority of Canadians Get Their News from Mainstream Sources, Study Shows." *CityNews—Ottawa*, September 28, 2022. https://ottawa.citynews.ca/2022/09/28/majority-of-canadians-get-their-news-from-mainstream-sources-study-shows-5882145/.

Corbett, Elisha. "No News Isn't Always Good News: Media Representation of Missing and Murdered Indigenous Women in Canada." Paper presented at the x Vancouver, BC, June 5, 2019.

Cotter, Adam. "Criminal Victimization in Canada, 2019." Canadian Centre for Justice and Community Safety Statistics, Statistics Canada, August 25, 2021. https://www150.statcan.gc.ca/n1/pub/85-002-x/2021001/article/00014-eng.htm.

Cowlishaw, Gillian. "Disappointing Indigenous People: Violence and the Refusal of Help." *Public Culture* 15, no. 1 (2003): 103–126. https://doi.org/10.1215/08992363-15-1-103.

Crown-Indigenous Relations and Northern Affairs Canada. "New Investments to Continue to Work to End the Tragedy of Missing and Murdered Indigenous Women, Girls and 2SLGBTQQIA People." Newswire, December 15, 2020. https://www.newswire.ca/news-releases/new-investments-to-continue-to-work-to-end-the-tragedy-of-missing-and-murdered-indigenous-women-girls-and-2slgbtqqia-people-893351711.html.

Eberts, Mary. "Being an Indigenous Woman Is a 'High-Risk Lifestyle.'" In *Making Space for Indigenous Feminisms*, 2nd ed., edited by Joyce Green. Fernwood Books, 2017.

Francis, Daniel. *The Imaginary Indian: The Image of the Indian in Canadian Culture*. Arsenal Pulp Press, 1992.

Gilchrist, Kristen. "'Newsworthy' Victims?: Exploring Differences in Canadian Local Press Coverage of Missing/Murdered Aboriginal and White Women." *Feminist Media Studies* 10, no. 4 (2010): 373–390. https://doi.org/10.1080/14680777.2010.514110.

Heidinger, Loanna. "Violent Victimization and Perceptions of Safety: Experiences of First Nations, Métis and Inuit Women in Canada." Canadian Centre for Justice and Community Safety Statistics, Statistics Canada, April 26, 2022. https://www150.statcan.gc.ca/n1/pub/85-002-x/2022001/article/00004-eng.htm.

Kane, Paul. *Wanderings of an Artist among the Indians of North America* (Radisson Society of Canada, 1859). Online at https://www.canadiana.ca/view/oocihm.35931/7.

Kauanui, J. Kēhaulani. "'A Structure, Not an Event': Settler Colonialism and Enduring Indigeneity." *Emergent Critical Analytics for Alternative Humanities* 5, no. 1 (2016). https://csalateral.org/issue/5-1/forum-alt-humanities-settler-colonialism-enduring-indigeneity-kauanui/#fn-351-3.

Koselleck, Reinhart, and Michaela Richter. "Crisis." *Journal of the History of Ideas* 67, no. 2 (2006): 357–400. https://doi.org/35910.1353/jhi.2006.0013.

Murdocca, Carmela. "'A Matter of Time and a Matter of Place': Colonial Inquiries and the Politics of Testimony." *Law, Culture and the Humanities* 13, no. 1 (2013): 1–23. https://ssrn.com/abstract=2351292.

National Inquiry into Missing and Murdered Indigenous Women and Girls. *Reclaiming Power and Place: The Final Report of the National Inquiry on Missing and Murdered Indigenous Women and Girls*. Volume 1a. National Inquiry on Missing and Murdered Indigenous Women and Girls, 2019. https://www.mmiwg-ffada.ca/final-report/.

Perreault, Samuel. "Criminal Victimization in Canada, 2014." Canadian Centre for Justice and Community Safety Statistics, Statistics Canada, November 23, 2015. https://www150.statcan.gc.ca/n1/pub/85-002-x/2015001/article/14241-eng.htm.

Razack, Sherene. "Memorializing Colonial Power: The Death of Frank Paul." *Law & Social Inquiry* 37, no. 4 (2012): 908–932. https://doi.org/10.1111/j.1747-4469.2012.01291.x.

Rosenthal, Uriel, R. Arjen Boin, and Louise K. Comfort. "The Changing World of Crises and Crisis Management." In *Managing Crises: Threats, Dilemmas, Opportunities*, edited by Uriel Rosenthal, R. Arjen Boin, and Louise K. Comfort. Charles Thomas, 2001.

Scott, Duncan Campbell. "The Onondaga Madonna." *CanLit Guides—University of British Columbia (Canadian Literature)*, October 23, 2013.

Simpson, Audra. "The Chiefs Two Bodies: Theresa Spence & the Gender of Settler Sovereignty: Unsettling Conversations." Keynote Address for the

Annual Critical Race and Anticolonial Studies Conference, March 14, 2014. https://vimeo.com/110948627.

Simpson, Audra. "The State Is a Man: Theresa Spence, Loretta Saunders, and the Gender of Settler Sovereignty." *Theory and Event* 19, no. 4 (2016). https://doi.org/10.3138/9781487532048-004.

Sturken, Marita. "The Remembering of Forgetting: Recovered Memory and the Question of Experience." *Social Text* 57 (1998): 103–125. https://doi.org/10.2307/466883.

Tuhiwai Smith, Linda. *Decolonizing Methodologies: Research and Indigenous Peoples* 2nd ed. Zed Books, 2012.

Wolfe, Patrick. "Settler Colonialism and the Elimination of the Native." *Journal of Genocide Research* 8, no. 4 (2006): 387–409. https://doi.org/10.1080/14623520601056240.

Wolfe, Patrick. *Settler Colonialism and the Transformation of Anthropology*. Cassell, 1999.

Zacher, Hannes, and Cort W. Rudolph. "Researching Employee Experiences and Behavior in Times of Crisis: Theoretical and Methodological Considerations and Implications for Human Resource Management." *German Journal of Human Resource Management* 36, no. 1 (2022): 6–31. https://doi.org/10.1177/23970022211058812.

# The Battleford Hangings and the Rise of the Settler Colonial State

James Daschuk

I AM A SETTLER OF FRENCH-CANADIAN AND UKRAINIAN ancestry and a guest in Treaty 4 territory for the last three decades. In that time, I have worked to understand how Saskatchewan came to be such a racially divided place. A few years ago, while working with a group of men supported by All Nations Hope Network in Regina, we were asked to share the stories of our great-grandparents. Everyone in the circle related their family histories back at least to the signing of the treaties and before. As the last person to speak, I said that my grandfather came over on a boat and that was all I knew. Maybe our lack of roots, the amnesia of personal and family histories on the land, are a symptom of setter-colonial societies and the violence they perpetuate.

## Introduction

November 1885 was arguably the most significant month in the formation of the Canadian West. In the span of three weeks, a trio of events laid the foundation for the fractured and racially divided society that persists today. On November 7, the Canadian Pacific Railway (CPR), the backbone of the fledgling Dominion of Canada, was completed. The industrial scale of immigration that came with the railway made Saskatchewan the third most populous province in the dominion, with more than 900,000 inhabitants. Indigenous Peoples were all but invisible in public discourse.[1] The occupation of land by settlers and the institutionalized irrelevance of the Indigenous population were central to what Patrick Wolfe called the "logic of elimination," a key element of the formation of settler colonial societies.[2]

Days after the last spike, on November 16, Métis leader Louis Riel was executed for treason in Regina. His death ended the dream of a multi-ethnic society in the west, dispossessed the Métis Nation, and cemented political loyalties along ethnic and religious lines across the dominion for generations. The location of his execution remains unmarked by the Royal Canadian Mounted Police, a sign that his death is still contested; its commemoration—and race relations involving the force generally—are still sources of conflict in official and community circles.

The third formative event that fateful month in 1885, though largely unknown to most Canadians, signalled a new, ongoing, and violent phase in the relationship between First Nations and the Canadian state. On the cold wet morning of November 27, eight Indigenous men were hanged in a choreographed display of state-sanctioned killing before a crowd of settlers, police, and Indigenous Peoples, including students of the Indian Industrial School and other children compelled to attend the mass execution.[3]

Six of the condemned were nêhiyaw (Cree) who had turned on the whites who had brutalized them at Frog Lake.[4] Their community, led by mistahimusqua (Big Bear), was among the last to submit to treaty in the winter of 1882–83 after years of struggle and hardship and hunger. His granddaughter succumbed to hunger just days before mistahimusqua traded his freedom for food. Conditions for his people only worsened under dominion supervision. Thomas Quinn, the sub-agent at Frog Lake, was a "brutal wretch" who physically, psychologically, and sexually abused the people he oversaw.[5] Driven by hunger and desperation, the nêhiyaw turned on their oppressors. Quinn's cruelty led to his death and unleashed a maelstrom of violence that left ten dead. The killings were a reckoning for the years of cruelty and abuse that the nêhiyaw had suffered from Canadian authorities. Near Battleford, two Nakoda men, Itka and Waywahnitch, exacted revenge on the farm instructor and a local settler who had starved and tormented members of their community.[6] Almost five decades ago, Métis scholar Howard Adams stressed that the deaths were "not an act of revenge" but "a struggle against colonization."[7]

## The Battleford Hangings

The trials for those executed on November 27, 1885, were part of a larger slate of legal proceedings held in the aftermath of the regional violence of the previous months. Many of the accused were incarcerated in Regina, where the trials of Riel and other high-profile Indigenous leaders had taken place.[8] Regina was hundreds of kilometres from the violence. There, the legal proceedings included defence counsel and the appearance of due process and resulted in only a single execution, that of Riel for the crime of high treason. Although the propriety of his execution has been challenged by politicians and historians alike, Riel was put to death only after three separate appeals were exhausted.[9]

The Indigenous leaders tried in Regina—kahpahyakasocum (One Arrow), mistahimusqua (Big Bear), and pîhtokahanapiwiyin (Poundmaker)—were charged with treason felony, an offence that did not carry the death penalty.[10] The choice to prosecute the men on the lesser charge was politically motivated though still part of the Dominion's plan to decapitate Indigenous leadership.[11] pîhtokahanapiwiyin was the adopted son of Siksika Chief Isapo-Muxipa (Crowfoot), and government officials were concerned that his execution would drive the Niitsitapi to war.[12] To avoid creating martyrs and sparking further violence, they sentenced the Chiefs to three-year terms at the Manitoba penitentiary.[13] They avoided the gallows, but all three contracted tuberculosis, a slower but just as certain sentence of death. In 2019, the federal government acknowledged the wrongful conviction of pîhtokahanapiwiyin and posthumously exonerated him.

The men tried and hanged at Battleford in the fall of 1885 received no such pardon. They accepted their fate. Only three spoke on their behalf at the trials.[14] A witness of the events, Robert Jefferson, wrote that the accused "all voluntarily surrendered themselves to the authorities; had they chosen to evade punishment for their crimes, it is more than doubtful that they would ever have been caught."[15] When the inevitable came, they sang a death song as they prepared to go to the other side. As warriors, they had done their duty, turning on their tormentors when the opportunity arose. Today the hanged men are remembered by the nêhiyaw as the "great eight"[16] for their resistance to the brutality of the dominion government.

The violence at Frog Lake was tabloid fodder across the country.[17] Because the men were not high-profile leaders known (and sometimes sympathized with) by the public in the east, they were considered expendable.

There were significant differences between the trials in Regina and those in Battleford.[18] The settlers who months earlier panicked and sought safety during the so-called "Siege of Battleford" were out for blood.[19] Outside Battleford, vigilante justice prevailed. In reporting the killing of ten Nakoda men, the *Saskatchewan Herald* shrugged: "Whether they proved fatal on the battle field or the reserve is not known; nor is it material."[20]

The townsfolk sought revenge for what they saw as the pillaging of the community when officials who cowered within the palisades refused to meet with the Indigenous delegation who then helped themselves to food and supplies. Judge C.B. Rouleau, accused of cowardice for bolting with his family at the first sign of trouble, called for the harshest penalties possible even before the trials began. Sandra Bingaman observed that everyone in Battleford, including Rouleau, "had been so directly affected by the rebellion that it was impossible to find impartial men to decide guilt or innocence."[21] Three days before the executions, a telegram from Ottawa concluded that Rouleau "should not have been allowed to preside at the trial of the prisoners."[22] Many called for the executions on reserve as an example to any others pondering violence, which Indian Commissioner Edgar Dewdney opposed because of the possibility of their abandonment given the "superstitious nature" of the reserve population.[23]

## The Purpose of the Battleford Trials

The goal of the hangings, the largest mass execution in Canadian history, was articulated by Prime Minister Macdonald in a November 1885 letter to Commissioner Dewdney, "to convince the Red Man that the White Man governs."[24] Prior to the executions, there had been only two hangings in the Canadian Northwest. Riel was hanged in Regina earlier in the month. Six years prior, ka ki si kutchin (Swift Runner) had been executed for cannibalism.[25] It is likely that none of the Indigenous witnesses at Battleford had seen a state-sanctioned killing, so the hangings would have had a profound and traumatic effect on those present.

The executions were designed as a powerful piece of political theatre even though public executions had been banned since 1868.[26] Assistant Indian Commissioner Hayter Reed—who considered Indigenous Peoples the "scum of the Prairies"[27]—wrote to his superior Edgar Dewdney on September 6, 1885, that the executions ought to be a "public spectacle" to "cause them to meditate…on the sound thrashing" meted out by the Dominion and to "have [an] ocular demonstration of the fact."[28] The gallows, twenty feet long and ten feet high, made the executions visible from outside the palisade of the fort, a macabre stage for the drama to unfold.[29] The grandstand built in front of the gallows enhanced the spectacle for those in attendance.[30] The audience included "large numbers of Indians...from the neighboring reserves"[31] and the students of the newly established Industrial School[32] to ensure that the message of the hangings was conveyed to its intended audience. One hundred and fifty armed police under the command of Major Crozier were stationed outside the stockade and "ringed three sides of the gallows."[33]

The executions culminated in the bodies swinging in the wind for fifteen minutes, and certainly had the desired effect. Jefferson reported the contractor hired to dispose of the bodies "objected to handling them.... The conflict between duty and inclination was compromised by his placing the boxes below the scaffold, so that when he cut the ropes by which they were suspended the dead Indians dropped into their respective 'caskets.' They were then hauled to the [river] bank and buried in the sand."[34] The indignities to the bodies and the haphazard burials were purposeful. Had the corpses been released to their families, the executed would have been glorified as warriors.

Days after the hangings, the editor of the *Herald* wrote, "It is devoutly to be hoped that the Indians at large will be duly impressed with the certainty with which punishment has overtaken their deluded followers, and recognizing the power of the law, settle down and make the most of their opportunities to improve their condition."[35] The *Regina Leader* echoed the sentiment: "It is believed the executions will have a wholesome effect upon the Indian tribes and tend largely to the preservation of the peace."[36]

By the 1950s, soil erosion exposed some of the remains of the men, and the burial site was capped with concrete. Generations after the hangings, the trauma of the day still resonates with the descendants of the executed or those forced to watch the killings. Oral histories underscored "the silent horror" of those who witnessed the executions.[37] Elder Paul Chicken of Sweetgrass First Nation shared the morbid fear of arrest and trial before "Hanging Judge Rouleau."[38] The grandson of Dressyman, one of those acquitted, stated that his grandfather and several other men had been forced to watch the executions and threatened with the same if there was further trouble: "They didn't like the hanging.... The law [had] overdone it."[39] Moreover, that the Dominion of Canada used the mass execution to terrorize schoolchildren, known even in the fall of 1885 to be malnourished,[40] seared the trauma of the event into the collective memory of Indigenous Peoples in the region. Conversely, the settlers of Battleford and beyond inherited a convenient collective amnesia of the hangings and a view that the establishment of their society was a peaceful and orderly process.

Bill Waiser described the conduct of the Canadian government in the aftermath of the resistance as being "as if Ottawa had declared war on the First Nations—a war that it was determined to win, at whatever the cost. And in the long run it has."[41] Indeed, while settler colonialism is acknowledged to be a structure rather than an event,[42] the hangings at Battleford were an unmistakable signal that the state could now act with impunity in their dealings with First Nations.[43]

By the end of 1885, the nêhiyaw were a subjugated people.[44] Wolfe argues that the land and its occupation by newcomers comprise "the specific irreducible element" of settler colonialism.[45] The unfettered and often illegal actions undertaken by the dominion government, the most egregious being the Indian residential school system, continue to fuel trauma, poverty, discord, and violence in the twenty-first century. The federal government has provided billions of dollars in compensation for the loss of land and other rights promised in the treaties during generations of government lawlessness after 1885.[46]

## The Numbered Treaties

In the years before 1885, the Crown was compelled to enter into treaties with Indigenous nations as a precondition for newcomers' entry and residence on the land. Without the numbered treaties, the establishment of Euro-Canadian society on the prairies would have been a legal impossibility. Kahkewistahaw Elder Joe Crowe made that point that "if the white man has any right to be in this country then the treaty is the source of that right."[47] To representatives of the Crown, treaties were a legal hurdle to overcome, a political and diplomatic nuisance necessary to open the land to white settlement, an imperative since the end of the Seven Years' War. The *Royal Proclamation of 1763* formally acknowledged that land not already occupied by European colonies would be set aside as "Indian Territory," recognition that Indigenous Peoples held title to their lands.[48] Since 1763, the expansion of settler territory has largely followed the negotiation or imposition of treaties between the British (or American) sovereign and the Indigenous nations whose lands were soon to be occupied.[49]

The territory that became Western Canada is covered by the numbered treaties completed between 1871 and 1877. As Sheldon Krasowski and others have shown, the Prairie treaties were not agreements that initiated the relationship between the Crown and Indigenous title holders of the territory.[50] Rather, negotiations took place after Canadians had trespassed on what they knew to be Indigenous Lands. Until the election of the second Macdonald government in 1878, there was no grand vision for the development of the west. The completion of each numbered treaty was the resolution of a local or regional dispute rather than the large-scale preparation of the land for imminent European settlement.[51] First Nations leaders knew that they could not stop the tide of newcomers from flooding into their territories. They saw treaties as creating a kinship relationship with whites, with mutual benefits and responsibilities, so that both societies could prosper on the land that they shared. As nêhiyaw writer Harold Johnson described it, it was a kind of mutual adoption, the creation of a new kind of family relationship.[52]

When the treaties were completed, the Crown did not have the military strength to conquer the west. To J.R. Miller, the Red River Resistance of 1869–70 was the result of Canadian expansion without the legal sanction afforded by a treaty.[53] Simply put, Canada was forced into treaties by First Nations that asserted their ownership of the land.[54] Although the Liberal government of Alexander Mackenzie completed Treaties 4 through 7, it had no real plan to settle the west. The election of the Conservatives under the banner of the "National Policy" changed the political and historical trajectory of the west forever. Completion of the CPR was the new government's priority. Prime Minister Macdonald took on the added responsibility of Indian Affairs to personally manage what he saw as the greatest impediment to the progress of the railway. His choice of the two portfolios underscores the view that Indigenous Peoples were understood as a threat and that they needed to be controlled to ensure the swift establishment of the settler state.

## The Provisions of Treaty 6

Battleford is located on the North Saskatchewan River in the heart of both nêhewayak and Treaty 6 territory. As with earlier treaty negotiations, the settlement of Treaty 6 was prompted by Canadian infringement on nêhiyaw territory.[55] The negotiations at Fort Carlton took place just weeks after the Battle of the Little Big Horn, the greatest defeat of the US Army in the west. No one wanted violence at Carlton, but knowledge of the bloodshed in Montana informed the proceedings.[56] The strength and foresight of the nêhiyaw leadership resulted in the most detailed and innovative terms of all the numbered treaties.[57] After days of discussion, three new provisos were added to the completed agreement, to the consternation of officials in Ottawa.[58]

In 1869–70, as Canada annexed Rupert's Land, smallpox killed over three thousand people across the plains. The experience of the epidemic prompted Chief kamiyistowesit (Beardy) to advocate for the inclusion of medical relief, almost certainly in the form of vaccination, resulting in the inclusion of the "medicine chest clause" in the text of the treaty. Between 1877 and 1880, thousands of Indigenous Peoples were vaccinated against smallpox, a procedure that protected both them and settlers who would someday arrive in the territory.[59] This was perhaps the only treaty innovation earnestly carried out by Canadian officials.

Indigenous leaders knew that the bison economy would not continue forever and recognized that farming was a bridge to a secure and prosperous future on the land that they would share with the newcomers. During the negotiations for Treaty 6, they secured a greater level of support for the conversion to farming than that provided in earlier agreements. Despite the optimism and good faith among the nêhiyaw and other nations regarding the new agrarian economy, reserve agriculture proved to be an unmitigated failure. Aidan McQuillan showed that in 1884 only 770 of more than 20,000 Indigenous Peoples in the west were not dependent on government relief.[60] The widespread failure of reserve agriculture was soon used as the rationale for the implementation of a permit system that required Indigenous farmers to secure written permission from an Indian Department official to sell their produce. This bureaucratic barrier to entry into the agrarian economy remained in place for generations. Harold LeRat, who farmed on Cowessess First Nation, explained that "Indians were not allowed to market their own produce without a permit. If you grew grain or cut wood on the reserve or raised cattle, they had to get a permit in order to sell it. The Indian Agent was in charge of issuing permits."[61]

Reserve agriculture was essentially a large-scale social experiment intended to have Indigenous Peoples go through the motions of farming rather than find a real path to economic independence and prosperity in the new economy.[62] Imposition of the "peasant" farming policy in 1888, which barred the use of mechanical implements and forced the use of hand tools such as scythes for harvesting, was perhaps the most harmful initiative contributing to the failure of reserve agriculture.[63] Residential school students deemed the best and brightest were placed by government officials in an "experimental colony" on expropriated reserve land in the File Hills, fuelling hardship and conflict for a century.[64] Along with a formal apology, Marc Miller, the minister of Crown-Indigenous Affairs, recently provided the affected communities with $150 million in compensation in 2022.[65] Other policies, such as the Soldier Settlement program, cleaved thousands of hectares of land from reserves and transferred them to non-Indigenous war veterans.[66] During the Laurier administration, 20 percent of reserve lands were surrendered in a number of questionable dealings that often profited Liberals and further impoverished First Nations.[67]

Coercive oversight and outright cruelty by dominion officials doomed reserve agriculture almost from the start. They had what amounted to unbridled control over every aspect of reserve life. Punishment for perceived insubordination or simply questioning authority could result in the withholding of food for entire communities. Previous studies have shown that entry into treaty undermined the health of communities while the non-treaty Dakota flourished without the continual interference of Indian Department officials in their daily affairs.[68]

The third significant addition to the terms of Treaty 6 was also made on the insistence of Chief kamiyistowesit. He successfully negotiated the inclusion of a "famine and pestilence" clause, ensuring the delivery of humanitarian aid in times of crisis if the bison were to disappear. After a lengthy negotiation, Lieutenant Governor Alexander Morris agreed that assistance would be provided by the Crown if such a situation were to occur. Less than two years later, the bison disappeared from Canadian territory.[69] The Dominion's initial response, though woefully inadequate, was driven by genuine concern for those experiencing hunger. The election of the Conservative Party in the fall of 1878 and its promise to quickly build the CPR changed Canada's response to the famine. Hunger provided the Macdonald government with the opportunity to force the thousands of Indigenous holdouts into treaties, onto reserves, and under the control of government officials directed to limit the supply of rations, to the point that food rotted in storehouses as the malnourished sickened and, in many cases, died.[70] The famine and pestilence clause was weaponized by officials who used hunger to ethnically cleanse the southwestern portion of Saskatchewan of thousands of Indigenous Peoples who sought sanctuary and reserves in the Cypress Hills.[71] By 1885, the commitment of humanitarian aid in times of famine was all but forgotten by Macdonald in his role as superintendent general of Indian Affairs. In Parliament, he quipped that "it can't be considered a fraud on the Indians because they have no right to that food. They are simply living on the benevolence and the charity of the Canadian Parliament, and, as the old adage says, beggars can't be choosers."[72] Coupled with the failure of reserve agriculture and other draconian regulations imposed on the treaty reserves, government rations perpetuated malnutrition and poor health for a century in the land celebrated as "the bread basket of the world."

Other commitments laid out in the treaty were ignored or manipulated to suit the agenda of the dominion government. The promise "to maintain schools for instruction in such reserves hereby made as to Her Government of the Dominion of Canada may seem advisable, whenever the Indians of the reserve shall desire it,"[73] served as the catalyst for the Indian residential school system. The treaty also ensured the free movement of Indigenous Peoples in the pursuit of their livelihood on the lands and waters. During the resistance of 1885, a proposal by General Middleton to confine First Nations to their reserves was considered legal overreach.[74] Dewdney told Macdonald that controlling the movement of Indigenous Peoples violated the terms of the treaty, and "to compel Indians to live wholly on their Reserves our Treaty must be altered."[75] In his annual report for 1889, Assistant Indian Commissioner Hayter Reed admitted that Indigenous Peoples are "not compelled by the terms of [the] treaty to stay on their reserves."[76] The violence that accompanied enforcement of the pass system had no basis in law. Yet by 1886 all Indigenous Peoples found off reserves were questioned by the police. Management of the force shifted from the Department of the Interior to the Department of Indian Affairs in 1883, and the RCMP reluctantly took on the role of enforcer of dominion Indian policy.[77]

Filmmaker Alex Williams has shown that, despite the absence of legislation, the confinement of Indigenous Peoples to their reserves persisted at least until the 1950s, undermining their participation in the commercial economy and creating generational food insecurity as those interned were forced to subsist on gophers and other small game.[78] The illegality of the system was no secret to the bureaucrats who enforced it. The prohibition on Indigenous Peoples hiring legal counsel between 1927 and 1951 perpetuated the program that turned treaty reserves into de facto internment camps.[79] Sickness within reserve populations was so widespread that limiting their mobility was seen as a public health precaution for the settler population. In 1932, Dr. J.J. Heagarty wrote to Dr. E.L. Stone of the Department of Indian Affairs that "if the Indians were not segregated on reservations we should be compelled to take better care of him [*sic*] for our own protection."[80] Communities banned Indigenous Peoples whom they perceived to be threats to health.[81] By the mid-twentieth century, as the pass system quietly fell into disuse, a form of "voluntary segregation" kept communities apart in Battleford and towns like it. In 1963, Peter Gzowski wrote that "practically no white citizen of North Battleford even knows an Indian to talk to."[82] The Saskatchewan government's recent amendment to the *Trespass Act* now includes an exception to the duty of care obligation, so if a trespasser is shot, the property owner is not compelled to provide assistance.[83] In *nipawistamasowin: We Will Stand Up*, nêhiyaw filmmaker Tasha Hubbard (Peepeekisis First Nation) connected the Battleford hangings to the killing of Colten Boushie in what she described as "conflicted land."[84]

Although it has yet to be subjected to the scrutiny of the courts, the surrender clause of the numbered treaties is by far the most important aspect of the newcomers' desire to control the land. From the perspective of governments, corporations, private property owners, and others, the treaties ceded all but a fraction of a percent of what was recognized as First Nations territory to the Crown in exchange for a series of legally binding commitments (including those listed above). The surrender clause is the cornerstone of settler occupation and ownership of the land, and without its inclusion in the treaties the land would remain in the hands of Indigenous Peoples, and there would be no private property.

The written version of Treaty 6 describes the transfer of title as follows: "The Plain and Wood Cree Tribes of Indians, and all the other Indians inhabiting the district hereinafter described and defined, do hereby cede, release, and yield up to the Government of the Dominion of Canada, for Her Majesty the Queen and Her successors forever, all their rights, titles and privileges, whatsoever, to the lands included within the following limits."[85] This statement has served as the bedrock of settler property relations and governance in western Canada for a century and a half. The problem, however, is that it may not have reflected the reality of the oral negotiations for Treaty 6 and the other numbered treaties. Krasowski triangulated oral and written accounts of the spoken negotiations, and nowhere did he find a spoken description of the surrender clause as presented in the official written version of the treaty. For Treaty 6, several eyewitness accounts of the negotiations were recorded and published that "contradict" the account published by Alexander Morris and reproduced in government documents.[86]

Although antithetical to the long-held view that over 99 percent of Indigenous territory was surrendered to the Crown, the depth of Krasowski's research makes his analysis hard to simply discount as hyperbole. His findings mirror the shock among southern Alberta Elders when they were informed of the surrender clause by researchers as they collected oral histories of Treaty 7.[87] Other scholars, both Indigenous and non-Indigenous, have argued convincingly that the land was to be shared between communities rather than handed wholesale from one group to the other. Nêhiyaw legal scholar Sharon Venne wrote,

> Now seriously, what kind of people would agree to give up these things? There are five thousand Indigenous Peoples camped at Fort Carlton. There are thirty non-Indigenous Peoples sitting at the table in their red uniforms saying, "put your pen to this paper and you give up everything." Be logical, does that make any sense? Yet, over and over, government officials say to us, "You gave up everything. You gave up the land, you gave up your law, and you gave up your government."[88]

Anishinaabe-Métis academic Aimée Craft was adamant that "at no point in the negotiations is it recorded, in any document or in the oral histories, that the parties discussed the concepts of land surrender or sale."[89] The issue of surrender is more than an academic or semantic debate; it is at the core of settler society in Western Canada.

## Conclusion

By the end of 1885, Canadian officials were in full control of the northern Great Plains, and the Indigenous population was almost completely settled on reserves, the small plots of land that would serve as "prisons of grass." Many sought solace in exile.[90] What crops reserve farmers managed to produce were kept from the market through a permit system that remained in place until the 1960s. Children were increasingly placed into residential institutions whose stated purpose was the elimination of Indigenous identity, family structure, and traditional governance. The *Indian Act*, passed in Parliament in 1876 without consultation of those affected, continues to frame the lives of Indigenous Peoples to this day.[91] Religious practices such as the Sundance were criminalized as part of a century-long enforced social experiment intended to recast identity, economy, and thought under the authoritarian control of government officials and the religious orders that served as their proxies.

The legacy of "Indian policy," which served to advance the interests of settlers to the detriment of First Nations, continues to undermine Indigenous health and well-being. In 2018, a Liberal cabinet minister identified a fifteen-year difference in the life expectancy between Indigenous Peoples and the wider Canadian population.[92] The Treaty Land Entitlement process in Saskatchewan,[93] and the hundreds of ongoing legal actions based upon the abrogation of treaty or inherent Indigenous Rights across the country, underscore the depth of dominion lawlessness that began almost as soon as the treaties were completed. Canadians raised on the myth of the "peaceable kingdom" must now deal with the legacy of thousands of unmarked graves at former Indian residential schools and so many other horrors that continue to fuel trauma from generation to generation. Instead of creating a "just society," the actions of the Canadian government in the wake of the treaties are increasingly characterized as genocide.[94] From the starvation and forced relocations that came with the extirpation of the bison, to the violent control of reserves, the permit and the pass systems, the horrors of residential schools, the Alabama-like segregation of the 1960s, to the killing of Colten Boushie and its aftermath, the racialized violence in Saskatchewan persists like a wound that refuses to heal. The executions at Battleford stand as a testament to the brutality employed in the establishment of the settler society in Western Canada.

## Notes

1 Most settler colonizers wanted the Indigenous Peoples to simply "go away." See Veracini, "Introducing Settler Colonial Studies," 2–3.

2 Wolfe, "Settler Colonialism."

3 Stonechild and Waiser, *Loyal till Death*, 223–224.
4 "Apishaskoos (Little Bear) Speech Before Dying." See page 5 for a list of the condemned and their offences.
5 Daschuk, *Clearing the Plains*, 152–155.
6 Daschuk, *Clearing the Plains*, 155–156.
7 "Their war was against those white men who held them in subjugation, and not against white people in general. They knew precisely who were their colonizers." See Adams, *Prison of Grass*, 108.
8 By July, seventy men were imprisoned in Regina and another sixty were held in Battleford. See Bingaman, "The North-West Rebellion Trials, 1885," 14.
9 Stonechild and Waiser, *Loyal till Death*, 221.
10 Stonechild and Waiser, *Loyal till Death*, 199.
11 Waiser, "The White Man Governs," 465.
12 Bingaman, "The North-West Rebellion Trials," 50.
13 pîhtokahanapiwiyin served only eight months before his release on medical grounds, and mistahimusqua served two years. See Bingaman, "The North-West Rebellion Trials," 93.
14 Bingaman, "The North-West Rebellion Trials," 127.
15 Jefferson, *Fifty Years on the Saskatchewan*, 152–153. Some—such as imases (Little Bear), Little Poplar, Lucky Man, and about a hundred other nêhiyaw—sought refuge in the United States. Dempsey, "Little Bear's Band."
16 Milton Tootoosis, personal communication, May 24, 2022.
17 Bingaman, "The North-West Rebellion Trials," 122.
18 In Battleford, hearsay evidence was allowed, there were no proper defence summations, and "the defendants were left to their own devices." Bingaman, "The North-West Rebellion Trials," 129–130.
19 "Settlers Express Their Views on the Situation and Demand that Justice Be Done, Great Unanimity of Feeling," *Saskatchewan Herald*, June 8, 1885.
20 *Saskatchewan Herald*, June 15, 1885.
21 Bingaman, "The North-West Rebellion Trials," 131.
22 "Judging a Judge," *Saskatchewan Herald*, December 14, 1885.
23 Dewdney to Macdonald, September 3, 1885, Saskatchewan Archives, Sir John A. Macdonald Papers, Transcripts R-70, 371. See also "Battleford Hangings," 5.
24 Waiser, "The White Man Governs," 475.
25 Pfeifer and Leyton-Brown, *Death by Rope*, 42–43.
26 Pfeifer and Leyton-Brown, *Death by Rope*, 42–43.
27 Roach, *Canadian Justice, Indigenous Injustice*, 35.
28 McCoy, "Legal Ideology," 186.
29 Waiser, "The White Man Governs," 475–477.
30 Bingaman, "The North-West Rebellion Trials," 129.
31 "The Execution: Indians Hanged at Battleford. They Sing Their Last Death Song and Are Not Afraid to Die," *Prince Albert Times and Saskatchewan Review*, November 27, 1885.
32 "Executions," *Saskatchewan Herald*, November 30, 1885.
33 Stonechild and Waiser, *Loyal till Death*, 224.

34 Jefferson, *Fifty Years on the Saskatchewan*, 153.
35 "Executions," *Saskatchewan Herald*, November 30, 1885.
36 "Indian Murderers Hanged," *Regina Leader*, December 3, 1885.
37 Stonechild and Waiser, *Loyal till Death*, 226.
38 Stonechild and Waiser, *Loyal till Death*, 226.
39 Stonechild and Waiser, *Loyal till Death*, 226–227.
40 See "The Indian Policy," *Saskatchewan Herald*, March 20, 1885. Between 1883 and 1892, 19 of 156 children died at the school, with 4 others unaccounted for. Roach, *Canadian Justice, Indigenous Injustice*, 36.
41 Waiser, "The White Man Governs," 476.
42 Kauanui, "'A Structure, Not an Event.'"
43 The policy of "sheer compulsion" developed by Reed in July 1885 served as a template for the administration of Indian Affairs in the field for decades. See Stonechild and Waiser, *Loyal till Death*, 215–218.
44 Tobias, "Canada's Subjugation of the Plains Cree."
45 Wolfe, "Settler Colonialism," 388.
46 Canadian Press, "'I Do See the Tide Turning'"; Harif, "Peepeekisis Cree Nation Celebrates"; NNL Digital News Update, "Land Claim Settled."
47 Roach, *Canadian Justice, Indigenous Injustice*, 25.
48 MacKinnon, "*Royal Proclamation of 1763*."
49 A significant exception is British Columbia, where only a tiny portion of the province was covered by treaties.
50 Krasowski, *No Surrender*.
51 Krasowski, *No Surrender*, 87–127. Treaty 4 was negotiated in an atmosphere of acrimony based upon a number of Canadian transgressions. A sign of the mistrust at the negotiations was the absence of a pipe ceremony. See also Daschuk, *Clearing the Plains*, 94–95.
52 Johnson, *Two Families*.
53 Miller, "Building the Foundations of Western Canada."
54 Treaty 4 was the result of an armed standoff resulting from the trespass of a Geological Survey of Canada party in 1873 in what is now southern Saskatchewan. Daschuk, *Clearing the Plains*, 94–95.
55 Treaty 6 was completed after the construction of a telegraph line across nêhiyaw territory had been stopped the previous year. Daschuk, *Clearing the Plains*, 96. See also Krasowski, *No Surrender*, 176.
56 Daschuk, *Clearing the Plains*, 97.
57 Canada was motivated by "mounting development pressures and the fear that warfare on the frontier would take place if Plains Indian needs and demands were not met promptly." Ray, Miller, and Tough, *Bounty and Benevolence*, 146–147.
58 Alexander Morris was censured for committing the Dominion of Canada government to added support for the nêhiyaw. Krasowski, *No Surrender*, 276.
59 Daschuk, *Clearing the Plains*, 105.
60 McQuillan, "Creation of Indian Reserves," 292; Sarah Carter's classic *Lost Harvests* remains the most detailed and sophisticated study of the failure of reserve agriculture.

61 LeRat with Ungar, *Treaty Promises*, 84.
62 Hildebrandt, *Views from Fort Battleford*, 94–96.
63 Carter, "Two Acres and a Cow."
64 Desnomie, "Voices of the File Hills Colony"; Bednasek, "Aboriginal and Colonial Geographies."
65 Patterson, "Ottawa Tells Saskatchewan Cree Nation.'"
66 Carter, "'An Infamous Proposal.'"
67 Waiser and Hanson, *Cheated*, 5.
68 Daschuk, Hackett, and MacNeil, "Treaties and Tuberculosis"; Elias, *The Dakota of the Canadian Northwest*.
69 Daschuk, *Clearing the Plains*, 106–126.
70 Daschuk, *Clearing the Plains*, 110–124.
71 Tobias, "Canada's Subjugation of the Plains Cree," 519–548. The nêhiyaw were not the only people forced from the Cypress Hills. The Nakoda, who had a surveyed reserve in place, were driven hundreds of kilometres east to their current location at Carry the Kettle First Nation; Tanner, Tanner, Miller, and McGuire, *Owóknage*.
72 House of Commons Debates, fifth Parliament, third Session (July 11, 1885), online at "Official Report of the Debates of the House of Commons of the Dominion of Canada," Canadiana.ca, at page 3319 (Hon. John A. Macdonald), https://www.canadiana.ca/view/oocihm.9_07186_3_4/763.
73 Duhame, "Copy of Treaty No. 6."
74 Dewdney to Middleton, May 7, 1885. Library and Archives Canada, Dewdney Papers, Northwest Rebellion, 1884–1885, MG 27, ICA, vol. 4, 1775–1776. I thank Rob Nestor for providing me with this reference.
75 Dewdney to Macdonald, Sir John A. Macdonald Papers, Saskatchewan Archives, September 9, 1885, Transcript R-70, 376.
76 Story, "The Pass System in Practice," 137–138.
77 Turner, *The North-West Mounted Police*, 284.
78 Williams, dir., *The Pass System*. With few exceptions, historians were slow to recognize the importance of the pass system. See Carter, "Controlling Indian Movement," and Barron, "The Indian Pass System."
79 Bob Joseph, *21 Things You May Not Know*.
80 Dr. J.J. Heagarty to Dr. E.L. Stone, "Epidemiology, Diseases, Tuberculosis, Tuberculosis among Indians," Library and Archives Canada, RG 29, National Health and Welfare, vol. 1225, November 16, 1932, file 311.
81 The Municipality of Weldon passed a resolution against keeping so many tubercular Indigenous Peoples on the James Smith Reserve because it was "resulting in the infection of white neighbours." Quote from *Saskatoon Star* clipping in Library and Archives Canada, RG 29, National Health and Welfare, Series A-2, vol. 2915, August 11, 1937 file 850-1-A105.
82 Gzowski, "This Is Our Alabama." These "voluntary" practices included settlers using the front seats of buses while Indigenous Peoples rode in the back and the refusal of service to Indigenous Peoples at local restaurants.
83 From *The Trespass to Property Act*: "Liability of an occupier, 17.1 An occupier owes no duty of care to a person entering onto the premises of the occupier

in contravention of this Act except the duty not to: (a) create a danger with the deliberate intent of doing harm or damage to the person; and (b) do a wilful act with reckless disregard of the presence of the person."

84 Hubbard, dir., *nipawistamasowin: We Will Stand Up*. See also Roach, *Canadian Justice, Indigenous Injustice*, 16–35.

85 See Duhame, "Copy of Treaty No. 6."

86 Krasowski, *No Surrender*, 176.

87 Treaty 7 Tribal Council, with Hildebrandt, Rider, and Carter, *The True Spirit and Original Intent of Treaty 7*.

88 Venne, "Treaties Made in Good Faith," 7–8.

89 Craft, *Breathing Life into the Stone Fort Treaty*, 109.

90 Stonechild and Waiser, *Loyal till Death*, 228–230.

91 Joseph, *21 Things You May Not Know*.

92 Canadian Press, "Lifespan of Indigenous People."

93 The return of land promised but not delivered by the treaties began in the province in 1992 and is not expected to be completed for several decades. So far, more than $680 million has been transferred to the thirty-six First Nations involved in the process. Those First Nations represent almost half of the reserve communities in Saskatchewan. See Government of Saskatchewan, "Treaty Land and Entitlements."

94 After the confirmation of 215 graves at the Kamloops residential school, the Canadian Historical Association stated that "The History of Violence Against Indigenous People Fully Warrants the Use of the Word 'Genocide.'" Soon after, more than fifty historians signed a document decrying the CHA's position. "Historians Rally vs. Genocide Myth."

## Sources

Adams, Howard. *Prison of Grass: Canada from the Native Point of View*. Fifth House, 1975.

"Apishaskoos (Little Bear) Speech Before Dying." *Saskatchewan Indian* 3 (1972).

Barron, F. Laurie. "The Indian Pass System in the Canadian West, 1882–1935." *Prairie Forum* 13, no. 1 (1988): 25–42.

"Battleford Hangings," *Saskatchewan Indian* 3 (1972).

Bednasek, C. Drew. "Aboriginal and Colonial Geographies of the File Hills Farm Colony." PhD dissertation, Queen's University, 2009.

Bingaman, Sandra. "The North-West Rebellion Trials, 1885." MA thesis, University of Saskatchewan, 1971.

Canadian Historical Association. "The History of Violence Against Indigenous People Fully Warrants the Use of the Word 'Genocide.'" Accessed October 14, 2024. https://cha-shc.ca/advocacy/the-history-of-violence-against-indigenous-peoples-fully-warrants-the-use-of-the-word-genocide/.

Canadian Press. "'I Do See the Tide Turning': Siksika First Nation Signs $1.3 B. Land Claim with Feds." *APTN News*, June 3, 2022. https://www.aptnnews.ca/national-news/i-do-see-the-tide-turning-siksika-first-nation-signs-1-3b-land-claim-with-feds/.

Canadian Press. "Lifespan of Indigenous People 15 Years Shorter than That of Other Canadians, Federal Documents Say." CBC News, January 23, 2018. https://www.cbc.ca/news/health/indigenous-people-live-15-years-less-philpott-briefing-1.4500307#.

Carter, Sarah. "Controlling Indian Movement: The Pass System." *NeWest Review* 10 (1985): 8–9.

Carter, Sarah. "'An Infamous Proposal': Prairie Indian Reserve Land and Soldier Settlement after World War One." *Manitoba History* 37 (1999): 9–21. https://www.mhs.mb.ca/docs/mb_history/37/infamousproposal.shtml.

Carter, Sarah. *Lost Harvests: Prairie Indian Reserve Farmers and Government Policy*. McGill-Queen's University Press, 1990.

Carter, Sarah. "Two Acres and a Cow: 'Peasant' Farming for the Indians of the Northwest, 1889–1897." *Canadian Historical Review* 70 (1989): 27–52.

Craft, Aimée. *Breathing Life into the Stone Fort Treaty: An Anishinabe Understanding of Treaty One*. Purich Publishing, 2013.

Daschuk, James. *Clearing the Plains: Disease, Politics of Starvation, and the Loss of Indigenous Life*. University of Regina Press, 2013.

Daschuk, J.W., Paul Hackett, and Scott MacNeil. "Treaties and Tuberculosis: First Nations People in Late 19th Century Western Canada, a Political and Economic Transformation." *Canadian Bulletin of Medical History* 23, no. 2 (2006): 307–330. https://doi.org/10.3138/cbmh.23.2.307.

Dempsey, James. "Little Bear's Band: Canadian or American Indians?" *Alberta History* 41 (1993): 2–10.

Desnomie, Chayenne. "Voices of the File Hills Colony." MA thesis, University of Regina, 2018.

Duhame, Roger. "Copy of Treaty No. 6 between Her Majesty the Queen and the Plain and Wood Cree Indians and other Tribes of Indians at Fort Carlton, Fort Pitt and Battle River with Adhesions." Government of Canada. Queen's Printer and Controller of Stationery, 1964. https://www.rcaanc-cirnac.gc.ca/eng/1100100028710/1581292569426.

Elias, Peter Douglas. *The Dakota of the Canadian Northwest: Lessons for Survival*. University of Manitoba Press, 1988.

Government of Saskatchewan. "Treaty Land and Entitlements." Accessed October 14, 2024. https://www.saskatchewan.ca/residents/first-nations-citizens/treaty-land-and-entitlements.

Gzowski, Peter. "This Is Our Alabama." *Maclean's*, July 6, 1963.

Harif, Afsa. "Peepeekisis Cree Nation Celebrates Signing of Historic Land Claim Settlement." CTV News, August 11, 2022. https://regina.ctvnews.ca/peepeekisis-cree-nation-celebrates-signing-of-historic-land-claim-settlement-1.5542665.

"Historians Rally vs. Genocide Myth." *Dorchester Review*, August 12, 2021. https://www.dorchesterreview.ca/blogs/news/historians-rally-vs-genocide-myth.

Hubbard, Tasha, dir. *nipawistamasowin: We Will Stand Up*. National Film Board, 2019. 98 min. https://www.nfb.ca/film/nipawistamasowin-we-will-stand-up.

Jefferson, Robert. *Fifty Years on the Saskatchewan*. Canadian North-West Historical Society, 1929.

Johnson, Harold. *Two Families: Treaties and Government*. Purich Publishing, 2007.

Joseph, Bob. *21 Things You May Not Know about the Indian Act: Helping Canadians Make Reconciliation with Indigenous Peoples a Reality*. Indigenous Relations Press, 2018.

Hildebrandt, Walter. *Views from Fort Battleford: Constructed Visions of an Anglo-Canadian West*. AU Press, 2008.

Kauanui, J. Kēhaulani. "'A Structure, Not an Event': Settler Colonialism and Enduring Indigeneity." *Emergent Critical Analytics for Alternative Humanities* 5, no. 1 (2016). https://csalateral.org/issue/5-1/forum-alt-humanities-settler-colonialism-enduring-indigeneity-kauanui/#fn-351-3.

Krasowski, Sheldon. *No Surrender: The Land Remains Indigenous*. University of Regina Press, 2019.

LeRat, Harold, with Linda Ungar. *Treaty Promises, Indian Reality: Life on a Reserve*. Purich Publishing, 2005.

MacKinnon, Leslie. "*Royal Proclamation of 1763*, Canada's 'Indian Magna Carta' Turns 250." CBC News, last updated October 7, 2013. https://www.cbc.ca/news/politics/royal-proclamation-of-1763-canada-s-indian-magna-carta-turns-250-1.1927667.

McCoy, Ted. "Legal Ideology in the Aftermath of the Rebellion: The Convicted First Nations Participants, 1885." *Histoire sociale/Social History* 42, no. 84 (2009): 175–201.

McQuillan, D. Aidan. "Creation of Indian Reserves on the Canadian Prairies, 1870–1885." *Geographical Review* 70, no. 4 (1980): 379–396. https://doi.org/10.2307/214075.

Miller, J.R. "Building the Foundations of Western Canada: Confederation and the Numbered Treaties." Public lecture, University of Regina, October 19, 2017.

NNL Digital News Update. "Land Claim Settled for Mitaanjigaming First Nation in Treaty 3." *NetNews Ledger*, August 24, 2022. https://www.netnewsledger.com/2022/08/24/land-claim-settled-for-mitaanjigamiing-first-nation-in-treaty-3/.

Patterson, Dayne. "Ottawa Tells Saskatchewan Cree Nation It's 'Deeply Sorry' for Assimilative 'Colony Scheme.'" CBC News, August 3, 2022. https://www.cbc.ca/news/canada/saskatchewan/canadian-government-apologize-peepeekisis-cree-nation-file-hills-colony-1.6539734.

Pfeifer, Jeffrey, and Ken Leyton-Brown. *Death by Rope: An Anthology of Canadian Executions, Volume 1 (1867–1923)*. Centax Books, 2007.

*Prince Albert Times and Saskatchewan Review*, November 27, 1885.

Ray, Arthur J., Jim Miller, and Frank Tough. *Bounty and Benevolence: A History of Saskatchewan Treaties*. McGill-Queen's University Press, 2000.

*Regina Leader*, December 3, 1885.

Roach, Kent. *Canadian Justice, Indigenous Injustice: The Gerald Stanley and Colton Boushie Case*. McGill-Queen's University Press, 2019.

Saskatchewan Archives. Sir John A. Macdonald Papers, Transcripts R-70.

*Saskatchewan Herald*, March 20 through December 15, 1885.

Stonechild, Blair, and Bill Waiser. *Loyal till Death: Indians and the North-West Rebellion*. Fifth House, 1997.

Story, Kenton. "The Pass System in Practice: Restricting Indigenous Mobility in Western Canada, 1885–1915." *Ethnohistory* 69, no. 2 (2022): 137–161. https://doi.org/10.1215/00141801-9522152.

Tanner, Jim, Tracey Tanner, David R. Miller, and Peggy Martin McGuire. *Owóknage: The Story of Carry the Kettle First Nation*. University of Regina Press, 2022.

Tobias, John L. "Canada's Subjugation of the Plains Cree, 1879–1885." *Canadian Historical Review* 64 (1983): 519–548. https://gladue.usask.ca/sites/gladue1.usask.ca/files/gladue//resource28-2c4f0414.pdf.

Treaty 7 Tribal Council, with Walter Hildebrandt, Dorothy First Rider, and Sarah Carter. *The True Spirit and Original Intent of Treaty 7*. McGill-Queen's University Press, 1996.

*The Trespass to Property Act*, SS 2009, c T-20.2. https://canlii.ca/t/5637c.

Turner, John Peter. *The North-West Mounted Police, Volume 2*. King's Printer, 1950. https://archive.org/details/northwestmounted01turn.

Venne, Sharon H. "Treaties Made in Good Faith." In *Natives and Settlers Now and Then: Historical Issues and Current Perspectives on Treaties and Land Claims in Canada*, edited by Paul W. DePasquale. University of Alberta Press, 2007.

Veracini, Lorenzo. "Introducing Settler Colonial Studies." *Settler Colonial Studies* 1, no. 1 (2011): 1–12. https://doi.org/10.1080/2201473X.2011.10648799.

Waiser, Bill. "The White Man Governs: The 1885 Indian Trials." In *Canadian State Trials, Volume III: Political Trials and Security Measures, 1840–1914*, edited by Barry Wright and Susan Binnie. University of Toronto Press, 2009.

Waiser, Bill, and Jennie Hanson. *Cheated: The Laurier Liberals and the Theft of First Nations Reserve Land*. ECW Press, 2023.

Williams, Alex, dir. *The Pass System*. Tamarack Productions, 2015. 50 min.

Wolfe, Patrick. "Settler Colonialism and the Elimination of the Native." *Journal of Genocide Research* 8, no. 4 (2006): 387–409. https://doi.org/10.1080/14623520601056240.

# Match and Exceed

## *Why Recognizing Genocide in Canada Is Only the First Step in Promoting Indigenous Self-Determination*

David B. A. MacDonald

BELIEVE IT OR NOT, CANADA HAS BECOME ONE OF THE world's most genocide-aware countries in the past decade, and potentially the most publicly repentant. We are the only western settler country to formally recognize in our national legislature that our state has committed genocide against Indigenous Peoples, following on a 2022 admission by Catholic Pope Francis that genocide took place in the Indian residential schools system (IRS). Canada is also the only country where a sitting head of government (Justin Trudeau) recognized continuing genocide by the state against Indigenous Peoples, following the conclusions of the National Inquiry into Missing and Murdered Indigenous Women and Girls (2019). As well, Canada is one of very few countries to pass a law incorporating the United Nations Declaration on the Rights of Indigenous Peoples into federal legislation (in 2021). At some level all of this seems precedent-setting and *could* lay the basis for major decolonizing change, including self-determination for Indigenous Peoples. Yet fine words have not translated into concrete action.

This chapter reflects on the Liberal legacy, which was at times potentially well-meaning and progressive, and at other times potentially hypocritical and undermining of Indigenous Peoples. In retrospect, the

Trudeau Liberal government engaged in a patchwork of conciliation-oriented[1] reforms, rhetorically advancing some commitments, following through with action on some issues, casting others aside, while simultaneously pursuing an agenda that often seemed anti-Indigenous and anti-reconciliation (especially when legal proceedings are involved). The overall context was the continuation of neoliberal settler colonialism and the further entrenchment of corporate control over the state. In this chapter, I follow Martin Lukacs's analysis in seeing the Trudeau administration as a textbook case of "extreme centrism." Such regimes are epitomized by a "continued support for privatization, deregulation, corporate tax cuts, and a slow withdrawal of the welfare state," while at the same time they "tinker around the edges to give their conservative economic policies a patina of emancipatory progressivism."[2]

Lukacs traced a "public consensus" that emerged under the Trudeau Liberals, where overt racism was condemned, Indigenous cultural expression was promoted, and "the language of Indigenous liberation" was used to frame government policies. However, this rhetoric disguised "several great unmentionables: land, resources, power, and the sharing of any of it." The government was seeking, as Lukacs put it appositely, to "contain and silence the transformative potential of Indigenous rights—held over vast territories, posing barriers to reckless extraction, and grounded in a vision of a different relationship to each other and the natural world."[3]

Whatever party is in power in future years, the settler state will continue, most likely ruled successively by the same two parties who created Canada and the IRS system, the same two parties whose governments committed genocide against Indigenous Peoples. We must consistently demand a higher standard from our orders of government. In their 2021 Action Plan on the National Inquiry into Missing and Murdered Indigenous Women and Girls, the National Family and Survivors Circle signally observed that "The efforts to end the genocide, to repair the harm caused and heal individually and collectively, must now match, and exceed, the intentions and actions that fueled the genocide."[4] This injunction to "match and exceed" is the necessary standard to which we need to hold the state and our settler-dominated governments. This call by the Circle sets the tone of my chapter.

I begin by defining what genocide is before exploring examples of the crime in settler colonial Canada. I take space to provide a history of the evolution of genocide recognition, through the work of Indigenous authors, the Truth and Reconciliation Commission, and the work of activists and political leaders. This sets us up to try to answer key questions many readers may have: So what? Does recognizing genocide actually change anything in Canada? Can it help support Indigenous self-determination? Can it bring about decolonization? I argue that, yes, it *can* provide useful leverage, but it won't directly impel action. For change to take place we need to act, and part of that is refusing as settlers to accept the status quo—to refuse to accept our institutions of government as inherently legitimate and neutral. Genocide must also be understood as a concerted and multistage war on Indigenous Peoples, their laws, political systems, and governments. Genocide recognition can and must provide further leverage for Indigenous self-determination—and demonstrate that the settler state has been a malign actor in the lives of Indigenous Peoples and nations.

We need to take a stand against denialism and promote memory, abandoning the myths Paulette Regan has identified: our front-facing image of "a nation of peacemakers," commensurate with a "myth of innocence" over the foundations of the country.[5] It also involves promoting Indigenous Peoples and presentations of their history. Linda Tuhiwai Smith (Ngāti Awa, Ngāti Porou) in her celebrated *Decolonizing Methodologies* promotes the need for Indigenous Peoples to engage in "rewriting and rerighting our position in history."[6] We must also avoid falling into the trap of the depravity narratives we discuss in this volume's introduction, what Eve Tuck (Unangax̂, St. Paul Island) terms "damage-centered research" and "deficit models." It was *never* right to present Indigenous Peoples as "broken" and Indigenous communities as "sites of disinvestment and dispossession."[7] We must now more than ever promote research that centres the strength, "survivance," and self-determination of Indigenous Peoples within a context of colonialism, occupation, and genocide.[8]

This chapter is written from the positionality of a mixed-race Indo-Trinidadian and Scottish settler. While Canada has been founded on whiteness and remains a settler state dominated by European-origin settlers, there is considerable demographic change that is colouring the nature of Canadian settler democracy. Racialized peoples can and do express solidarities with Indigenous Peoples and can share some experiences of settler racism, and, yet, they may echo settler stereotypes of Indigenous Peoples as part of their journey to integrate into what they understand as mainstream Canada. My ancestors were brought to Trinidad from British India to cut sugar cane as indentured labourers in the 1850s and '60s. They were

Muslims and Hindus; many were converted by missionaries in order to get a formal education. I am mindful of George Lipsitz's observation that "non-white people can become active agents of white supremacy" and that "one way of becoming an insider is by participating in the exclusion of other outsiders."[9] My own identity as an unsettled Brownish settler in a majority-white environment forms the backdrop to this analysis.

## What Is Genocide?

In my work involving Indian residential schools, I have often heard survivors use the term *genocide* to describe the IRS system. The creator of the term, the Polish Jewish lawyer Raphaël Lemkin, defined it in 1944 as "a coordinated plan of different actions aiming at the destruction of the essential foundations of the life of national groups, with the aim of annihilating the groups themselves."[10] Yet, genocide was not just about mass murder, and Lemkin's understanding included forms of colonization, the theft of Indigenous Land, and attempts to destroy Indigenous Peoples, cultures, languages, spiritualities, and relationships. By 1948, the United Nations passed the Genocide Convention, portions of which we reproduced in the introduction to this volume.

It would not be difficult to match up the crimes of the settler state with the Genocide Convention, and numerous scholars and activists have done so. Unfortunately, but not unexpectedly, Indigenous genocide denial has been a fairly routine aspect of settler statecraft. Steven Newcomb (Shawnee/Lenape) outlines how "a colonising nation or people will tend not to interpret or characterise its political system as one of domination."[11] Nêhiyaw legal theorist Tamara Starblanket writes that the biggest challenge to achieving genocide recognition has been "the oppressive dominating and dehumanizing framework internationally and domestically infested with the rubric of denial."[12]

Key reasons to recognize genocide include stopping genocidal practices and promoting redress. The TRC also sought to honour Indigenous survivors—of residential schools; the Sixties Scoop; gender-based violence, including abduction, physical and sexual abuse, and sterilization, amongst other crimes. For the late Murray Sinclair, former judge and chair of the Truth and Reconciliation Commission, tracing the applicability of genocide to the IRS system honoured the truths conveyed by survivors, who made use of the term to engage with their own experiences.

Sinclair promoted genocide acknowledgement, as he stated recently, "because, first and foremost, Survivors themselves raised the issue. For many of them, recognition of colonial malevolence is necessary for the process of reconciliation to move forward."[13] When I interviewed TRC Commissioner Marie Wilson, she noted to me that genocide was on the minds of survivors throughout the country. They "came forward to us [and] talked about it and qualified their own experience as genocide."[14] Honouring the survivors became a key aspect of why the TRC engaged with the topic.

At another level, recognizing genocide helps bring about change because it allows us to understand the truth about our institutions of settler government—why they were formed, how they functioned historically, and why and how they function now to continue to perpetuate crimes against Indigenous Peoples. Only with the truth can we bring about institutional change. For those of us who study political science, the truth of genocide must be widely recognized in our discipline so that we no longer make the error of studying institutions of the state with the unspoken and tacit assumption that they are benign, neutral containers, representing the cultures, values, and governance traditions of Indigenous Peoples.

## Genocide in Canada

When we think of genocide in Canada, there are numerous historical instances that might come to mind. Both Emily Grafton and I have served as members of the Reconciliation Committee of the Canadian Political Science Association. In 2021, we drafted a statement that recognized fourteen different instances of genocide against Indigenous Peoples in Canada.[15] Word count restrictions prohibit me from engaging too deeply, but I can offer a few examples.

In the Atlantic region, the deliberate killing of Mi'kmaq peoples by the British in the eighteenth century is documented through the work of Mi'kmaq historian Daniel Paul.[16] Settler historian James Daschuk has documented how the federal government deliberately starved Plains Indigenous Peoples during the late nineteenth century, using violence to take their lands and waters and push them onto small reserves.[17] I will discuss the IRS in a moment, but it is also important to contextualize this system as part of an ongoing genocidal project by the settler state and its orders of government. This included what became known as the Sixties Scoop, and I have included some details about this in the book's introduction. From the 1930s and '40s, thousands of Indigenous children were taken from their parents and sent for adoption or to foster homes, the majority to white homes, an approach that some argue continues through contemporary child welfare apprehension practices. A number of scholars suggest that genocide occurred here, a conclusion I support.[18]

The most prominent discussions of genocide relate to the network of Indian residential schools, established and run by the federal government with the enthusiastic collaboration of the four mainline Christian churches. These operated from the 1880s to the 1970s, with the last of the schools closing only in 1996.[19] A coherent system of Indian residential schools was established by the mid-1880s. The Catholic Church ran the majority, followed by schools run by the Anglicans, and the Presbyterian, Methodist, and United Churches.[20]

I have focused much of my research on forcible transfer, namely Article 2(e) of the UNGC,[21] and I have highlighted legislation, for example, such as the 1920 amendment to the *Indian Act*, which made school attendance compulsory for all status First Nations children aged seven to fifteen. This meant in practice that a large proportion were forced to attend residential schools located a considerable distance from their homes, as day schools near or on reserves were few in number.[22]

Claims of genocide are hardly new—they stretch back many decades. Roland Chrisjohn and Sherri Young,[23] Dean Neu and Richard Therrien,[24] and Agnes Grant, among others, all used the Genocide Convention in their analyses of the IRS system.[25] In the second edition of his *Unjust Society* (1999), noted nêhiyaw historian Harold Cardinal similarly cast the IRS experience as a form of genocide.[26] The Assembly of First Nations made a determination in 2002 that the UNGC applied, specifically citing "the forcible transfer of children from one racial group to another with the intent to destroy the group" as being central to the operation of the IRS system.[27]

The Truth and Reconciliation Commission (2009–2015) concluded that cultural genocide had been committed, outlining some of the goals of the Canadian government as "to eliminate Aboriginal governments; ignore Aboriginal rights; terminate the treaties; and, through a process of assimilation, cause Aboriginal peoples to cease to exist as distinct legal, social, cultural, religious, and racial entities in Canada."[28] Why did the TRC not find Canada guilty of genocide as described in international law?

The primary reason was the post-judicial mandate of the TRC under the Settlement Agreement. The commissioners were prohibited from finding the federal government or the churches guilty of breaking any law in Canada, either domestic or international.[29]

Nevertheless, Justice Sinclair made frequent and public statements that the UNGC was violated and sought to make this conclusion in the *Final Report*, only to be dissuaded by his legal team.[30] Sinclair later noted that if the TRC had stretched beyond their mandate, there could have been negative repercussions in the Canadian court system: "We were concerned that if we simply used the term genocide—which surely we could have—the government or somebody would have asked a court to wipe out that part of the report. And the court, in its heavy-handed way, would likely have simply deleted those findings. So we couched it as carefully as we could, but as clearly as we could, by referencing the term cultural genocide."[31]

This strategy of getting *cultural genocide* accepted worked well in the sense that it did not provoke widespread settler denial, although the Conservative government of Stephen Harper was not pleased. Both the Liberals and NDP recognized cultural genocide in 2015 and pledged a range of policies to promote reconciliation. In a poll of Canadians taken shortly after the release of the TRC reports, 70 percent of respondents felt that "cultural genocide" accurately described the IRS system.[32] This recognition of cultural genocide in turn laid the basis for further discussion of genocide as prohibited under international law. Noted Indigenous academics and activists also made ample use of the Genocide Convention in their TRC-era analyses of the IRS system in particular and settler colonialism in general. Mi'kmaq legal theorist and activist Pam Palmater, for example, asserted that "what happened to our people on Turtle Island fits every criteria of the international definition of genocide."[33] Bev Sellars, former chief of the Xat'sull First Nation, specifically referenced forcible transfer in her conclusion of genocide.[34] Joyce Green (Ktunaxa and Cree-Scots Métis) notes, too, that "the historical record of settler states shows that all of these acts have been committed by the states or their agents against Indigenous Peoples."[35] To this body of work, Tamara Starblanket added a detailed analysis of genocide in Canada in her 2018 book, *Suffer the Little Children*.[36]

All of this suggested that Canada was indeed guilty of genocide. When should full government accountability have kicked in? Arguably from November 4, 2015, when Justin Trudeau formed the first Canadian government led by a party that recognized cultural genocide. Yet no steps were taken to do anything specific to atone or provide redress for genocide. Efforts within the Liberal caucus went nowhere. For example, Liberal backbench MP Robert-Falcon Ouellette (Métis and Cree, Red Pheasant Cree Nation) introduced a private member's bill, C-318, calling for an IRS Memorial Day, and for Parliament to recognize UN-defined genocide for "the actions taken to remove children from families and communities to place them in residential schools."[37] While this federal bill had its first reading in October 2016, it proceeded no further and had no backing from the Liberal government.

However, in keeping with its "extreme centrism" and contradictory approach to Indigenous Rights, the Liberals took with one hand and gave with the other. While not endorsing a genocide finding, they did create a permissive political climate for extensive discussions of the topic. In 2016, the government established the National Inquiry into Missing and Murdered Indigenous Women and Girls, which would make important inroads into genocide recognition. The National Inquiry's discussions of genocide helped lay the basis for Winnipeg's Canadian Museum for Human Rights to finally recognize genocide. The museum's leadership had long refused to weigh in on the issue.[38] However, in the new political climate, the museum released a statement in 2018 recognizing that "the colonial experience in Canada, from first contact to the present, constitutes genocide against Indigenous Peoples. The Indian residential school system was one key component of this genocide."[39]

From 2016 to 2019, the National Inquiry carried out hearings throughout the country, documenting the violence of the settler state, especially against Indigenous women and girls, who are twelve times more likely than other women in Canada to go missing or be killed. In 2019, the National Inquiry made the case for considering "the application of genocide in both legal and in social terms, and as it persists today."[40] Overall they identified a "race-based genocide of Indigenous Peoples, including First Nations, Inuit and Métis, which especially targets women, girls, and 2SLGBTQQIA people." They deployed genocide widely to encompass the history of colonization and its ongoing practices and processes, including contemporary problems of "increased rates of violence, death, and suicide in Indigenous populations." The NIMMWG identified "the unique nature of 'colonial genocide,'" which is unlike the traditional understanding of genocide derived from the "Holocaust prototype."[41]

Eventually, with some pressure, Trudeau accepted the verdict of ongoing genocide. This was probably the first time a sitting head of government recognized that his government and his country were continuing to commit genocide against distinct peoples within the state, in violation of the UN convention. Law professor Bruno Gélinas-Faucher noted at the time, "A court could say, under current rules of international law, that the state has accepted responsibility under international law for the crime of genocide.... That's a big deal."[42] Big deal or not, there was no follow-through by the Trudeau government on this issue, no apology for genocide, and no plans for redress specifically related to this recognition.

## The Deaths of Children, Unmarked Burials, and Genocide Recognition

Indigenous families and communities knew from the beginning that their children died in large numbers in residential schools, and sometimes later on reserves, as a consequence of horrendous health conditions in the schools. The TRC confirmed 3,201 deaths from 1867 to 2000 but observed this number was probably too low, given the limited time and resources they had to investigate.[43] Commissioner Wilson notes that, of the named deaths, "at least double that number is suspected, in addition to the many that the records show were sent home, or sent to Indian hospitals in the final stages of illness to die there."[44] In May 2021, the Tk'emlúps te Secwépemc First Nation was the first to publicly announce the presence of up to 215 unmarked potential burials at the location of the Kamloops Indian Residential School. Further unmarked grave sites were identified from 2021 to 2023, in BC, Alberta, Saskatchewan, Manitoba, and Ontario.[45] We are now compiling the evidence of mass deaths in the schools, as many First Nations actively search these lands using ground penetrating radar. In 2021, Murray Sinclair articulated the belief that the death toll of Indigenous children may reach twenty-five thousand.[46]

It is during this period that New Democratic Party MP Leah Gazan (Winnipeg Centre) introduced the first of two non-binding motions to the House of Commons, a process that echoed Ouellette's bill of 2016. The first, in June 2021, would have recognized the IRS system as genocide. It required unanimous consent of the House and failed to get the support needed.[47] Due to media coverage of the unmarked burials as well as public outcry and some political pressure, Pope Francis journeyed to Canada in summer 2022 to deliver a formal apology to survivors. The apology was very meaningful for some, but for others it fell short as the Vatican did not assume responsibility for the co-creation and perpetuation of the system. Indeed, the apology seemed designed to evade legal responsibility for the crimes of the Catholic Church, which included running approximately 70 percent of residential schools.[48]

The apology masked the Catholic Church's integral role in the development and continuation of the IRS system, even during periods when the federal government sought other options. Still today, the church refuses to pay full compensation to survivors and has been reticent to open its archives. Nevertheless, and potentially in an effort to shield the Vatican from blame, the late Pope Francis recognized *state*-sponsored genocide. When subsequently confronted with a question about why he did not mention genocide, the Pope remarked, "But I described genocide. I apologised, I asked forgiveness for this activity, which was genocide."[49]

On the heels of the papal apology and genocide recognition, Gazan introduced a second motion: "That in the opinion of the House, this government must recognize what happened in Canada's Indian residential schools as genocide, as acknowledged by Pope Francis and in accordance with article II of the United Nations Convention on the Prevention and Punishment of the Crime of Genocide."[50] This one was passed unanimously in the House of Commons, and marks an important milestone in how the IRS system will be understood and commemorated. Now this system and its continued legacies will stand alongside the other genocides that are officially recognized.

Soon after, Canadians were polled on their views of whether genocide took place in their country. A June 2023 Leger poll yielded some interesting results: Of Canadian respondents, 60 percent "accept that Indigenous Peoples were the target of some form of genocide in Canada... 29 per cent strongly agreed and 31 per cent agreed somewhat." At the same time, such a belief did not impact most people's sense of personal accountability for what happened. Indeed, "almost 80 per cent of respondents across the country said they strongly disagree with the notion they bear personal responsibility for past injustice."[51] We might accept 60 percent as a good outcome, but the poll also indicates that a quarter of respondents disagreed with a finding of genocide.

Of these a proportion engage in denialism, not only of genocide but some also of the nature of the IRS system and settler colonialism itself.

Created in 2021 after the public disclosure of unmarked graves, the Office of the Independent Special Interlocutor for Missing Children and Unmarked Graves and Burial Sites investigated the extent of Indigenous children's deaths within the IRS system. Denialism was an important theme in their 2023 *Interim Report*, which observed that "a core group of Canadians continue to defend the Indian Residential Schools System. Some still deny that children suffered physical, sexual, psychological, cultural, and spiritual abuses, despite the TRC's indisputable evidence to the contrary. Others try to deny and minimize the destructive impacts of the Indian Residential Schools."[52]

I have documented settler denialism in my 2019 book, and a number of types come to mind here. The first is definitional, not necessarily denying the crimes but refusing to label them as *genocide*. Human rights lawyer Payam Akhavan is a notable example. He refused to recognize both cultural genocide and genocide, suggesting instead the term "persecution," a type of crime against humanity, which is of the "same genus as genocide."[53] While similar, the key difference lies in the specific intent, which must be present in genocide but need not be present in persecution. He tacitly implied that the genocide debate was a waste of effort, getting in the way of "the urgency of national reconciliation with Canada's indigenous people."[54]

A second type of denialism of claims that IRS administrators, teachers, and others had primarily negative intentions. While conceding some negative aspects of the schools, the argument goes that the positives should not be overshadowed. The TRC is blamed for promoting an unfair and overly negative narrative. The most obvious proponent of this denialist argument was former Conservative Senator Lynn Beyak, who famously praised the "kindly and well-intentioned men and women" who ran the schools, while lamenting that their "remarkable works, good deeds and historical tales in the residential schools" had gone unacknowledged.[55]

Another type of denial focused on settler colonial goals of control and assimilation, which were sometimes and disingenuously presented as antithetical to genocide. The well-known historian of the IRS system James R. Miller saw a "fixation" on genocide as "pointless and distracting," acting only to impede reconciliation by causing settlers to "tune out."[56] Earlier, Miller, with Donald B. Smith, opined that "the goal of policies we now consider horrific...was to control Indigenous people but not to eradicate them." The conclusion was "if Canada had wanted to destroy them, it would not have devoted so much effort to trying to turn them into Euro-Canadians."[57]

Statements like these distort the meaning of genocide, since the efforts to forcibly convert Indigenous Peoples into "Euro-Canadians" is indeed an aspect of genocide and is recognized as a violation of international law.

Genocide is also denied by arguing that its recognition is just a form of virtue signalling, wokeness, or political correctness—a performance and an exercise in hypocrisy. Writing in the *National Post*, Chris Selley put it that while officially the Liberal government accepted the NIMMIWG's finding of genocide, "obviously neither Miller nor Prime Minister Justin Trudeau actually believe the latter, ridiculous notion," and the path of least resistance for them was to agree, given that "it's actually less stressful for a politician to admit spurious charges of genocide than try to defend himself."[58] Thus, genocide recognition was positioned as a sort of mantra that progressives were forced to repeat, in contrast to the more "honest" conservatives.

We cannot know whether Justin Trudeau or his ministers believed genocide took place in Canada, and polls provide only a suggestive snapshot of public opinion. However, while we don't know the extent of denialism, we do know a few things for certain. The Office of the Special Interlocutor made several important points. The first is that any successful reconciliation between Indigenous Peoples and settlers depends on our ability to accept the truth of genocide. Special Interlocutor Kim Murray noted that "failing to acknowledge the deliberate genocidal harm inflicted on Indigenous children becomes a barrier to reconciliation and reinforces a culture of denialism in the Canadian population."[59] Second, there are demonstrable impacts on Indigenous Peoples, especially survivors, that are exacerbated by genocide denialism. The special interlocutor's 2022 report highlighted problems of "disenfranchised grief," defined as grief that "occurs when our losses are not acknowledged or accepted as legitimate by the society around us."[60] And third, we must be clear, following the words of the special interlocutor, that "denialism is a uniquely non-Indigenous problem; it therefore requires non-Indigenous people to actively work to counter denialism and to create and implement strategies to do so."[61]

Currently, there is little effort to ensure that denialism is actively combatted. Genocide recognition pushes us to a higher standard of behaviour. Recall the words of the National Family and Survivors Circle in the chapter introduction: "The efforts to end the genocide, to repair the harm caused and heal individually and collectively, must now match, and exceed, the intentions and actions that fueled the genocide."[62] What needs to change?

Recognition of genocide implies recognizing ongoing wrongs and malignancy on the part of the state. The state is responsible and state institutions that caused the harm cannot be trusted. It is an admission of guilt—that the settler state sought to dismantle and destroy Indigenous governments. It must be understood as a basis on which to call for full scale capacity-building for self-determination on Indigenous terms and including forms of collective self-determination involving multiple First Nations communities. As Audra Simpson (Kanien'kehá:ka) articulates, Indigenous Peoples need to be understood as "nationals with sovereign authority over their lives and over their membership and living within their own space."[63] If Indigenous Peoples have not had the ability to fully exercise their self-determining rights, the federal government must be responsible for making changes. Naomi Metallic rightly observes that if "Canada's slow and piecemeal recognition of self-government relates to concerns about Indigenous peoples' capacity," action is the obvious solution to "ensure that Indigenous groups are growing capacity." Thus, we should "expect Canada to currently be investing more resources and placing greater emphasis on capacity building towards self-government."[64]

A good start to self-determination is the return of Indigenous Lands. Indigenous nations require land bases in order to ensure their well-being and livelihood. As Katsi'tsakwas Ellen Gabriel (Kanehsatà:ke Nation, Turtle Clan) observes, "Land dispossession remains a key issue as it disrupts the relationship we have with Mother Earth and all our relations. The pillars of our identity—our languages, customs, health, ceremonies, and traditional forms of governance—are all inter-related and interdependent upon the health of our environment."[65] The late Arthur Manuel (Ktunaxa and Secwépemc Nations) articulated a vision of how Indigenous self-determination might look, based on control over sufficient land bases to "protect our languages, cultures, laws and economies." The focus of land back, then, is to "provide Indigenous Peoples with the right to make and influence economic development choices because of our increased governance over our larger land base."[66]

The settler state has enriched itself because it has usurped those lands. Almost 90 percent of Canada's territory is Crown land, divided between the federal and provincial governments. Overall, reserve communities comprise a meager 0.2 percent of the country's landmass, and while more government funding for services will help in the short term, ultimately the state must give back land—there is no other viable solution. Indigenous Lands were taken for the establishment of the railroad, and also taken and given over to European settlers as farmland and urban space. Crown land more recently has been used to generate tremendous wealth for the settler state and society. This includes control of waters, which have been used to construct hydroelectric infrastructure such as dams, with Canada producing the third-largest amount of hydroelectricity in the world. More than $80 billion annually is derived from the mining and processing of over sixty metals and minerals, accounting for approximately 20 percent of Canada's exports. In 2017, the forestry sector generated almost $25 billion, while the production and shipping of fossil fuels (oil, natural gas, and coal) has greatly enriched Alberta and Saskatchewan. Over 80 percent of water usage is tied to the natural resource sectors.[67]

Despite recognition of genocide in 2022, little of the settler colonial dynamic of controlling land, waters, and other Indigenous territories has changed. Self-determination is not speeding along, and no orders of settler government are admitting liability. The Liberal government moved forward only very slowly on the TRC's ninety-four calls to action, most of which remained unrealized in 2025. Reflecting on reconciliation in early 2023, Douglas Sinclair (Peguis First Nation) of the Indigenous Watchdog organization noted four main types of problems:

> Lack of political will to tackle the hardest issues, specifically issues around land and self-government; structural, legislative and institutional barriers embedded in colonial governance systems; systemic racism and discrimination entrenched within multiple sectors of society; failure to collect and disseminate quality data that makes accurate reporting difficult.[68]

Even when the Liberal government sought to promote Indigenous interests, they have had to contend with the provinces and territories, many of which have right-of-centre governments who can be hostile to Indigenous concerns. Sinclair has traced a concerted provincial agenda against the federal government. Six provincial governments have taken legal action in the courts against *Bill C-15*, the federal act to implement the United Nations Declaration on the Rights of Indigenous Peoples. Further, ten provinces and territories are "fighting Indigenous people in all levels of the court system over Aboriginal Rights and Title, Land

Claims, Duty to Consult/Free Prior and Informed Consent."[69] Clearly, we have a long way to go because our governments are often headed in the wrong direction.

## Conclusions

At some levels, the Trudeau government's "extreme centrism" was ambitious, with legislation to create an Indigenous languages act, a bill incorporating the UN Declaration on the Rights of Indigenous Peoples into domestic federal law (*Bill C-15*), and a range of other initiatives. At the same time, the new rights to be enshrined for Indigenous Peoples did little to reduce the coercive power of the settler state. The state continues to hold most of the political and economic cards and there will be little return of stolen land. Bruce McIvor rightly noted in 2020, "Reconciliation continues to fail because it rests on a foundation of systemic racism. It is predicated on the denial of Indigenous peoples' inherent rights and the willingness of the Canadian state to use violence to suppress the exercise of Indigenous rights."[70]

The Trudeau government was concerned primarily with the politics of balance—that is, balancing settler interests with those of Indigenous Peoples. Part of the balance involved pandering to settler fragility, especially in the difficult post-Covid economic climate. The government was therefore looking for a win-win situation in which Indigenous lives improved within Canada but primarily through means that legitimated existing settler colonial political, economic, educational, and legal institutions.

In this chapter I have argued for a higher standard—we must call out settler institutions for their genocidal foundations and continued genocidal actions. Justice Sinclair some time ago noted that for the status of Indigenous Peoples to improve, the behaviour of the perpetrator must change and patterns of victimization must stop: "It's not enough to say I'm sorry for what I did in the past and I'm going to keep abusing you."[71] We need to pressure our governments in power to cede at least some of their illegitimate control and to ensure that Indigenous Peoples have the lands, waters, and political and economic space needed to develop their own governments without the continued paternalistic control of the settler state. Only then can any real form of conciliation be possible after genocide and only then might we discuss an end to genocide.

## Acknowledgements

My thanks for their guidance to Michael Cachagee, Harvey Trudeau, Andrew Woolford, Murray Sinclair, Paulette Regan, Sheryl Lightfoot, Tricia Logan, James Daschuk, Ry Moran, Bernie Farber, Michael Dan, Len Rudner, Mike DeGagné, Jonathan Dewar, Matt James, Jennifer Preston, Lori Ransom, and Karine Duhamel, with special thanks to Emily Grafton for her editorial skills. This publication was supported by SSHRC Insight Grants 430413 and 430855.

## Notes

1 I use the term *conciliation* here (rather than *reconciliation*), since there has never been an initial period of conciliation historically.
2 Lukacs, "Is It Still Business as Usual?"
3 Lukacs, "Reconciliation."
4 National Inquiry into Missing and Murdered Indigenous Women and Girls [NIMMWG], "National Action Plan," 32.
5 Regan, *Unsettling the Settler*, 106.
6 Tuhiwai Smith, *Decolonizing Methodologies*, 29.
7 Tuck, "Suspending Damage," 409, 412.
8 Tuck, "Suspending Damage," 415, 422.
9 Lipsitz, *The Possessive Investment in Whiteness*, viii.
10 Lemkin, *Axis Rule in Occupied Europe*, 79.
11 Newcomb, "Domination in Relation to Indigenous ('Dominated') Peoples," 21.
12 Starblanket, *Suffer the Little Children*, 29.
13 Independent Special Interlocutor, "Sacred Responsibility," 10–11.
14 MacDonald, *The Sleeping Giant Awakens*, 106.
15 CPSA Reconciliation Committee, "Briefing Note on Genocide."
16 Paul, *We Were Not the Savages*, 45, 108, 165, 182.
17 Daschuk, "Acknowledging Patriarch's Failures," 44–45.
18 Episkenew, *Taking Back Our Spirits*, 67; Liebenberg and Ungar, *Resilience in Action*, 296.
19 Truth and Reconciliation Commission of Canada [TRC], *Final Report: The History, Part 1*, 66.
20 Milloy, *A National Crime*.
21 MacDonald and Hudson, "Contextualizing Aboriginal Residential Schools in Canada," 597–613.
22 Legacy of Hope Foundation, "Remembering the Children."
23 Chrisjohn, Young, and Maraun, *The Circle Game*, 17.
24 Neu and Therrien, *Accounting for Genocide*, 11–13.
25 Grant, *No End of Grief*, 24.
26 Cardinal, *The Unjust Society*, xv.

27 Assembly of First Nations, "Human Rights Report," 3.
28 TRC, *Final Report: The History, Part 1*, 3–4.
29 TRC, "Our Mandate."
30 MacDonald, *The Sleeping Giant Awakens*, 106.
31 Jewell and Mosby, eds., *Calls to Action—Accountability*, 7.
32 Angus Reid Institute, "Truth and Reconciliation."
33 Palmater. *Indigenous Nationhood*, 118.
34 Sellars, *Price Paid*, 101.
35 Green, "Introduction," 2.
36 Starblanket, *Suffer the Little Children*, 2018.
37 House of Commons, *Bill C-318*.
38 Logan, "Memory, Erasure, and National Myth."
39 Young, "Confronting Genocide in Canada."
40 NIMMWG, "Reclaiming Power and Place," 52–53.
41 NIMMWG, "A Legal Analysis of Genocide," 1.
42 Alhmidi, "Trudeau's Acknowledgment ."
43 TRC, "Honouring the Truth, Reconciling for the Future," 95–96.
44 Wilson, "Foreword," xiv.
45 Independent Special Interlocutor, "Sacred Responsibility," 10–11.
46 See Murray Sinclair's discussion with Rosanna Deerchild on "Reconciliation Reality Check."
47 CityNews, "NDP Motion."
48 Canadian Press, "'I Am Deeply Sorry.'"
49 Pullella, "Pope Says Genocide."
50 Hansard, "House of Commons Debates 44th Parliament, 1st Session."
51 Humphreys, "Even Those Saying Indigenous Land Acknowledgments."
52 Independent Special Interlocutor, "Sacred Responsibility," 104.
53 Akhavan, "Cultural Genocide: Legal Label or Mourning Metaphor?," 65.
54 Akhavan, "Cultural Genocide: When We Debate."
55 Kirkup, "Lynn Beyak Removed."
56 Miller, "Genocide, Macdonald and Canadian History."
57 Smith and Miller, "No Genocide."
58 Selley, "Liberals Consider."
59 Independent Special Interlocutor, "Sacred Responsibility," 133.
60 Independent Special Interlocutor, "Addressing Trauma," 17,
61 Independent Special Interlocutor, "Sacred Responsibility," 106.
62 NIMMIWG, "National Action Plan," 32.
63 Simpson, *Mohawk Interruptus*, 16.
64 Metallic, "Ending Piecemeal Recognition."
65 Gabriel, "Untethering Colonial Rule."
66 Manuel, "Until Canada Gives."
67 Pasternak, King, and Yesno, *Land Back*, 26.
68 Indigenous Watchdog, "Where Are the Successes."
69 Sinclair, "Why Reconciliation Is Absolutely Necessary."
70 McIvor, "Reconciliation as a Massive Failure."
71 Kennedy, "Q and A."

## Sources

Akhavan, Payam. "Cultural Genocide: Legal Label or Mourning Metaphor?" *McGill Law Journal* 62, no. 1 (2016): 244–70. https://lawjournal.mcgill.ca/article/cultural-genocide-legal-label-or-mourning-metaphor/.

Akhavan, Payam. "Cultural Genocide: When We Debate Words, We Delay Healing." *Globe and Mail*, February 10, 2016. http://www.theglobeandmail.com/opinion/cultural-genocide-when-we-debate-words-we-delay-healing/article28681535/.

Alhmidi, Maan. "Trudeau's Acknowledgment of Indigenous Genocide Could Have Legal Impacts: Experts." CTV News, June 5, 2021. https://www.ctvnews.ca/canada/trudeau-s-acknowledgment-of-indigenous-genocide-could-have-legal-impacts-experts-1.5457668.

Angus Reid Institute. "Truth and Reconciliation: Canadians See Value in Process, Skeptical about Government Action." July 9, 2015. http://angusreid.org/aboriginal-truth-and-reconciliation/.

Assembly of First Nations. "Human Rights Report to Non-Governmental Organizations: Redress for Cultural Genocide; Canadian Residential Schools." 2002. https://web.archive.org/web/20081124201833/http://www.turtleisland.org/news/afnrezschools.pdf.

Canadian Press. "'I Am Deeply Sorry': Full Text of Residential School Apology from Pope Francis." CBC News, July 25, 2022. https://www.cbc.ca/news/canada/edmonton/pope-francis-maskwacis-apology-full-text-1.6531341.

Cardinal, Harold. *The Unjust Society: The Tragedy of Canada's Indians*. M.G. Hurtig, 1969.

Chrisjohn, Roland, Sherri Young, and Michael Maraun. *The Circle Game: Shadows and Substance in the Indian Residential School Experience in Canada*. Theytus Books, 1997.

CityNews. "NDP Motion to See Commons Recognize Residential Schools as Genocide Fails." June 10, 2021. https://vancouver.citynews.ca/2021/06/10/ndp-motion-to-see-commons-recognize-residential-schools-as-genocide-fails/.

CPSA Reconciliation Committee. "CPSA Reconciliation Committee's Briefing Note on Genocide." September 30, 2021. https://cpsa-acsp.ca/cpsa-reconciliation-committee/.

Daschuk, James. "Acknowledging Patriarch's Failures Will Help Canada Mature as a Nation." *Canadian Issues* (2015): 39–46. https://acs-aec.ca/wp-content/uploads/2019/05/CITC-2015-Summer.pdf.

Episkenew, Jo-Ann. *Taking Back Our Spirits: Indigenous Literature, Public Policy, and Healing*. University of Manitoba Press, 2009.

Gabriel, Katsi'tsakwas Ellen. "Untethering Colonial Rule for Canada's 150th Birthday." *National Observer*, July 1, 2017. http://www.nationalobserver.com/2017/07/01/opinion/untethering-colonial-rule-canadas-150th-birthday.

Grant, Agnes. *No End of Grief: Indian Residential Schools in Canada*. Pemmican Publications, 1996.

Green, Joyce. "Introduction: Honoured in Their Absence: Indigenous Human Rights." In *Indivisible: Indigenous Human Rights*, edited by Joyce Green. Fernwood Publishing, 2014.

Hansard. "House of Commons Debates 44th Parliament, 1st session." No. 119, October 27, 2022. https://www.ourcommons.ca/DocumentViewer/en/44-1/house/sitting-119/hansard.

House of Commons of Canada. *Bill C-318: An Act to Establish Indian Residential School Reconciliation and Memorial Day*, 1st Session, 42nd Parliament (first reading on October 31, 2016). https://www.parl.ca/DocumentViewer/en/42-1/bill/c-318/first-reading.

Humphreys, Adrian. "Even Those Saying Indigenous Land Acknowledgments Don't Feel Personal Responsibility for Injustices: Poll." *National Post*, July 1, 2023. https://nationalpost.com/news/canada/canada-indigenous-poll.

Independent Special Interlocutor for Missing Children and Unmarked Graves and Burial Sites. "Addressing Trauma in the Search and Recovery of Missing Children: Summary Report." Office of the Independent Special Interlocutor , 2022. https://osi-bis.ca/wp-content/uploads/2023/03/OSI-SummaryReport_Winnipeg_Nov2022_web.pdf.

Independent Special Interlocutor for Missing Children and Unmarked Graves and Burial Sites. "Sacred Responsibility: Searching for the Missing Children and Unmarked Burials Interim Report." Office of the Independent Special Interlocutor , 2023. https://osi-bis.ca/.

Indigenous Watchdog. "Where Are the Successes and Failures in Reconciliation: 2022 Year in Review." January 23, 2023. https://www.indigenouswatchdog.org/2023/01/23/where-are-the-successes-and-failures-in-reconciliation-2022-year-in-review/.

Jewell, Eva, and Ian Mosby, eds. *Calls to Action—Accountability: A 2022 Status Update on Reconciliation*. Yellowhead Institute, 2022. https://yellowheadinstitute.org/wp-content/uploads/2022/12/TRC-Report-12.15.2022-Yellowhead-Institute-min.pdf.

Kennedy, Mark. "Q and A: Murray Sinclair on How Residential Schools Taught Aboriginal Children They Were Heathens." *Ottawa Citizen*, September 26, 2014. https://ottawacitizen.com/news/politics/q-and-a-murray-sinclair-on-how-residential-schools-taught-aboriginal-children-they-were-heathens.

Kirkup, Kristy. "Lynn Beyak Removed from Senate Committee over Residential School Comments." *Globe and Mail*, April 5, 2017. https://www.theglobeandmail.com/news/politics/beyak-removed-from-senate-committee-over-residential-school-comments/article34610016/.

Legacy of Hope Foundation. "Remembering the Children." June 1, 2008. http://www.rememberingthechildren.ca/.

Lemkin, Raphaël. *Axis Rule in Occupied Europe: Laws of Occupation, Analysis of Government, Proposals for Redress*. Carnegie Endowment for International Peace, 1944.

Liebenberg, Linda, and Michael Ungar. *Resilience in Action*. University of Toronto Press, 2008.

Lipsitz, George. *The Possessive Investment in Whiteness: How White People Profit from Identity Politics*. Temple University Press, 2018.

Logan, Tricia E. "Memory, Erasure, and National Myth." In *Colonial Genocide in Indigenous North America*, edited by Andrew Woolford, Jeff Benvenuto, and Alexander Laban Hinton. Duke University Press, 2014.

Lukacs, Martin. "Is It Still Business as Usual?" *Policy Alternatives* (2020). https://www.policyalternatives.ca/publications/monitor/it-still-business-usual.

Lukacs, Martin. "Reconciliation: The False Promise of Trudeau's Sunny Ways." *Walrus*, September 19, 2019. https://thewalrus.ca/the-false-promise-of-.trudeaus-sunny-ways/.

MacDonald, David B. A. *The Sleeping Giant Awakens: Genocide, Indian Residential Schools, and the Challenge of Conciliation*. University of Toronto Press, 2019.

MacDonald, David, and Graham Hudson. "Contextualizing Aboriginal Residential Schools in Canada: How International and Domestic Law Can Help Us Interpret Genocide Claims." *Canadian Journal of Political Science* 45, no. 2 (2012): 597–613.

Manuel, Arthur. "Until Canada Gives Indigenous People Their Land Back, There Can Never Be Reconciliation." *Rabble*, January 18, 2017. http://rabble.ca/blogs/bloggers/views-expressed/2017/01/until-canada-gives-indigenous-people-their-land-back-there-ca#.WIAw9l1F2Ko.twitter.

McIvor, Bruce. "Reconciliation as a Massive Failure." *Bar Talk: Indigenous Matters*, August 1, 2020. https://www.cbabc.org/BarTalk/Articles/2020/August/Columns/Reconciliation-as-a-Massive-Failure.

Metallic, Naiomi. "Ending Piecemeal Recognition of Indigenous Nationhood and Jurisdiction: Returning RCAP's Aboriginal Nation Recognition and Government Act." In *Renewing Relationships: Indigenous Peoples and Canada*, edited by Karen Drake and Brenda L. Gunn. Native Law Center, 2019.

Miller, J.R. "Genocide, Macdonald and Canadian History." *National Post*, January 8, 2021. https://nationalpost.com/opinion/j-r-miller-genocide-macdonald-and-canadian-history.

Milloy, John. *A National Crime: The Canadian Government and the Residential School System, 1879 to 1986*. University of Manitoba Press, 1999.

National Inquiry into Missing and Murdered Indigenous Women and Girls. "A Legal Analysis of Genocide: Supplementary Report of the National Inquiry into Missing and Murdered Indigenous Women and Girls." 2019. https://www.mmiwg-ffada.ca/wp-content/uploads/2019/06/Supplementary-Report_Genocide.pdf.

National Inquiry into Missing and Murdered Indigenous Women and Girls. "National Action Plan." June 3, 2021.

National Inquiry into Missing and Murdered Indigenous Women and Girls. *Reclaiming Power and Place: The Final Report of the National Inquiry into Missing and Murdered Indigenous Women and Girls*. Indigenous Law Web Archive, 2019. https://www.loc.gov/item/lcwaN0028038/.

Neu, Dean, and Richard Therrien. *Accounting for Genocide: Canada's Bureaucratic Assault on Aboriginal People*. Fernwood Publishing, 2003.

Newcomb, Steven. "Domination in Relation to Indigenous ('Dominated') Peoples in International Law." In *Indigenous Peoples as Subjects of International Law*, edited by Irene Watson. Routledge, 2017.

Palmater, Pamela. *Indigenous Nationhood: Empowering Grassroots Citizens*. Fernwood Publishing, 2015.

Pasternak, Shiri, Hayden King, and Riley Yesno. *Land Back: A Yellowhead Institute Red Paper*. Yellowhead Institute, October 2019.

Paul, Daniel N. *We Were Not the Savages*. Fernwood Publishing, 2000.

Pullella, Philip. "Pope Says Genocide Took Place at Church Schools in Canada for Indigenous Children." Reuters, July 30, 2022. https://www.reuters.com/world/pope-says-genocide-took-place-church-schools-canada-indigenous-children-2022-07-30/.

"Reconciliation Reality Check with Murray Sinclair." *Unreserved with Rosanna Deerchild*. CBC Radio, September, 23, 2021. https://www.cbc.ca/listen/live-radio/1-105-unreserved/clip/15868493-reconciliation-reality-check-murray-sinclair.

Regan, Paulette. *Unsettling the Settler Within: Indian Residential Schools, Truth Telling, and Reconciliation in Canada*. University of British Columbia Press, 2010.

Sellars, Bev. *Price Paid: The Fight for First Nations Survival*. Talon Books, 2016.

Selley, Chris. "Liberals Consider Making It a Hate Crime to 'Deny' Residential School 'Genocide.'" *National Post*, February 22, 2023. https://nationalpost.com/opinion/liberals-free-speech-genocide.

Simpson, Audra. *Mohawk Interruptus: Political Life Across the Borders of Settler States*. Duke University Press, 2014.

Sinclair, Douglas. "Why Reconciliation Is Absolutely Necessary for Indigenous Peoples." Indigenous Watchdog, June 8, 2023. https://www.indigenouswatchdog.org/2023/06/19/why-reconciliation-is-absolutely-necessary-for-indigenous-peoples/.

Smith, Donald B., and J.R. Miller. "No Genocide: It's Not the Right Word for the History Books." *Literary Review of Canada*, October 2019. https://reviewcanada.ca/magazine/2019/10/no-genocide/.

Starblanket, Tamara. *Suffer the Little Children: Genocide, Indigenous Nations and the Canadian State*. Clarity Press, 2018.

Truth and Reconciliation Commission of Canada. "Honouring the Truth, Reconciling for the Future: Summary of the *Final Report of the Truth and Reconciliation Commission of Canada*." 2015. https://ehprnh2mwo3.exactdn.com/wp-content/uploads/2021/01/Executive_Summary_English_Web.pdf.

Truth and Reconciliation Commission of Canada. "Our Mandate: Schedule N of the Indian Residential Schools Settlement Agreement." Accessed October 14, 2024. http://www.trc.ca/websites/trcinstitution/index.php?p=7.

Truth and Reconciliation Commission of Canada. *Truth and Reconciliation Commission of Canada Final Report: The History, Part 1*. McGill-Queen's University Press, 2015.

Tuck, Eve. "Suspending Damage: A Letter to Communities." *Harvard Educational Review* 7, no. 3 (2009): 409–427.

Tuhiwai Smith, Linda. *Decolonizing Methodologies: Research and Indigenous Peoples*. 2nd ed. Zed Books, 2012.

Wilson, Marie. "Foreword." In *Missing Persons: Multidisciplinary Perspectives on the Disappeared*, edited by Derek Congram. Canadian Scholars' Press, 2016.

Young, John. "Confronting Genocide in Canada." Canadian Museum for Human Rights, April 26, 2018. https://humanrights.ca/news/confronting-genocide-canada.

# Unsettled Arrivants

## *Stolen People on Stolen Land*

Malissa Bryan

THE POSITIONING OF ANTI-BLACK RACISM WITHIN COLONIAL structures continues to have a direct impact on the ways that Black bodies are imagined and situated in Canada. Anti-Black racism is a normalized reality; it shows up in policies and is embedded in practices across institutions in Canada. Anti-Black racism knows no bounds: it is embedded in the social fabric of Canada's belief systems, attitudes, biases, discrimination, and oppression that directly targets people of African descent.[1] Anti-Black racism (a term coined by Akua Benjamin) is a distinct form of racism that stems from Canada's history of enslaving African peoples and their descendants.[2] The impact of anti-Black racism is evident in highly disproportionate negative outcomes for Black populations in relation to but not limited to social, economic, health care, education, and political spheres, and beyond.[3] In Canada, Black people have certainly arrived, yet continue to be unsettled, and face exclusion, dehumanization, and discrimination in many aspects of Canadian life.

There are many ways in which the Black body exists within the settler colonial state, including Black identity in and against relations with Indigenous Peoples and other people of colour. Black peoples, however, have distinct experiences that differ from other racialized populations (i.e., Asian, Brown, and other settlers). The term BIPOC (Black, Indigenous, and people of colour) further demonstrates the push to recognize Black and Indigenous experiences of racialization as distinct. Oppressive ideologies directed at Black and Indigenous Peoples are key to fulfilling the colonial project in which white supremacy thrives. The extraction of Indigenous Peoples' lands in collaboration with the exploitation of Black labour and the criminalization of Black bodies creates an ideal environment for potential Black and Indigenous solidarity and resistance.

I am a Black–multi-racial and multi-ethnic person of Jamaican descent born in Canada to Jamaican immigrants. I am a descendant of Africans enslaved in Jamaica, subjected to chattel slavery. This chapter has six small sections that build on one another to understand the relationality of Black and Indigenous Peoples to one another and to settlers. The first section reflects on the crisis of identity that is born from slavery. This is followed by settler colonialism, the post-abolition era, the transition from slaves to arrivants, the failure of Canada to fully settle Black populations, and, lastly, an exploration of reflections of Black and Indigenous solidarities.

## Slavery and the Crisis of Identity

To know who you are is to know where you are going and why. To know where you come from is to know where you have been and how to find your way home. So, where is home for Caribbean descendants of enslaved people? Where is home for the many people who cannot neatly trace their roots back to a specific place, people, or nation? According to the United Nations, between 12 and 20 million Africans were enslaved and forcibly brought to the Western hemisphere of the world. During the six- to eight-week sail across the Atlantic Ocean, nearly 20 percent of enslaved Africans were killed or died from the unsanitary and inhumane conditions. The European captors did not consider enslaved Africans to be human beings or as inherently deserving of rights; instead, they were considered to be cargo and property. Disease and death were both expected and accepted as the status quo. Approximately 40 percent of the 12 to 20 million Africans enslaved were brought to the Caribbean. The use of chattel slavery and the implementation of the *Slave Codes* across the Caribbean ingrained the dehumanization of not only enslaved Africans but their descendants for generations, with the impact still felt with descendants today.[4]

Slavery within the Caribbean was rife with complicated relations and overlapping traumas from peoples who existed, lived, and died within a socially constructed racial hierarchy under the myth of superiority and inferiority. According to Kehinde Ayo, African people in the Caribbean have many painful traumas to contend with, including that they were violently, brutally ripped from their homes, countries, cultures, families, traditions, languages, religions, and lands through collaboration with their own kinfolk and white slavers in a process that was both dehumanizing and deadly.[5] This death was not just one of a physical sense but also one that stripped the descendants of African enslaved people who did survive of their languages, cultures, sense of self, histories, family structures, and traditions.[6]

Enslaved Africans essentially were deprived of their identity and reduced to a status akin to cattle. Europeans in the Caribbean were able to depend on and bring much of their cultural heritage and maintain relations with their European roots and import this to be consumed and embodied at their will. Descendants of African enslaved people were taken to lands that had been colonized; Africans, too, had been colonized. African enslaved people and their descendants did not have their lands settled; instead, Europeans violently assumed control over their bodies, lineages, and selves. Blackness is in a sense lost through slavery, which transformed people into property in an extreme, depraved form of colonization. Through a different lens, colonization can be seen as a reduced form of slavery, and, indeed, in the Americas, Indigenous Peoples were often enslaved by the Spanish and Portuguese, leading to mass death.[7]

Slavery cannot be separated from colonialism in the same way that colonialism cannot be severed from slavery. In truth they are born of projects that interdepend on one another to function, exist, and exploit. In this sense groups of people do not experience processes of racialization in the same way, and while some groups benefit to varying degrees from their group placement, Black people are perpetually stigmatized and are positioned as the extreme Other in relation to all bodies, at times even within their own communities, through acts of colourism and internalized anti-Black oppression. The commodification of African enslaved bodies linked the worth of Black people to a profit-driven model. In other words, the auction blocks and the slave ships represent not just bondage but profits in a manner that violently robbed African enslaved people of their autonomy, agency, and right to exist as beings separate from that of their commodified worth.

In his book *Afropessimism*, Frank Wilderson describes social death related to slavery as a process in which enslaved Black people experience the stripping away of social life, human rights, recognition, and empathy, essentially reducing them socially and legally to non-human status. At the core of this stripping away is the alienation experienced at infancy, childhood, and throughout all life cycles through callous separation of individuals from their mothers, fathers, children, siblings, spouses, and meaningful community connections.[8]

Chattel slavery perpetually enslaved Africans as well as their offspring, with additional production and reproduction of slaves through the breeding of African enslaved women with enslaved men as well as with their European slave masters. In these ways, reproductive means were exploited to reinforce the commodification of enslaved Africans and heighten the dehumanizing process of human commodification. The positioning of Black bodies as products to be reproduced and sold based on physical attributes and perceived value differs from the experiences of other racialized people brought to the Caribbean as indentured servants. These peoples, primarily of Indian and Chinese descent, also faced hardships and abuse, losing much of their autonomy over their labour, freedom, and personal lives. However, they were often able to keep many aspects of their identities, cultures, and languages and participate with autonomy in the capitalist system in a limited manner.[9] By contrast, African enslaved family structures and kinship were dismantled during the era of slavery, and, in many cases, mixed race Black and white babies were taken from their mothers soon after birth.[10]

What does enslavement mean for the Indigenous inhabitants of lands that enslaved Africans were forcibly brought to? Further, what does it mean when formerly enslaved Africans and their descendants move between lands that are colonized? Are they also settlers like the descendants of former European slavers? How are African enslaved descendants positioned in such places as Canada, which has a legacy of more than two hundred years of African slavery? Have African descendants from the Caribbean truly settled in Canada? What about descendants of Africans enslaved in Canada? These are some of the key questions I grapple with throughout this chapter with the understanding that there are many overlapping histories of oppression. These struggles and axes of oppression are intricately connected and should be explored singularly and together to understand the parallels.

## Settler Colonialism

African Caribbeans and their descendants who migrated to Canada entered a country rife with the marks of colonialism, displacement, genocide of Indigenous Peoples, and a history of African enslavement. Canada is far from being the land of the free, and as a settler colonial state it is directly complicit in the slave trade, racial disenfranchisement, and settler colonial domination. Glen Coulthard (Yellowknives Dene) states, "I conceptualize settler colonialism as a structure of domination that is partly predicated on the ongoing dispossession of Indigenous peoples' lands and the forms of political authority and jurisdiction that govern our relationship to these lands."[11]

According to Emma Battell Lowman and Adam J. Barker, there is a deep-rooted refusal by settlers to see colonization as an ongoing process, and instead it is situated in the consciousness of the vast majority of settlers as being in the distant past.[12] As explained by Eve Tuck and Wayne Yang, settlers come with the intention of making a new homeland and becoming the dominant power over all things and all people on that land. Settler colonialism is rooted in the extraction of natural resources, and colonial appropriation of the land is often accompanied by the violent displacement of Indigenous Peoples. Settler colonial violence is an ongoing, present process, and Indigenous Peoples are still under occupation today.[13]

Settler colonialism goes beyond the unsettling relationship between Indigenous Peoples and European settlers. As stated by Eve Tuck, Allison Guess, and Hannah Sultan, "settler colonialism fuses a set of (at least) tripled relationships between settlers/settlement, chattel/enslavement and Indigenous/erasure."[14] The relationships between Indigenous Peoples, African formerly enslaved people, and European settlers must be evaluated when negotiating who is and who is not a settler. Enslaved Africans were not only legally made into property but were also socially conceptualized as inferior, non-human, animalistic, and less than "persons." Africans held neither the power, the status, nor the agency to occupy the role of settler during the early colonial era. Further, colonial settler states were dependent on the interactive relationship between the triad. Indigenous Land was appropriated and used for resettlement and the reimagination of a European homestead, and African chattel slavery was used as a source of free labour to grow European settlers' profit and solidify their "top" position in the settler state. This creates a relationship wherein African labour was wanted and "needed" to fulfill the colonial project but African people themselves are unwanted, despised, and treated and deemed as disposable.

According to Maynard, slavery did not just achieve the subjugation and dehumanization of Black bodies, it imprinted ideologies of Black people as inferior, criminal, unintelligent, unattractive, and undesirable. Long after slavery officially ended in 1834 across the British Empire, the idea of Blackness and all the negative connotations that were attached to Black bodies had been ingrained in the psyche of Canadian life. Black people became free from the physical bondage of slavery but were not free from the social bondage of widespread ideologies and constructions of Blackness. Indeed, the weight and meanings attached to Blackness still hold a frightening resemblance to the ideas in which the enslaved African was first conceptualized and therefore acted on.[15] An uneasiness accompanies Blackness, as Black people are over-surveilled and criminalized, undervalued and underserved. In this hostile environment, Black people are always made aware of their Blackness, with how and when they can move through spaces simultaneously experiencing hyper-visibility and hyper-invisibility.

Slavery and the colonization of African people have in fact not ended, but have been repackaged and repurposed, as the colonial project continues to adapt to the social climate and laws of the day.[16] In other words, the legality of African enslavement ended across the British Empire, but the ideologies and cultural belief systems of slavery remain. The terminology shifted from *enslaved African* to *Black*, and with it the idea of "Blackness" as an inferior race. Does this mean that the descendants of African enslaved people cannot participate in settler colonialism? Does the history of slavery erase or diminish current-day Black people's responsibilities in maintaining settler colonialism or profiting from the dispossession and displacement of Indigenous Peoples and their lands? What about Indigenous Peoples: Are they free from participating in and benefitting from anti-Black racism?

## Post-Abolition Era: From Slaves to Arrivants

Jodi Byrd adopted African Caribbean poet Edward Kamau Brathwaite's word *arrivant* in place of *chattel slave*.[17] The word *arrivants* provides a broad description of people who were brought violently to the Americas in the process of colonialism. Discussions about settlers and arrivants must position African descendants of enslaved people through a historical lens that considers the impacts of colonization, displacement, and ongoing entrenched marginalization in Canadian and global society. Black people, unable to change their positioning in the racial hierarchy, are promised the hope of ownership of property and participation in the extraction of Indigenous Lands.

The term *arrivants* clearly highlights the role of all settlers in the settler colonial project while simultaneously underscoring the unsettled social and systemic status held by descendants of enslaved Africans. Settlers and arrivants (including Black populations) can participate in the colonial project through direct and indirect displacement of Indigenous Peoples from their lands. In addition, all non-Black people, including Indigenous Peoples can participate in anti-Black racism and discrimination.[18] The unique positioning of Black people as both oppressed and participants in the separation of Indigenous Peoples from their lands in the continued project of colonialism demonstrates a complex relationship. Persistently, Black people are positioned as the farthest "Other" from the perceived normativity of the white "settler," and the continued devaluation of Black bodies and peoples creates a dual social location.

## Unsettled in Canada

I further conceptualize arrivants not just as inhabiting a social location but as part of the unfinished story of formerly enslaved Africans who arrived in the Americas and moved between colonized lands looking for a place to call home. There is yet to be a point in history where Black people have "settled" within Canada because, in the colonial sense, settling necessitates both power and acceptance of that power or position of normativity. Black people in Canada systemically have had neither of these characteristics attributed to them. According to Maynard,

> Though formalized Black bondage was officially over, the meaning of Blackness had been consolidated under slavery and remained intact in the post-abolition period. In the end, slavery had accomplished more than an economic subjugation, it had created particular meanings of what it meant to be Black—meanings that were attached to Black people's bodies. The fact of Black enslavement altered the signification of Black skin and features, regardless of the legal status of freedom or unfreedom.[19]

In other words, Blackness had been marked beyond an identity into a permanent social location embedded into the psyche and functioning of Canadian society. The social location of Blackness created barriers and informed what freedom meant for people who occupied the social location of Black. African people were relabelled as "black," which went beyond a physical identifying characteristic and instead carried the weight of the former social location of enslaved Africans. Anti-Black racism is the foundation on which settler colonialism stands today; it is an ongoing process, an evolving relationship between the triad of native, settler, and chattel slave. It is simply the next chapter of the ongoing colonial story of Canada. After slavery was officially abolished in Canada in 1834, segregation was practised in Ontario, Alberta, and Nova Scotia. Black children were physically separated from white children and sent to under-resourced schools that provided an inferior education. Black schools subjected the Black population to economic exclusion in comparison to white Canadians. In communities where segregated schools were not officially backed by the law, white Canadians would frequently physically bar Black children from entering white schools.[20]

"Freedom" for descendants of African slaves did not mean equality with white settlers, including freedom from physical violence and segregation, freedom of movement, economic freedom, freedom to access social resources, freedom from criminalization, or freedom from the implications of Blackness. Freedom from chattel slavery simply meant white settlers would not outright own Black people, but whiteness would still control them, shower violence on them, subjugate them to widespread poverty, criminalize them, imprison them, and kill them with impunity. Anti-Black racism is normative in settler colonialism, according to Sharpe:

> The ongoing state-sanctioned legal and extralegal murders of Black people are normative and, for this so-called democracy, necessary: it is the ground we walk on. And that it is the ground lays out that, and perhaps how, we might begin to live in relation to this requirement for our death.... What happens when we proceed as if we know this, antiblackness, to be the ground on which we stand, the ground from which we attempt to speak, for instance, an "I" or a "we" who know, an "I" or a "we" who care?[21]

In essence, anti-Black racism is embedded in Canadian institutions and can be seen and felt across sectors. The available data demonstrates the legacy of slavery and the pervasiveness of anti-Black racism in Canada today. The Black Canadian National Survey of 2021 documented that 70 percent of Black Canadians reported facing racism regularly or occasionally, 91 percent of Black Canadians felt that racism is a problem, 66 percent of Black Canadians had been treated with suspicion within the twelve months prior to the study being conducted, 67 percent of Black Canadians had reported being treated as lacking intelligence, and 91 percent of Black Canadians felt that racism is a problem in the health-care system.[22] The day-to-day lives of Black Canadians are riddled with having to navigate anti-Black racism across systems, communities, and spaces. According to Statistics Canada, Black populations experienced more than 40 percent of the total sum of reported hate crimes in Canada, with a 28 percent increase of incidents from 2021 to 2022.[23] The statistics on anti-Black racism in policing across Canada are harrowing. Although Black people only make up 8.8 percent of Toronto's population, out of 244 Special Investigation Unit (police watchdog) cases analyzed between 2013 and 2017, Black populations were grossly overrepresented: Black people made up 25.4 percent of all investigations, 61.5 percent of police use of force cases resulting in civilian death, and 70 percent of police shootings resulting in death. According to the Ontario Human Rights Commission, white people physically threatened the police significantly more than Black people. In police shootings, 20 percent of white civilians were carrying a gun versus 11.1 percent of Black civilians.[24]

The legacy of slavery, of the dehumanization and commodification of Black bodies, has shifted and evolved over time but has always been a constant reality in Canada and is not confined to the past. Particularly looking at anti-Black racism, this includes various vehicles of control including incarceration, ghettos, hoods, school-to-prison pipelines, underfunding of social services, segregation, surveillance, criminalization, and so on.[25] Indigenous Peoples are faced with internal colonialism in the form of reserves, unclean drinking water, criminalization, missing and murdered Indigenous women, discrimination in and lack of children's services, inferior access to health care, and the continued extraction of Indigenous Lands.

Whiteness is as powerful now as it was during chattel slavery and the early days of settler colonialism. Conversations addressing the impact of colonialism and chattel slavery are difficult, as white people are often hesitant to take accountability for the past and current roles of "whiteness" in settler colonialism, chattel slavery, and the ongoing degradation of Black and Indigenous Peoples.[26] Reforms to address the impact on Indigenous and Black people are slow and watered down, often simply performative. As Jodi Byrd states, "There remains a glancing away, an uncomfortable refusal, a too easy gesture of presumed affiliation and equivalency, or a persistent recentering of whiteness that intrudes. The possible conversations remain stymied, half-formed, guarded, and weary, with both sides."[27] Settler colonialism necessitates white silence, complicity, and amnesia.

## Black and Indigenous Solidarity: Imagined and in Practice?

Black and Indigenous Peoples both have been racialized and socially located in different, often opposing ways to reflect their social locations in the formation and continuation of settler colonialism. The "one drop rule," explicitly stated in the United States and implicitly practised in Canada, allowed for all offspring of enslaved parents to inherit the social location of chattel slave and later criminal. By contrast, Indigenous Peoples have been racialized in a very different, subtractive way to reduce the Indigenous population by imposing blood quantum thresholds, identification cards, and controlling who is legally Indigenous. The increase of the chattel slave population directly benefitted and increased the wealth of white settlers, while the decrease of Indigenous populations benefitted the colonial settler project of extracting, stealing, exploiting, and owning Indigenous Lands.[28]

Settler colonialism is centred around a preoccupation over land ownership, and Africans were enslaved to support the fulfillment of this project. African chattel slaves and their descendants point to the soaking of the colonized land with their blood and the blood of their ancestors as flawed proof of African entitlement to Indigenous Lands.[29]

Black and Indigenous solidarity requires the reimagining of self and community externally to the white colonial gaze. This includes consideration for Afro-Indigenous Peoples who hold both heritages and are often erased as they break the narrative of mutually exclusive identities that never overlap.[30] Reframing the descendants of enslaved Africans as arrivants/survivants[31] retells the story, shifting history away from a focus on the dehumanization of Black people and the creation of "Blackness" as a negative mark. The concept of arrivants describes the story of enslaved

Black people who were indigenous to places across Africa, who had histories and attachments to lands, peoples, traditions, and ways of understanding themselves in relation to others, who were violently brought to foreign shores on lands belonging to other Indigenous Peoples.

Arrivants continuously participate in a process of arriving, arriving to new truths and new stories, creating new histories, traditions, and languages such as Ebonics (an African American language in its own right) and patois (languages created by the fusion and mixing of many languages). It is a process of both undoing and doing; a renaming and reclaiming of self and a recognition of the past, traditions, histories, and cultures that have been lost while building what can be gained for a future. The term *arrivants* does not erase the history of early settler colonialism but instead provides an opportunity to redefine Blackness outside the confines of the white settler imagination. It is within this space of imagining and acceptance that Black and Indigenous Peoples can share one another's stories and find solidarity.

The common experience of oppression through colonial structures can create avenues of increased understanding and empathy between Black and Indigenous Peoples in Canada. As stated by Mike Alexander (Anishinaabe, Swan Lake First Nation), "When I hear about Black struggles, I think of my own life trying to make my way in a country that can be intolerant and discriminatory. I can relate to the pain and anger experienced by Black folks who live with systemic as well as overt examples of racism on a daily basis."[32] The common experience of marginalization and oppression at the hands of colonial racist structures and practices have created opportunities and conditions for Indigenous and Black solidarity to be demonstrated. According to a statement from Idle No More organizers Nickita Longman and Alex Wilson, "Black activists have supported the resiliency of Indigenous Peoples time and time again. It is our turn to show up, take instruction, and trust in the Black Lives Matter movement at this time, and always."[33]

In 2016 Black Lives Matter activists organized a fifteen-day encampment outside Toronto Police Headquarters in protest after learning that there would be no criminal charges for the officer who shot and killed Andrew Loku, a Sudanese refugee who was experiencing a mental health crisis at the time. In response, Indigenous activists organized and supported the Black Lives Matter encampment. Weeks later First Nations people occupied the offices of Indigenous and Northern Affairs Canada, in protest of the conditions that led to a wave of suicides in the Cree Attawapiskat community. Black Lives Matter activists showed up in solidarity and support and followed the lead of Indigenous activists.[34] The solidarity between Black and Indigenous Peoples in Canada has been not only organic but beneficial as an avenue to increase knowledge mobilization, to share resources and methods, to gain larger platforms, and to extend the reach of information sharing and community and political networks. Black and Indigenous Peoples have long-standing histories of struggle and resistance beginning at first contact with Indigenous Peoples and the beginning of the enslavement of Africans. Throughout history the struggle is a direct response to state-sanctioned violence, capitalism, settler colonialism, and anti-Black and anti-Indigenous racism. These histories are deeply connected. Whether the movement is called an uprising, Black Lives Matter, or Idle No More, the root causes remain the same: the human need for freedom.[35]

## Conclusion

Anti-Black racism must be conceptualized through an understanding of its foundations in colonization and the enslavement of Africans. Black people were stolen and reduced to property while Indigenous Lands and Peoples were colonized, controlled through stolen lands, and subjected to violence; these are both processes that are ongoing and that underpin Canadian society. Black arrivants in Canada are a stolen people on stolen Indigenous Land. This common struggle against colonialism and racist structures allows for continued opportunities for increased solidarity between Black and Indigenous Peoples in Canada. There may not be a clear image of how solidarity between Black and Indigenous populations will evolve, but we do know that Black initiatives, struggle, and resistance must be Black-led and Indigenous initiatives and struggles must be Indigenous-led. Solidarity work between Black and Indigenous Peoples has always honoured the tradition of following the lead of the people directly impacted. Exploring ways to co-lead joint movements while drawing on historical significance to both Indigenous and Black populations may be the future direction as this struggle for and work towards freedom evolves and continues.

## Notes

1 City Manager, "The Toronto Action Plan."
2 Black Health Alliance, "Anti-Black Racism."
3 Ontario Human Rights Commission, *Human Rights Under Pressure.*
4 Sherman-Peter, "The Legacy of Slavery."
5 Ayo, "Edward Brathwaite's *The Arrivants.*"
6 Brathwaite, *The Arrivants.*
7 Byrd, "Weather with You," 207.
8 Wilderson, *Afropessimism.*
9 Kehinde, "Edward Brathwaite's *The Arrivants,*" 183.
10 Maynard, *Policing Black Lives.*
11 Coulthard and Betasamosake Simpson, "Grounded Normativity," 251.
12 Lowman and Barker, *Settler.*
13 Tuck and Yang, "Decolonization Is Not."
14 Tuck, Guess, and Sultan, "Not Nowhere."
15 Maynard, *Policing Black Lives*, 31.
16 Colourism and a preference for lighter skin in connection with proximity to whiteness is an ongoing phenomenon.
17 Byrd. "Weather with You."
18 Tuck and Yang, "Decolonization Is Not."
19 Maynard, *Policing Black Lives.*
20 Maynard, *Policing Black Lives*, 34.
21 Christina, Sharpe." In the Wake on Blackness and Being" 2016. Duke University Press. Durham and London.
22 Foster, Park, McCague, Fletcher, and Sikdar, "Black Canadian National Survey."
23 Statistics Canada, "Police Reported Hate Crime."
24 Wortley, Laniyonu, and Laming, "Use of Force."
25 Tuck and Yang, "Decolonization Is Not," 6.
26 Whiteness here is referred to in an abstract manner. The ideology and social construction of whiteness has yet to claim responsibility for the past and current exclusion of Black and Indigenous people.
27 Byrd, "Weather with You," 207.
28 Tuck and Yang, "Decolonization Is Not," 12.
29 Daggar, "Review of *Native Land Talk.*"
30 Daggar, "Review of *Native Land Talk.*"
31 I utilize the term *survivants* as a play on *survivance* to describe descendants of enslaved Africans who both survived and arrived. The word *survivants* demonstrates the complex relationship that many African descendants of enslaved people have with North American Indigenous Lands.
32 Alexander, "As an Indigenous Person."
33 Canadian Press, "Supporting Role."
34 Democracy Now, "Occupied Canada."
35 Simpson, Walcott, and Coulthard, "Idle No More and Black Lives Matter."

## Sources


Alexander, Mike. "As an Indigenous Person, I Empathize with Black Struggles." *Broadview*, June 25, 2020. https://broadview.org/black-lives-matter-indigenous.

Ayo, Kehinde. "Edward Brathwaite's *The Arrivants* and the Trope of Cultural Searching." *Journal of Pan African Studies* 1, no. 9 (2007): 182–198.

Black Health Alliance. "Anti-Black Racism." https://blackhealthalliance.ca/home/antiblack-racism/.

Brathwaite, Kamau. *The Arrivants: A New World Trilogy*. Oxford University Press, 1986.

Byrd, Jodi A. "Weather with You: Settler Colonialism, Antiblackness, and the Grounded Relationalities of Resistance." *Critical Ethnic Studies* 5, no. 1–2 (2019): 207–214. https://doi.org/10.5749/jcritethnstud.5.1-2.0207.

Canadian Press. "Supporting Role: Indigenous Activists Want Focus to Stay on Black Demonstrators." CBC News, June 5, 2020. https://www.cbc.ca/news/canada/kitchener-waterloo/indigenous-activists-idle-no-more-black-lives-matter-1.5599669.

City Manager. "The Toronto Action Plan to Confront Anti-Black Racism." City of Toronto, November 15, 2017. https://www.toronto.ca/legdocs/mmis/2017/ex/bgrd/backgroundfile-109126.pdf.

Coulthard, Glen, and Leanne Betasamosake Simpson. "Grounded Normativity/Place-Based Solidarity." *American Quarterly* 68, no. 2 (2016): 249–255. https://doi.org/10.1353/aq.2016.0038.

Daggar, Lori. "Review of *Native Land Talk: Indigenous and Arrivant Rights Theories*, by Yael Ben-Zvi." *Early American Literature* 54, no. 2 (2019): 533–537. https://doi.org/10.1353/eal.2019.0040.

Democracy Now. "Occupied Canada: Indigenous & Black Lives Matter Activists Unite to Protest Violence & Neglect." May 20, 2016. https://www.democracynow.org/2016/5/20/occupied_canada_indigenous_black_lives_matter.

Foster, Lorne, Stella Park, Hugh McCague, Marcelle-Anne Fletcher, and Jackie Sikdar. "Black Canadian National Survey Interim Report 2021." Institute for Social Research, York University, 2021. https://www.researchgate.net/publication/359176213_Black_Canadian_National_Survey_Interim_Report_2021.

Lowman, Emma Battell, and Adam J. Barker. *Settler: Identity and Colonialism in 21st Century Canada*. Fernwood Publishing, 2015.

Maynard, Robyn. *Policing Black Lives: State Violence in Canada from Slavery to the Present*. Fernwood Publishing, 2017.

Ontario Human Rights Commission. *Human Rights Under Pressure: From Policing to Pandemics, Annual Report 2020–2021*. https://www.ohrc.on.ca/sites/default/files/ohrc%202020-21%20Annual%20Report%20final%20en.pdf.

Sharpe, Christina. *In the Wake: On Blackness and Being*. Duke University Press, 2016.

Sherman-Peter, A. Missouri. "The Legacy of Slavery in the Caribbean and the Journey Towards Justice." *United Nations Chronicle*, March 24, 2022. https://www.un.org/en/un-chronicle/legacy-slavery-caribbean-and-journey-towards-justice.

Simpson, Leanne Betasamosake, Rinaldo Walcott, and Glen Coulthard. "Idle No More and Black Lives Matter: An Exchange." *Studies in Social Justice* 12, no. 1 (2018): 75–89. https://doi.org/10.26522/ssj.v12i1.1830.

Statistics Canada. "Police Reported Hate Crime in Canada, 2022." March 13, 2014. https://www150.statcan.gc.ca/n1/pub/11-627-m/11-627-m2024006-eng.htm.

Tuck, Eve, Allison Guess, and Hannah Sultan. "Not Nowhere: Collaborating on Selfsame Land." *Decolonization: Indigeneity, Education & Society* (2014). https://www.academia.edu/10363027/Not_nowhere_Collaborating_on_selfsame_land.

Tuck, Eve, and K. Wayne Yang. "Decolonization Is Not a Metaphor." *Decolonization: Indigeneity, Education & Society* 1, no. 1 (2012): 1–40.

Wilderson, Frank B., III. *Afropessimism*. Liveright Publishing, 2020.

Wortley, Scot, Ayobami Laniyonu, and Erick Laming. "Use of Force by the Toronto Police Service, Final Report." Ontario Human Rights Commission, July 2020. https://www.ohrc.on.ca/sites/default/files/Use%20of%20force%20by%20the%20Toronto%20Police%20Service%20Final%20report.pdf.

# Labouring and Living in and Beyond Canada

## *An Unlikely Archive of Chinese Arrivant and Immigrant Women Writing*

Angie Wong

Canadian settler colonialism is a distinct triadic formation that comprises Indigenous Peoples, white European settlers, and racialized non-Indigenous people of colour. This third group of peoples, called *arrivants* in some postcolonial discourse, is what makes settler colonialism distinctly different from classical colonialism, which more commonly has a dyadic relationship between colonized/colonizer or settlers/Indigenous Peoples. The first generations of Chinese racialized, non-Indigenous subjects (often forced out of their own homelands by imperialism) to emigrate and settle in Canada from the mid-nineteenth into the early twentieth century are analytically positioned and discussed throughout this chapter as arrivants. These early arrivants are to be distinguished from the discussion of later twentieth-century Chinese immigrant women writing.

Racialized peoples not Indigenous to these lands migrated and settled in these locales through diverse movements (sometimes voluntary, sometimes forced and coercive). They have been historically shaped by the same European forms of colonization on their own homelands, which resulted in their forced migration to new lands such as Turtle Island. They are characterized by their major contributions to settler colonial projects that were in high demand of Asian racialized labour: arrivant labour expedited settler expansionism. They are also critical to deeper understandings of the nuance of settler colonial policies, occupation, and culture.

Arrivant is a term used by African Caribbean poet Kamau Brathwaite and redeveloped by scholars such as Jodi Byrd to refer to the forced movements of people into the Americas "through the violence of European and Anglo-American colonialism and imperialism around the globe."[1] In a Canadian context, male Chinese labourers who entered Canada from the mid- to late-nineteenth century to the early twentieth century have been studied as arrivants for the ways in which they interacted with both Indigenous Peoples and settlers.

By way of their movements around the globe through trans-Atlantic and trans-Pacific movements, arrivants are critical placeholders within a triad of relations who work to tease out processes of racialization (such as xenophobic immigration policies) from colonization (such as the continued theft of Indigenous Lands and resources) by mapping out a third space between the settler and native. The experiences of arrivants signals how "not all migrations are settler migrations and not all colonialisms are settler colonial."[2] Yet, the term *arrivant* can also highlight the ways in which they resisted or participated in projects of settler colonialism.[3] Most arrivants arrived in the nation as labourers who were manipulated to complete economic tasks and consolidation for settler colonial national projects. The unilateral relationship between classical colonial formations of colonized and colonizer or native and settler typically do not account for the third classification of peoples on these lands (those who make up the triad of settler colonialism), thereby missing a key analytical lens that decentres the myth of the sojourner—the assumption that Asian racialized labourers came/come only under temporary work contracts.[4] There were, of course, some who came on their own through voluntary movements and interests (unfortunately, there is no time in this chapter to highlight those exceptions). As such, arrivant histories, perspectives, and exchanges exist, and they do so in idiosyncratic spaces that evaded the prying eyes of immigration agents. Latter-twentieth-century immigrant women counterparts are the last vestiges of an era of settler colonial Canada that fumbled its crisis response to Chinese men, whose labour, rather than families, the state sought.

The memories and voices of Chinese labourers and Chinese women are expressed in unlikely places to produce alternative archives that highlight a lesser-known twentieth-century Canada. Here, I will look at two types of text that capture an altogether different side of the Canadian experience at the beginning and end of the twentieth century. This approach offers the perspectives of both men and women from various class strata and political perspectives. David Lai's contribution to *The Asianadian: An Asian Canadian Magazine* (1978–85) is a discussion of Victoria's Chinese immigration prison and the writings and etchings of poetry and lamentation left behind in the prison cells. The first edited collection on Chinese women's experiences in Canada, *Jin Guo: Voices of Chinese Canadian Women* (1992), was edited by the Women's Book Committee of the Chinese Canadian National Council. On the one hand, the experience of Chinese men arriving at the turn of the century showcases the imperial realities of forced migration, surveillance, and censorship under settler immigration policy. This encompasses class antagonisms inside immigration prison spaces.

The voices of Chinese women in *Jin Guo* exhibit dynamic worldviews that were shaped by gender perceptions in China and Canada, movement, imperialism, and family separation. It is among the first texts that gave voice to Chinese women to speak for themselves. Sentiments of isolation and loneliness echo those of Chinese arrivant men nearly a century earlier. In examining these temporal traces of the impacts of settler colonialism, I consider the ways in which settler colonial perspectives on labour, gender, and class came together and intersected to systemically control Chinese arrivants and shape latter immigrant experiences under a newly veiled multicultural Canada. The intricacies of these texts have the potential to reveal *why* anti-immigrant policy bolstered settler occupation and *how* processes of racialization using anti-immigrant policy support continued theft of Indigenous Lands.

## Arrivants: A Third Relation

Arrivants have been theorized as global racialized labourer subjects who experience modes of external imperialism through movement and migration between homeland and new lands. Jodi Byrd's *Transit of Empire* introduces this important idea of how global racialized non-Indigenous Peoples experience both colonialism and racial oppression. These experiences are further shaped by their encounters, exchanges, and relationships with Indigenous nations and people and with white settlers.[5] One example is Renisa Mawani's reading of Chinese arrivants living in proximity to Indigenous nations in Western Canada. She suggests how the intermingling between Chinese men on Indigenous reserves through the illicit sale of liquor was seen as a threat to the futurity of settler colonialism.[6] The kinship relations that inevitably formed between Indigenous and Chinese peoples as a result of proximity and repeated encounters threatened a puritanical settler society. As such, these real-life interactions position the descendants of arrivants in conflictual ways, according to Byrd, to carry out responsibilities unique to Indigenous Peoples and their decolonization efforts.[7]

Edward Kamau Brathwaite's collection of poems *The Arrivants* (1973) makes the case that stolen Africans who were forced into slave labour are autochthonous arrivants. Brathwaite locates stolen Black arrivant subjects and identities as distinctly pushed into exile (migration) through imperialism.[8] This historically colonial impetus has the potential to "conceal the unique positioning of Blackness in settler colonialism and the complicity of white people and nonwhite people ... in anti-Blackness."[9] In their seminal work "Decolonization Is Not a Metaphor," Eve Tuck and K. Wayne Yang consider that "people of colour who enter/are brought into the settler colonial nation-state also enter the triad of relations between settler-native-slave," usually through the colonial pathways prescribed under immigration policy.[10] Although they note that in some cases "the refugee/immigrant/migrant is invited to be a settler in some scenarios, given the appropriate investments in whiteness,"[11] it was not historically the case for arrivants to receive the same invitations to participate in settler society. Rather, the blatant racial profiling and the predominant incarceration of Black people suggests that "once colonized people outlive their utility, settler societies can fall back on the repertoire of strategies"[12] to continually sequester unwanted or undesirable citizen/subjects spatially.

While Patrick Wolfe explains that "the Red man's land would be mixed with Black labour to produce cotton, the white gold of the Deep South,"[13] he argues elsewhere that, "ubiquitously, therefore, settlers bring their labor with them, usually already coerced, whether as slaves, convicts, indenturees, *Mizrahim*, or other subordinated categories."[14] Arrivants thus exist in relation to Indigenous nations and Peoples and settlers. They became an important and substantial supplemental low-wage labour force in the wake of "the murderous activities of the frontier rabble," which came to "constitute its principal means of expansion"[15] and eventual white settlement. Settler colonial anxieties about racial difference, amalgamation, assimilation, and miscegenation are grounded in the paranoia of classical colonialism and prompted the insatiable European dependency on the slave labour of the transatlantic slave trade. To thwart these percolating anxieties, "between 1838 and 1900 Britain, France, Germany, Austria, Japan, the United States, Italy, and Russia engaged in a series of wars with China in her territories and succeeded in securing trading and other rights from the Chinese government."[16]

This Eight-Nation Alliance performed a series of land and sea invasions in China, which forced the country to open ports and trade agreements with its invaders. This was one of many responses to the abolishment of slavery across the British Empire: imperialize elsewhere. This triggered a mass exodus of Chinese labourers, who moved far beyond the traditional routes to the South Asian Pacific where their ancestors had gone. While Black labour was still a considerable source of super-cheap labour,[17] Chinese labour became classified along similar economic and social vectors of dispensability. African peoples were colonized and stolen from their homelands to generate the plantation economies of the Deep South of the United States. In similar but different ways, Chinese people were imperialized and forced to leave their homelands to become the new supplemental low-wage labour. Both are indicative of empire's unending appetite for the luxuries that were wrought by the coerced labour of colonized or stolen people.[18] Within the triad framework of settler colonialism, arrivants and Indigenous Peoples are bound to interact, regardless of settler control and censorship.

## Apprehensive Arrivals and Apprehending Arrivant

Settlers perceived Chinese arrivants as people who were incompatible with the desired white settler order of Canada. While their labour was desired, their families were not. Chinese people who arrived in Canada at the turn of the twentieth century were the first and only group to be federally head-taxed for entry into the nation. That is, until they were altogether excluded from entry into the nation between 1923 and 1947.[19] The *Chinese Immigration Act* of 1885 introduced a $50 head tax. A second amendment in 1900 increased the tax to $100, and a final amendment in 1903 increased the head tax to $500, until 1923 when the *Act* was amended to prohibit all Chinese immigration (with minor exceptions for diplomats, merchants, students, and children born in Canada returning from China). The *Act* of 1885 exploited the labour of men, while the 1923 *Act* specified the exclusion of women. Both contributed to financial insecurity and family separation, interrupted educational opportunities, and established a massive state archive containing records from this era of anti-Asian surveillance. Under these conditions of separation and censure, Chinese arrivants and then their later twentieth-century counterparts captured their apprehensive arrivals in the nation through writing, poetry, and personal testimony, which reveals an altogether different kind of lived reality in Canada not fully captured by mainstream narratives of national emergence.

At the turn of the century, the state had developed several structural and juridical means to conduct surveillance and track the movements of arrivants (using Chinese Immigration Certificates). Even before Chinese men could enter the nation to perform any actual labour, federally mandated and municipally enforced immigration laws and their infrastructural counterparts, immigration prisons, suggest a nascent internal aporia to Canadian settlement. Asian people and their labour exist in proximity to Euro-Canadian settlers and their desires for "white Canada forever,"[20] which inform the state's historic attitudes towards primarily desiring the labour capacities of Asian men to complete national projects with speed and efficiency. This desire was always alongside the discriminatory expectation that Asian men would work for half the pay they were promised, for seasonal and irregular work, and they could not bring their families. These temporary conditions fed into the myth of the sojourner, which characterized the socio-cultural construction of Asian labourers as perpetually foreign, non-belonging, fortifying the assumption that they merely came to work rather than live. From the perspectives of early Chinese arrivants discussed below, however, Canada was hostile and racist. By the end of the twentieth century, the country drastically altered its laws and exhibited the adoption of new attitudes; yet many Chinese immigrants, namely women, were skeptical of the country's newfound remorse. Rather, arrivant and immigrant perspectives offer alternative ways of relating to Canada, ones not typically found in mainstream masculinized narratives of the nation's emergence.

## Immigration Prisons and Settler Colonial Immigration Control

According to David Lai, immigration buildings were constructed in Victoria to process Chinese immigrants travelling from the Pacific because Canadian immigration offices did not exist in Hong Kong or in China at the time.[21] One such building was erected in 1908 in Victoria and operated as a detention hospital until it was demolished in 1977. The immigration building was called many things, but "it was notoriously known to the Chinese as *Chu-tsai-uk* (pigpen)," which referred to the nineteenth-century practice of recruiting, buying, and selling Chinese coolie labour[22] to Singapore.[23] The confinement of the labourers into a small lodging while they waited to be bought or sold, Lai argues, was a situation similar to those imprisoned in the Canadian immigration building. When Chinese labourers arrived at the West Coast in passenger ships, they were detained and escorted directly from Rithet's Piers outside Victoria to the immigration building. Here, their head taxes were hastily processed before they were confined into prison-like cells "where they could see their dreamland only through barred windows."[24]

Lisa Mar notes that many arrivants "languished in jail cells for days, weeks, or months while officials questioned them about their identity and background."[25] The extent to which officials interrogated and scrutinized detainees was immense. Arrivants were expected to know the "minute details of their hometowns, families, friends, and associates in China, in Canada, and in the United States."[26] Mar further explains that luggage was searched, letters were inspected, and personal belongings were examined for consistency with their owners' claims. This type of acute regulation over Chinese bodies, according to Nayan Shah, recoded them as subjects "haphazardly and unevenly" fostered in coherent state programs, producing them as "social problems with consequences for national well-being."[27] This was the first time that many had left their villages in China, so to encounter Canada first through detainment and incarceration was confusing, distressing, and demoralizing. The carceral space of the immigration prison, much like its descendent in immigration border control, served the larger purpose of surveillance, censorship, and punitive control over the movements of arrivant/immigrant subjects, or those seen as undesirable/unwanted.

The interpersonal transactions and surveillance conducted inside the building match its grim infrastructure. City records indicated the building was a detention hospital or immigration hospital, which "explains why the building [had] unusually thick exterior walls and a prison-like layout."[28] Lai adds how the building was constructed with "five columns of red bricks and measured slightly over twenty inches thick," which was "unnecessary for an immigration building... unless it [was] used for special purposes such as a prison."[29] Before it was razed in the 1970s, Lai spoke with demolition workers and asked if they noticed any Chinese characters or writing inside the building. Upon closer inspection during his own archaeological examination of the site, Lai discovered that there were Chinese writings and etchings hidden beneath layers of paint in the prison cells on the second floor. That the writings were hidden under layers of paint reveals the lengths to which immigration authorities attempted to hide arrivant recordation of humanity and resistance. These writings and etchings contain the dynamic consciousness of Chinese arrivants who arrived in Canada not merely as labourers but as poets, writers, artistic souls.

## The Writing on the Wall

The writing on the walls of the immigration prison cells contains spectral lamentations of loss, misfortune, disappointment in both the homeland and Canada, and perseverance. They describe the hopelessness and humiliation of detainees from isolation and loneliness inside the prison cells. Yet, under the precarious conditions of imprisonment, some called for perseverance and self-determination to expose "state mechanisms of control," which helps to "[disentangle] practices of punishment from values of justice and benevolent society by which they are often promoted."[30] Roxanne Rimstead and Deena Rymhs here note the significance of using a transnational lens when studying prison writing because such an approach "might also reveal the ways in which prison systems are... transformed by global capitalism."[31] The Eight-Nation Alliance invasion of China is a primary example of the ways in which networks of Euro-American imperialism instigated early stages of global capitalism through labour manipulation and exploitation. A poem from 1919 sharply carved into the wall captures the transnational class antagonisms of this period of global capitalist emergence:

> I have always yearned to go to the Gold Mountain
> But instead it is hell, full of hardships. I was detained in a prison and
> tears rolled down my cheeks.
> My wife at home is longing for my letter... I cannot sleep because
> my heart is filled with
> hate. When I think of the foreign barbarians
> my anger will rise sky high. They put me in jail
> and make me suffer this misery.

I moan until the early dawn,
But who will console me here.[32]

This poem insightfully depicts Canada's nascent economic development, which appeared void of tolerant attitudes towards invited and coerced racialized labourers who were tasked with accomplishing settler projects and economic consolidation. Imprisonment was an unpleasant and unexpected welcome to *gum san* or "Gold Mountain" (the historic metaphor used colloquially to discuss the mineral wealth of Canada and the United States during their gold rush eras). The gossip around gum san was a hopeful rhetoric that romanticized settler lands that were cleared for occupation as a place to get rich quick and seen as a convenient opportunity by many Chinese to escape the poverty provoked by imperialism. Instead, what took place inside the immigration prison (confinement, isolation, interrogation) broke men psychologically: "although they may not have been physically abused, many must have been shaken psychologically by the incarceration experience."[33] The bitterness expressed towards Canadian immigration officials who "put me in jail / and make me suffer this misery"[34] is a critical perspective echoed by other poet/labourers to describe the draconian practices of wrongful imprisonment and unnecessary long-term confinement.

The poet/labourer calls Canadian immigration authorities "foreign barbarians," inverting the perception of this term commonly used by European colonizers to label the non-European, non-Anglo people they attempted to colonize. Moreover, he is worried about his wife. Such a simple statement that captures the poet's care for his spouse is an example of the consequences of the demand for a network of global capitalism, namely family separation. This single poem comprises the plenitude of personal and political problems associated with settler immigration policy towards a single group of arrivants. While this poem describes the encounter with Canada as "hell" and "full of hardships," others left behind less lamenting and more direct warnings of their imprisonment.

The following prose piece was written anonymously and is undated. It grieves family separation, disparages poverty, and describes a humiliating medical examination:

> Leaving my parents, wife and children, I have come to the Gold Mountain because I am poor. By various means, I managed to gather a thousand and some odd dollars and bought my passage to Canada.

> Unexpectedly I was confined in the Customs Office where I was subjected to a medical checkup. They examined my eyes, forced me to strip to my waist and take off my pants to lay bare my body. What crimes have I committed? Why am I confined here like a prisoner?[35]

This record of physical humiliation speaks to how "racial difference itself was perpetuated through systems of public health practice,"[36] which reinforced differences between the working class and healthy citizens. The embarrassment and physical discomfort of the medical examination psychologically marked the poet, who then textually (re)marked upon the walls of the immigration building that confined him the record of his humiliation. The arrivant poet concludes with a reflection that is permeated by kinship and self-determination: "Sitting / alone in the cell, I always think of my parents. / My dear fellow country men, work hard here! / After you are financially successful, return / to your motherland and help build your mother / country strong and rich."[37] In noting how "I always think of my parents," the arrivant poet captures a uniquely Chinese worldview that adopts filial piety and meaningful familial relationships as central to human development.

In its mode of poetic expression, the walls of the prison cells became the textual surface to contain the reality of a hostile land, of a "version of the world that is peculiarly one-sided, that is known only from within the modes of ruling, and that defines the objects of its power."[38] While immigration officials selected which "bodies of knowledge"[39] were targeted for state collection, arrivants developed their own sites of knowledge in writing on the walls of their prison cells. The writings on the walls are traces of a nascent counter-hegemonic cultural production that muddy the national claims to a monolithic European and benevolent emergence. Lai's discovery of the prison poems is a significant find in Chinese Canadian and Canadian history, offering a glimpse into the nascent race relations of the state.

## *Jin Guo* and Writing Chinese Women's Experience

*Jin Guo: Voices of Chinese Canadian Women* was published in 1992 and is widely regarded as the first Chinese Canadian women's oral history text. It contains oral testimonies and interviews, extensively transcribed by editor Momoye Sugiman, with women born in Canada and those from China,

Hong Kong, and Taiwan who emigrated to Canada after the 1947 repealing of the *Chinese Immigration Act*. The *Act* of 1923 categorized Chinese women as an excluded class of immigrant and was informed by fundamental cultural assumptions that Chinese women were promiscuous, a hygienic threat to the racial purity of the white settler nation, and thus unfit—unworthy, even—for entry and integration into the nation. These racist assumptions were coupled with systemic powers of the state and meant that some families did not reunite for nearly twenty-five years.[40]

This legislated exclusion accounts for the absence of Chinese women in mainstream archives. While the women of *Jin Guo* did not express themselves under the coercion of confinement and isolation in an immigration prison, many women reference family members who were detained in immigration prisons during the era of exclusion. *Jin Guo* is organized according to major themes such as identity, marriage, parents, education, surviving war (referring to the twentieth-century Chinese Civil War, as well as the First and Second World Wars), settlement, and transnational movement between China, Hong Kong, Taiwan, and Canada.

*Jin Guo* is particularly significant for its memory work in its regard for oral testimony, which "lies in the truth of experience—of letting people speak for themselves about their daily lives and communities, their thoughts and feelings."[41] While arrivant poets recorded the urgency of their duress and immediate conditions, implicit within the voices of the women in *Jin Guo* are sombre thoughts of missing home, isolation, and loneliness.

Chinese women in the late twentieth century were asked to share their experiences of Canada through oral testimony, voicing similar circumstances of forced relocation. Their modes of expression, however, were not recorded under the duress of detainment and confinement.[42] And while the interviewees of *Jin Guo* were not writing themselves, they did participate in acts of memory retrieval that had yet to be acknowledged or recognized as critical testimonies.

Containing a plenitude of Chinese Canadian women's voices, participants such as SKY Lee stated in her interview: "I want all of our community art and writing to become part of mainstream culture. But we shouldn't have to change. Canadian attitudes should change... 'Canadian' is not just hockey or apple pie. It means all kinds of things—anything from immigrant, new or old—because we are all immigrants here. None of us have been in Canada long enough to set cultural standards for other people."[43] Given Canada's newly adopted multicultural face, Lee's comments are extraordinarily different compared to the commentary made in the writing on the walls of the immigration prison a century earlier. The anachronistic references to hockey and apple pie showcase that this is an altogether different Canada, yet she also unsettles the myth of nativism. These fresh perspectives about being Canadian are balanced by the realities of global movement and family reunification.

Although some women were compelled by geopolitical and patriarchal forces to relocate to Canada, they all shared different experiences and perspectives about movement. The traditional gender roles of Chinese culture and society further shaped the path that Chinese men took to go abroad to work for a better life, a path that was not open to Chinese women.[44] While patriarchy and gender in both places shaped family and prolonged separation, some women recognized that "back in China they didn't know how hard the old men worked here."[45] Deborah Madsen's analysis of the exclusion of Chinese women in the United States notes how "both their bodies and their work [were] circumscribed by patriarchal efforts at nation building exerted from both sides of the Pacific."[46] Chinese women in Canada, therefore, cannot be defined under the monolith of their exclusion given their dynamic intra-Canadian experience and transnational movements.

## How Chinese Canadian Women Are Not Limited to One Voice

Chinese Canadian women's experiences ought to be read in their multiplicity and not be limited to geography and the transit of their movements from mainland China to Pacific Canada.[47] Rather, similar to their arrivant counterparts at the start of the century, Chinese Canadian women at the end of the twentieth century were versatile subjects.

One segment of the amended 1923 *Chinese Immigration Act* states that no Chinese women could enter the country without being either a wife of a merchant or a prostitute dependent on a man. An overbearing white settler male fantasy was at the root of this inherent sexualization of Chinese women.[48] The exclusion of Chinese women subsequently limited the establishment of stable family structures and engendered prolonged family separation. While the Canadian state wanted Chinese labour, it did not want Chinese families. Fearing miscegenation while desiring racial purity and racialized labour at the same time, Canadian immigration rendered Chinese women legally subjectless and male-serving even before they entered the country. The institution of such racist gender reform was first and foremost deployed upon Indigenous women and their families, and later redeployed against undesirable groups.[49]

Imposed racial difference and the geographical (thus implicitly cultural) distance of China were only partially responsible for turning Chinese women into victims of Canadian immigration policy. Although the *Chinese Immigration Act* was repealed in 1947, family reunification activist Jean Lumb notes the hesitancy of the government to reunite families: "they kept giving us little changes, but not enough until 1957. The main thing we wanted was family reunification."[50] Lumb was a part of a delegation of Chinese Canadians seeking full family reunification. Her committee effectively disabled restrictive legislation (that tried to limit the age of reunifying family members) and expedited conditional family reunification. The success of her efforts in reuniting families contests a deeply problematic nature rooted in the assumption that Chinese women were not fit to be mothers for a nationalized generation.

Other women reveal how although the male-dominated family clan system put immense pressure on women to remain in China, some found independence in the absence of their husbands. In the southern Guangdong region of China, for instance, women were seen as exceptionally independent as it was common practice for men to travel to South and Southeast Asia for work contracts. With the intergenerational practice of local migration, travelling overseas was considered acceptable and "the strength of the family allowed villages to function in the absence of men."[51] Others beyond this specific Guangdong region describe their experiences in less optimistic terms. An interviewee who chose to go by the name of "Kim" was born in China in 1937. She explains how she was raised in a traditional feudal family household with hardened gender roles and recalls how her father "used to talk about the 'pig house' where immigrants were detained like prisoners."[52] Kim's experience further highlights the intergenerational impacts of colonial policy and patriarchal forces. She and others express the tension of being in both worlds and struggling with belonging as Chinese, Canadian, and in between.

## Conclusion: Labouring and Living at the Beginning and End of the Twentieth Century

Although the general situation of arrivant labourers at the start of the twentieth century was very different from the women who shared their experiences in *Jin Guo*, we can nevertheless see common threads of thought associated with homeland, new homeland, family, and belonging. That these elements of labour and living in Canada are reinforced and reiterated at multiple sites of temporal and geographical experience demonstrate the remarkably vast networks of transnational movement induced by imperialism. They further affirm that arrivant insight is critical to deeper understandings of racialization and colonization that exist beyond classical colonial situations.

Settler colonial Canada's desire for racial and ethnic purity led to the subsequent social construction of Chinese people as a threat to the nation, and it formed legalized family separation and fracture that were first practised on Indigenous nations and people. As the writing on the walls and oral testimony reveal, the lived realities of Chinese arrivant men and their latter-twentieth-century immigrant women counterparts stand in unique juxtaposition to settler fantasies of benevolent emergence. As "most historians saw Canada as a European settler nation," Mar notes, "they did not deeply inquire into Chinese Canadian perspectives,"[53] thus their distinct absence from the colonial archive. Instead, by inscribing on the walls of their immigration prison cells and using their voices to write themselves into being, alternative archives were produced to tell a different story of Canadian emergence. The prison cells of the immigration building and the inaugural Chinese Canadian women's anthology became third spaces[54] of articulation that challenge the veil of a predominantly white, rugged, Christian, masculine proto-Canada. These Chinese-language documents and English-language records reveal the gradual and conflictual process of colonialism, migration, and family separation under settler colonial formations. And though they do not speak directly to relationships with Indigenous Peoples, the recordation of their humiliation and harassment highlights the iterative process of settler colonial crisis management. The triadic relationship between Indigenous Peoples, settlers, and arrivants is complex partly due to the traumatic historic emergence of these categories of subjecthood through colonization and forced migration. More than anything, these unlikely archives are a collection of life experiences that attest to a dynamic humanism, ones that are shaped not merely by their labour but by living and being beyond their capacities as labour contributing to settler colonial national projects.

## Notes

1 Byrd, *Transit of Empire*, xix.
2 Veracini, *Settler Colonialism*, 3.
3 Tuck, Guess, and Sultan, "Not Nowhere." For conversations on the ways in which racialized arrivants are made or have been complicit in forms of Asian settler colonialism, see considerations by Saranillio, "Why Asian Settler Colonialism Matters."
4 See Chan, *Gold Mountain*.
5 See Byrd, *Transit of Empire*. Also see Ben-Zvi, *Native Land Talk*.
6 Mawani, *Colonial Proximities*, 124.
7 See Byrd, *Transit of Empire*.
8 See Brathwaite, *The Arrivants*.
9 Tuck, Guess, and Sultan, "Not Nowhere."
10 Tuck and Yang, "Decolonization Is Not," 17.
11 Tuck and Yang, "Decolonization Is Not," 17.
12 Wolfe, "Settler Colonialism," 392.
13 Wolfe, "Settler Colonialism," 404.
14 Wolfe, "The Settler Colonial Complex," 2.
15 Wolfe "Settler Colonialism," 392.
16 Li, *The Chinese in Canada*, 13.
17 Wolfe, "Settler Colonialism," 404.
18 While Wolfe draws examples from the development of plantation economies in America's Deep South, Afua Cooper conceives of the history of slavery in Canada in *The Hanging of Angélique*. Also see Maynard, *Policing Black Lives*.
19 See Chan, *Gold Mountain*. Also see Wong, *Laughing Back at Empire*.
20 Ward, *White Canada Forever*.
21 Lai, "A 'Prison,'" 17.
22 *Coolie labourers* were low-wage labourers, historically from South or East Asia. See Lai, "A 'Prison,'" 17–18. In the nineteenth-century colonization of India by Britain, the term described the system of contract labour on sugar plantations in the Caribbean, which supplanted enslaved African labour. See Jung, *Coolies and Cane*.
23 Lai, "A 'Prison,'"17.
24 Lai, "A 'Prison,'"18.
25 Mar, "Beyond Being Others," 20.
26 Mar, "Beyond Being Others," 21.
27 Shah, *Contagious Divides*, 8.
28 Lai, "A 'Prison,'" 17.
29 Lai, "A 'Prison,'" 16.
30 Rimstead and Rymhs, "Prison Writing," 6.
31 Rimstead and Rymhs, "Prison Writing," 2.
32 Lai, "A 'Prison,'" 18–19.
33 Lai, "A 'Prison,'" 19.

34 Lai, "A 'Prison,'" 19.
35 Lai, "A 'Prison,'" 18.
36 Shah, *Contagious Divides*, 76.
37 Lai, "A 'Prison,'" 18.
38 Smith, *The Conceptual Practices*, 83–84.
39 Smith, *The Conceptual Practices*, 84.
40 See Li, "Reconciling with History."
41 Women's Book Committee, eds., *Jin Guo*, 12.
42 Agnew, "History and Identity," 111.
43 Women's Book Committee, eds., *Jin Guo*, 97.
44 Women's Book Committee, eds., *Jin Guo*, 17.
45 Women's Book Committee, eds., *Jin Guo*, 17.
46 Madsen, "Sexing the Sojourner," 36.
47 See Chen, *The Many Dimensions*.
48 See Chao, "*Bachelor-Man*." Also see Poy, *Passage to Promise Land*.
49 See Oikawa, *Cartographies of Violence*.
50 Women's Book Committee, eds., *Jin Guo*, 48.
51 Women's Book Committee, eds., *Jin Guo*, 18.
52 Women's Book Committee, eds., *Jin Guo*, 69.
53 Mar, "Beyond Being Others," 13.
54 In reference to Homi K. Bhabha's "third space of enunciation," in Bhabha, *The Location of Culture*.

## Sources

Agnew, Vijay. "History and Identity." In *Diaspora, Memory, and Identity: A Search for Home*. University of Toronto Press, 2005.

Ben-Zvi, Yael. *Native Land Talk: Indigenous and Arrivant Rights Theories*. Dartmouth College Press, 2018.

Bhabha, Homi K. *The Location of Culture*. Routledge, 2004.

Brathwaite, Kamau. *The Arrivants: A New World Trilogy*. Oxford University Press, 1986.

Byrd, Jodi A. *The Transit of Empire: Indigenous Critiques of Colonialism*. University of Minnesota Press, 2011.

Chan, Anthony B. *Gold Mountain: The Chinese in the New World*. New Star Books, 1983.

Chao, Lien. "*Bachelor-Man*: 'A Silence Crying Out to Be Broken' in Canadian Theatre." In *Beyond Silence: Chinese Canadian Literature in English*. TSAR Books, 1997.

Chen, Ya-Chen. *The Many Dimensions of Chinese Feminism*. Palgrave Macmillan, 2011.

Cooper, Afua. *The Hanging of Angélique: The Untold Story of Canadian Slavery and the Burning of Old Montreal*. HarperCollins Canada, 2011.

Jung, Moon-Ho. *Coolies and Cane: Race, Labor, and Sugar in the Age of Emancipation*. Johns Hopkins University Press, 2006.

Lai, David Chuen-Yan. "A 'Prison' for Chinese Immigrants." *Asianadian* 2, no. 4 (1979): 16–19.

Li, Peter. *The Chinese in Canada*. Oxford University Press, 1988.

Li, Peter. "Reconciling with History: The Chinese Canadian Head Tax Redress." *Journal of Chinese Overseas* 4, no. 1 (May 2008): 127–140. https://dx.doi.org/10.1353/jco.0.0010.

Madsen, Deborah. "Sexing the Sojourner: Imagining Nation / Writing Women in the Global Chinese Diaspora." *Contemporary Women's Writing* 1, no. 2 (2008): 36–49.

Mar, Lisa Rose. "Beyond Being Others: Chinese Canadians as National History." *BC Studies* 156/157 (Winter 2007/Spring 2008): 13–34. https://doi.org/10.14288/bcs.v0i156/7.608.

Mawani, Renisa. *Colonial Proximities: Crossracial Encounters and Juridical Truths in British Columbia, 1871–1921*. University of British Columbia Press, 2010.

Maynard, Robyn. *Policing Black Lives: State Violence in Canada from Slavery to the Present*. Fernwood Publishing, 2017.

Oikawa, Mona. *Cartographies of Violence: Japanese Canadian Women, Memory, and the Subjects of the Internment*. University of Toronto Press, 2012.

Poy, Vivenne. *Passage to Promise Land: Voices of Chinese Immigrant Women to Canada*. McGill-Queen's University Press, 2013.

Rimstead, Roxanne, and Deena Rymhs. "Prison Writing/Writing Prison in Canada." *Canadian Literature*, no. 208 (2011): 6–11.

Saranillio, Dean Itsuji. "Why Asian Settler Colonialism Matters: A Thought Piece on Critiques, Debates, and Indigenous Difference." *Settler Colonial Studies* 3, nos. 3–4 (2013): 280–294. https://doi.org/10.1080/2201473X.2013.810697.

Shah, Nayan. *Contagious Divides: Epidemics and Race in San Francisco's Chinatown*. University of California Press, 2001.

Smith, Dorothy. *The Conceptual Practices of Power: A Feminist Sociology of Power*. University of Toronto Press, 1990.

Veracini, Lorenzo. *Settler Colonialism: A Theoretical Overview*. Palgrave Macmillan, 2010.

Ward, Peter. *White Canada Forever: Popular Attitudes and Public Policy Toward Orientals in British Columbia*. 2nd ed. McGill-Queen's University Press, 1990.

Wolfe, Patrick. "The Settler Colonial Complex: An Introduction." *American Indian Culture and Research Journal* 37, no. 2 (2013): 1–22.

Wolfe, Patrick. "Settler Colonialism and the Elimination of the Native." *Journal of Genocide Research* 8, no. 4 (2006): 387–409. https://doi.org/10.1080/14623520601056240.

Women's Book Committee, Chinese Canadian National Council, eds. *Jin Guo: Voices of Chinese Canadian Women*. Women's Press, 1992.

Wong, Angie. *Laughing Back at Empire: The Grassroots Activism of the Asianadian Magazine, 1978–1985*. University of Manitoba Press, 2023.

PART TWO

# Logics of Empire, Colonialism, and Unsettlement

# Imperial Circulation, Implicatedness, and Co-Conspiracy

## *Racialized Interruptions of Settler Colonialism in Canada*

Liam Midzain-Gobin

THIS CHAPTER AIMS TO DEVELOP OUR UNDERSTANDING of the relationship racialized individuals hold to settler coloniality and decolonization. From the perspective of a Brown settler, I discuss settler coloniality in what is today Canada as a project of possessive white supremacy aimed at dispossessing Indigenous Peoples. Historically, Canada has been an important and constituent part of the British Empire, primarily as one of the white settler colonies, and among the first to achieve self-determination and independence. Of course, this whiteness is not absolute: from its beginning what we today call Canada has been a multiracial state that has deliberately sought to incorporate non-white peoples into the settler colonial project by having them support Indigenous dispossession. While this has been uneven and imperfect, the multicultural state we envision today owes much to this history of British imperial circulation.

This history, and our present, shows that racialized peoples in contemporary Canada are implicated in the settler colonial project. However, this implication does not require that we accept a role in upholding it. Instead, through understanding our existence here as an outcome of global colonial processes, I suggest Canadians of colour especially have an important role to play as "co-conspirators," aligning ourselves with Indigenous Peoples to interrupt settler colonialism and build a decolonial future. I make this case through a personal reflection of my own, trying to make sense of settler colonialism through research, teaching, and organizing.

## Introduction

I am a settler, but one who is very used to facing the question "where are you from?" Somehow my answer—"southern British Columbia, just outside Vancouver" to anyone who I guess doesn't know the area—isn't normally as satisfying to them as I hope it will be in the moment.

Perhaps it's because I'm Brown.

That's to say, while things are changing (slowly), I'm not what comes to mind when people think of "old-stock Canadians" in former Prime Minister Stephen Harper's notorious turn of phrase.[1]

For those wondering, when the phrase "old-stock Canadians" was uttered, it raised images of white Canadians. Indeed, after the 2015 federal election debate in which Harper made the comment there was an outcry from many who immediately understood who the comment was referring to.[2] It wasn't addressing "multicultural" Canadians, or the recently arrived.

Perhaps it was the tip line for "barbaric cultural practices" that Harper's Conservatives had proposed earlier in the campaign that made the meaning clear.

What I'm trying to say is that even if, as Harper claims, he was describing "old-stock Canadians" as anyone here for one generation or longer, there was an understanding that he was referring to those white folks who settled the country earlier. That means those who left Ukraine to settle and take up farming across the Prairies, or those who left Italy or Portugal to settle in cities like Hamilton, Ontario, and work in factories and other industries. They settled here and have built lives and families across generations. Even if they didn't arrive white (in the "Anglo Saxon" sense of the term), they have been absorbed into whiteness over that time.

Settling and building a life in the longer-term, across multiple generations, does not necessarily mean that you are "old stock" in the popular view, however. Instead, our racial order remains, with only some able to climb the hierarchy. I understand this in two important ways. First, because it has been part of my intellectual, academic studies. Second, it comes from my lived experience.

I mention those who left Ukraine in part because that is part of my own heritage, even if it does not visibly define me. My mother's father arrived from Ukraine and built a life and family in Manitoba and British Columbia. They have been absorbed into whiteness, with my mother not really questioning it. My own father, however, has very much not been absorbed. Born to South Asian parents in Georgetown, Guyana, at the very end of British imperial rule there, he arrived in Manitoba in his teens. That is, he wouldn't be "old stock," but I would be if not for my Brownness.

Canada likes to frame itself as a "multicultural mosaic."[3] Broadly speaking, this may be true, but the mosaic is also a useful image to think of how I see whiteness shaping our racial order within Canada. It is there in the discussion of "old stock"—those who can attain that status are those in close proximity to whiteness, like one side of my family. They can claim a Canadianness and find a place within the country's mosaic that is unquestioned. On the other hand, those of us of colour fit within the mosaic somewhat differently, put into cultural boxes to belong, shaped and moulded into the correct shape so as to not dramatically shift the underlying (settler colonial) relations of power. But these underlying relations of power present the problem. Instead of trying to fit into the mosaic, I argue that we should be working to undermine it. As I outline below, we can do so by moving away from implicated subjecthood to standing alongside Indigenous Peoples as "co-conspirators" working to abolish what Goenpul scholar Aileen Moreton-Robinson describes as white possessiveness, or that "excessive desire to invest in reproducing and reaffirming the [white] nation-state's ownership, control and domination."[4] That is, we can work to affirm Indigenous sovereignty.

## Canada Within Empire

What I want to suggest in discussing my own background is not only that white possessiveness as a relational and property-centric logic organizes Canadian political culture. It does, as we also see in other settler colonial contexts.[5] However, what I aim to unpack here is how this came about and why it is not only about the colour of one's skin. Canada is interesting because of its place within with what historian Kenton Storey refers to as "British imperial networks."[6] Looking at these networks helps us understand the connectivity of the British Empire on material and subjective as well as imaginative levels. They show that rather than understanding the British Empire as a collection of independent colonies, rigidly controlled by the British metropole through London, we can focus on how the "web-like structure" of empire[7] was stitched together, in particular through flows of information, imaginaries, people, and practices. For those working in this area of new imperial history, these flows connect metropole to colony, colony to metropole, and colony to colony if not freely, at least not in the unidirectional ways that previous histories would suggest.

Canada has been a point within this structure. We are a bilingual, multicultural nation built out of an imperial competition between the British and French. Both were, and remain, colonial powers. This history shapes Canada, however, as a white dominion, specifically constructed to extend Anglo sovereignty. Indeed, it has been an important part of the British Empire that is both constituted by and also constitutive of it. This is to say that Canada's existence in the world is mediated by an Anglo imperialism[8]—historically the British, contemporaneously the American.[9] We do not oftentimes think of ourselves in this way, preferring instead to consider ourselves the tolerant, multicultural nation that is a leader within the rules-based international order. However, that mosaic I referred to earlier is in part a result of our connections to the British Empire. If not for empire, migration flows would have been different. My own family may have looked quite different if they had not come through the migration pathways established by the legal order prevailing throughout the empire, and the migration flows that accompanied this order and the connected systems of slavery and indentured servitude.[10]

## Imperial Accumulation Through Dispossession

If Canada was established within and through the British Empire, it is useful to think of it as an "Other England" in Sarah Hogan's terms,[11] or a "neo-Britain" in James Belich's,[12] in that it was understood to mirror a specific (utopian) vision of Britain and constituted through settler colonial "explosions." Canada, then, is more than just a material entity. It also brings together ideas: cosmological, political, and economic imaginaries with material logics of capital. These ideas shape our understandings of where we fit in the universe, how we ought to govern ourselves—who that "we" even is—and how we will create, trade, and materially survive. So, creating Canada was a sort of utopian process of transposing Britain (as an idea) into a new space. This can be seen in the naming of towns, mountains, and other features after British places and individuals and also through the bringing of political institutions and social mores. Materially, the imperative towards land and resource accumulation played such an important role in imperial expansion and as a justification for the migration and population flows I referred to above—both intentional and forced.[13] Looking at settler colonialism within Canada as an ongoing project calls on us to take seriously the ways it is upheld. The existing literature engages with this in two registers: the material and the subjective. I want to outline both briefly before suggesting one way to understand their interconnectedness.

Materially, the settler colonial project is a question of land and dispossession. One of the core features of a specifically *settler* colonialism is that those who arrived from Europe stayed,[14] seeking to reproduce much of European society and extending European (settler) sovereignty over the lands of Indigenous nations. This extension of settler sovereignty is not uniform. In some places, it meant claiming so-called "unused" or "open" land; in others, it meant forcibly relocating existing communities that were established in locations settlers wanted access to. In each case, claiming, settling, and extending European sovereignty over the land was the key purpose. The intent was accumulating land[15] and then "developing" it to facilitate European economies. Indeed, it is through the absorption of the land into European (primarily British) sovereignty that we see the remaking of Britain in an external space within which British sovereigns reigned and that provided for European economic needs.

This process of dispossession continues into the present day: while some Anglo settler states (including Canada) have put in place systems of Aboriginal or Indigenous title, Indigenous Peoples continue to identify ways that contemporary settler states rely on their dispossession. Settler economies were built on the exploitation of Indigenous People and lands,[16] and to take one example, First Nations occupy only 0.2 percent of the lands that make up Canada.[17] This is to say that the economic imperative of dispossession remains today. Resource extraction and other economic development regularly proceed contrary to the expressed wishes of the Indigenous nations who are impacted by them. Oftentimes, this further undermines the possibility of Indigenous communities maintaining their food security, access to clean water, or ability to maintain their own economies. Instead, economies are oriented around capitalist imperatives.[18]

This also remains true for those migration flows that brought so many non-Indigenous peoples of colour to Canada. While the individual flows are different, migration politics still so often bring people in as workers, with legal regimes maintaining precarity and barriers for those in racialized fields such as temporary foreign agricultural workers and caregivers, among others.

Not only a material process, this dispossession also impacts subjectivities as those understandings of self, and people's relationalities as well. Land remains central, but rather than understanding access to land as a way of ensuring life it can instead be understood as the framework through which the relationships that make up our place in the world exist.[19] These are ontological and cosmological questions about our relationships to the earth, other (non-human) beings, and the spiritual realm. Taking Indigenous philosophies and ways of understanding the world seriously means seeing humanity as deeply connected to, part of, and not authoritative over, the natural world around us. This need not move us towards repeating the "mythical" or "natural" stereotype that underpins the *Doctrine of Discovery* and understanding of the lands that comprise North America as terra nullius. These logics, used by early settlers to justify dispossession, deliberately dissuade us from understanding the relationality at the heart of Indigenous philosophies.[20] Instead, we should understand our embeddedness in the natural world as responsibilities to beings other than ourselves. Understanding them this way leads us to ask how these responsibilities might be enacted, questions that form the basis of many Indigenous political and legal orders.

The subjective level is important to settlers as well. Speaking of Canada specifically, we as settler Canadians have tied our own self-understanding to this landscape. One illustration of this comes in the form of our national anthem, which opens with (and includes) the following lines:

O Canada!
Our home and native land!
True patriot love in all of us command.
...
God keep our land glorious and free!
O Canada, we stand on guard for thee.[21]

What becomes apparent in the anthem is how our own mythology is tied to the land that comprises the contemporary state of Canada. This creates, in the words of anthropologist Eva Mackey, a form of "settled expectations" of settler ownership and authority,[22] or what Mark Rifkin calls a "settler common sense."[23] In such a context, territory, and the common sense of exclusive settler sovereignty, is intimately tied to our own national self-image, underpinning what Marie Battiste (Mi'kmaq) describes as "cognitive imperialism."[24]

Of course, land remains central to Indigenous Peoples' own sense of self and place in the world (cosmology), too, but in a very different way. As mentioned before, whereas we settlers tie ourselves to the land through an understanding of ourselves as mastering or conquering territory—and thus, literally inscribing our authority into the landscape—land remains a fundamental source of reciprocal relationships in many Indigenous cosmologies. Without wanting to overgeneralize and homogenize all Indigenous Peoples into one, nations from as far apart as the Dene[25] to the north, the Anishinaabe[26] to the centre, the Mi'gmaq[27] to the east, and the Songhees, Huu-ay-aht, and WSANEC[28] to the west all share understandings of the importance of human relationships with the non-human world. These are well-described through the concept of "grounded normativity," which through the work of Leanne Betasamosake Simpson (Michi Saagiig Nishnaabeg) and Glen Coulthard (Yellowknives Dene) understands land as a sort of container for our relations, positing not only that Indigenous Peoples have rights to the land but also responsibilities to it and the rest of Creation.[29] Humans take from the rest of Creation but also give and help maintain. In this way, land is important not only for the material sustenance of Indigenous nations but also for spiritual and political sustenance. Legal and political orders, and governance systems, are organized around and incorporate these rights and responsibilities. Breaking these reciprocal relationships underlines governance mechanisms and Indigenous nationhood. It is this that Coulthard refers to when he writes of the creation of "Indigenous subjects of empire."[30]

These registers—the material, cosmological, and political/legal—come together in the logic of possession through which colonialism operates. Without access to land (especially the nations' own lands) and the ability to maintain these reciprocal relationships, Indigenous nationhood is severely damaged. In its place we see the construction of settler sovereignty through the implementation of Moreton-Robinson's white possessive logics that affirmed and reproduced European possession of, and control over, Indigenous Lands and bodies.[31] Within the context of the British Empire, this creates a form of "ontological belonging"[32] for settlers organized around whiteness and settler ownership and control over the territory. To take one concrete example, in 2002 the Government of British Columbia, then led by Premier Gordon Campbell, put forward the Treaty Negotiations Referendum.[33] The referendum was meant to get support for the government's approach to treaty-making with First Nations in the province. It asked residents for their views on eight principles, which, when read together, offer a concrete illustration of the kinds of possessive logics outlined above. Particularly notable were mentions of First Nations powers being "delegated from Canada and British Columbia" (Principle 6) and maintaining property arrangements (both public and private) that affirmed settler authority (Principles 1 through 4). The purpose of the referendum, as pointed out at the time and supported by First Nations opposition, was to provide popular backing for the provincial government's position in treaty negotiations that settler accumulation of land was legitimate and appropriate.

## Implicated Within Empire

When we look to questions of land and belonging within Canada, we find a process of settler colonial accumulation through Indigenous dispossession, with land at its centre. Even though we settlers of colour are not white, we can still uphold and entrench the type of white possessiveness sketched out above. Before moving to this argument, though, I want to show how settlers of colour may (even unwittingly) support ongoing processes of accumulation. I think this support in part derives from what I have elsewhere called "settler comfort,"[34] a term that draws from Michael Rothberg's "implicated subject" that is "neither a victim, nor a perpetrator."[35] Here, I want to focus in on the relationship of settlers of colour to settler colonial accumulation, pointing out how we can work from our position to support Indigenous assertions of sovereignty.

First, who is the implicated subject? Notably, such a figure is distinct from a complicit actor. According to Rothberg, "implicated subjects occupy positions aligned with power and privilege without being themselves direct agents of harm; they contribute to, inhabit, inherit, or benefit from regimes of domination but do not originate or control such regimes" as would one who is complicit.[36] Rather than being the perpetrator of an action, the implicated subject continues to (at times indirectly) maintain support for the regime. Thinking through questions of implication does not deny belonging within society, but rather recognizes that inclusion within society cannot impose a one-size-fits-all approach when it comes to apportioning responsibility. By emphasizing the implicated nature of the subject, we can see how members of a society are related to the exercise of power even when they are not the ones doing the exercising. In this sense, implicated subjects are proximate to power, they benefit from it but importantly are not the ones exercising it. My other work shows this beneficial relationship with reference to the Canada Pension Plan, but the 2002 referendum from above offers an illustration of this as well. Settler residents in the province would maintain their preferential access to Crown lands under the proposed principles, even if they did not vote and had no part to play in the preparation of the questions or negotiating of treaties.

There is, of course, a grey area here, one raised by the specifics of who precisely can be seen to exercise power. Who exactly is implicated in settler colonialism? And how might this differ from being complicit in its perpetuation? I want to be cautious of being overly deterministic or of focusing too closely on individuals while missing the structural and systemic relationships within which they live and make choices, and so I make my own case with that in mind. However, in my analysis the line between implicated and complicit subjecthood lies at the point at which one's actions actively *extend* white possessiveness and settler accumulation or deny Indigenous nations' sovereignty.[37] That is, to be complicit is to do more than benefit from colonization—it also requires its active reproduction.

If we think of this relationship and map it onto settler colonial relations within Canada, it is the everyday Canadian citizen that I identify as implicated. Unlike government officials—and even public servants, to a degree—citizens in and of themselves are not actively making decisions that further settler colonial accumulation of the type outlined above. For example, they are not elected officials determining the legal frameworks of project permitting, nor are they government lawyers arguing in court against Indigenous jurisdiction. Instead, they are the recipients of the benefits associated with Canadian citizenship, both subjective and material. Subjective, in the form of belonging and identity; material, in the form of access to land and resources. These are the characteristics associated with white possessiveness, and without other work to undermine settler colonial power citizens end up affirming it by continuing to lend support.

Importantly, as discussed above, citizenship and belonging within Canada is now more inclusive, with racialized individuals existing within the mosaic. While we may not be the shapers of the settler colonial state, we also do not evade responsibility. This is because the relationship of implication is apparent among those non-white subjects within imperial Canada. Like white settlers, we maintain an identity, property, and access to the subjective and material benefits of dispossession even if, unlike white settlers, those of us of colour never quite reach the heart of the Canadian nation. Put differently, Canada retains a structural white supremacy[38] that, even while displaying a remarkable (settler) fragility, nonetheless continues to structure hierarchies of belonging within the state. As Ajay Parasram notes in discussing scholarship on white supremacy, racial fragility, and settler colonialism in Canada, this creates an arrogance among the "old stock" that assumes white Canadian superiority as the foundational logic of the Canadian state.[39] This arrogance reflects Mackey's framing of settled expectations from above and blinds white settler Canada to the ongoing existence and legitimacy of Indigenous sovereignty. It also results in moves to violence when what the Anishinaabe and Haudenosaunee know as Turtle Island appears.[40]

So, where does this leave non-Indigenous Peoples of colour in Canada? Of course, even if we are not the organizing force of settler coloniality, we can still play a productive role within it by taking on, and implementing, the kinds of white possessive logics that I have outlined above. Importantly, I think it has to do with not only an individual's role within society but also the impacts of the work they do. Take, for example, those individuals of colour in decision-making roles in police forces who disproportionately target Indigenous communities and continue to attack Indigenous expressions of self-determination, or those who have taken up positions within the government and/or public service that determine how to manage resources or the directions of policy. To the extent that their work further undermines Indigenous self-determination and the regeneration of Indigenous legal and political orders, these subjects may be less implicated than they are complicit.[41]

In other cases, we are implicated in the ways that we accumulate the benefits associated with dispossession. This is the case even as our existence here results from the migratory flows and networks constructed by imperialism. Nisha Nath and Willow Samara Allen develop the concept of "settler socialization" that is useful to describe the ways that we become invested—ontologically, but also materially—in settler colonialism.[42] We may see racism as a normative harm, but we don't align ourselves against the system and logics that perpetuate it.

## Co-Conspiracy

However, there are other ways we can understand, and practise, our relationship to settler colonialism. Instead of maintaining epistemological and ontological commitments to white possessiveness, I want to turn to relational work that tries to understand the interactions between racialization and colonization, and, importantly, how the state benefits from these processes. In particular, Rita Dhamoon's analytical framework of "relational Othering" is instructive. For Dhamoon, relational Othering is "the interactive processes of re/making, re/organizing, and managing *subjugating formations of difference which operate not only in contexts of dominance but in relation to one another as well*."[43] What Dhamoon is suggesting is that racialized subjects and Indigenous Peoples both exist as Others, and that the relations of power through which they are each Othered are interactive. Taking this, we can see ways in which these processes of racialization and colonization are mutually supportive, with the state maintaining and furthering its own claims to sovereignty and material benefits of Indigenous dispossession through the combined forces of these processes.

This relational analysis shows us the importance of seeking to align ourselves *against* these processes of colonial and imperial violence. In conclusion, I want to make the normative point that we as people of colour (racialized subjects) ought to reject existing (settler) colonial systems. Even more so, it is incumbent upon us to attempt to put our efforts towards their unmaking. Indeed, where relational Othering opens us to seeing the interactive natures of racialization and colonization, seeking to act as co-conspirators with Indigenous nations lets us work together for our collective liberation by replacing these imperial networks and logics.

Why co-conspiracy? While allyship is important, the idea of co-conspiracy comes out of abolitionist thought and describes collective action whereby peoples and communities work together to not only undermine violent and colonial power relations but to develop decolonial futures.[44]

This has traditionally centred Black thought, and especially Black-Indigenous relationalities. However, many of us, perhaps most poignantly those of us with family histories of indenture, should see ourselves as implicated in these struggles as well. In the context of settler colonialism in Canada, it means not only trying to disrupt settler colonial continuity but also pursuing a positive vision of Indigenous self-determination outside of (Canadian) colonial control.

How might this co-conspiracy be achieved? How might we align ourselves against the power of the settler state and white possessiveness? I think a good starting point is to reflect on the impacts of our professional lives. Of course we cannot know every possible outcome of our work, but we can and should be reflecting on the ways that our actions may contribute to ongoing Indigenous dispossession. I recognize this as a fraught assertion, considering my own position of (relative) power within a university—an institution that has historically played a constitutive role in shaping and promoting colonial practices. However, given Canada's position within the imperial networks outlined above, and given that many racialized subjects have rights within this space as a result of the white possessive logics that underpin the Canadian state, we as racialized subjects have a responsibility to act. Our own liberation can be achieved only through realizing that of Indigenous Peoples. One of the core lessons I have learned through my work is how Indigenous Peoples are not seeking the removal of non-Indigenous folks. Instead, to live within Indigenous sovereignty is a call to build futures alongside one another, but without imposing our own ways of governing or living onto each other. That is, we don't have to reject our vision of a mosaic, but we need to rebuild it outside of the (colonial) strictures placed on it by white possessiveness that ultimately harm us all in different ways. The legitimacy of the settler state of Canada increasingly relies on claims that racial multiculturalism and economic prosperity allow us to collectively achieve justice. Insofar as multiculturalism and economic prosperity are shaped by Indigenous dispossession and white possessiveness, though, they do not substantially alter the underlying power relations. Making us more diverse while continuing to maintain colonial authority can't be the answer.

How might we approach enacting liberatory practices? From my position, and from speaking to others participating within educational and research roles, I think we can enact these relations through our teaching and research. Community-engaged (or participatory/partnership-based) scholarship has a crucial role to play. Rather than being driven by the interests of the researcher, this kind of scholarship centres the needs of the community involved with a research project co-developed between the researchers and community participating—and with clear benefits for the community.[45] It is research intended to directly address a problem identified by the community, and which places the community in the position of knower, not just known. Moreover, it is the kind of work being demanded by Indigenous communities and scholars themselves.[46]

While research does indeed have a difficult history with Indigenous communities,[47] we are increasingly seeing that work dealing with Indigenous communities is required to engage with them from funding bodies such as the Social Sciences and Humanities Research Council and others. This is a positive step, and, further, I want to foreground the importance of working through the legal and political orders, mechanisms, and systems of each community involved. To help build the kinds of futures we want to see, community-based projects need to practise those relations and should operate on the basis of Indigenous sovereignty and law. Working through Indigenous Peoples' own governance protocols and systems offers concrete opportunities to work against colonial erasure to not only support but help further affirm Indigenous authority. It also offers us the opportunity to continue supporting communities in revitalizing these systems, working from the position of their own knowledges to further their own authority and jurisdiction. In doing this type of "insurgent" research,[48] settlers of colour can align themselves against the white possessiveness and the ongoing reproduction of settler coloniality. This would move them away from implicated subjecthood and instead towards acting as co-conspirators alongside Indigenous Peoples against the (white) settler assemblage.

While this work need not be done only by racialized individuals—nor from within a university—I want to suggest that it is particularly important for scholars of colour to align ourselves against this white possessiveness. Indeed, as Dhamoon outlines, "In failing to pursue how we complicitly consent to the conditions that structure processes of relational Othering, we fail to undo our own subordinations."[49] This is because, as I pointed out above, our status as racialized and existence on these territories are both produced and shaped by the imperial networks that extended white possessiveness across the globe. To build those decolonized futures outside of colonial control thus requires us to stand in solidarity with Indigenous nations. Working to undo settler coloniality, including by affirming Indigenous sovereignty, is a concrete step that we can take.

In the interest of being self-reflexive, I have been more and less successful at achieving this in different projects I have been a part of and led. So, this is not a call for an all-or-nothing approach. However, aligning ourselves against colonial power, or working ourselves into positions to undo it, remains an important objective if we are going to realize our decolonial potential.

So, to return to the beginning: Where am I from? For now, Chilliwack, a little city outside of Vancouver.

But if we align ourselves against white possessiveness and return land and authority to the Stó:lō Nation, the answer would be S'ólh Téméxw.[50]

## Notes

1 CBC News, "Stephen Harper Explains."
2 Edwards, "'Old Stock Canadians' Comment."
3 Midzain-Gobin, "Reimagining the Mosaic."
4 Moreton-Robinson, *The White Possessive*, xii.
5 Bell, ed., *Empire, Race and Global Justice*; Moreton-Robinson, *The White Possessive*.
6 Storey, *Settler Anxiety*, 9.
7 Ballantyne, *Orientalism and Race*.
8 Dunton, "Willing to Serve."
9 See Mackey, *The House of Difference*.
10 Lowe, *The Intimacies of Four Continents*; Nath, "Curated Hostilities."
11 Hogan, *Other Englands*.
12 Belich, *Replenishing the Earth*.
13 Day, *Alien Capital*; Leroy, "Black History in Occupied Territory."
14 Veracini, *Settler Colonialism*.
15 Coulthard, *Red Skin, White Masks*; Estes, *Our History Is the Future*; Simpson, "Under the Sign of Sovereignty."
16 Yellowhead Institute, *Cash Back*.
17 Manuel and Grand Chief Derrickson, *Unsettling Canada*.
18 Coulthard, "For Our Nations."
19 Coulthard, *Red Skin, White Masks*; Coulthard and Simpson, "Grounded Normativity."
20 For examples, see Ambers and George, "Fluid Internationalisms"; Corntassel, "Toward Sustainable Self-Determination"; Todd, "Fish Pluralities."
21 Government of Canada, "National Anthem of Canada" (emphasis mine).
22 Mackey, *Unsettled Expectations*.

23 Rifkin, *Settler Common Sense.*
24 Battiste, "Maintaining Aboriginal Identity," 192–208.
25 Coulthard, *Red Skin, White Masks.*
26 Simpson, *Dancing on Our Turtle's Back.*
27 Ladner, "Up the Creek."
28 Cook, Vallance, Lutz, Brazier, and Foster, eds., *To Share, Not Surrender.*
29 Coulthard and Simpson, "Grounded Normativity."
30 Coulthard, "Subjects of Empire."
31 Moreton-Robinson, *The White Possessive,* 49–50.
32 Moreton-Robinson, *The White Possessive,* 4.
33 Elections BC, "Report of the Chief Electoral Officer."
34 Midzain-Gobin, "Comfort and Insecurity ."
35 Rothberg, *The Implicated Subject,* 1.
36 Rothberg, *The Implicated Subject,* 1.
37 Here I'm drawing on Jafri, "Privilege vs. Complicity"; Nath and Allen, "Settler Colonial Socialization."
38 Razack, *Looking White People in the Eye*; Thobani, *Exalted Subjects.*
39 Parasram, "Pathological White Fragility."
40 Parasram, "Pathological White Fragility."
41 Lawrence and Dua, "Decolonizing Antiracism."
42 Nath and Allen, "Settler Colonial Socialization."
43 Dhamoon, "Relational Othering," 874; emphasis in original.
44 Love, *We Want to Do More Than Survive*; Habtom and Scribe, "To Breathe Together."
45 Fletcher, "Community-Based Participatory Research"; Goodman, Bird, and Gabel, "Towards a More Collaborative Political Science"; Israel, Schulz, Parker, and Becker, "Review of Community-Based Research"; MacKinnon, ed., *Practising Community-Based Participatory Research.*
46 Gaudry, "Insurgent Research"; Gaudry, "Next Steps," 254–258; MacKinnon, "Introduction," 3–13.
47 Tuhiwai Smith, *Decolonizing Methodologies.*
48 Gaudry, "Insurgent Research."
49 Dhamoon, "Relational Othering," 888.
50 S'ólh Téméxw Stewardship Alliance, "History."

## Sources

Ambers, Andrew, and Rachel yacaaʔał George. "Fluid Internationalisms: The Ocean as a Source and Forum of Indigenous International Law." *Borders in Globalization Review* 5, no. 1 (2024): 21–25. https://doi.org/10.18357/bigr51202421801.

Ballantyne, Tony. *Orientalism and Race: Aryanism in the British Empire.* Palgrave Macmillan, 2002.

Battiste, Marie. "Maintaining Aboriginal Identity, Language, and Culture in Modern Society." In *Reclaiming Indigenous Voice and Vision,* edited by Marie Battiste. University of British Columbia Press, 2000.

Belich, James. *Replenishing the Earth: The Settler Revolution and the Rise of the Angloworld*. Oxford University Press, 2009.

Bell, Duncan, ed. *Empire, Race and Global Justice*. Cambridge University Press, 2019.

CBC News. "Stephen Harper Explains 'Old-Stock Canadians' Comment." Last updated September 18, 2015. https://www.cbc.ca/news/politics/canada-election-2015-harper-debate-1.3233785.

Cook, Peter, Neil Vallance, John Lutz, Graham Brazier, and Hamar Foster, eds. *To Share, Not Surrender: Indigenous and Settler Visions of Treaty Making in the Colonies of Vancouver Island and British Columbia*. University of British Columbia Press, 2021.

Corntassel, Jeff. "Toward Sustainable Self-Determination: Rethinking the Contemporary Indigenous-Rights Discourse." *Alternatives* 33, no. 1 (2008): 105–132. https://www.jstor.org/stable/40645238.

Coulthard, Glen. "For Our Nations to Live, Capitalism Must Die." *Unsettling America* (blog), November 5, 2013. https://unsettlingamerica.wordpress.com/2013/11/05/for-our-nations-to-live-capitalism-must-die/.

Coulthard, Glen. *Red Skin, White Masks: Rejecting the Colonial Politics of Recognition*. University of Minnesota Press, 2014.

Coulthard, Glen. "Subjects of Empire: Indigenous Peoples and the 'Politics of Recognition' in Canada." *Contemporary Political Theory* 6, no. 4 (2007): 437–460.

Coulthard, Glen, and Leanne Betasamosake Simpson. "Grounded Normativity / Place-Based Solidarity." *American Quarterly* 68, no. 2 (2016): 249–255. https://dx.doi.org/10.1353/aq.2016.0038.

Day, Iyko. *Alien Capital: Asian Racialization and the Logic of Settler Colonial Capitalism*. Duke University Press, 2016.

Dhamoon, Rita Kaur. "Relational Othering: Critiquing Dominance, Critiquing the Margins." *Politics, Groups, and Identities* 9, no. 5 (2021): 873–892. https://doi.org/10.1080/21565503.2019.1691023.

Dunton, Caroline. "Willing to Serve: Empire, Status, and Canadian Campaigns for the United Nations Security Council (1946–1947)." *International Journal* 75, no. 4 (2020): 529–547. https://doi.org/10.1177/0020702020980764.

Edwards, Peter. "'Old Stock Canadians' Comment Gives Chills to Professor." *Toronto Star*, September 18, 2015. https://www.thestar.com/news/canada/2015/09/18/old-stock-canadians-phrase-chills-prof-ignites-twitter.html.

Elections BC. "Report of the Chief Electoral Officer on the Treaty Negotiations Referendum." September 9, 2002. https://www.elections.bc.ca/docs/rpt/2002-CEOReport-TreatyNegotiationsReferendum.pdf.

Estes, Nick. *Our History Is the Future: Standing Rock Versus the Dakota Access Pipeline, and the Long Tradition of Indigenous Resistance*. Verso, 2019.

Fletcher, Christopher. "Community-Based Participatory Research Relationships with Aboriginal Communities in Canada: An Overview of Context and Process." *Pimatisiwin* 1, no. 1 (2003): 27–62.

Gaudry, Adam. "Insurgent Research." *Wicazo Sa Review* 26, no. 1 (2011): 113–136.

Gaudry, Adam. "Next Steps in Indigenous Community-Engaged Research: Supporting Research Self-Sufficiency in Indigenous Communities." In *Towards a New Ethnohistory: Community-Engaged Scholarship Among the People of the River*, edited by Keith Thor Carlson, John Sutton Lutz, David M. Schaepe, and Naxaxalhts'i–Albert "Sonny" McHalsie. University of Manitoba Press, 2018.

Goodman, Nicole, Karen Bird, and Chelsea Gabel. "Towards a More Collaborative Political Science: A Partnership Approach." *Canadian Journal of Political Science* 50, no. 1 (2017): 201–218. https://doi.org/10.1017/S000842391700004X.

Government of Canada. "National Anthem of Canada." January 5, 2018. https://www.canada.ca/en/canadian-heritage/services/anthems-canada.html#a11.

Habtom, Sefanit, and Megan Scribe. "To Breathe Together: Co-Conspirators for Decolonial Futures." Yellowhead Institute, June 20, 2020. https://yellowheadinstitute.org/2020/06/02/to-breathe-together/.

Hogan, Sarah. *Other Englands: Utopia, Capital, and Empire in an Age of Transition*. Stanford University Press, 2018.

Israel, Barbara A., Amy J. Schulz, Edith A. Parker, and Adam B. Becker. "Review of Community-Based Research: Assessing Partnership Approaches to Improve Public Health." *Annual Review of Public Health* 19 (1998): 173–202. https://doi.org/10.1146/annurev.publhealth.19.1.173.

Jafri, Beenash. "Privilege vs. Complicity: People of Colour and Settler Colonialism." *Equity Matters* (blog), March 12, 2012. https://www.federationhss.ca/en/blog/privilege-vs-complicity-people-colour-and-settler-colonialism.

Ladner, Kiera L. "Up the Creek: Fishing for a New Constitutional Order." *Canadian Journal of Political Science* 38, no. 4 (December 2005): 923–953. https://doi.org/10.1017/S0008423905040539.

Lawrence, Bonita, and Enakshi Dua. "Decolonizing Anti-Racism." *Social Justice* 32, no. 4 (2005): 120–143.

Leroy, Justin. "Black History in Occupied Territory: On the Entanglements of Slavery and Settler Colonialism." *Theory & Event* 19, no. 4 (2016). https://muse.jhu.edu/article/633276.

Love, Bettina L. *We Want to Do More Than Survive: Abolitionist Teaching and the Pursuit of Educational Freedom*. Beacon Press, 2019.

Lowe, Lisa. *The Intimacies of Four Continents*. Duke University Press, 2015.

Mackey, Eva. *The House of Difference: Cultural Politics and National Identity in Canada*. Routledge, 1999.

Mackey, Eva. *Unsettled Expectations: Uncertainty, Land and Settler Decolonization*. Fernwood Publishing, 2016.

MacKinnon, Shauna. "Introduction: 'Research That Belongs to Us.'" In *Practising Community-Based Participatory Research: Stories of Engagement, Empowerment, and Mobilization*, edited by Shauna MacKinnon. Purich Books, 2018.

MacKinnon, Shauna, ed. *Practising Community-Based Participatory Research: Stories of Engagement, Empowerment, and Mobilization*. Purich Books, 2018.

Manuel, Arthur, and Grand Chief Ronald M. Derrickson. *Unsettling Canada: A National Wake-Up Call*. 2nd ed. Between the Lines Books, 2021.

Midzain-Gobin, Liam. "Comfort and Insecurity in the Reproduction of Settler Coloniality." *Critical Studies on Security* 9, no. 3 (2021): 212–225. https://doi.org/10.1080/21624887.2021.1936834.

Midzain-Gobin, Liam. "Reimagining the Mosaic." *International History and Politics Newsletter* (2020).

Moreton-Robinson, Aileen. *The White Possessive: Property, Power, and Indigenous Sovereignty*. University of Minnesota Press, 2015.

Nath, Nisha. "Curated Hostilities and the Story of Abdoul Abdi: Relational Securitization in the Settler Colonial Racial State." *Citizenship Studies* 25, no. 2 (2021): 292–315. https://doi.org/10.1080/13621025.2020.1859187.

Nath, Nisha, and Willow Samara Allen. "Settler Colonial Socialization in Public Sector Work: Moving from Privilege to Complicity." *Studies in Social Justice* 16, no. 1 (2022): 200–226. https://doi.org/10.26522/ssj.v16i1.2648.

Parasram, Ajay. "Pathological White Fragility and the Canadian Nation." *Studies in Political Economy* 100, no. 2 (2019): 194–207. https://doi.org/10.1080/07078552.2019.1646457.

Razack, Sherene H. *Looking White People in the Eye: Gender, Race, and Culture in Courtrooms and Classrooms*. University of Toronto Press, 1997.

Rifkin, Mark. *Settler Common Sense: Queerness and Everyday Colonialism in the American Renaissance*. University of Minnesota Press, 2014.

Rothberg, Michael. *The Implicated Subject: Beyond Victims and Perpetrators, Cultural Memory in the Present*. Stanford University Press, 2019.

Simpson, Audra. "Under the Sign of Sovereignty: Certainty, Ambivalence, and Law in Native North America and Indigenous Australia." *Wicazo Sa Review* 25, no. 2 (2010): 107–124. https://dx.doi.org/10.1353/wic.2010.0000.

Simpson, Leanne Betasamosake. *Dancing on Our Turtle's Back: Stories of Nishnaabeg Re-Creation, Resurgence and a New Emergence*. Arbeiter Ring Publishing, 2011.

S'ólh Téméxw Stewardship Alliance. "History." Accessed January 20, 2023. https://thestsa.ca/about-stsa/history/.

Storey, Kenton. *Settler Anxiety at the Outposts of Empire: Colonial Relations, Humanitarian Discourses, and the Imperial Press*. University of British Columbia Press, 2018.

Thobani, Sunera. *Exalted Subjects: Studies in the Making of Race and Nation in Canada*. University of Toronto Press, 2007.

Todd, Zoe. "Fish Pluralities: Human-Animal Relations and Sites of Engagement in Paulatuuq, Arctic Canada." *Études Inuit/Inuit Studies* 38, nos. 1–2 (2014): 217–238. https://www.jstor.org/stable/24368324.

Tuhiwai Smith, Linda. *Decolonizing Methodologies: Research and Indigenous Peoples*. 2nd ed. Zed Books, 2012.

Yellowhead Institute. *Cash Back: A Yellowhead Institute Red Paper* (2021). https://cashback.yellowheadinstitute.org/wp-content/uploads/2021/05/Cash-Back-A-Yellowhead-Institute-Red-Paper.pdf.

# A Contribution to Periodizing Settler Colonial History in Canada

Peter Kulchyski

## i.

AS THE CONCEPT OF SETTLER COLONIALISM DEVELOPS, it is possible to think about Indigenous Peoples' struggles for justice in a more particular light. Colonialism and imperialism are terms that deal with forms of domination largely defined by spatial difference and that attend to a variety of distinct oppressive historical forces and the struggles to counter them. Imperialism generally describes a situation where a single metropolitan entity (city-state, nation) dominates a variety of peripheral entities enough to be awarded a regular bribe (tithe, tribute). Colonialism describes a process of establishing a "beach-head" such that members of the colonial power occupy a peripheral site (whether or not it was previously occupied) and take political and economic control, oftentimes expanding or attempting to expand their small area of control and even to gain demographic preponderance. Removal of formal political ties of dominance in the post–World War II period led to the coining of the term *neo-colonialism* to describe a situation in which the colonial metropole surrendered its formal political control but continued to extract wealth through ongoing economic control.

The concept of internal colonialism is an early version of settler colonialism and has been used to describe colonial relations within a territorial entity (used in the 1970s and '80s to describe Canada's relation to its northern territories).[1] The term *postcolonialism* developed during the theoretical season of "posts," especially in the 1980s and '90s (poststructuralism and postmodernism are some other examples) and emphasized the ideological, symbolic, and cultural elements that propped up and continue to justify or otherwise support colonial relations. In the last few decades, *settler colonialism* was developed to describe the specific and complex situation in which a colonial population comes to have a lengthy, multigenerational control over the Indigenous prior occupants of a territory, often (though not always) demographically growing into a majority of the nation.

The theorists of settler colonialism, particularly Patrick Wolfe and Lorenzo Veracini, have tied it to the Marxist concept of primitive accumulation, which refers to a process of separating people from the land in order to use land to generate capital and to transform land-based people into dispossessed workers. In the process of their work, along with that of geographer and Marxist theorist David Harvey, the term *primitive accumulation* has been reshaped into *accumulation by dispossession* and has been applied far beyond the settler colonial context.[2] Among the precursors of settler colonial analysis are Frantz Fanon, arguably the leading theorist of colonialism, who described the "town of the settler" and the "town of the native" (1961) and interrogated the cultural and psychological dynamics of a settler colonial context in which the settlers were a minority (in Algeria). Fanon's sometime interlocutor, Jean-Paul Sartre, has a remarkable chapter with a nuanced analysis of colonialism in his *Critique of Dialectical Reason*, which also offered up striking characterizations of settler colonial "bad faith."[3]

In the Canadian context, although *settler colonialism* was not used until the last few decades, many Indigenous and non-Indigenous scholars and activists have described features of what we would now understand that term to mean. For example, the Dene Nation itself, and Mel Watkins in his work with them, characterized the Dene as a "colony within," which can now be seen as a specifically anti–settler colonialism gesture. Early Indigenous scholars or writers, such as Howard Adams, Harold Cardinal, Emma LaRocque, George Manuel and Michael Posluns, and Maria Campbell described and theorized features of settler colonial domination.

Hugh Brody's *The People's Land* offers an early and very nuanced description of settler colonial social dynamics in contemporary Inuit communities. This 1977 analysis is still almost unparalleled and is enormously relevant to the continued "settler colonial enclaves" that exist in most northern Canadian Indigenous communities.[4]

Periodization is itself a politicized interpretive gesture. It is not simply a matter of setting an arbitrary temporal boundary that links some events and excludes others, though it is that as well. An historical period involves acknowledgement that a degree of stasis around a particular social element (say the reign of Elizabeth I) allows for a temporally bounded sense that this element (who rules) lends a certain colour to many of the events within the boundary. Thus, British historians have categorized the "Elizabethan" era as having particular features that are distinct from say the "Jacobean" era that followed. Periodization allows a quick look into history, taking the endless chain of events and grouping them into analytically digestible moments. It is striking that, for example, Canadian history is largely told through the narrative of periods established in a European context (interwar, postwar, and so on).

What follows is an attempt to extend the emerging dialogue on settler colonialism in Canada by developing the historical, global features and historical pacing of settler colonialism, offering a new periodization as a key tool. I frame this discussion within the "progressive-regressive" method developed by Jean-Paul Sartre. Sartre deploys a dialectical materialist approach, a Marxist theory of history in which collective practices and the structures that inflect them are seen as determinative. This approach emphasizes the importance of adding analyses of psychological structures, affective flows, cultural constraints, and interventions to the political and economic concerns that command the attention of much Marxist critical thought. I start this chapter with a theoretical discussion of settler colonialism (those without an interest in theory may want to pass over this section), beginning with a focus on the progressive-regressive method and the concept of primitive accumulation. I will then turn to a periodization of settler colonial history, emphasizing why periodization itself may be such a "key tool" and offering a substantive analysis of distinct periods in what eventually became "Canada" as a way of establishing what Sartre would call the "progressive" context of current practice.

**ii.**

It is worth reminding ourselves that many of the early critiques of colonialism in general include extensive descriptions of specific settler colonial conditions and ideological constructions. Frantz Fanon's close investigations of psychological structures across the colonial divide in *Black Skin, White Masks*[5] and his descriptions of the two towns in *The Wretched of the Earth*—native and colonial—remain a rich source of thinking on settler colonialism "before the letter," as it were. Roland Barthes's critical unpacking of the Black African soldier image on the cover of *Paris Match* in his *Mythologies* likewise involves a careful reading of a settler colonial ideological gesture: the Black soldier fighting for France obviously suggests that Indigenous Algerians supported French control; they decidedly did not![6] In Canada, Hugh Brody's striking chapters on the colonial enclaves in contemporary Inuit communities from *The People's Land* represents another strong look at a micro settler colonial dynamic that could stand in as a metonymic (a part that represents the whole) description of the nation itself. These were all written in the period between the early 1950s and the 1970s, well before Wolfe and Veracini, but have important things to say about settler colonial ideology, sociality, and psychology.

Another key source from the same period is Sartre's well-known anti-colonial analysis. Elements of Sartre's theory of totalization features a number of theoretical innovations. In particular, Sartre highlights ways in which the world is reshaped to conform to the demands of capital, and he offers an analysis of alienated serial collectives as a social form, in which the banal everyday lineup reveals the deeply unethical logic of contemporary society. Further, his understanding of the "original violence" of colonialism, in which the violent attacks on colonialism as a strategy of resistance are a logical response to the violence that comes with the imposition of colonialism (all from the *Critique of Dialectical Reason*) remain critical conceptual tools for a historical materialism that orients itself towards the particular dynamics of settler colonial polities. In this chapter, I want to centre another aspect of Sartre's thinking—his "progressive-regressive method"—and offer a demonstration of its value. In doing so, we initially note that this method is not a paint-by-numbers, instrumentalist set of narrow orderly steps. Instead, given its strong oscillation between structure and agency, it is a properly dialectical (perhaps leaning into the speculative side of dialectics recently emphasized by Fredric Jameson[7]) and therefore "messier" guide to thinking about historical dynamics.

The progressive-regressive method is discussed by Sartre in *Search for a Method*, a kind of introduction/preface to his *Critique*, and demonstrated in *The Idiot of the Family*,[8] his last major work, a study of the French novelist Gustave Flaubert. At a very broad level, Sartre's methodological discussion is an attempt to think of the role and impact of individual and collective agency in history within the Marxist paradigm (one focused on economic class conflict within the capitalist mode of production as the primary motor of world history). Sartre began his chapter on the progressive-regressive method, interestingly, citing Friedrich Engels in a letter to Marx as saying, "men themselves make their history but in a given environment which conditions them" (85). It is somewhat curious that Sartre does not use the more well-known sentence of Marx's from the "Eighteenth Brumaire of Louis Bonaparte": "Men make their own history, but they do not make it as they please; they do not make it under self-selected circumstances, but under circumstances existing already, given and transmitted from the past."[9] These quotes both point to the problem of agency versus structure in historical analysis. In Sartre's *Critique* this will take the conceptual form of a dynamic between totalization (ongoing reshaping of the world) as structure and praxis (forms of activity including resistance to totalization) as agency, but it also inflects the progressive-regressive method. Sartre explains it this way: "The dialectical totalization must include acts, passions, work, and need as well as economic categories; it must at once place the agent or the event back into the historical setting, define him in relation to the orientation of becoming, and determine exactly the meaning of the present as such."[10]

The progressive-regressive method involves a progressive moment that attends to the broad "conditions" or structures that create restrictions and openings for agency, moves towards discussion of how individuals may be crushed or raised by those same structures in its regressive moment and how those conditioned actions themselves play a role in extending or dismantling or adapting the structure, which is then altered in ways that will enable or discourage continuing or different forms of agency. In Sartre, this in part means thinking through the relation of biography to history:

> The existentialist method . . . will have no other method than a continuous "cross reference"; it will progressively determine a biography

> (for example) by examining the period, and the period by examining the biography. Far from seeking immediately to integrate one into the other, it will hold them separate until the reciprocal involvement comes to pass of itself and puts a temporary end to the research.[11]

While Sartre means for this approach to inform his understandings of class struggle, it may be deployed in other political and historical contexts. Sartre was also himself invested in understanding the colonial struggles of his era in Algeria and Vietnam. Here we want to examine what light it can shine on a settler colonial context: taking a broad look at Canadian history as specifically a settler colonial story by proposing a periodization of Canadian history in which elements of the evolving colonial structure are foregrounded and current structural features are illuminated. This will be our version of a "progressive" analytical moment. The work of other scholars who turn to somatic, embodied, psychological elements embedded in our culture would in my reading offer strands of thinking around the "regressive" analytic moment.

## iii.

What follows in this section is an attempt to offer a settler colonial periodization as a progressive moment (broad history of collective agency that determines structures) of exploration within which analysis of individual biographies and agencies can be added as a regressive (individual affective developments, struggles, collaborations, and resistances) interpretive moment. Three major transformations in settler colonial totalizations are emphasized here: from economic (1500 to 1869) to political (1869 to present) spheres of engagement; within the political, from repressive (1869 to 1951) to ideological (1951 to present) mechanisms of social control; within the ideological, from exclusion (1869 to 1970) to appropriation (1970 to present). These transformations mark the period when Canada as an emerging nation—by which we refer to the legal-cultural container that the state constructs—takes over the leading role as driver of settler colonialism. It should be noted that this periodization is developed primarily around First Nations. Although Métis and Inuit histories have been influenced by the same forces, the pacing is significantly different.

At a very broad level, the first periodic distinction we draw is between an era when relations between Indigenous Peoples and emerging settler

| |
|---|
| 1500–1869: Economic Logic → 1869–present: Political Logic |
| 1869–1951: Repression → 1951–present: Ideology |
| 1869–1970: Exclusion → 1970–present: Appropriation |

FIGURE 7.1. Overall timeline and breakdown of political shifts

colonial subjects were motivated primarily by economic concerns (from about 1500 to about 1870), and then an era when political concerns become primary (1870 to the present). In the first few centuries of this era, "Canada" did not exist, but the precursors, New France and British North America, encountered and began to occupy parts of the territory that would become or include Canada, establishing many of the parameters of settler colonialism. The major motivation of Europeans who came to this land in the broad early period was the trade for furs. If an Indigenous person and a European were meeting somewhere, chances are they were meeting to trade Indigenous-produced furs for European-made goods. The nature, the pace, the style, and the geographic status of the fur trade all evolved over the nearly three-century-long growth and decline of the trade. Both periods involve subordinate periodizations, and these are consequential, especially, for our purposes, the recent ones: the repressive/ideological shift, and the exclusion/appropriation shift.

PERIODIZING SETTLER COLONIAL CANADA
PART ONE: THE ECONOMIC PERIOD

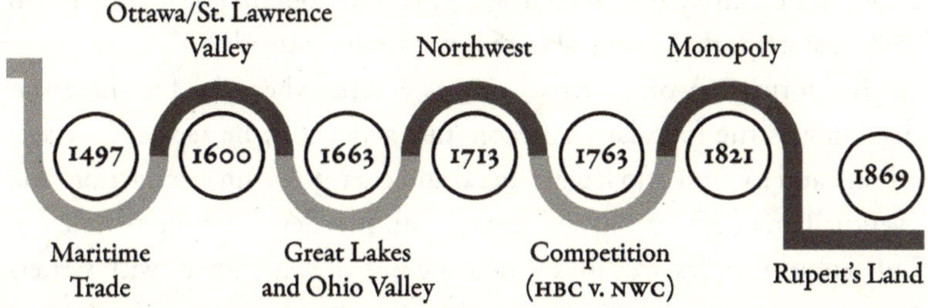


FIGURE 7.2. The economic period (drawn from Innis)

The initial period focused on economic exchange, though the forms and pacing of such exchanges assumed somewhat extra-economic dimensions (ceremonial practices and formal gift exchanges, for example). Periods (or subperiods, if you will) over the nearly three hundred years under discussion are divided by the geographic spread of the fur trade, in conjunction with the balance between English and French, and later British and Canadian, interests. Harold Innis's *The Fur Trade in Canada* (1931) has perhaps this much remaining as a lasting legacy: his periodization of the fur trade remains strong.[12] Hence, we see movement from a maritime (east coast), somewhat informal trade system (1497–1600) to the St. Lawrence Lowlands and a more systematized trade (1600–1663), to the middle ground of the Ohio valley trade (1663–1713), to the competitive period in which Hudson's Bay and North West Companies leapfrogged each other in pushing up into the north and west of the continent (1713–1763 and 1763–1821). What follows is a monopoly period after the merger of these two companies (1821–1869), and a modern trade (which still continues), or industry, that becomes more of a bit player in the overall struggle of Indigenous Peoples. However, we should note that it still remains an invaluable base of the practices and ethics that underlie Indigenous cultural expressions (see Figure 7.2). Each of these periods left its impacts on the people and territories into which its defining feature, the fur trade, moved. Among the overall results of the fur trade, some scholars (Arthur Ray and Anthony Hall,[13] for example) argue that it paved the way for dialogue between European settlers and Indigenous prior occupants. This helped each to see the value of peaceful treaties as a way to establish a mutually beneficial relationship (regardless of how, in the event, the treaties served more as a tool of colonial power in purporting to extinguish Indigenous Land rights). A more specific but lasting legacy involves the development (in its own interest by the HBC in the late nineteenth century) of a credit system, which would lay the foundation for the relief/welfare systems that emerged in the twentieth century.[14]

The formation of Canada came at a time when the fur trade was declining as the foundational economic activity, to be replaced by agriculture and forestry and later mineral and energy resource extraction, and eventually manufacturing and service industry development as well. For Indigenous Peoples, this meant that the line of engagement with settlers became a question of politics, involving (from the state's perspective) marginalizing Indigenous Peoples in order to totalize (assimilate or absorb) them. Since the late nineteenth century, as well as meeting traders and missionaries, Indigenous leaders increasingly found themselves negotiating with state functionaries: first policing officials, later Indian agents, and later still the whole panoply of community development agents, teachers, nurses, and welfare workers. On a daily basis, encounters and negotiations came to be with agents of the state. The fur trade had not required a massive transplant of labour, and the initial profits that made Canada economically viable were all secured on the bodies and backs of labour performed by Indigenous women and men as the primary producers. However, the new economic activities demanded larger populations. The demographic surge of newcoming settlers came to overwhelm the still shrinking Indigenous populations to such an extent that there would not be any negotiations in which nations met on level enough ground that they at least paid lip service to mutual respect. Instead, the situation was one in which the surviving Indigenous Peoples were to be paternalistically "managed": either absorbed by the larger population or marginalized to a degree where they posed no threat. This shift from an economic line of engagement to a political one has remained in place to the present day. Indigenous Peoples, while they may be sharply critical of private capital holders, largely fight on the terrain of the political, with blockades, hunger strikes, marches, and other actions focused on the state and on the courts: in law and policy-making, as well as in legal interpretation of treaty or Aboriginal Rights. These are all political questions, albeit with significant economic implications.

**iv.**

Within this political era, a sub-periodization would distinguish between, borrowing from the influential analysis established by French philosopher Louis Althusser, a repressive (1870 to 1951) and an ideological era (1951 to present;[15] see Figures 7.1 and 7.3). In the repressive era, Indigenous Peoples were subjected to state-sponsored policing and coercion as key or leading mechanisms of social control. In the ideological era (as will be demonstrated), beliefs and values became the targets of a concerted effort to change Indigenous Peoples' life ways, with education as the leading vehicle. In the repressive period, the most notorious elements of the *Indian Act* were adopted: sexual discrimination of females only around so-called out-marriage and leading to their and their children's forced removal from communities; pass laws that restricted First Nations citizens' travel rights; bans on the Sundance and the potlatch ceremonies; and bans on collecting funds for legal or political challenges to government actions. This array of legal sanctions was weighted towards the ban and incarceration threats associated with violating the ban. Although the historic numbered treaties were negotiated in this period (1871 to 1921)—itself a testament to the leading role of the state that had emerged and thus to the "political shift" described above—they were used by Canada as a tool of marginalization. The treaties became a weapon in establishing thinly disguised land theft, and the nation-to-nation element was honoured only in its consistent breach. That the process was "more peaceful" than that adopted by our neighbour to the south may offer some ethical consolation to those who studiously ignore the fact that the ultimate outcome on both sides of the border was apocalyptic. In Canada and the United States we see genocidal destruction of Indigenous Peoples through systematic reduction of their access to their land base coupled with determined attacks on cultural values, especially traditional spiritual ones. It should be noted that the first attempts to negotiate a modern political response were engaged by Indigenous leaders in this period, including, for example, the League of Indians of Canada (1919 to 1932).[16]

PERIODIZING SETTLER COLONIAL CANADA
PART TWO: THE POLITICAL PERIOD

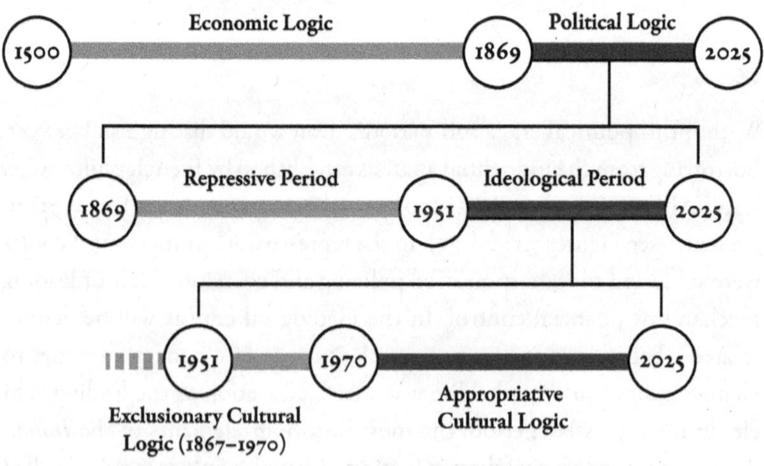


FIGURE 7.3. The political period

In 1951 the *Indian Act* was revised, and the worst restrictions were removed. This marks a shift towards ideology (still a tool of domination) and away from repression (physical restrictions) as the main tool of social control. The goal remained totalization: now more clearly aimed at assimilating Indigenous Peoples into the mainstream of the settler body politic as docile workers. However, instead of using the stick, the carrot would be the new weapon, and education became the critical tool. It should be noted that at least some historical observers have dismissed the 1951 *Indian Act* revisions as window dressing, arguing that the most salient aspects of the *Act*, including the wording, remained intact from its 1869 and 1876 originals.[17] My argument, grounded in recognizing the distinction between repression and ideology (pointed to, as noted earlier, by French Marxist theorist Louis Althusser as a key element of capitalist social reproduction), emphasizes that the dropping of the most repressive parts of the *Indian Act* was consequential. It led directly to a growing Indigenous migration to cities, playing a role in the politicization of Indigenous communities. In general, it established a new terrain of struggle in which Indigenous political leaders began organizing on a regional and national basis, and a growing set of institutional processes and linkages developed for formalizing a degree of ongoing political discussion.

## V.

A final periodic shift in the early 1970s, within the ideological, takes us to the present (see Figures 7.1 and 7.3). Cultural or ideological "exclusion" was the dominant motif in the slow development of Canada's national character (1867 to 1970). From the founding of the nation through to the early 1970s, scholars and artists alike searched for a Canadian "identity" by a rigid exclusion of Indigeneity. Harold Innis's *Fur Trade* (1931) is a telling example. In his book, Canada is given the waterways of the beaver (first chapter) and the civilization of Europe (last chapter) as its "natural" and "social" foundations respectively, with Indigenous Peoples not natural enough to be a natural foundation or civilized enough to be a social foundation.[18] Diamond Jenness's *The Indians of Canada*[19] appeared at nearly the same time (1932), and as I have argued elsewhere serves as an intellectual containment of Indigenous cultures, circumscribing them and making clear all the elements of (European) civilization that they lacked. The Group of Seven (landscape painters who created much of their work from 1920 to 1933) depicted an empty landscape, terra nullius, devoid of Indigenous presence and offering a "wilderness sublime"[20] to revel in. "Canada" defined itself as an exclusively "newcomer" (settler) nation and groped to characterize itself. By definition, this meant an absolute disregard for Indigenous contributions and a systemic attempt to position so-called liberal British benevolence as a defining feature (in supposed contrast to everywhere in the hemisphere to the south of Canada). In 1965, among settlers, if one had an Indigenous great-grandparent, one hid that fact. This was the skeleton in the closet, a secret weakness or, worse, a scandal. Indigenous culture was seen as a holdover from an embarrassing past and related images, styles, clothes, ceremonies, languages were all directly or implicitly shoved aside.

**vi.**

This would change at the time of the struggle over the Liberal government's 1969 *White Paper* (fully titled *Statement of the Government of Canada on Indian Policy*).[21] The actual transition likely can be said to unfold through the 1970s, but the *White Paper* struggle, in which the federal government was ultimately forced to completely back down on a formal version of a termination policy (ending recognition of Indigenous and even Treaty Rights) seems a propitious marker. In our view, exclusion as a cultural logic came to be replaced by appropriation. In the period from 1970 to the present, Canada started emphasizing Indigenous symbols and expressive arts. It began to take pride in claiming a major role in the global recognition of Indigenous Rights, and it moved away from the strict separation of "Canada" from Indigenous Peoples and cultures. Olympic ceremonies would begin with Indigenous expressive culture being showcased. Rather than being a skeleton in the closet, that Indigenous ancestor would become the most talked about person, and source of pride, to at least a section of the family. Some family members would even go so far as to ennoble their suburban pasts with generational suffering on an often very flimsy basis, demanding they be recognized as Indigenous.

While there are some ways in which the logic of exclusion had horrendous consequences (in terms of marginalization from the life of the nation), the logic of appropriation is more subtle but equally or more dangerous to the surviving and thriving of Indigenous culture. In short: appropriation's main tool is commodification. To transform some element of culture into a commodity is to allow the capitalist logic of exchange value into the inner sanctums of spirituality. This transforms the sacred medicine into a scent, the sacred drum into a wall hanging, the sacred ceremony into a spectacle. Sartre noted that "when Marx speaks of reification, he does not mean to show that we are transformed into things but that we are men condemned to live humanly the condition of material things."[22] The sacred spiritual person is transformed into a productive unit or as an unemployed charter member of the reserve army of labour. The appropriation of identity itself is the final extreme of this movement and the most ultimately threatening.

As the number of people identifying as Indigenous increased, it became clear that whole multi-generations that grew up in the mainstream are on a tenuous bloodline claim (sometimes even that being false) to be in a position to take advantage of the sometimes significant awards that Indigenous identity can now confer in certain institutional settings. This helps explain the growing number of scandals. Now, figures such as Mary Ellen Turpel-Lafond, Carrie Bourassa, Gina Adams, and Cheyanne Turions have joined Archie Belaney (a.k.a. Grey Owl) in a hall of identity infamy. The idea that practice, living within a set of particular values that are attached to bush life and to meaningful communities, is a basis of identity has entirely been lost in the gold rush of Indigenous identity claims. Indigenous identity, in an era of appropriation, confers enormous career value and has moved Indigeneity from a debased and marginalized subject position to a desired one, at least on the part of unscrupulous individuals who can see opportunities for advancement in institutions like universities. We also see the issue emerge as whole communities attempt to assert Indigeneity, while others strongly attempt to withhold it. This is especially prominent among Métis, where descent from Red River Métis has become a standard to uphold against other "mixed raced" communities. That "gold rush" can only be understood if we recognize a move from exclusion to appropriation within the ideological field and as a subperiod within the ideological period.

### vii.

In conclusion, it can be noted that these three major shifts—from economic to political; from repressive to ideological; from exclusion to appropriation—are not abrupt or absolute. Important political events happened in the period of economic relations (the *Royal Proclamation of 1763*, for example). The fur industry remains economically important in many northern Indigenous communities to this day. Similarly, repression did not disappear after 1951, nor was ideology invented then. The army was called into Kanesatake in 1990. E. Pauline Johnson was celebrated and performed to many audiences in the late nineteenth and early twentieth century. Archie Belaney was happily passing as "Indian" in the early twentieth century (selling large numbers of books and performing in Canada and Europe), while Indigenous Peoples continue to face barriers to participation in the mainstream in the twenty-first century. We mark these shifts as a structure of dominance, not an exclusive logic. Economic exchange dominates political negotiation in the earliest days, while the prominence of a political interface characterizes the last 150 years. But the most visible political struggles in Canada between Indigenous Peoples and the state have been around extraction industries, from Temagami to Haida Gwai to Denendeh. The oscillation between exclusion and appropriation, between marginalizing and absorbing, has been a feature of "Indian" policy since the *Gradual Enfranchisement Act of 1869*, which defined and marginalized "Indians" in the interest of ultimately "enfranchising" or absorbing them.

It should also be emphasized that the Indian residential school system, which played such a powerful role in advancing a colonial agenda, took place through most of the political period. It was a major mechanism associated with the effort of the state to turn First Nations people, as well as severing their connections to the land, into a docile part of the wage labour force.[23] Interestingly, the IRS system involved both ideological approaches (education, however poor) and repressive mechanisms (the harsh discipline, confining of bodies, forced separation from families, and, tragically, even many deaths). It was, though, fundamentally an effort to ideologically inculcate dominant values. The radical difference between these values and those of First Nations people, the underfunding and poor government support for the effort, and the racism and ethnocentrism that pervaded the mentality of those responsible, contributed to the degree of repression that became associated with the schools.

Settler colonialism in Canada, as elsewhere, was an element of what Marx called primitive (or original) accumulation of capital. Marx thought "primitive accumulation" involved two elements: 1) severing people from the land, and 2) leaving them no choice but to become wage labourers (creating a "free, rightless and rootless" body of workers). Marx points out that these processes took place at different times with different pacing in different places.[24] And primitive accumulation is only one of the ways, perhaps the most well-known, associated with capitalist totalization: the reshaping of space, time, subjectivity, knowledge, and language. Marx and Engels famously wrote in *The Communist Manifesto* of this process: "all that is solid melts into air."[25] The analysis and periodization offered here is an attempt to understand the specific dimensions and pacing of capitalist totalization, including primitive accumulation, in the particular historical imposition of "Canada" on the many Indigenous homelands that existed prior to the colonial encounter. Finally, the shifts are not simply a facet of institutional development or of a progressive society coming on its own to realize its mistakes. The shifts are rather in largest part due to active collective and individual resistances on the part of Indigenous activists, who contested the repressive regime and the exclusion of Indigeneity from the national self-representations. The continued survivance of Indigenous Peoples and cultures are the enduring testament of this rich history of resistance.



## Notes

1 See, for example, Watkins, ed., *Dene Nation.*

2 Wolfe, *Settler Colonialism*; Veracini, *Settler Colonialism*; Harvey, *The New Imperialism.*

3 Fanon, *The Wretched of the Earth*; Sartre, *Critique of Dialectical Reason.*

4 See Watkins, ed., *Dene Nation*; Adams, *Prison of Grass*; Cardinal, *The Unjust Society*; LaRoque, *Defeathering the Indian*; Campbell, *Half-Breed*; Manuel and Posluns, *The Fourth World*; Brody, *The People's Land.*

5 Fanon, *Black Skin, White Masks.*

6 Barthes, *Mythologies.*

7 Jameson, *The Hegel Variations.*

8 Sartre, *Critique*; Sartre, *Search for a Method*; Sartre, *The Family Idiot.*

9 Marx, "The Eighteenth Brumaire of Louis Bonaparte."

10 Sartre, *Search for a Method*, 133.

11 Sartre, *Search for a Method*, 135.

12 Innis, *The Fur Trade in Canada.* Though Innis's periodization remains largely intact, see also Ray, *Indians in the Fur Trade*; Ray and Freeman, *Give Us Good Measure*; Francis and Morantz, *Partners in Furs*; Krech, ed., *The Subarctic Fur Trade*; and Tough, *As Their Natural Resources Fail* for more recent analyses centring Indigenous Peoples in the trade.

13 See Ray, *Indians in the Fur Trade*; Hall, *The American Empire.*

14 Compare with Ray, "Period Shortages."

15 The repression-ideology distinction is key in Althusser, "Ideology and Ideological State Apparatuses."
16 See Kulchyski, "A Considerable Unrest."
17 See Frideres, *Aboriginal Peoples in Canada* on 1951 changes to the *Indian Act*.
18 Innis, *The Fur Trade*, 1–4, 386.
19 Jenness, *The Indians of Canada*. See also Kulchyski, "Anthropology at the Service of the State."
20 Bordo, "Jack Pine."
21 See Weaver, *Making Canadian Indian Policy*.
22 Sartre, *Search for a Method*, 105fn6.
23 See Milloy, *A National Crime*.
24 Marx, *Capital, Volume One*.
25 Marx and Engels, *The Communist Manifesto*.

## Sources

Adams, Howard. *Prison of Grass: Canada from the Native Point of View*. General Publishing, 1975.

Althusser, Louis. "Ideology and Ideological State Apparatuses." In *Lenin and Philosophy and Other Essays*, translated by Ben Brewster. Monthly Review Press, 1971.

Barthes, Roland. *Mythologies*. Translated by Annette Lavers. Paladin Press, 1973.

Bordo, Jonathan. "Jack Pine—Wilderness Sublime or the Erasure of the Aboriginal Presence from the Landscape." *Journal of Canadian Studies* 27, no. 4 (1993): 98–128. https://doi.org/10.3138/jcs.27.4.98.

Brody, Hugh. *The People's Land: Eskimos and Whites in the Eastern Arctic*. Penguin Books, 1977.

Campbell, Maria. *Half-Breed*. Goodread Biographies, 1983.

Cardinal, Harold. *The Unjust Society: The Tragedy of Canada's Indians*. M.G. Hurtig, 1969.

Fanon, Frantz. *Black Skin, White Masks*. Translated by Charles Lam Markmann. Grove Press, 1967.

Fanon, Frantz. *The Wretched of the Earth*. Translated by Constance Farrington. Grove Press, 1966.

Francis, Daniel, and Toby Morantz. *Partners in Furs: A History of the Fur Trade in Eastern James Bay, 1600–1870*. McGill-Queen's University Press, 1983.

Frideres, James. *Aboriginal Peoples in Canada: Contemporary Conflicts*. Prentice Hall, 1998.

Hall, Anthony. *The American Empire and the Fourth World: The Bowl with One Spoon, Part One*. McGill-Queen's University Press, 2003.

Harvey, David. *The New Imperialism*. Oxford University Press, 2005.

Innis, Harold. *The Fur Trade in Canada: An Introduction to Canadian Economic History*. University of Toronto Press, 1999.

Jameson, Fredric. *The Hegel Variations: On the Phenomenology of Spirit*. Verso Books, 2017.

Jenness, Diamond. *The Indians of Canada*. University of Toronto Press, 1977.
Krech, Shepard, III, ed. *The Subarctic Fur Trade: Native Social and Economic Adaptations*. University of British Columbia Press, 1984.
Kulchyski, Peter. "Anthropology at the Service of the State: Diamond Jenness and Canadian Indian Policy." *Journal of Canadian Studies* 28, no. 2 (1993): 21–50.
Kulchyski, Peter. "A Considerable Unrest: F.O. Loft and the League of Indians." *Native Studies Review* 4, nos. 1–2 (1988): 95–118.
LaRoque, Emma. *Defeathering the Indian*. Book Society of Canada, 1975.
Manuel, George, and Michael Posluns. *The Fourth World: An Indian Reality*. Collier Macmillan, 1974.
Marx, Karl. *Capital, Volume One*. Translated by Ben Fowkes. Vintage, 1977.
Marx, Karl. "The Eighteenth Brumaire of Louis Bonaparte." In *Surveys from Exile*, edited by David Fernbach. Vintage, 1978.
Marx, Karl, and Frederic Engels. *The Communist Manifesto*. Translated by L.M. Findlay. Broadview Press, 2004.
Milloy, John. *A National Crime: The Canadian Government and the Residential School System, 1879 to 1986*. University of Manitoba Press, 1999.
Ray, Arthur J. *Indians in the Fur Trade: Their Roles as Trappers, Hunters, and Middlemen in the Lands Southwest of Hudson Bay, 1660–1870*. University of Toronto Press, 2015.
Ray, Arthur J. "Period Shortages, Native Welfare, and the Hudson's Bay Company 1670–1930." In *The Subarctic Fur Trade*, edited by Shepard Krech III. University of British Columbia Press, 1984.
Ray, Arthur J., and Donald Freeman. *Give Us Good Measure: An Economic Analysis of Relations Between the Indians and the Hudson's Bay Company Before 1763*. University of Toronto Press, 1978.
Sartre, Jean-Paul. *Critique of Dialectical Reason*. Translated by Alan Sheridan-Smith. New Left Books, 1978.
Sartre, Jean-Paul. *The Family Idiot: Gustave Flaubert 1821–1857, Volume 1*. Translated by Carol Cosman. University of Chicago Press, 1981.
Sartre, Jean-Paul. *Search for a Method*. Translated by Hazel Barnes. Vintage, 1968.
Tough, Frank. *As Their Natural Resources Fail: Native Peoples and the Economic History of Northern Manitoba, 1870–1930*. University of British Columbia Press, 1996.
Veracini, Lorenzo. *Settler Colonialism: A Theoretical Overview*. Palgrave Macmillan, 2010.
Watkins, Mel, ed. *Dene Nation: The Colony Within*. University of Toronto Press, 1977.
Weaver, Sally. *Making Canadian Indian Policy: The Hidden Agenda, 1968–1970*. University of Toronto Press, 1981.
Wolfe, Patrick. *Settler Colonialism and the Transformation of Anthropology: The Politics and Poetics of an Ethnographic Event*. Cassell, 1999.

# Learning Settler Colonialism

## *Double Diaspora and Transnational Imperial Refraction*

Ajay Parasram

I AM A MULTIGENERATIONAL, TRANSNATIONAL BY-PRODUCT of the British Empire. My people came mostly from northern India; in the late nineteenth century they were brought to Kairi, the island territory of Lokano and Kalina peoples, misnamed "Trinidad" by a lost Italian thinking of the Catholic Father, Son, and Holy Ghost in 1498. My ancestors who crossed the *kala pani* (black water) often didn't know where they were headed, but those landing in British sugar colonies would have found themselves immediately in conflict with formerly enslaved, recently freed African labourers advocating for better working conditions post-emancipation.[1]

The "new" world of the Caribbean, South America, and Turtle Island knows the deep scars of European arrival, Indigenous genocide, African slavery, and anti-colonial resistance. Asian indentureship is less well-known and was not as widespread a practice, lasting from 1838 to 1917 across nineteen colonies and involving approximately 1.2 million people and their descendants. Over time, many of my ancestors worked their way out of the cane fields and secured Westernized and Christianized education for their children. Some then left to other settler colonies. I built a life on unceded Mi'kmaw, Algonquin, and Coast Salish territories.

This positionality informs how I understand colonialism and settler colonialism. The vectors through which descendants of Indian indentured labourers have arrived in Canada are many and differ from the majority of South Asians who came directly since the nineteenth century. Their connection to South Asia is clearer than those of us who have been disconnected for generations. Some came as temporary foreign agricultural workers in the 1960s and '70s, others as "points" immigrants in the 1980s and '90s, and others still as refugees and international students.[2] Just as our problematic arrival in the nineteenth century placed us into structural conflict with the free African population, our problematic arrival into twentieth-century settler colonial Canada puts us in structural conflict with Indigenous Peoples and Nations asserting sovereignty and self-determination.

To be clear, all newcomers, regardless of the conditions of their arrival, are structurally in conflict with peoples who have always been here. This is for a variety of reasons grounded in the configuration of colonial nationalism, territoriality, and international law opposite diverse forms of Indigenous nations, laws, and territoriality.[3] An aspect of the double-diaspora migration experience that is somewhat unique, however, is our sense of confusion and shame associated with being disconnected from the land that nurtured our people. It often manifests as imposter syndrome, questioning if we are South Asian at all, then melds with encountering the racism most non-white people experience upon arriving to Canada.

In this chapter, I explore how our intergenerational forms of surviving and resisting white supremacy worked to gloss over the inherently white supremacist values encoded into the Western modernity we learned to navigate. They are encoded in part through liberal concessions won by racialized peoples that enable a thin and fragile sense of cultural distinctiveness within the dominant white settler state structure, so long as it does not disturb the settler colonial, capitalist objectives of the post-imperial, still-colonial state. I am not making an argument about whether South Asians are "model migrants" in Canada.[4] Rather, I want to understand how the intergenerational, transnational experiences we carry may inadvertently fuel systemic white supremacy and further ongoing colonization of Indigenous Peoples. I am primarily concerned with how transnational intergenerational learning—what I am calling *imperial refraction*—has made the double-diaspora "desirable" immigrants in the context of multicultural settler colonial nationalism.

I focus on a particular imperial refraction connecting Canada and the Indo-Trinidadian community of which I am a part. Asian presence in the Caribbean is substantial, often taking people by surprise. East Asians,

South Asians, and Middle Eastern communities along with African and Indigenous communities and European communities comprise the multicultural demography of Trinidad and Tobago (TT). Guyana and TT are home to the largest concentration of South Asians in the total population. People of Indian and African descent comprise approximately 70 percent of the national population of TT, split nearly equally according to most recent census data, with the remaining 30 percent mostly comprising self-identified "mixed" people of East Asian, Middle Eastern, Indigenous, and European ancestry.

In the sections that follow, I describe experiences of surviving structural white supremacy in the movement from India to Trinidad, drawing on illustrative examples from plantations and from missionary schools established by Canadians in Trinidad that targeted the Indian population in the late nineteenth and early twentieth centuries. In all of these encounters, the values of white supremacy are established by normalizing "how the world is" in universal and Eurocentric terms. This is important because even instances of direct resistance to white supremacy have rarely taken the form of challenging the logics of colonial and white supremacist society itself. By stipulating "structural" white supremacy, I mean to differentiate between the individual forms of racial supremacy and focus on how white supremacy works at the level of structure.[5] In practice, structural white supremacy helped to naturalize institutions like plantation capitalism, church, state, school, and courts. These become taken for granted, inevitable, and at times even desirable forms of organizing society when Asians can navigate and excel within them.[6]

The processes that colluded to break our connection to our traditional lands and land-based practices in India are precisely what helped condition us to be "model" minorities. In the final section of the chapter, I explore imperial refraction as an ongoing process in the still-colony. We have opportunities to build solidarity with anti-colonial Indigenous sovereignty-asserting movements as a means of restoring land-based practices within diaspora communities—ways to de-link from hegemonic structural white supremacy.

A well-established literature examines how the racial category of "Brown" has been used to legitimize structural white supremacy in various imperial and colonial contexts.[7] Race is an imagined and enforced social construct that has had enormous social, political, cultural, and economic consequences over the last half-millennium. *Brown* is defined by negation—not white, not Black, often not Indigenous. In this chapter, I'm interested in understanding how multigenerational by-products of empire—defined as Asians displaced from their homelands to two or more other sites of the British Empire, the double diaspora—have been an essential part of sustaining structural white supremacy in Canada through "refracting" imperial sensibilities like white supremacy and development.

By *imperial refraction*, I mean how imperial values of structural white supremacy, developmental modernity, and racial hierarchies have been learned and at times bent/transformed and internalized by people like me. We can then fit into the logic of structural white supremacy presenting Brown migrants as "model minorities" that help to legitimize the existing political economic situation of settler colonialism based in ongoing Indigenous dispossession.[8] The term *model minority* places the burden of integration and accommodation squarely on the newcomer to demonstrate their willingness to conform to the expectations of a host country that does not need to change. To "model" how to be a migrant means conforming to the cultural and political conventions of the host country with gratitude. This is especially problematic in settler colonies because the "host" society is not actually Indigenous to the land in question, and this essential illegitimacy renders settler society both deeply fragile and hyper-focused on ignoring its complicities in genocide, both historical and ongoing. In presenting structural white supremacy as a condition of the past and using reasonably well-integrated non-white settlers as evidence of Canada's multicultural present, the Canadian state becomes a neutral actor while ongoing genocide, racism, and ecocide are blamed on individuals—not the structurally racist processes of settler state formation and expansion. Importantly, my intent is not to suggest that "model minorities" get an easy ride in Canada.[9] I neither seek to denigrate double-diasporic South Asian migrants nor celebrate us but to describe how our transnational and multigenerational migration process fits into Canadian structural white supremacy and settler colonial nationalism.

This is significant for settler colonial studies in two ways: 1) it helps to describe lateral racial violence as a symptom of intergenerational trauma, and 2) it suggests that if the break with migrants' land-based and ontologically distinct forms of knowledge makes us susceptible to internalizing white supremacy, then discovering ways to reconnect with it may build the racial resilience of racialized people. Thus, we may find in one another solidarity instead of competition. Racial competition between Africans and Indians in Trinidad or among various non-white peoples in Canada has only served the interests of structural white supremacy. This is rarely discussed explicitly in the literature, which often expresses the sentiment in terms of "communalism" or "ethnonationalism" or competition for scarce resources. These approaches are often inattentive to how the values of white supremacy are present precisely in the absence of racialized language. Whiteness is most present in its absence from racial considerations, which is why studying it explicitly is important to understanding the role of white supremacy in conditioning global expectations of what is "normal," from gender binaries to state territoriality.

## White Supremacy Crossing the Black Waters

The period of Indian indentureship in the British Empire lasted from 1838 until 1917 (1845 to 1917 in Trinidad). Building on older coercive labour practices under the rule of the British East India Company, Indian recruiters were often contracted to help indenture labourers. In principle this was a consent-based process, meaning that potential labourers agreed to a period of servitude usually between five to twenty years with the promise of returning to India or later remaining with a small plot of land. "Consent" needs to be interpreted through the coerced conditions of British de-industrialization of India. British imperial political economic policies created the conditions for poverty and famines from the mid-nineteenth to the early twentieth century, rendering "choice" an inaccurate framing for indentureship.[10] Men, women, and children departed India following a medical examination in Calcutta, later Madras. Many records of the period note people were often categorized as healthy enough to survive the three-month voyage, despite being clearly too ill or malnourished.

Nineteenth-century Christian missionaries were often of the opinion that Indians would very quickly cascade into Christianity, in large part because the missionaries were ontologically incapable of understanding that in many Indian traditions there's no conflict in accepting a Christian god.[11] While Buddhism, Islam, and Sikhism share with Christianity a sense of universal applicability across time and place, Hinduism is place-based in its development, historically integrating local gods; the god of Christianity could be incorporated.[12]

## On the Plantations

The British were deliberate in preventing indentured workers from meeting with one another, or with other members of the island community, for fear it could foment organized resistance and undermine the plantation economy. Indian workers were not permitted to leave the plantation to which they were indentured without a pass. Especially in the early days of indentureship, punishment and discipline were extremely harsh and violent.[13] Above all the British feared cross-racial solidarity between the African and Indian populations.

Racial animosity was routinely stoked on the plantations, and there are many accounts of white plantation owners—sometimes with African and/or Indian foremen—beating and whipping indentured workers to death without their having been convicted or at times even prosecuted.[14] There were also cases in which indentured Indians attacked plantation owners, as well as the African and Indian foremen who worked on their behalf.[15] State violence as a means of blocking solidarity came to a head in the inquiry into the 1884 Muharram Massacre (also called the Hosay Riots), in which indentured Indians openly defied the government to mark the Shia commemoration of the Battle of Karbala that claimed the life of the Prophet's grandson Imam Hussain.[16] On their march into the city of San Fernando they were joined by Afro-Trinidadians. The colonial troops fired on the procession, killing more than twenty and injuring upwards of a hundred people. In the inquiry that followed, the colonial government noted the Afro-Trinidadians who participated may have also been involved in earlier riots, which concerned them because it implied cross-racial solidarity.

Indentured Indians articulated their resistance to colonialism through their cultural adherence, which included largely refusing to convert to Christianity despite state and economic pressure. Multigenerational attempts to eradicate Indian culture and religion inspired forms of cultural resistance in Trinidad, centrally featuring aspects of Hindu stories and Bhojpuri folk songs describing life in exile.[17] By the time of independence in Trinidad (1962) a great many of the Indian population were still first- and second-generation migrants who had close affinity with the Indian independence movement. In other words, holding their identity as Indians was sometimes a source of contention in the context of nationalist activism that sought to establish a firmly "Trinidadian" identity and the growth of Black power and pan Africanism in the region. While Caribbean intellectuals like Walter Rodney clearly articulated a materialist understanding of Blackness connected to labour and history that necessarily included indentured Indians, not all individuals were as inclusive in their reasoning, and Indians themselves were suspicious of what were perceived to be continued efforts to erase their Indianness.[18] In the post-independence era, this legacy remains. While both major parties identify as multicultural national parties, there remains a party of predominantly Indo-Trinidadians (currently the United National Congress) and a party of predominantly Afro-Trinidadians (the People's National Movement).

## Structural White Christian Supremacy, Pedagogy, and Patriarchy in the Canadian Mission

In the nineteenth and early twentieth centuries, Trinidad—like most parts of the British Empire—unapologetically favoured whiteness and Christianity. Hindu and Muslim marriages were not considered to be lawful, and pundits and imams could not register marriages until well into the twentieth century. This had material consequences for legal transfers of land to surviving family members. Until the 1940s, the colonial government only offered support to Christian schools; Hindu and Muslim communities were not able to open their own schools until the late colonial period.[19] The first Canadian Presbyterian Mission schools in Trinidad were established by Canadian Rev. John Morton and his wife, Sarah Morton—schools for boys by the 1870s, located near the plantations; for girls by the 1890s.

The racial cleavages on the island between Africans and Indians, while grounded in economic conflict, were substantial and well-known by the missionaries. White supremacy is premised on anti-Blackness—though it has no scientific basis, this racial binary has tremendous sociological relevance.[20] The discursive connection between the orientalist production of knowledge and varying ways of responding to it (Black nationalism, Pan-Africanism, Brownness) help to normalize structural white supremacy as a framework within which politics functions as opposed to epistemic and ontological violence that produces material consequences.

With civilizational hierarchical thinking in mind, the Canadian missionaries in Trinidad were willing to learn Hindi and preach/teach in that language, effectively excluding African children from the classroom. Such accommodation worked to deepen already-seeded racial tension.[21] That white people would teach and preach in Hindi while "allowing" Indian clothing and some customs into churches and schools helped to make the fear of cultural annihilation less acute for many workers, especially those who were parents. In general, South Asian parents across the late British Empire understood the importance of "civic Christianity" (conforming to Christian expectations in the public realm and retaining Hindu, Islamic, Sikh, or Buddhist expectations at home).[22]

As feminist scholars have long explained, structural forms of oppression like race and gender are always operating in tandem, and the gendered politics of white supremacy are very important in the Canadian Mission's maneuvering.[23] Girls' education was understood as derivative of the more important boys' education, and its purpose was to build Christian households and break the girls' connection to Hinduism and Islam.

The matrons and teachers at the girls' school would also engage in the practice of arranging marriages between the students and converts, allowing for Indian-style feasting and festivities to happen after the Christian services were performed. By organizing weddings in this way, the sacredness of Hindu and Islamic traditions are subordinated to Christian spirituality both in religious and legal terms, but they are "tolerated" in a depoliticized and strictly cultural manner.[24] In creating intergenerational space that offered a mild recognition of Indian culture through the Hindi language and the possibility of education without conversion, the relationship between Indians and the Mission can perhaps be described as mutually advantageous. Most Indian pupils retained their connection to Hinduism and Islam, though many developed a sense that this knowledge was "traditional" and "private." Away from their parents, the children experienced religious destruction, skill building, and preparation for living in Western Christian culture—a complex mix of positive and negative experiences at the level of the individual. At the level of structure, however, the institutions of schools, plantations, and law worked to normalize structural white supremacy and lateral racial competition, calcify a gendered division of labour and family, and shift struggle away from colonial capitalism while emphasizing that competition and hard work result in material progress.[25]

My purpose in dwelling here is to think about how the work of "benefitting" pupils relied on acclimating them to structural white supremacy. The time my ancestors spent in the "middle" migration point (Trinidad) was substantial relative to the short time we have spent in Canada, but the imperial refractions of critical survival lessons learned in Trinidad have arguably made our integration into the settler project of Canada successful from the vantage point of Canadian nationalists.

## Imperial Refraction in the Second Migration

Much has been written on indentureship and what it has meant to individuals in shaping the Trinidadian nation-state, but the significance of intergenerational imperial learning—and how it is refracted through subsequent migration—is not as well understood.

White supremacy was an organizing principle in the founding of the Canadian state, and though it, too, has shifted forms over the last sixty years, we can see evidence of it in everyday issues such as migration policies, state denial of Indigenous laws and sovereign rights, settler denialism of genocidal Indian residential schools, and much more.[26] Simply *existing* as culturally distinct people in post-British places (be it Trinidad, Canada, or elsewhere in the former empire) requires us to be grateful eating our pholourie and doubles or worshipping without having to build a mandir in the ocean, as Siewdass Sadhu had to do to avoid anti-Hindu laws in Trinidad (National Trust of Trinidad and Tobago).

In the independence era in Trinidad many people of different races began to emigrate to Canada as temporary foreign workers and later as economic migrants and international students. By the time Indo-Trinidadians began to arrive in large numbers in the 1960s, debates in Canada had shifted away from explicit white supremacy in policy towards liberal multiculturalism and a general agreement to simply ignore discussions of race rather than confront the legacies of racism.[27] Of course, it wasn't only Indo-Trinidadians coming during this time. As Nishant Upadhay argues, South Asian (im)migrants occupying a relatively high class and caste position tend to play the role of the model minority in Canada.[28] Drawing on fieldwork with upper-caste and upper-class white-collar workers in Fort McMurry, Alberta, Upadhay shows how Indians apply their own racist assumptions about Adivasi and tribal people in India to make generalized assumptions that Indigenous Peoples in Canada are primitive or lazy.[29] Asked about the relative lack of presence of Indigenous workers in tar sands operations (though they do comprise roughly 5 percent of workers) Indian informants expressed little more than shoulder shrug answers to explain the absence of Indigenous Peoples, often defaulting to assumptions about Indigenous unsuitability for "developed" town-based life, simultaneously erasing Indigenous workers from the tar sands and playing into the settler colonial narrative of "empty land."[30] Following Vijay Prashad's engagement with W.E.B. Du Bois in his book *Karma of Brown Folk*, the position of the upper-caste professionalized South Asian in settler colonies like Canada is to be presented as "the solution" that proves discrimination is not systemic. Instead, there must be something wrong with non-white peoples who cannot "make it" in settler colonial societies.[31] The trope of the model minority is realized in part through keeping one's head down, turning inward to one's community, succeeding economically, and not complaining. But simply accepting the platitude that "working hard pays off" does not confront the intergenerational trauma of colonial migration.

South Asians indeed face racism of a structural nature—especially visibly Muslim and Sikh ones and those of non-dominant caste and class position. Like other racialized migrants to Canada, South Asians have been victims of white supremacist public policy since they began arriving in substantial numbers around the turn of the twentieth century. Anti-Asian sentiment, especially on the West Coast, took the form of organized efforts to curtail immigration such as the 1907 formation of the Anti-Asiatic League, who catalyzed white supremacist riots in the streets of Vancouver (targeting mainly the Chinese and Japanese communities but also impacting the Indian community). No laws or guidelines restricted the migration of imperial subjects of Great Britain, and early Indian migrants were Sikh men with strong military and agricultural backgrounds. Prior to the riots, Asians of all varieties were being laid off by white employers; following the riots, many businesses were destroyed and looted by white mobs. In response, the premier of British Columbia formally disenfranchised South Asians and the federal government introduced the "continuous journey regulation" of 1908 that stipulated one could only lawfully arrive in Canada if arriving in one continuous journey—technologically impossible crossing the Pacific Ocean at that time. Vancouver City Council followed suit, and to highlight the centrality of white supremacy to these efforts, exception was made to allow people born in India who were white to continue to exercise their franchise—these policies were explicitly intended to hurt Asian communities and benefit white ones.[32]

It wasn't until 1947, after considerable domestic and international pressure from the newly independent government of India that Asians in Canada would have voting rights restored; Indigenous Peoples had to wait even longer.[33] After 1947, Canada had its first *Citizenship Act*, though Prime Minister Mackenzie King was unequivocally clear that its intent was to maintain the white and Christian character of the Canadian state. White supremacy was a central aim of Canadian immigration and citizenship policy until it was formally changed in the 1977 *Citizenship Act*.[34] From the 1970s onwards, Canada's points-based immigration system has traded racial profiling for class profiling, preferring to recruit as potential citizens university-educated working professionals. Seemingly "positive" racial stereotyping about Indians and Asians being "good at school" offers second generation children in Canada a means through which to differentiate their otherness.[35]

Of course, there is as much diversity in the broader South Asian Canadian community as there would be in any community; West Coast Punjabi communities present in trade unionism since the early twentieth century obviously articulate their politics differently than would a recently arrived upper-caste neurosurgeon in New Brunswick. When people of colour—especially women of colour—do not conform to the expected behaviour of a grateful model minority as explained in the preceding section on British-controlled Trinidad, but also here in settler colonial Canada, they are vilified and attacked in ways both institutional and public. The fragility and the violence of settler colonial nationalism is easily triggered when those who ought to be "model minorities" do not conform.[36] Their enactment of anti-colonial solidarity, however, takes control over how their embodied subjectivity is manipulated within Canada.

## Imperial Refraction Through Anti-Colonial Land-Based Solidarity

According to *Merriam-Webster*, refraction is defined as "the deflection from a straight path undergone by a light ray or energy wave in passing obliquely from one medium (such as air) into another (such as glass) in which its velocity is different." As we passed from India, across the Atlantic, into Kairi-turned-Trinidad and to Turtle Island-turned-Canada, we transnational by-products refract and transform with a great deal of imperial learning. Imperialism has been refracted in our intergenerational experiences through diverse ways. For many it was resistance through cultural resilience, anchoring to a reading of what Hinduism or Islam was to shape how these traditions would evolve in the double diaspora. For others it emerged through retaining folk music and adapting food, a new kind of postcolonial national pride. For others still, strategic (or genuine) conversions offered leverage to escape intergenerational oppression within their own communities by adopting and adapting practices of the empire's religion.

Part of the imperial refractions are also the diverse ways we have extracted lessons from white and Christian supremacist institutions to "code-switch" or conform to public expectations outwardly while acting and thinking differently in the relative safety of the private realm.[37] That learning came through the refraction of our pre-colonized identities being reduced to merely a religious identity rather than a set of place-based practices. In the process of refracting through the medium of nineteenth-century race "science," the concept of "Brownness" emerged as something defined by negation—not white, not Black, not Indigenous, and not limited to a particular religion. Historically, being "closer" to white within the imaginary but materially significant hierarchy of race has provided some individual benefits. Through capitulating to these small mercies, however, we cede ground to the logic of white supremacy as a "normal" structure within which the modern world operates. Aspiring to whiteness is perhaps the most egregious form of colonization, and much ink has been spilled by Caribbean intellectuals to resist it.[38]

Hierarchies and injustice were not inventions of white supremacist modernity, and Indians are no strangers to hierarchy, which is especially visible through caste. There is a contradiction and an irony in how we double-diaspora folks have navigated white supremacy—the intergenerational processes through which we survived have normalized structures like the state, religious bureaucracy and institutions, capitalism, and settler nationalism in the second country, Canada. These institutions are the very same ones that organized colonial genocide on these lands and continue to conscript settlers into the ongoing work of settler colonial accumulation by dispossession.[39] This is not a question of "fault" so much as it is an accounting of transnational, multigenerational migration that can help shatter the bonds that anchor us to structural white supremacy and the odious category "model minority."

Upon arrival, grateful integration into Canada is taught as a survival and coping mechanism from those who migrated just a little earlier. I still remember the outrage my parents felt when well-meaning members of the Trinidadian diaspora warned them to give their four kids "Canadian" names to help us assimilate. The allure of integrating into Canada's settler-nationalist system despite its problems and working to make modest changes within it represents the somewhat privileged position of the model minority within my demographic. I was not taught to understand things like intergenerational trauma from colonialism until I saw it reflected in the heavy eyes of relatives (Hindu, Christian, and Muslim alike), felt its tug in my own struggles to parent, and discovered that friends and allies from other racialized backgrounds had similar experiences. The common denominator in our experiences is structural white supremacy. The *numerators* are all different, but structural white supremacy is the denominator of how our various entanglements, migrations, and displacements have separated us from our lands, mutilated our cultures and cosmologies, and then repackaged it all into a developmentalist history of progress and consumer durables like turmeric pills and yoga pants.

Refraction has no end point, however. We did not conclude our journey by arriving in Canada; in fact the refractions continue as we learn to move beyond only Canada and into places like Mi'kma'ki and other Indigenous sovereign spaces across Turtle Island. Imperial refraction in my own life has meant realizing that Canada is not a post-colony but a still-colony. As I began learning from Indigenous Peoples on the West Coast defending land and asserting sovereignty in the face of what can only be described as brutal and disproportionate settler colonial state violence, it became very clear that when Indigenous Peoples enact their sovereign rights, it strikes a blow deep into the intergenerational inertia of settler colonialism; it forces all people who have arrived here through many imperial refractions to grapple with the inherited conundrum of being simultaneously in Canada and Turtle Island.

Learning through solidarity-building with others who are themselves learning to reconnect with their land-based practices can be an enormously and at times unexpectedly powerful way of thinking about our complex positionalities and how to put our transnational imperial learning to work. Since returning to Mi'kma'ki in 2016, I have had the good fortune of working in support of projects led by Mi'kmaq grassroots grandmothers, warriors, and allies. This has taken many different practical forms, including bringing students to help work on building a "treaty truckhouse" in congruence with the eighteenth-century Peace and Friendship Treaties, transporting resources and people, sharing food, participating in demonstrations, and working on gardens.[40] In the process of being engaged in these activities, there has been a great deal of anti-colonial learning. While I expected some of this to be the case based on previous experiences, I now see a way I might become more than a "by-product" of British colonialism.

Refraction isn't a sieve for trauma alone; it is the bending and transforming of energy. Part of passing through the medium of "Canada" via Trinidad and India and into Mi'kma'ki has been seeing the similarities between land-based ceremonies and prayers I have witnessed in many places. This is not to reduce the differences but to demonstrate that land itself offers ways to understand diasporic transformations that honour the practices that have developed in particular lands and peoples. Through learning more about Mi'kma'ki and concepts explained by Mi'kmaq scholars and activists—like M'sɨt No'kmaq, Netukulimk, Etuaptmumk, and treaty as a process into which white Europeans entered only after thousands of years of international development—I have been rethinking Indian concepts such as dharma, which I was taught to understand as an obligation to protect a cosmic balance that has different meaning and demands depending on where you are.[41] Balance and equilibrium are as important in a small pond as they are in a large country or in a droplet of water, and the decentring of humanity, interestingly, helps me to reconnect with my own humanity. If the colonial encounter has been, as Robbie Shilliam describes it, fundamentally a project of "categorical separation" from our genealogies, then decolonial repair is quite possible if we find ways to intergenerationally reconnect and refuse the logic of separation.[42] I recognize that we are all in different places, carrying different experiences of intergenerational trauma from our imperial refractions, but just as structural white supremacy was the common link in our categorical separation from our land and one another, those of us who are not indigenous to the lands on which we live have a unique opportunity to work alongside Indigenous Peoples who are fighting to defend their ways of living, under threat by the same imperial forces that ripped us from our lands generations ago.

## Conclusion

Imperial refraction as a means of understanding migration offers a nuanced picture of historical experiences of double-diaspora communities that simultaneously allows for critical introspection from within the community and a structural way of explaining why settler colonial nationalism continues to exert so much power over racialized newcomers to Canada. Through looking at different historical periods in the transnational and multigenerational journey of Indo-Trinidadians to Canada, I have signposted critical junctures that show how the articulation of resistance to empire has favoured religious, educational, and economic modes of "success" in India, the transatlantic passage, Trinidad, and Canada. The work of refraction is important because it empowers migrants to be more than the sum of survival strategies over the past two hundred years. It offers a method through which to "take control" of refraction, choosing to move beyond "Canada" and its settler colonial limit and into relationships of Indigenous solidarity on the same land claimed by Canada. While this sounds complex and abstract, it really can be as simple as turning up when invited to help with the multitude of Indigenous solidarity and sovereignty movements—the lifelong practice of horizontal solidarity building.[43]

Horizontal solidarity and relationship building with Indigenous Peoples in the areas that I've lived as an adult (Algonquin, Coast Salish, and Mi'kmaq territories) has opened the possibility of finding new ways, rather than old ways, of reconnecting with land and ancestors without idealizing or romanticizing or dwelling so much on the enormity of structural white supremacy in the colonial present. Shilliam has described this process of accessing the "uncolonized hinterlands" in his work on the subject, and I must admit that I did not know what to make of this assertion for years.[44] But the labour of horizontal solidarity building has offered a way to make meaning and to exercise agency over how my "Brownness" is used by the state. By learning about how white supremacy placed us in conflict with our African brothers and sisters in Kairi, I believe that Trinis of all stripes can refuse the table scraps offered by official Canadian multiculturalism in favour of building horizontal solidarity with Indigenous Peoples who are still fighting the same colonialism that brought us here in the first place. This can't happen passively; we newly arrived people need to commune with our ancestors whose struggle ensured our survival and draw guidance from these varied struggles to embrace the obligations of decolonization. This is necessary therapy for intergenerational colonial healing in this post-British still-colony, with significance well beyond the Indo-Trinidadian community.

## Notes

1 Rodney, *The Groundings with My Brothers*; Samaroo, "The Presbyterian Canadian Mission."

2 A newcomer's experience in Canada is related to whether they are categorized as an economic migrant, refugee, temporary foreign worker, or international student. Canada's immigration system has specific criteria for temporary workers and students, different criteria for asylum seekers and refugees (often requiring a tremendous amount of legal processing prior to arrival), and still different processes for irregular arrivals, including detention centres that can place undocumented people into a legal limbo, unable to work or even leave while their cases languish for years. While this describes the legal parameters, the social parameters are also inflected by whether the person is seen to be a "desirable" immigrant to Canada and its many provinces and territories. Anti-Black and anti-Asian racism have deep cultural and political histories across Canada, and Islamophobia has been particularly on the rise in the twenty-first century. For more, see Walia, *Undoing Border Imperialism*; Choudry and Smith, eds., *Unfree Labour?*; Henaway, *Essential Work, Disposable Workers*; Parasram and Mannathukkaren, "Imperial Afterlives."

3 Dhamoon, "A Feminist Approach to Decolonizing Anti-Racism"; Lawrence and Dua, "Decolonizing Anti-Racism."

4 Chun, "I Ain't Your F*Cking Model Minority!"; Liu, Wang, Nguyen, and Sun, "The Model Minority Myth"; Zhou and Bankston III, "The Model Minority Stereotype"; Kim and Kirpalani, "The Model Minority Myth."

5 White supremacy operates at both the level of individuals (e.g., Nazis in the streets) and at the level of structure (e.g., legal assumptions about what land "is" or the intergenerational harm associated with residential schools). For more on how structural white supremacy is the organizing logic of Canadian society, see Parasram and Khasnabish, *Frequently Asked White Questions*; Thobani, *Exalted Subjects*.

6 Saranillio, "Why Asian Settler Colonialism Matters."

7 Prashad, *Karma of Brown Folk*; Thobani, *Exalted Subjects*; Parasram and Mannathukkaren, "Imperial Afterlives."

8 Coulthard, *Red Skin, White Masks*.

9 Stasiulis and Jhappan, "Fractious Politics"; Parasram, "Seeing Whiteness in the Margins"; Yu, "Global Migrants"; Kim and Kirpalani, "The Model Minority Myth."

10 Rodney, *The Groundings*; Parasram, *Beyond Survival*.

11 Christianity did not come to India via European colonialism alone—for thousands of years Indians have been practising Christianity of a very different nature and political purpose than that devised by nineteenth-century white missionaries. See Thomas, *Christians and Christianity*.

12 Jayawardena, *The White Woman's Other Burden*; Parasram, *Pluriversal Sovereignty and the State*.

13 Wahab, *Disciplining Coolies*; Mahase, "'Plenty a Dem Run Away.'"
14 Brereton, "The Historical Background."
15 Brereton, "The Historical Background."
16 Webb, "137 Years Later"; TMV Team, "What Happened During the 1884 Hosay Massacre."
17 Although focusing on Guyana, this collection of translated poetry of Lalbihari Sharma from 1916 is an excellent example. See Sharma, *I Even Regret Night*.
18 Rodney, *The Groundings*, 16.
19 Brereton, "Contesting the Past."
20 Thame, "Racial Hierarchy"; Parasram and Mannathukkaren, "Imperial Afterlives"; Chatterjee, *The Nation and Its Fragments*; Chatterjee, *Nationalist Thought*.
21 Christianity did not come to India initially through European colonization. India was always well-connected with the rest of the ancient world, and the mythology of European exploration and "discovery" makes no sense in light of this. Nevertheless, the kind of Christianization that came with European colonization is of a very different nature than the older forms.
22 Parasram, *Pluriversal Sovereignty and the State*.
23 Choudhry and Nair, eds., *Power, Postcolonialism*; Snyder "Indigenous Feminist Legal Theory"; Mohanty, "'Under Western Eyes' Revisited."
24 Barsh, "Aboriginal Peoples and Canada's Conscience," 270–291.
25 Teelucksingh, *Beyond the Legacy of the Missionaries and East Indians*.
26 Parasram, "Pluriversal Sovereignty"; MacDonald, *The Sleeping Giant Awakens*.
27 Thobani, *Exalted Subjects*; Parasram and Mannathukkaren, "Imperial Afterlives."
28 Upadhyay, "Making of 'Model.'"
29 Upadhyay, "Making of 'Model.'"
30 Upadhyay, "Making of 'Model,'" 158–59.
31 Prashad, *Karma of Brown Folk*.
32 Bains and Sandhra, "The Battle."
33 Bains and Sandhra, "The Battle"; Dhamoon, Bhandar, Mawani, and Bains, eds., *Unmooring the Komagata Maru*.
34 Yu, "Global Migrants.; Parasram and Mannathukkaren, "Imperial Afterlives."
35 Parasram, *Take d Milk, Nah?*; Thobani, *Exalted Subjects*; Prashad, *Karma of Brown Folk*.
36 Parasram, "Pathological White Fragility."
37 This safety is relative because with the division of public and private realms in the context of Western modernity has come rigid gendered expectations and patriarchal dominance of the private realm. While the "private" realm might offer reprieve from the indignities of public white supremacy, this is precarious at best because of the unnatural power such a division confers to patriarchs. See Spivak, "Can the Subaltern Speak?"; Chatterjee, *The Nation and Its Fragments*.
38 Césaire, *Discourse on Colonialism*; Fanon, *Black Skin, White Masks*; Williams, *British Historians and the West Indies*.

39 Coulthard, *Red Skin, White Masks.*
40 Parasram, "Solidarity Is a Verb," 149–166.
41 No'kmaq et al., "'Awakening the Sleeping Giant'"; Shani and Behera, "Provincializing International Relations"; Bernard, "Reconciliation and Environmental Racism"; Peters, "Settler Forgetting."
42 Shilliam, *The Black Pacific.*
43 Parasram and Khasnabish, *Frequently Asked White Questions.*
44 Shilliam, *The Black Pacific.*

## Sources


Bains, Satwinder Kaur, and Sharanjit Kaur Sandhra. "The Battle for the South Asian Right to Vote." *British Columbia History* 52, no. 1(2019): 18–24. https://www.ufv.ca/media/assets/sasi/bchf-Story-on-the-Vote-(final).pdf.

Barsh, Russel Lawrence. "Aboriginal Peoples and Canada's Conscience." In *Hidden in Plain Sight: Contributions of Aboriginal Peoples to Canadian Identity and Culture*, edited by David R. Newhouse, Cora J. Voyageur, and Dan Beavon. University of Toronto Press, 2005.

Bernard, Dorene. "Reconciliation and Environmental Racism in Mi'kma'ki." *Kalfou* 5, no. 2 (2018): 297–303.

Brereton, Bridget. "Contesting the Past: Narratives of Trinidad & Tobago History." *New West Indian Guide* 81, nos. 3–4 (2007): 169–196.

Brereton, Bridget. "The Historical Background to the Culture of Violence in Trinidad & Tobago." *Caribbean Review of Gender Studies* 4 (2010): 1–16.

Césaire, Aimé. *Discourse on Colonialism*. Monthly Review Press, 1972.

Chatterjee, Partha. *Nationalist Thought and the Colonial World: A Derivative Discourse?* Oxford University Press, 1986.

Chatterjee, Partha. *The Nation and Its Fragments: Colonial and Postcolonial Histories*. Oxford University Press, 1993.

Choudhry, Geeta, and Sheila Nair, eds. *Power, Postcolonialism and International Relations: Reading Race, Gender and Class*. Routledge, 2003.

Choudry, Aziz, and Adrian Smith, eds. *Unfree Labour? Struggles of Migrant and Immigrant Workers in Canada*. PM Press, 2016.

Chun, Christian. "I Ain't Your F*Cking Model Minority! Indexical Orders of 'Asianness', Class, and Heteronormative Masculinity." *Applied Linguistics Review* (2023). https://doi.org/10.1515/applirev-2023-0021.

Coulthard, Glen. *Red Skin, White Masks: Rejecting the Colonial Politics of Recognition*. University of Minnesota Press, 2014.

Dhamoon, Rita. "A Feminist Approach to Decolonizing Anti-Racism: Rethinking Transnationalism, Intersectionality, and Settler Colonialism." *Feral Feminisms* 4 (2015): 20–37.

Dhamoon, Rita, Davina Bhandar, Renisa Mawani, and Satwinder Kaur Bains, eds. *Unmooring the Komagata Maru: Charting Colonial Trajectories*. University of British Columbia Press, 2020.

Fanon, Frantz. *Black Skin, White Masks*. Translated by Charles Lam Markmann. Grove Press, 1967.

Henaway, Mostafa. *Essential Work, Disposable Workers: Migration, Capitalism and Class*. Fernwood Publishing, 2023.

Jayawardena, Kumari. *The White Woman's Other Burden: Western Women and South Asia During British Rule*. Routledge, 1995.

Kim, Sunny, and Amrit Kirpalani. "The Model Minority Myth: A Threat to Asian Canadians in Higher Education." *Canadian Medical Education Journal* 13, no. 3 (2022): 79–80. https://doi.org/10.36834/cmej.74344.

Lawrence, Bonita, and Enakshi Dua. "Decolonizing Anti-Racism." *Social Justice* 32, no. 4 (2005): 120–143.

Liu, Clifford, Eileen Wang, Don Nguyen, and Mary Sun. "The Model Minority Myth, Data Aggregation, and the Role of Medical Schools in Combating Anti-Asian Sentiment." *Academic Medicine* 97, no. 6 (2022): 797–803. http://dx.doi.org/10.1097/acm.0000000000004639.

MacDonald, David B. A. *The Sleeping Giant Awakens: Genocide, Indian Residential Schools, and the Challenge of Conciliation*. University of Toronto Press, 2019.

Mahase, Radica. "'Plenty a Dem Run Away'—Resistance by Indian Indentured Labourers in Trinidad, 1870–1920." *Labor History*, 49 no. 4 (2008): 465–480.

Mohanty, Chandra Talpade. "'Under Western Eyes' Revisited: Feminist Solidarity Through Anticapitalist Struggles." *Signs* 28, no. 2 (2003): 499–535. https://doi.org/10.1086/342914.

No'kmaq, M'sɨt, Albert Marshall, Karen F. Beazley, Jessica Hum, shalan joudry, Anastasia Papadopoulos, Sherry Pictou, Janet Rabesca, Lisa Young, and Melanie Zurba. "'Awakening the Sleeping Giant': Re-Indigenization Principles for Transforming Biodiversity Conservation in Canada and Beyond." *Facets* 6, no. 1 (2021): 839–869. https://doi.org/10.1139/facets-2020-0083.

Parasram, Ajay. "Pathological White Fragility and the Canadian Nation." *Studies in Political Economy* 100, no. 2 (2019): 194–207. https://doi.org/10.1080/07078552.2019.1646457.

Parasram, Ajay. *Pluriversal Sovereignty and the State: Imperial Encounters in Sri Lanka*. Manchester University Press, 2023: 356–67.

Parasram, Ajay. "Pluriversal Sovereignty and the State of IR." *Review of International Studies* 49, no. 3 (2023): 356–67. http://dx.doi.org/10.1017/S0260210523000165.

Parasram, Ajay. "Seeing Whiteness in the Margins." *Journal of Narrative Politics* 8, no. 1 (2021): 7–9. https://jnp.journals.yorku.ca/index.php/default/article/view/146/146.

Parasram, Ajay. "Solidarity Is a Verb: Teaching Development Activism on Stolen Land." In *Subversive Pedagogies: Radical Possibilities in the Academy*, edited by Kate Schick and Claire Timperley. Routledge, 2021.

Parasram, Ajay, and Alex Khasnabish. *Frequently Asked White Questions*. Fernwood Publishing, 2022.

Parasram, Ajay, and Nissim Mannathukkaren. "Imperial Afterlives: Citizenship and Racial/Caste Fragility in Canada and India." *Citizenship Studies* 28, no. 3 (2021): 301–324. https://doi.org/10.1080/13621025.2021.1984494.

Parasram, Jai. *Beyond Survival: Indians in Trinidad and Tobago, 1845–2017*. Hansib Publications, 2017.

Parasram, Jivesh. *Take d Milk, Nah?* Playwrights Canada Press, 2021.

Peters, Mercedes. "Settler Forgetting in Saulnierville: The Sipekne'katik Mi'kmaw Fishery as Reminder." *NiCHE*, October 19, 2020. https://niche-canada.org/2020/10/19/settler-forgetting-in-saulnierville-the-sipeknekatik-mikmaw-fishery-as-reminder/.

Prashad, Vijay. *Karma of Brown Folk*. University of Minnesota Press, 2001.

Rodney, Walter. *The Groundings with My Brothers*. Miguel Lorne Publishers, 2001 (1969).

Samaroo, Brinsley. "The Presbyterian Canadian Mission as an Agent of Integration in Trinidad During the Nineteenth and Early Twentieth Century." *Caribbean Studies* 14, no. 4 (1975): 41–55.

Shani, Giorgio, and Navnita Chadha Behera. "Provincializing International Relations Through a Reading of Dharma." *Review of International Studies* 48, no. 5 (2021): 1–20. http://dx.doi.org/10.1017/S026021052100053x.

Sharma, Lalbihari. *I Even Regret Night: Holi Songs of Demerara*. Translated by Rajiv Mohabir. Kaya Press, 2020.

Shilliam, Robbie. *The Black Pacific: Anti-Colonial Struggles and Oceanic Connections*. Bloomsbury, 2015.

Snyder, Emily. "Indigenous Feminist Legal Theory." *Canadian Journal of Women and the Law* 26, no. 2 (2014): 365–401. https://doi.org/10.3138/cjwl.26.2.07.

Spivak, Gayatri Chakravorty. "Can the Subaltern Speak?" In *Colonial Discourse and Post-Colonial Theory: A Reader*, edited by Patrick Williams and Laura Chrisman. Routledge, 2015.

Stasiulis, Daiva, and Radha Jhappan. "The Fractious Politics of a Settler Society: Canada." In *Unsettling Settler Societies: Articulations of Gender, Race, Ethnicity and Class*, edited by Daiva Stasiulis and Nira Yuval-Davis. Sage, 1995.

Thame, Maziki. "Racial Hierarchy and the Elevation of Brownness in Creole Nationalism." *Small Axe* 21, no. 3 (2017): 111–123. https://doi.org/10.1215/07990537-4272031.

Thobani, Sunera. *Exalted Subjects: Studies in the Making of Race and Nation in Canada*. University of Toronto Press, 2007.

Thomas, P. *Christians and Christianity in India and Pakistan: A General Survey of the Progress of Christianity in India from Apostolic Times to the Present Day*. Routledge, 2020 (1954).

TMV Team. "What Happened During the 1884 Hosay Massacre in the Caribbean?" TMV (The Muslim Vibe), August 27, 2023. https://themuslimvibe.com/faith-islam/in-history/what-happened-during-the-1884-hosay-massacre-in-the-caribbean.

Upadhyay, Nishant. "Making of 'Model' South Asians on the Tar Sands: Intersections of Race, Caste, and Indigeneity." *Journal of Critical Ethnic Studies* 5, nos. 1–2 (2019): 152–173.

Wahab, Amar. *Disciplining Coolies: An Archival Footprint of Trinidad, 1846*. Peter Lang Publishing, 2018.

Walia, Harsha. *Undoing Border Imperialism*. AK Press, 2014.
Webb, Yvonne. "137 Years Later—Sod Turned for Hosay Massacre Monument." *Trinidad and Tobago Newsday*, October 31, 2021. https://newsday.co.tt/2021/10/31/137-years-later-sod-turned-for-hosay-massacre-monument/.
Williams, Eric. *British Historians and the West Indies*. Andre Deutsch, 1966.
Yu, Henry. "Global Migrants and the New Pacific Canada." *International Journal* 64, no. 4 (2009): 1011–1026. https://doi.org/10.1177/002070200906400410.
Zhou, Min, and Carl L. Bankston III. "The Model Minority Stereotype and the National Identity Question: The Challenges Facing Asian Immigrants and their Children." *Ethnic and Racial Studies* 43, no. 1 (2020): 233–253. http://dx.doi.org/10.1080/01419870.2019.1667511.

# Settler Natures

## *Becoming Settler Against Waters*

Andrew Woolford

THIS CHAPTER EXPLORES HOW SETTLER IDENTITIES ARE fashioned from, and quite often against, the more-than-human world. I argue that a settler is something one becomes rather than an identity dependent on the mere fact of location. Moreover, this becoming is neither solely the result of an isolated individual shaping a sense of self, nor of a process of socialization into settler patterns of thinking and being. Instead, it is through what Karen Barad refers to as "intra-action" that the settler emerges from a complex, entangled world.[1] To make this argument in this chapter more concrete, I begin by focusing on a specific entanglement—settler relationships with water—to demonstrate how settlers become settlers by taking *from* and working *against* water. I further illustrate this process in the next section by drawing on my childhood memories as a settler of learning about water. This experience is contrasted to collective identity formation processes that take place *alongside* and *with* water. To emphasize this difference, the chapter turns to examples of how residential schools sought to destroy Anishinaabe relationships with *nibi* (or water) and assimilate Indigenous young people to settler water regimes. Based on this analysis, I conclude by identifying entryways for reconfiguring settler relationships *with* water.

## Being and Becoming Settler

Settler, as a social location, could suggest a position of permanence and fixity. One may be defined as settler by being born into a family that settled or through the mobility that brought the individual to Turtle Island to benefit from the settler colonial system.[2] In either case, "settler colonizers come to stay," Patrick Wolfe tells us,[3] dispossessing Indigenous Peoples of their lands. Therefore, land is settler colonialism's "irreducible element."[4] Based on these criteria, one might be inclined to view settler identity as nothing more than the product of a material relationship between the dispossessor and the dispossessed.

Yet there is a danger in reifying settler identities through this framing. And, in doing so, we risk forgetting the remaining portion of this often-quoted passage from Wolfe, namely that settler invasion is "a structure and not an event."[5] The notion of structure introduces an element of process; settler colonialism, and its logic of elimination, involves making and remaking settler society, and therefore of making and remaking the settler. For Wolfe, this process occurs primarily through efforts to erase and replace Indigenous Peoples, drawing on strategies such as resocialization, religious conversion, and frontier homicide to destroy all that obstructs an unrivaled settler claim to the land. With this framing, Wolfe's analysis focuses on the macro-level creation of settler society through processes of dispossession, elimination, and settler colonial consolidation, and, therefore, less attention is given to the everyday making of the settler.

The structural reproduction of settler society is, of course, the overarching motive force of settler colonialism. For this reason, the everyday fashioning of settler identities may seem a less pressing concern. One could rightfully ask, if settlers are settlers by virtue of their presence on Indigenous Lands, why is it necessary to account for practices of day-to-day settler reconstitution? Here, Paulette Regan's pedagogy of unsettlement is instructive, as it turns our attention to how "settler colonialism has shaped [our] ways of seeing and knowing the world" and resulted in the subsequent need to "unsettle the settler within."[6] Unmaking settlers will not by itself redress land dispossession as a material practice.[7] But it does counter settler colonial hegemony, which undergirds and feeds settler colonial patterns of dispossession and elimination.[8]

When thinking about the everyday making of settlers and the goal of unsettling, a challenge arises that is based in the liberal individualist worldview that travelled with settlers to Turtle Island. We tend to view the settler as an isolated individual, that is, either as a preformed self or a self that takes shape through anthropocentric socialization, rather than as a being always already interconnected with a world of other beings. Reflecting on the work of Red River Métis scholar Zoe Todd, Anishinaabe scholar Deborah McGregor, nêhiyaw scholar and filmmaker Tasha Hubbard, Diné scholar Kelsey Dayle John, and Dakota scholar Kim TallBear, for example, Indigenous ontologies suggest otherwise, placing human beings within an intricate web of life defined by a multitude of relations.[9] Indigenous legal orders also present tools to understand and evaluate processes of becoming in a vibrant world in which humans are not the only actors who matter.[10] But settlers, as Yellowknives Dene scholar Glen Coulthard rightly notes, are not grounded in such ontologies, and we, as settlers, often fail to obtain a full understanding of their significance.[11]

As settlers, we thus need to take a more arduous route to gain this knowledge and overcome our anti-natural tendencies. Wolfe's work has helped us comprehend that there is a material reality to being a settler in that one lives on and through the resources of stolen Indigenous Lands. But each settler also constructs out of this reality an identity that fits the settler world. This happens quite naturally, in the sense that we do not actively think about it, since the dominant ways of seeing and being in society are settler ways. It also happens anti-naturally as we often act as though the more-than-human world is outside of or secondary within processes of settler identity formation even though domination of the natural world is, in fact, central to becoming settler.

The work of unsettling settler identity formation processes is enhanced through grappling with and centring Indigenous knowledges. As well, some contemporary non-Indigenous approaches to multi-entity relationality, which go by names such as the "ontological turn" or "new materialisms,"[12] can be helpful to deconstruct the anthropocentric—or human-centred—binaries we have long employed to categorize our world. I make no claim that these perspectives are original, and I share concerns that they, at times, appropriate Indigenous knowledges and repackage them as European theory. However, because we are grounded within settler processes of seeing and knowing the world, we also need tools to help us critique settler colonialism from within so that we may create space for new ways of engaging our world. My use of Karen Barad's "agential realism" is therefore not intended to prioritize non-Indigenous scholarship but rather is a means to undercut dominant logics of settler science and sociology and find pathways towards productive overlap with Indigenous ontologies. In particular, I am on this journey because I want to explore how I have become settler in relationship to waters as well as the violence enacted through settler efforts through residential schools to impose new water relationships on Indigenous Peoples.

Barad draws on quantum physics to argue that agents are entangled with all that surrounds them, and each must actively work to separate themselves and fashion a discrete sense of self.[13] For Barad, this work of world-making is material and not solely symbolic; "matter" is what it does, meaning it is always in the process of change and becoming through relations with other bits of matter. This is true for humans, who "(like everything else) always partly constitute and are partly constituted by that which they observe."[14] In effect, our sense of self is performatively constructed through connections among a host of lively actors. We are not separate or outside of all that surrounds us, as is imagined by René Descartes's thinking self who isolates himself from the world around him; we are always already part of this world, and it acts upon us just as we act upon it. In Barad's emphasis on entanglement, action and agency are not understood in anthropocentric terms; rather these terms refer to the specific ways different entities engage in the practices of separation through which they distinguish themselves from others. This is a continuing process, which is why we speak of "becoming" as an ongoing rather than "being" as a fixed state.

This processual understanding holds true for the formation of collective entities, like settlers. We can better understand the making of settlers through what Barad terms "intra-action" rather than imaging them as pre-established and autonomous entities that interact with a world that is external to them.[15] Whereas *interaction* presupposes separation, *intra-action* acknowledges the necessity of relationality. As Barad writes, "In other words, relata do not preexist relations; rather, relata-within-phenomena emerge through specific intra-actions. Crucially then, intra-actions enact *agential separability*."[16] Here, "relata" refer to the presumed separate bits of matter, what we are prone to see as separate and discrete actors, who exist entangled with one another rather than independently. A notion of the self, or of collective identity, emerges from such entanglements of which it is already a part. This emergence is continuous, thereby propelling the formation and reformation of identity out of material intra-actions.

The remainder of the chapter will illustrate this complex process of becoming with nature through the example of relationships with water. However, an example might help further clarify this theoretical framework. Khmer Cambodians have long created their world in companionship with rice and rice fields. The Khmer word *pisa bei*, which is used in the same manner we would say "to eat" in English, literally translates as "to eat rice." Indeed, rice is entwined with Khmer family and spiritual life as the basis of the family meal, a fundamental component of rituals such as marriages, and a means of connecting with spirits. To this extent, it is difficult to think of Khmer without thinking of them *with* rice, and one gets a better sense of the devastation wrought by the Cambodian genocide by the Khmer Rouge when one understands how the revolution disrupted Khmer relations with rice by enforcing collectivization and increased rice production.[17]

Similarly, understanding of how one becomes settler is enhanced through recognizing the series of everyday material relations involved in making the settler. If we view the settler simply as the product of a macro-level material relationship between dispossessor and dispossessed, whereby a settler subject dominates a passive natural world object, we in fact maintain a very settler colonial way of seeing the world. We imagine the settler category as clearly demarcated, bordered by sharp lines akin to borders on colonial maps of a neatly divided world. We do not capture that this is a category that must be made and remade through intra-action with a variety of other beings, establishing multiple relations of domination and connection with human and more-than-human others. Collectivities, such as settlers, are in fact forms of doing, or performances, within these intra-actions, stabilizing as groups, but always in relation with other material participants in their processes of becoming. To this extent, the group is not just a product of human representations of identity; it is always an ongoing performance of human and more-than-human world-making.

## Settlers and Their Surroundings

To make this more concrete, a brief auto-ethnographic excursus will help. We live in a watery world. We are water, we need water, we enjoy and use the water. Water is not something external to who I am, and it has been a participant in shaping my identity. If I were born Anishinaabe rather than white settler, I might have been guided to understand the diversity and complexity of water relations.[18] In contrast, thinking back on water stories, and their role in my Christian-settler-Canadian upbringing, water was most often reduced to its role in serving human existence. I recall learning the Biblical story of Noah's ark and the great flood at Sunday school at the Nazarene church I attended in Esquimalt, British Columbia. The rains fell for forty days and forty nights before the world was cleansed of sin. The flood was God's punishment, a curse upon humanity for our evil hearts. But when the ark came to rest on Mount Ararat,[19] and the dove returned to Noah with the olive leaf, God sent Noah, his family, and their crew of animals from the ark to repopulate the world. Another story from Sunday school was of Moses parting the Red Sea. In the Book of Exodus in the Old Testament, we learn of Moses helping the Israelites flee from the Egyptians, holding out his staff as they reached the Red Sea and opening a path through the waters so the Israelites could cross, leaving the Egyptians to be caught in the sea. In both these stories, water is an inanimate tool of God, manipulated to deliver *His* punishment or blessing.

Nazarenes also engage in baptism as a sacrament and as the sign of a new covenant with Jesus Christ. In my case, this sacrament never occurred, as my parents viewed it as a choice I would make at a more mature age. I instead left the church when I was twelve. Nonetheless, I received the message of water as a means of cleansing one's sins and for purification of the soul. The expression "cleanliness is next to godliness," much loved by Victorian moralists, resounded throughout my early religious life, and I fussed miserably over the dirt that often covered my hands. I sought to be clean, pure, and sacred, until the fear of hell became too much and drove me away from religion.

In my secular education, water was also part of the story. We learned of the "founding" of Canada, as explorers braved the vast ocean to "discover" the "new" world. We wrote essays and dreamed of engaging in similar acts of exploration. When our attention turned to the science of water, and the creatures therein, it was a matter of uncovering the mysteries of their operation. We learned about all the parts of the sockeye salmon, including how their gills enabled the exchange of oxygen and carbon dioxide. We even took a field trip to observe salmon spawning at Goldstream Park and felt the shock of seeing their carcasses litter the riverbank after their journey was complete. This was part of the salmon lifecycle we were to learn about, with few tools provided to address feelings of wonder and mourning.

What these stories, both Biblical and secular, communicated was a becoming of the Christian and settler Canadian *against* water. Though water was all around us, and part of us, we worked to separate it, to recreate it as something to manage. Water was punishment, weapon, and obstacle; a separate and passive object to be used, transcended, examined, and categorized by the brave and faithful. It was part of a process of symbolic boundary-making between the human and non-human worlds, allowing us to define the settler as above nature in a hierarchy of existence.[20] These water stories were part of an intra-action that allowed for the performance of a settler identity outside and above nature. We were never separate from water, but we were taught to remove ourselves from its entanglement and rule over it. Like Moses, the explorers, scientists, or even God, we envisioned ourselves in control of water.

This settler nature was not my only intra-action with water, and different ways of relating to water emerged, though I was not fully ready to grasp them. Some of my intra-actions with water were intimate. As a teen, my friends and I would go hiking in the many forest areas outside Victoria. We were seldom well-prepared—no compass or emergency supplies. But we always knew that we could follow a river or stream and then easily retrace our steps. We hiked with water, relying on its guidance and enjoying its icy coldness on warm summer days. The ocean was also always no more than a bike ride away and was there for pensive and confusing times when one just needed to sit with water, hear the pulse of the waves, and stare out towards islands and mountains. In such instances, I felt water speaking to me, consoling me, but I lacked a cosmology to articulate such a relationship.

These illustrations are few but emblematic of the tensions between becoming *against* and *with* water that beset the settler self. I fashioned myself as a Canadian, as belonging among the land and waters of Vancouver Island, primarily through socio-cultural frames that placed me as separate from and dominating the waters surrounding me. But water also reached out, offered to unsettle me, if I would only accept the invitation.

## Settler Destruction of Indigenous Water Relations

Understanding my becoming settler against water also opens me to consideration of how water relations were at stake in the Canadian settler colonial project of forced assimilation and genocide. Settler domination of nature could not fully assert its claimed superiority when Indigenous worldviews suggested different water relations. In making settlers, and ensuring their continuing domination, Indigenous ontologies had to be unmade.

Indigenous children were removed from lives with water and a concerted attempt was made to force upon them lives against water. Part of the destructiveness of settler colonialism is its effort to destroy symbiogenesis—the way we become who we are in relationship or intra-action with the more-than-human world. Indigenous lives were enriched by multiple meaningful relationships with more-than-human entities, and assimilation operated to sever such connections, weakening bonds between the human and more-than-human so the latter became more open to exploitation. Several examples from the statements taken by the Truth and Reconciliation Commission of Canada illustrate this point. All the examples discussed below are from Survivors located in Manitoba or who were incarcerated at a residential school in Manitoba. The speakers are primarily Anishinaabe.

Upon entry into residential school, Anishinaabe children were confronted with the caustic power of water, as school staff sought to scrub, bathe, scald, and disinfect their Indigeneity away. As one Survivor who attended the Fort Alexander Indian Residential School recounts, "they took me, and they took us upstairs. So, it was called the little boys' dormitory, and they scrubbed us in there, and they used lye soap. I guess it was supposed to be purified, and then they, they just rubbed this thing down on us, and [it] burnt like hell, what, you know, so that was, that was the first day."[21] Another told the TRC of a rough washing and disinfecting of his body upon entry to the school: "When I got to residential school, that first day I remember, they stripped us of our clothes. They hosed us down, and they put powder on our bodies. I don't know what kind of powder that was."[22] The water used to clean the students was often too hot rather than comforting: "And then they chopped my hair off, my long hair; threw me in a hot tub—it was scalding hot. She was angry with me because I was crying."[23] With each such action, the life-giving capacity of water is replaced with its potential for violence. Where once lives were nourished and sustained in daily relationships with *nibi*, or waters, now their bodies are tormented with it, as water is deployed to convey the message that they are unclean, dirty, and profane. An Anishinaabe Survivor from Sagkeeng First Nation describes the feeling of impurity as follows: "I started to question my own, you know, my own being, like why am I here? You know, why is a dirty, savage, heathen here?... You hear it enough times you, you start to believe it."[24]

Several Survivors also recall being forbidden from crying no matter what punishment they endured. An Anishinaabe man who suffered sexual molestation at the hands of a nun recounts, "She hit [me] in the groin... and that really hurt, and she hit me again, and she says, 'I'm gonna keep on 'til you learn not to cry.'"[25] This is a lesson that stuck with him, and he refused to shed tears during the regular violence of life at Fort Alexander Residential School until another staff member decided to extract tears from him: "He says, 'Cry, or I'm not gonna let you go.' I said, 'No.' So finally, and then he put his knee into my, the back of my head, and then he just stomped me into the, to the floor. Well, that hurt, and my nose started to bleed. So, I finally gave into that one that one time, you know."[26] The relationship with water, and his body's capacity to shed tears to contend with sorrows, is manipulated by the staff. Tears no longer can flow naturally but only when permitted by his overseers. One Survivor remarks on reclaiming the power to cry, "I couldn't cry. Now, I'm okay. I can laugh. I can laugh... and I can cry."[27] Another still struggles to allow himself to shed tears: "I just didn't want to cry. You know, I don't know why. I, I believe that was one of the things from the residential school; if you showed any kind of emotion you were punished."[28]

Washrooms and showers were not safe places for students; under the guise of cleaning students, sexual predators frequently molested their victims in these areas. A Survivor reports, "You know I remember being in the shower room. See we used to shower, boys together, boys, maybe they would be about six, six or eight of us in one big shower stall. And that same nun would be there watching us.... And she would touch them, she would touch me too."[29] These patterns were picked up by older students, who added to the danger of washing and showering facilities within the schools: "Where the nuns' bedroom was, there was the bathrooms. And that, one side of it was the bathing corners and the other piece was, was sinks and the toilets. There was visible sexual abuse happening in there that the nuns never stopped, from other kids doing where they, 'coz they would be the ones bathing, bathing us, eh."[30]

Residential schools, like the students themselves, needed to be kept clean. In a project I worked on with several Fort Alexander Residential School Survivors, we sought to create a virtual reality version of their residential school; the Survivors rejected an early prototype of the school because the designers had made it look too filthy. Hearing the stories of the hardship of life within this school, the designers had imagined that the space would match their experiences and be dismal and dirty. But the Survivors corrected them, noting how much time they had to spend cleaning Fort Alexander. In addition to being a regular chore, cleaning was also assigned to them as a punishment. Using cleaning as a punishment allowed staff not only to offload the school's upkeep onto the students, but also to communicate to them messages about European standards of cleanliness and domesticity. The staff also applied cleaning as a form of torment: "I... had to scrub the stairs with a toothbrush, the little toothbrush, you know. Scrub the stairs with that."[31]

Residential school students did not simply stand by and allow their relationships with water to be destroyed. They instead sought to protect these relationships where they could, allying themselves with water to counter the assimilative pressures of these institutions. Water acted as a partner in their potential escape. A Survivor recalls staring out from the window of her dorm, day-dreaming about crossing the river to return to her family: "I see the river and then I got lost in my thoughts. I kind of, I believe I was so afraid I disassociated. I, I just stared out and pretended I was going across to my, to my Kookom's and my Mushoom's."[32] Another Survivor similarly thought about how he might walk from the school to get to Lake Winnipeg, from whence he could find his home.[33] An Elder told me how he and his fellow students connected with the frozen water on which they played hockey; their smooth and fluid motions on the ice were a reminder of the flow of water and of the difficulty of containing something intent on moving.[34]

In these and other ways, residential school students sought to preserve Anishinaabe ways of becoming with water. Astrida Neimanis describes this as the "hydro-logic" of water, or how we think through and with water, including how its fluidity and ability to reflect and diffract represent water's resistance to categorization and containment.[35] Indigenous students trapped in residential schools thought through water towards their freedom. Assimilative education on and around water sought to counter such Indigenous hydro-logics, pushing students to accept the mastery and colonization of water as a resource shapable to the human will. These efforts would continue after residential school, as students returned to communities affected by hydro dams, amplifying the settler dream of bending water to human will.

In general, residential schools sought to ensure that the lives of Indigenous children would lose their flow. What was once a world of watery relations, self-discovery, and interconnection became a system of obstruction, engineered passageways, and controlled movement. The bells and whistles designating when to move and when to sit tried to channel the students into engineered canals, from class to hall to refectory. In the latter, dry hard tack and lumpy porridge further symbolized a change in water relations as many Survivors recall choking back ill-textured food, hoping to keep it down for fear of having to eat their regurgitated meal should they happen to vomit. Powdered milk and eggs added to the sense of disgust felt by many students, as the rehydrated foods lacked the taste and consistency of traditional meals.[36] A Survivor testified that "there was a lot of times there I seen other students that threw up, you know; and they were forced to eat their own, their own vomit."[37]

Despite the attempted recalibration of the relationship with water, and the flow of Indigenous life more broadly, Survivors did not entirely forget their relations with water. Rather than master water, using it to feed crops or harnessing its power, Survivors often found themselves going back to old ways of working alongside water. Water was there as part of the healing journey many took after residential schools, participating in their reclamation of Indigenous identities.[38]

In this section, many potentially familiar indignities of residential school—the domestic chores, the incessant washing, the punishments for bed-wetting and tears—can be understood more holistically as part of residential schools' efforts to transform Indigenous relations with water. Instead of the liveliness of nibi, with both its dangers and gifts, they learn to relate to water as a source of purification as well as a resource to be controlled. The Roman Catholic rush to baptize Indigenous children is another example of a shifting water logic imposed on Indigenous families, as baptism of children was understood by the Church to place a claim in these children, compelling them to attend Catholic residential schools.[39] More than isolated and arbitrary cruelties, these actions show an attempt to rewrite Indigenous becoming *with* water and elevate settler becoming *against* water. Against this violence, Indigenous young people were able to draw on their relationships with nibi, and their attendant hydro-logics, to try to preserve their connections to self, family, and community.

## Recalibrating Water Relations

Now, living in the Anthropocene, the epoch defined by human-caused impact on Earth's ecosystems, and amid devastating ecological change, it is becoming clear that settler certainty about the need to dislodge Indigenous relations with water was mistaken. Settlers would have done better to learn from and aspire towards Indigenous relationships with the more-than-human. As Martin Crook and Damien Short note with respect to the combined threats of genocide and ecocide, "the role traditional owner-conservators play could prove crucial in our ability to survive and adapt to climate change."[40] Western colonialism and capitalism have brought widespread destruction to ecosystems, making settler efforts to overwrite Indigenous ecologies all the more problematic.

In my own life, I was too often unable to heed the lessons of water, though they were ever-present, such as through the wayfinding with water I discovered as a teen or the solace I took in the ocean at multiple points in my life. I was not equipped to understand water as a living entity with which we humans have an intricate relationship.

Unsettling the settler requires rediscovering a liquid symbiogenesis, whereby we recognize the vibrancy of water and its multiple roles in constitution of the human. It requires understanding settler identity not only as a product of an imbalance of material relations but as an ongoing performance of settler becoming through which we enact our separability from the world of water. It is this day-to-day making of ourselves as settler that allows us to project ourselves as dominating waters, despite waters frequently refusing our dominion. As I write this, the fields, roadways, communities, and parks are experiencing severe flooding in my current home province of Manitoba. Sandbags and Tiger Dams are being assembled to interrupt the flows of water, including around homes on the Peguis First Nation (around two hundred kilometres north of Winnipeg). This was a community that in 1907 was relocated from what is now Selkirk, Manitoba, to a flood plain after an illegal land transfer. In such circumstances, we cannot ignore the need to redress the material relations of settler colonialism that have dispossessed Indigenous Peoples, like the Peguis First Nation, leaving them more at the mercy of water. But such actions must take place alongside countering settler processes of becoming against the natural world that perpetuate hydro-logics of domination in a time when we desperately need to learn to live with waters.

## Notes

1 Barad, "Posthumanist Performativity," 815.
2 Manuel and Grand Chief Derrickson, *Unsettling Canada*; Regan, *Unsettling the Settler*; Veracini, *Settler Colonialism*; Lowman and Barker, *Settler*.
3 Wolfe, "Settler Colonialism," 388.
4 Wolfe, "Settler Colonialism," 388.
5 This argument is also presented in Wolfe, *Settler Colonialism*,163.
6 Regan, *Unsettling the Settler*, 313–314.
7 Tuck and Yang, "Decolonization Is Not."
8 For further discussion of hegemony and the need to dismantle it in transformative struggle, see Gramsci, *Selections*.
9 See, for example, Todd, "Fish Pluralities"; McGregor, "Mino-Mnaamodzawin"; Hubbard, "Buffalo Genocide,'" 292–305; John, "Animal Colonialism";TallBear, "An Indigenous Reflection."
10 Todd, "An Indigenous Feminist's Take"; Rosiek, Snyder, and Pratt, "The New Materialisms"; Bignall, Hemming, and Rigney, "Three Ecosophies."
11 Coulthard, *Red Skin, White Masks*.
12 Conty, "The Politics of Nature"; Gamble, Hanan, and Nail, "What Is New Materialism?"; Haraway, *Staying with the Trouble*; Kohn, *How Forests Think*.
13 Barad, "Posthumanist Performativity," 801–830; Barad, *Meeting the Universe Halfway*.
14 Gamble, Hanan, and Nail, "What Is New Materialism?"
15 Barad, "Posthumanist Performativity," 815. See also Barad, *Meeting the Universe Halfway*; Juelskjaer and Schwennesen, "Intra-Active Entanglements."
16 Barad, "Posthumanist Performativity," 815.
17 Woolford, June, and Um, "'We Planted Rice and Killed People.'"
18 Daigle, "Resurging Through Kishiichiwan"; Anderson, Clow, and Howarth-Brockman, "Carriers of Water"; McGregor, "Mino-Mnaamodzawin."
19 Armenian Christian culture treats Mount Ararat as more than a static object. Ararat is likened to the mother and heartbeat of this nation. See Woolford, "'To Make It Belong.'"
20 On symbolic boundary-making, see Douglas, *Purity and Danger*.
21 Truth and Reconciliation Commission of Canada [TRC], "02-MB-16JU10-065," 12.
22 TRC, "07-MB-24FB10-001," 26.
23 TRC, "02-MB-16JU10-041," 1–2.
24 TRC, "2011-0291," 12.
25 TRC, *Honouring the Truth*, 14.
26 TRC, *Honouring the Truth*, 35.
27 TRC, *Honouring the Truth*, 18.
28 TRC, *Honouring the Truth*, 30.
29 TRC, *Honouring the Truth*, 4.
30 TRC, *Honouring the Truth*, 9.
31 TRC, *Honouring the Truth*, 8.

32 TRC, *Honouring the Truth*, 2–3.
33 TRC, *Honouring the Truth*.
34 Interview with Elder Rudy Okemaw, November 21, 2021.
35 Neimanis, "Feminist Subjectivity, Watered."
36 See, for example, TRC, "2011-0089," 7.
37 TRC, *Honouring the Truth*, 33–34
38 See, for example, TRC, *Honouring the Truth*, 15.
39 TRC, *Final Report*, 631–632.
40 Crook and Short, "Developmentalism and the Genocide–Ecocide Nexus."

## Sources

Anderson, Kim, Barbara Clow, and Margaret Howarth-Brockman. "Carriers of Water: Aboriginal Women's Experience, Relationships and Reflections." *Journal of Cleaner Production* 60 (2013): 11–17.

Barad, Karen. *Meeting the Universe Halfway: Quantum Physics and the Entanglement of Matter and Meaning*. Duke University Press, 2007.

Barad, Karen. "Posthumanist Performativity: Toward an Understanding of How Matter Comes to Matter." *Signs: Journal of Women in Culture and Society* 28, no. 3 (2003): 801–830. https://doi.org/10.1086/345321.

Bignall, Simone, Steve Hemming, and Daryl Rigney. "Three Ecosophies for the Anthropocene: Environmental Governance, Continental Posthumanism and Indigenous Expressivism." *Deleuze Studies* 10, no. 4 (2016): 455–478. http://dx.doi.org/10.3366/dls.2016.0239.

Conty, Françoise. "The Politics of Nature: New Materialist Responses to the Anthropocene." *Theory, Culture, & Society* 35, nos. 7–8 (2018), 73–96. https://doi.org/10.1177/0263276418802891.

Coulthard, Glen. *Red Skin, White Masks: Rejecting the Colonial Politics of Recognition*. University of Minnesota Press, 2014.

Crook, Martin, and Damien Short. "Developmentalism and the Genocide–Ecocide Nexus." *Journal of Genocide Research* 23, no. 2 (2021): 162–188. https://doi.org/10.1080/14623528.2020.1853914.

Daigle, Michelle. "Resurging Through Kishiichiwan: The Spatial Politics of Indigenous Water Relations." *Decolonization: Indigeneity, Education & Society* 7, no. 1 (2018): 159–172.

Douglas, Mary. *Purity and Danger: An Analysis of the Concepts of Pollution and Taboo*. Routledge, 1966.

Gamble, Christopher N., Joshua S. Hanan, and Thomas Nail. "What Is New Materialism?" *Angelaki* 24, no. 6 (2019): 111–134. https://doi.org/10.1080/0969725x.2019.1684704.

Gramsci, Antonio. *Selections from the Prison Notebooks*. International Publishers, 1971.

Haraway, Donna J. *Staying with the Trouble: Making Kin in the Chthulucene*. Duke University Press, 2016.

Hubbard, Tasha. "Buffalo Genocide in Nineteenth-Century North America: 'Kill, Skin, and Sell.'" In *Colonial Genocide in Indigenous North America*, edited by Andrew Woolford, Jeff Benvenuto, and Alexander Laban Hinton. Duke University Press, 2014. https://doi.org/10.1515/9780822376149-015.

John, Kelsey Dayle. "Animal Colonialism—Illustrating Intersections Between Animal Studies and Settler Colonial Studies Through Diné Horsemanship." *Humanalia: A Journal of Human/Animal Interface Studies* 10, no. 2 (2019): 42–68. https://humanimalia.org/article/view/9501/10041.

Juelskjaer, Malou, and Nete Schwennesen. "Intra-Active Entanglements—An Interview with Karen Barad." *Kvinder, Køn & Forskning* nos. 1–2 (2012): 10–23. https://doi.org/10.7146/kkf.v0i1-2.28068.

Kohn, Eduardo. *How Forests Think: Toward an Anthropology Beyond the Human*. University of California Press, 2013.

Lowman, Emma Battell, and Adam J. Barker. *Settler: Identity and Colonialism in 21st Century Canada*. Fernwood Publishing, 2015.

Manuel, Arthur, and Grand Chief Ronald M. Derrickson. *Unsettling Canada: A National Wake-Up Call*. 2nd ed. Between the Lines Books, 2021.

McGregor, Deborah. "Mino-Mnaamodzawin: Achieving Indigenous Environmental Justice in Canada." *Environment and Society* 9, no. 1 (2018): 7–24. https://doi.org/10.3167/ares.2018.090102.

Neimanis, Astrida. "Feminist Subjectivity, Watered." *Feminist Review* 103 (2013): 23–41. https://www.jstor.org/stable/41819667.

Regan, Paulette. *Unsettling the Settler Within: Indian Residential Schools, Truth Telling, and Reconciliation in Canada*. University of British Columbia Press, 2010.

Rosiek, Jerry Lee, Jimmy Snyder, and Scott L. Pratt. "The New Materialisms and Indigenous Theories of Non-Human Agency: Making the Case for Respectful Anti-Colonial Engagement." *Qualitative Inquiry* 26, nos. 3–4 (2019): 331–346. https://doi.org/10.1177/1077800419830135.

TallBear, Kim. "An Indigenous Reflection on Working Beyond the Human/Not Human." *GLQ: A Journal of Lesbian and Gay Studies* 21, nos. 2–3 (2015): 230–235. https://muse.jhu.edu/article/582037.

Todd, Zoe. "Fish Pluralities: Human-Animal Relations and Sites of Engagement in Paulatuuq, Arctic Canada." *Études/Inuit/Studies* 38, nos. 1–2 (2014): 217–238. https://doi.org/10.7202/1028861ar.

Todd, Zoe. "An Indigenous Feminist's Take on the Ontological Turn: 'Ontology' Is Just Another Word for Colonialism." *Journal of Historical Sociology* 29, no. 1 (2016): 4–22. https://doi.org/10.1111/johs.12124

Truth and Reconciliation Commission of Canada. "02-MB-16JU10-065." National Centre for Truth and Reconciliation Archives, June 16, 2010.

Truth and Reconciliation Commission of Canada. "07-MB-24FB10-001." National Centre for Truth and Reconciliation Archives, February 24,2010.

Truth and Reconciliation Commission of Canada. "2011-0089." National Centre for Truth and Reconciliation Archives, March 2, 2011.

Truth and Reconciliation Commission of Canada. "Honouring the Truth, Reconciling for the Future: Summary of the *Final Report of the Truth and Reconciliation Commission of Canada*." 2015. https://ehprnh2mwo3.exactdn.com/wp-content/uploads/2021/01/Executive_Summary_English_Web.pdf.

Truth and Reconciliation Commission of Canada. *Truth and Reconciliation Commission of Canada Final Report: The History, Vol 1*. McGill-Queen's University Press, 2015.

Tuck, Eve, and K. Wayne Yang."Decolonization Is Not a Metaphor." *Decolonization: Indigeneity, Education & Society* 1, no. 1 (2012): 1–40.

Veracini, Lorenzo. *Settler Colonialism: A Theoretical Overview*. Palgrave Macmillan, 2010.

Wolfe, Patrick. "Settler Colonialism and the Elimination of the Native." *Journal of Genocide Research* 8, no. 4 (2006): 387–409. https://doi.org/10.1080/14623520601056240.

Wolfe, Patrick. *Settler Colonialism and the Transformation of Anthropology: The Politics and Poetics of an Ethnographic Event*. Cassell, 1999.

Woolford, Andrew. "'To Make It Belong to Who I Was, to Who I Became': Atom Egoyan's *Ararat* and Symbiogenesis Among the Diaspora of the Armenian Genocide." *American Review of Canadian Studies* 52, no. 1 (2022): 29–45. https://doi.org/10.1080/02722011.2022.2028247.

Woolford, Andrew, Wanda June, and Sereyvothny Um. "'We Planted Rice and Killed People': Symbiogenetic Destruction in the Cambodian Genocide." *Genocide Studies and Prevention* 15, no. 1 (2021): 44–67. https://doi.org/10.5038/1911-9933.15.1.1805.

PART THREE

# Settler Colonial Society

*Relating, Reckoning, and Unreconciliation*

# Reckoning and Unreconciled

## *Neil Stonechild, Starlight Tours, and Racialized Policing in the Settler State*

Chris Lindgren and Michelle Stewart

How do you tell the story of the Starlight Tours—a form of racialized policing that targets Indigenous Peoples and has resulted in freezing deaths in Canada? This is the challenge presented to Chris and Michelle during a phone call to discuss a proposed documentary they are working on together. The documentary will focus on the death of Neil Stonechild, an Indigenous youth, and the legacy of the Starlight Tours with a producer who is not from Canada. A producer became aware of Neil's freezing death and wants to create a documentary about the "lesser-known histories" of Canada for an international audience. Here *lesser known* stands in for histories of ongoing violence related to settler colonialism. Michelle and Chris are discussing how to tell the story.

Chris is Neil Stonechild's brother. Chris is an Indigenous man and a Sixties Scoop survivor, which means he was taken from his Indigenous mother and adopted by a white family. Chris reconnected with his family when he was a young adult. Chris thinks of Neil's death and the Starlight Tours through this lens and his lived experiences. Michelle, on the other hand, has a complex history related to the *Indian Act* in Canada but was raised as a settler and has white privilege. Michelle has worked on issues related to systemic racism and racialized policing as a researcher and a grassroots community advocate, and she teaches on these topics as a professor. So, while Chris and Michelle are both thinking about the same topic—the Starlight Tours—they do so based on different experiences that shape how they understand the issues. There is a difference in perspective, and that difference is key and must be attended to. Where to start?

Chris points out that telling the story would need to start "with Christopher Columbus coming over, he fucked us up." Silence for a moment. Quiet agreement? There is a not a shared *us* on the call. The conversation wanders for a bit. Chris circles back: "This all started when the white settlers came to North America," he interjects. "I am sorry, Michelle, but that is the truth."

"Agreed," Michelle responds.

The statement of where it starts serves to mark distinction. It tests for awareness of the problem. It also calls for self-recognition of "social location" (think here of the role of one's class, race, gender, ability). By marking Columbus and using the language of settlers, there is an implicit test for white settler fragility. This conversation is about settler colonialism. Agreement does not erase distinction, social location, fragility, and settler colonialism. And as such, we will start here with some shared language and definitions before digging deeper into context and background.

## Shared Language

Articles and chapters about racialized policing and the settler state are themselves littered with jargon. To find shared language and understanding requires that we dismantle jargon. The words, unpacked, can form shared understanding. So, we will start first with the title of this chapter and then add a few more words we want to explore. Title: "Reckoning and Unreconciled: Neil Stonechild, Starlight Tours, and Racialized Policing in the Settler State."

### *Reckoning*

This term can sometimes make one think of calculations or perhaps a person's perspective. It can also make one think of wrestling with something. Diane Nelson speaks about the ways that reckoning "promises a fixed position, from which to decide," and she notes "it also has several definitions: (i) to count, figure up; (ii) to measure possibilities for the future; (iii) to settle rewards or penalties."[1] For our purposes, *reckoning* will include the idea of a calculation or judgment. More specifically, it is also a verb—it is action based.

*Unreconciled*

Thinking about the definition, there is the concept of deduction or what cannot be reconciled. If we think about the idea of things that cannot be reconciled, we can think of a definition that focuses on a way to restore friendly relations, resolve, or settle.[2] By extension, if something cannot be reconciled, then it can remain in a liminal—or an in-between—space. Something that is unreconciled, then, could be a space in which friendly relations are not possible, cannot be resolved. A space that is always unsettled.

*Neil Stonechild*

Neil Stonechild was Chris's brother. The following is taken from an article Michelle wrote in 2019 after talking to Chris on the twenty-ninth anniversary of Neil's death:

> On Nov. 29, 1990, the body of Neil Stonechild, a Saulteaux First Nation teen, was found frozen in a field on the outskirts of Saskatoon. It was -28°C. He was just 17-years-old at the time of his death. He was found wearing only jeans and a light jacket and was missing one shoe.
>
> Teenager.
> Face down.
> Light jacket.
> Jeans.
> One shoe.
> -28°C.
>
> On Dec. 5, 1990, the Saskatoon Police Service closed the investigation into the death of Neil Stonechild. Despite visible injuries to the body of the Indigenous teenager, the file was closed. The investigation closed prior to receiving the Coroner's Report, prior to receiving the toxicology report and prior to completing interviews with all witnesses.[3]

*Starlight Tours*

This is a documented police practice in which Indigenous individuals are dropped off on the outskirts of cities and forced to walk back, often during freezing weather, that has resulted in injuries and death. Starlight Tours are often traced back to Saskatchewan, Canada, and the "freezing deaths" of Indigenous men outside the city of Saskatoon. These practices were captured during the Commission of Inquiry into the Death of Neil Stonechild, who was just seventeen years old when he died. While the practice is often linked to actions of the Saskatoon Police Service, there have been documented incidents of this form of police violence elsewhere, including a recent incident in Eastern Canada in 2024.[4]

*Racialized Policing*

Taking the terms apart, there is connection between race and policing. Racialized policing can present in many ways. Elizabeth Comack distinguishes between racial profiling and racialized policing and notes that race and racism impact police actions as well as public analysis and discourse[5]—which means how policing is understood is also impacted. The term *racialized policing* includes a wide range of practices. For example, over-policing is when racialized minorities experience increased police presence or scrutiny. Under-policing can refer to the lack of police investigation when the victim is BIPOC (Black, Indigenous, and people of colour). Seen this way, there are different forms of policing that become available for white and non-white community members. Krista Stelkia of the Yellowhead Institute argues, "The notion of police being there to serve and protect in times of need often does not apply to Indigenous, Black or other racialized minorities in Canada. The notion of 'help' more often resembles harm."[6]

*Settler Colonialism and Racial Terror*

This book is about settler colonialism, and we build from work that appears throughout and underscore Patrick Wolfe's argument that this form of colonialism "is a structure not an event."[7] This means that settler colonialism is a set of systems, not an incident. It also means this form of colonialism is not a thing of the past; settlers came to settle, and the occupation of Indigenous Land is an ongoing act. This form of colonialism, thinking through Wolfe, means that the structures help to maintain the occupation. Thinking about structures, one can think about specific practices in education, health, and justice that are grounded in settler colonial ideologies. Sherene Razack presses further into the structures and shares the following observation:

> A white settler society targets Indigenous land *and* Indigenous people. In this regard, police shootings of Indigenous people and the legal response to police use of force (along with everyday settler violence) are a part of the racial terror that is a central part of settler colonialism. As an ongoing racial project of accumulation, settler colonialism requires the enforcement of colonial lines of force.[8]

This chapter focuses on the violence that necessarily surrounds settler colonialism and how different structures are intertwined in such a way that one system reinforces another. Police play a particular role in the settler state. Razack points to racial terror; we can also think about racialized policing. At the centre is violence and dispossession. This chapter will look at these systems while thinking about Neil Stonechild.

Before moving forward, we ask readers to pause for a moment. Depending on who is flipping through this chapter, you are being asked to step into a space of violence. For the Indigenous reader, we offer caution. This chapter will discuss the freezing death of an Indigenous teenager and other Indigenous Peoples. Take care as you read; move to another chapter if that is better for you. For the settlers, take care and read slowly and with intention. A key part of your privilege is being able to opt in and out of discussions or engagement. Please check that privilege. If your pace is fast or distracted, come back later. Take time to read and become unsettled.

## Terms and Context

Chris notes that to tell the story of Neil Stonechild to a wider audience, the documentary filmmaker(s) would need to move back and forth in time. Chris outlines a narrative that would include Sitting Bull and the US Cavalry; residential schools and the Sixties Scoop; social determinants of health; the persistence of trauma, grief, and anger. In other words, to tell the story of the Starlight Tours and Neil Stonechild requires understanding the broader contexts that allow for the freezing death of an Indigenous youth. To tell that story here, we will trace stories through the language that was just explored.

Sitting Bull was an Indigenous Chief for the Hunkpapa Sioux. The Sioux were granted the Black Hills in treaty negotiation with the United States, but soon settlers, including prospectors, attempted to extract from the land. Sitting Bull defeated George Custer and the US Cavalry in the Battle of the

Little Big Horn (in what is now Montana). This battle can be understood to be an ongoing battle against white settlement and western expansion of settlers—it can also be understood to have come about because of broken treaty agreements. Following the battle, Sitting Bull fled to Canada to seek refuge in the Cypress Hills (now in Saskatchewan). Sitting Bull was assured he could stay in Canada, but soon American and Canadian officials took actions to force him back to the United States, as Canada would not grant him access to land (reserve) or resources (rations). He would later be returned to the US and murdered by "a group of Indian police who were attempting to issue a warrant for his participation in the Ghost Dance."[9]

This narrative of movement and control is also captured by Jesse Wente (Anishinaabe, Serpent River First Nation),[10] Indigenous author and artist, when he notes land configurations and right to movement was entirely a product of the state, including how concentrations of Indigenous Peoples and land were formed and then managed through the settler's imaginary, including the development of the reserve system.

Returning to Chris's comment about the necessary backgrounds, he speaks also about the residential school system and the Sixties Scoop. The residential school system in Canada was a product of collusion between church and state to forcibly remove Indigenous children from their homes under the auspices of civilizing Indigenous Peoples.

As Jesse Wente notes, the focus of the schools found the Canadian state clearly outlining a vision of Indigenous Peoples as servants and labourers.[11] The intersection of settler colonialism and capitalism at once stripped children away from their homes to live in residential schools, sometimes for years on end, with limited access to their culture and family. Instruction was in English and speaking one's own language was punished viciously. To produce compliance—language, culture, behaviour—violence was at the heart of the practice. Structural but also physical, sexual, and emotional violence. Chris notes, "priests and nuns beat us. They raped our women and beat them. The nuns were ruthless. Through the years our people had tried to escape and they were beaten and killed." The ripple effect of these educational practices saw generation after generation pulled from home. Some never to return and with the intention of all to be forever transformed. Violence and trauma stood at the foundation of this transformation. Thousands of children died or went missing because of this school program, and unmarked graves outside the schools are being investigated to this date.[12]

For each generation that "survived" being in residential school, their relationships were forever changed from the experience. Researchers, community members, and advocates have explored a range of impacts of the residential schools that operated for over 150 years in Canada. These, along with many other practices of settler colonialism, produced trauma. Maria Yellow Horse Brave Heart is recognized as coining an approach to understanding intergenerational impacts of historic trauma, "the collective and compounding emotional and psychological injury over the lifespan that is multigenerational and resulting from a history of genocide."[13] This collective and compounding impact for Indigenous Peoples occurs within and between generations. And while these impacts compounded, the Canadian state continued to focus on Indigenous children—and their removal from family, home, and community.

Chris notes the need to speak about the Sixties Scoop. For Chris, the Sixties Scoop and impacts of residential school are an intimate part of the story of Neil Stonechild because Neil's family experienced both. Chris was taken from his mother, Stella, and sent to live with a family in the United States of America. Chris was taken when he was five years old. Like many children taken at this time—in the 1960s—Chris was first moved from foster home to foster home. He would later find himself adopted to a family in Minnesota. Moving farther and farther from his home and his community, Chris came to know himself primarily through his adopted family. During this time period there were agencies that would broker adoptions, there were regular ads in newspapers advertising Indigenous children for adoption, and programs that facilitated the removal of Indigenous children under the auspices of "child welfare." During this time period, Chris shares that his adoptive mother was working at Children's Aid and was involved in getting Indigenous children adopted all over the world. Chris was listed as "on the register" for getting adopted in Winnipeg. Chris, like many other Indigenous children, was subject to a policy of being taken and having his connection to family severed:

> An alarmingly disproportionate number of Aboriginal children were apprehended from the 1960s onward. By the 1970s, roughly one third of all children in care were Aboriginal. 70 percent of the children apprehended were placed into non-Aboriginal homes, many of them homes in which their heritage was denied. In some cases, the foster or adoptive parents told their children that they

> were French or Italian instead. Government policy at the time did not allow birth records to be opened unless both the child and parent consented. This meant that many children suspected their heritage but were unable to have it confirmed.[14]

With no outside assistance in the form of formal agencies or supports, Chris traced out his roots and found his mother and his biological family when he was twenty-two years old. Chris notes that all he and his adoptive family had to work with was his birth certificate that stated who his biological mother and father were. Chris went to Winnipeg seeking out answers and received no support until he made contact with one woman from Indian Affairs who helped him. Chris remembers she was Indigenous and her help was critical in connecting him with his family.

Chris returned to Saskatoon, Canada, in 1989. Chris made an immediate connection with his younger brother, Neil, as they both loved wrestling. Chris recalls that Neil was a funny and caring person. Chris gave Neil his letterman's jacket prior to taking a trip to Ontario. Chris had hoped that Neil would join on the trip to go pick up a car, but Neil changed his mind and remained in Saskatoon while Chris travelled. Neil would later be found in this same jacket. Frozen in a field. Images circulated of Neil in the letterman's jacket:

> Given the sentimental importance of the jacket, Chris went to the police after the investigation concluded to request Neil's belongings including the jacket. The Saskatoon Police told him they couldn't find it. "I don't even know if this has been told publicly," says Chris. "But we couldn't find any of his stuff." The jacket and Neil's other possessions were never returned. Chris tells me his mom, Stella, "was heartbroken."[15]

Reflecting on the investigation, Chris shares, "they didn't take it serious." Chris continues, "Neil wasn't the first one." In January 2000, Darrell Night would survive a Starlight Tour, and two other men would die launching a renewed call for investigations:

> Darrell Night, a Saulteaux First Nation member and survivor of a Starlight Tour, best describes the horrifying nature of these tours. He said of the experience, "I thought I was dead. All those rumours

I heard in the past, they were all coming true." On January 28, 2000, two officers took Night out of town and left him stranded. He was wearing only a light denim jacket in -25 Celsius weather. Night told the officers, "I'll freeze to death out here" to which one officer replied, "That's your f-ing problem." Night survived after walking to a nearby power plant and pounding on the door for nearly 30 minutes until a worker heard him. Days after the incident, the frozen bodies of two other Indigenous men—25-year-old Rodney Naistus and 30-year-old Lawrence Wegner—were found close to where Night was left.[16]

This same month the body of Lloyd Dustyhorn was also discovered. An article in the *Washington Post* in February 2000 noted "troubles" in a Canadian city and discussed these recent events thusly (racialized language is included to mark the tenor of reporting on the issue):

> It had become almost commonplace: young Indian men, half-naked, found dead and frozen in fields or alongside the road on the outskirts of town. The general assumption was that such misfortune was what happened when poverty and substance abuse mixed with the frigid Canadian winter. But after two more deaths last month and a shocking story told by an out-of-work Indian bricklayer, this prairie city of churches and pickup trucks has been forced to confront a more sinister possibility: that some of those drunk or drug-addled Indians may have been left out there by police.[17]

The following year, Saskatoon Police Service Officers Dan Hatchen and Ken Munson were convicted of assault and unlawful confinement of Darrell Night.[18] Munson and Hatchen were sentenced to six months.[19] Within hours, the officers were fired from the police force, and days later the Saskatchewan government announced an inquiry into the treatment of Indigenous Peoples; the inquiries, however, "into the deaths of Naistus and Wegner made no conclusive statements."[20] No one was charged in these deaths.

In February 2003, the Government of Saskatchewan established the Commission of Inquiry into Stonechild's death.[21] The inquiry concluded in May 2004, and the final report was released later that year, in October.[22] The purpose of the inquiry was to examine the circumstances surrounding the death of Neil Stonechild, including the role that Saskatoon police officers played, and the ensuing investigation.[23] The final report included eight recommendations regarding improving police relations with Indigenous populations and individuals.[24] The inquiry found that the original investigation into Stonechild's death had been "superficial and totally inadequate."[25] Saskatoon Police Service Constables Brad Senger and Larry Hartwig were fired following the release of the report, as Stonechild had been in their custody on the night of his death.[26] Neither was charged criminally for the death of Neil Stonechild.[27]

For the police involved, Chris notes that they got "a slap on the wrist. You know 'you can't be a police [officer] anymore.'" Chris was present for different parts of the inquiry and can still vividly recall how Hartwig presented himself on the stand. Chris shares that his sister would regularly nudge him during the proceedings, and they would whisper about his smirk. Chris remembers approaching Hartwig, patting him on the shoulder, and saying, "you may think you have everyone else fooled here... but you don't have me fooled." The inquiry into the freezing death of Neil Stonechild found that both officers were with Neil on the night he died and discussed injuries that were consistent with bruising from handcuffs. It is understood that the two police officers were the last to see him alive and that Neil died as a result of a Starlight Tour, which is a form of racialized policing.

As Razack argues, "There is a popular term [Starlight Tour] is testimony to the fact that it happened more than once. The practice of drop-offs is a lethal one when the temperature is −28°C and if the long walk back to town is undertaken without proper clothing and shoes."[28] And a further review of other incidents in Saskatoon alone affirms the statement from Razack. In 2003, during the time period of the inquiry into Neil Stonechild's death, the Saskatoon Police Chief noted that these practices could be traced back as far as 1976.[29] Media reports included a story about three Indigenous Peoples, including a woman who was eight months pregnant, being dropped on the outskirts of town and forced to walk back. The officer was given a $200 fine.[30] In other examples, media reported that a retired police officer wrote a news column describing a Starlight Tour that was published in 1997.[31] In 2015, a young Indigenous woman alleged that police in another part of the province took her on a Starlight Tour; her complaint was dismissed, and it was implied other allegations could face litigation.[32] GPS was reviewed as part of the investigation, and while police claimed vindication, it was left unexplained why it was that "she could have seen the refinery during the trip"[33] to the police station.

The following year, a student completing a university paper on police brutality discovered that the Wikipedia page about the Saskatoon Police Service had information about the Starlight Tours removed; it was later found that the edits came from an IP address at the Saskatoon Police Service.[34] Disclosure, investigation, erasure. The patterns of abuse and commitments to white supremacy and settler colonialism start prior to, and extend beyond, the scope and intent of an inquiry or inquest. Inquests and inquiries, as pointed out by Razack[35] and others, are products of the settler state. Commissions, inquiries, and other entities can explore acts of systemic and state violence, but they are not equipped—or intended—to bring about remedy.

Jesse Wente[36] discusses three national commissions or inquiries in Canada, each of which had large and sweeping mandates to take on an investigation into systemic racism and inequality impacting Indigenous Peoples. Accordingly, each investigated symptoms and impacts of settler colonialism:

- The Royal Commission on Aboriginal Peoples was established in August of 1991 and ran for five years, with the final report being published in 1996.[37] The report consisted of five volumes that outlined 440 recommendations concerning the relationship between First Nations and the federal and provincial governments.[38] The final report suggested a twenty-year timeline in which to implement changes.[39] At the conclusion of the twenty-year timeline, no significant changes had occurred. In 2021, Prime Minister Justin Trudeau stated that the commission helped pave the way for the Indian Residential Schools Settlement Agreement and the Truth and Reconciliation Commission.[40]

- The Truth and Reconciliation Commission of Canada (TRC) is often framed as a proactive approach to reconciliation. However, the TRC is the "result of protracted litigation by survivors of the IRS system against the government and churches that ran the schools."[41] The TRC was established in 2007 and concluded in 2015.[42] The final report consisted of six volumes and included ninety-four calls to action regarding reconciliation between Indigenous Peoples and Canadians.[43] While there has been some headway in addressing the calls to action, there has also been much criticism for the slow progress in which the calls are being addressed,[44] with one review estimating that the completion of all calls to action may not occur until 2057 or later.[45]

- The National Inquiry into Missing and Murdered Indigenous Women and Girls was launched in 2016,[46] with an extension announced in 2018, and the final report being published in 2019.[47] The final report outlined eighteen main calls for justice, each with multiple subsections, bringing the total number of calls for justice to 231.[48] A report by the Canadian Broadcast Corporation stated in June of 2023 that only 2 of the 231 calls for justice have been completed, with fewer than half of them having even been started.[49]

Wente notes that each of these entities released findings and recommendations that were stop-gap measures to address the impacts of systemic racism. However, the ideologies that drive settler colonialism build interlocking systems of violence and dispossession in Canada focused on the erasure of Indigenous Peoples from the land. As such, each inquiry is limited in its capacity as it is not seeking to dismantle the system—settler colonialism—but to address the symptoms.

In the absence of dismantling the entire structure, families and communities continue to experience violence. Chris reflects in one conversation that "it's always going to be hard. I never thought thirty years later I would still be dealing with this." In another conversation, he expands the footprint: "I always thought that I was done with this—[but] I will always be pissed off. It will never go away." Trauma, grief, and anger linger at the core of experience and animate this chapter. Neil's death, and the Starlight Tours, remain unreconcilable.

## Conclusion

This chapter was an experiment. It brought together a family member and an academic to discuss the Starlight Tours. Each author, Chris and Michelle, has their own unique social location that shapes how they think about the Starlight Tours. Chris is Neil's brother and set the framework for this chapter, which is meant to serve as an invitation to the reader to learn more as most citations are accessible resources meant to encourage further reading. The goal was to offer a blended discussion about the Starlight Tours from different social locations and for a diverse audience.



Taken together, and returning to the title, "Reckoning and Unreconciled: Neil Stonechild, Starlight Tours, and Racialized Policing in the Settler State," this chapter explored the ways in which racialized policing practices play out in a settler state with particular focus on the Starlight Tours, and the death of Neil Stonechild, as a practice of setter colonialism that must be reckoned with. The chapter also explored the ways in which his death will remain necessarily unreconciled. Neil Stonechild's death and the Starlight Tours are but one of many examples of the ongoing violence that surrounds settler colonialism. This chapter placed an emphasis on different perspectives and the need for broader concepts and contexts by which to understand the Starlight Tours. Chris argued that all issues can be traced back to the arrival and ongoing impact of settlers. And so here we can end with a provocation: the need for accomplices.

We will close by speaking directly to settlers. As stated earlier, settler colonialism is an active system and it is a structure. For structures to come down, they must be dismantled. Settlers continue to benefit from the violence and dispossession of settler colonialism. Whiteness follows and serves as the foundation of those benefits. As Jesse Wente notes,

> One of the reasons whiteness is so alluring, after all, is that built-in sense of entitlement. And why should that not be its default attitude? When you've murdered and stolen so that you can be centred in everything, you are going to feel authorized to watch the whole world revolve around you. And when your great grandchildren have never known anything but their comfortable place at the centre of things, they'll willingly overlook the oppression of others that is necessary to keep it.[50]

This chapter traced out a short overview of key contexts that serve as the background and allow for racialized policing practices, including Starlight Tours. There are many who have only known "their comfortable place at the centre of things" and were not aware of these acts of police violence in the settler state. Now you know—what are you willing to overlook moving forward? Indigenous Action argues that accomplices "aren't afraid to engage in uncomfortable/unsettling/challenging debates or discussions."[51] Chris tested Michelle's literacy about context and her capacity to see herself within the framework of settler colonialism and as someone who occupies a space of white privilege. We must be willing to explore these issues, recognize our location and privilege, and find a path forward lest we continue on this same path of violence and dispossession.

## Notes

1 Nelson, *Reckoning.*
2 *Merriam-Webster*, s.v. "reconcile (v)."
3 Stewart, "Remembering Neil Stonechild."
4 Armstrong, "'Starlight Tour.'"
5 Comack, *Racialized Policing.*
6 Stelkia, "Police Brutality in Canada."
7 Wolfe, "Settler Colonialism."
8 Razack, "Settler Colonialism, Policing."
9 The information in this paragraph and the closing quotation are from Nestor, "Sitting Bull."
10 Wente, *Unreconciled.*
11 Wente, *Unreconciled.*
12 Austen, "How Thousands of Indigenous Children Vanished."
13 As cited in Tracey, Kellogg, Sanchez, and Keenan, eds., "Addressing Historical, Intergenerational, and Chronic Trauma," 37.
14 Hanson, "Sixties Scoop."
15 Stewart, "Remembering Neil Stonechild."
16 For further details, consider reading Hausch, "Canada's Best-Kept Secret."
17 Pearlstein, "Indian Deaths Compound Troubles."
18 Pearlstein, "Indian Deaths Compound Troubles."
19 Cecco, "Left to Freeze."
20 Legal Aid Saskatchewan, "Freezing Deaths."
21 Wright, "Report of the Commission."
22 CBC News, "Who Was Neil Stonechild?"
23 Wright, "Report of the Commission."
24 Wright, "Report of the Commission."
25 Wright, "Report of the Commission," 9.
26 James, "Grief, Memories."
27 CBC News, "Fired Police Officers."
28 Razack, "'It Happened More Than Once.'"
29 Windspeaker Staff, "Saskatoon Police Chief Admits."
30 MtPleasant, "Ernie Louttit."
31 Pearlstein, "Indian Deaths Compound Troubles."
32 Knox and Smith, "Police Did Nothing."

33 Silva, "Chief on Facebook Allegations."
34 CTV Saskatoon, "Police Accused of Deleting."
35 Razack, *Dying from Improvement.*
36 Wente, *Unreconciled.*
37 "Report of the Royal Commission on Aboriginal Peoples."
38 Trudeau, "Statement by the Prime Minister."
39 Troian, "20 Years Since Royal Commission."
40 Trudeau, "Statement by the Prime Minister."
41 Stanton, "Canada's Truth and Reconciliation Commission."
42 Government of Canada, "Truth and Reconciliation Commission of Canada."
43 Government of Canada, "Truth and Reconciliation Commission of Canada."
44 Monkman, "5 Years After Report."
45 Jewell and Mosby, "Calls to Action Accountability."
46 Government of Canada, "Backgrounder—National Inquiry."
47 National Inquiry into Missing and Murdered Indigenous Women and Girls [NIMMWG], "Reclaiming Power and Place."
48 NIMMWG, "Reclaiming Power and Place."
49 CBC News, "A Report Card."
50 Wente, *Unreconciled.*
51 Rudy, "Accomplices Not Allies."

## Sources

Armstrong, Lyndsay. "'Starlight Tour': Mi'kmaq Fisher Allegedly Dumped Without Boots or Phone Feared Death." *City News*, last updated April 23, 2024. https://halifax.citynews.ca/2024/04/03/starlight-tour-mikmaq-fisher-allegedly-dumped-without-boots-or-phone-feared-death/.

Austen, Ian. "How Thousands of Indigenous Children Vanished in Canada." *New York Times*, March 28, 2021. https://www.nytimes.com/2021/06/07/world/canada/mass-graves-residential-schools.html.

CBC News. "Fired Police Officers Challenge Stonechild Findings." Last updated September 24, 2007. https://www.cbc.ca/news/canada/saskatchewan/fired-police-officers-challenge-stonechild-findings-1.649376.

CBC News. "A Report Card on the MMIWG Inquiry's Calls for Justice." June 5, 2023. https://www.cbc.ca/newsinteractives/features/cfj-report-cards.

CBC News. "Who Was Neil Stonechild?" November 3, 2005. https://www.cbc.ca/news2/background/stonechild/.

Cecco, Leyland. "Left to Freeze by Canada Police, Darrell Night Exposed Their Deadly 'Starlight Tours.'" *Guardian*, April 25, 2023. https://www.theguardian.com/world/2023/apr/25/darrell-night-who-exposed-canada-police-freezing-deaths-scandal-dies-at-56.

Comack, Elizabeth. *Racialized Policing: Aboriginal People's Encounters with the Police*. Fernwood Publishing, 2012.

CTV Saskatoon. "Police Accused of Deleting 'Starlight Tours' Section from Wikipedia Page." *CTV News*, March 31, 2016. https://saskatoon.ctvnews.

ca/police-accused-of-deleting-starlight-tours-section-from-wikipedia-page-1.2840924.

Government of Canada. "Backgrounder—National Inquiry into Missing and Murdered Indigenous Women and Girls." November 26, 2020. https://www.canada.ca/en/women-gender-equality/news/2019/06/backgrounder-national-inquiry-into-missing-and-murdered-indigenous-women-and-girls.html.

Government of Canada. "Truth and Reconciliation Commission of Canada." September 29, 2022. https://rcaanc-cirnac.gc.ca/eng/1450124405592/1529106060525.

Hanson, Erin. "Sixties Scoop." Indigenous Foundations, accessed July 31, 2023. https://indigenousfoundations.arts.ubc.ca/sixties_scoop/.

Hausch, Madalynn. "Canada's Best-Kept Secret: Starlight Tours." *Spheres of Influence*, June 2, 2023. https://spheresofinfluence.ca/canadas-best-kept-secret-starlight-tours/.

James, Thia. "Grief, Memories, and a Starting Point: 30th Anniversary of Neil Stonechild's Death." *Saskatoon StarPhoenix*, November 25, 2020, https://thestarphoenix.com/news/local-news/30th-anniversary-of-neil-stonechilds-death.

Jewell, Eva, and Ian Mosby. "Calls to Action Accountability: A 2020 Status Update on Reconciliation Executive Summary." Yellowhead Institute, December 17, 2020. https://yellowheadinstitute.org/2020/12/17/calls-to-action-accountability-a-2020-status-update-on-reconciliation/.

Knox, Shawn, and Kim Smith. "Police Did Nothing Wrong in Arrest of Brooke Watson; Public Complaints Commission." *Global News*, May 14, 2015. https://globalnews.ca/news/1998455/police-did-nothing-wrong-in-arrest-of-brooke-watson-public-complaints-commission/.

Legal Aid Saskatchewan. "Freezing Deaths: The Starlight Tours." Gladue Rights Research Database, accessed July 31, 2023. https://gladue.usask.ca/node/2860.

*Merriam-Webster*. s.v. "reconcile (v)." Accessed July 31, 2023. https://www.merriam-webster.com/dictionary/reconcile#.

Monkman, Lenard. "5 Years After Report, Truth and Reconciliation Commissioners Say Progress Is 'Moving Too Slow.'" CBC News, December 15, 2020. https://www.cbc.ca/news/indigenous/trc-5-years-final-report-1.5841428.

MtPleasant, Jen. "Ernie Louttit and the Investigation into 'Starlight Tours.'" *Two Row Times*, January 29, 2014. https://tworowtimes.com/news/national/ernie-louttit-and-the-investigation-into-starlight-tours/.

National Inquiry into Missing and Murdered Indigenous Women and Girls. *Reclaiming Power and Place: The Final Report of the National Inquiry on Missing and Murdered Indigenous Women and Girls*. Volume 1a. National Inquiry on Missing and Murdered Indigenous Women and Girls, 2019. https://www.mmiwg-ffada.ca/final-report/.

Nelson, Diane M. *Reckoning: The Ends of War in Guatemala*. Duke University Press, 2009.

Nestor, Rob. "Sitting Bull (1836–90)." Indigenous Saskatchewan Encyclopedia, University of Saskatchewan, accessed July 31, 2023. https://teaching.usask.ca/indigenoussk/import/sitting_bull_1836-90.php#.

Pearlstein, Steven. "Indian Deaths Compound Troubles in a Canadian Prairie City." *Washington Post*, February 27, 2000. https://www.washingtonpost.com/archive/politics/2000/02/28/indian-deaths-compound-troubles-in-a-canadian-prairie-city/17b52b30-d637-47ae-b1fb-5a43e90b1aef/.

Razack, Sherene. *Dying from Improvement: Inquests and Inquiries into Indigenous Deaths in Custody*. University of Toronto Press, 2015.

Razack, Sherene. "'It Happened More Than Once': Freezing Deaths in Saskatchewan." *Canadian Journal of Women and the Law* 26, no. 1 (2014): 51–80. https://doi.org/10.3138/cjwl.26.1.51.

Razack, Sherene. "Settler Colonialism, Policing and Racial Terror: The Police Shooting of Loreal Tsingine." *Feminist Legal Studies* 28, no. 1 (2020): 1–20.

"Report of the Royal Commission on Aboriginal Peoples." Library and Archives Canada, accessed July 31, 2023. https://www.bac-lac.gc.ca/eng/discover/aboriginal-heritage/royal-commission-aboriginal-peoples/Pages/final-report.aspx.

Rudy. "Accomplices Not Allies: Abolishing the Ally Industrial Complex." Indigenous Action, May 4, 2014. https://www.indigenousaction.org/accomplices-not-allies-abolishing-the-ally-industrial-complex/.

Silva, Steve. "Chief on Facebook Allegations: GPS Proves Police Stayed Within City." *Global News*, January 6, 2015. https://globalnews.ca/news/1758628/chief-on-facebook-allegations-gps-proves-police-stayed-within-city/.

Stanton, Kim. "Canada's Truth and Reconciliation Commission: Settling the Past?" *International Indigenous Policy Journal* 2, no. 3 (2011). https://doi.org/10.18584/iipj.2011.2.3.2.

Stelkia, Krista. "Police Brutality in Canada: A Symptom of Structural Racism and Colonial Violence." Yellowhead Institute, July 15, 2020. https://yellowheadinstitute.org/2020/07/15/police-brutality-in-canada-a-symptom-of-structural-racism-and-colonial-violence/.

Stewart, Michelle. "Remembering Neil Stonechild and Exposing Systemic Racism in Policing." *Conversation*, December 5, 2019. https://theconversation.com/remembering-neil-stonechild-and-exposing-systemic-racism-in-policing-128436.

Stewart, Michelle. "The Space Between the Steps: Reckoning in an Era of Reconciliation." *Contemporary Justice Review* 14, no. 1 (2011): 43–63.

Tracey, Sarah M., Erin Kellogg, Clarissa E. Sanchez, and Wendy Keenan, eds. "Addressing Historical, Intergenerational, and Chronic Trauma: Impacts on Children, Families, and Communities." In *Achieving Behavioral Health Equity for Children, Families, and Communities: Proceedings of a Workshop*. National Academies Press, 2019. https://www.ncbi.nlm.nih.gov/books/NBK540764/#.

Troian, Martha. "20 Years Since Royal Commission on Aboriginal Peoples, Still Waiting for Change." CBC News, March 3, 2016. https://www.cbc.ca/news/indigenous/20-year-anniversary-of-rcap-report-1.3469759.

Trudeau, Justin. "Statement by the Prime Minister on the 25th Anniversary of the Final Report of the Royal Commission on Aboriginal Peoples." Prime Minister of Canada, November 21, 2021. https://www.pm.gc.ca/en/news/statements/2021/11/21/statement-prime-minister-25th-anniversary-final-report-royal-commission#.

Wente, Jesse. *Unreconciled: Family, Truth, and Indigenous Resistance*. Penguin, 2021.

Windspeaker Staff. "Saskatoon Police Chief Admits Starlight Cruises Are Not New." *Windspeaker Publication* 21, no. 4 (2003). https://www.ammsa.com/publications/windspeaker/saskatoon-police-chief-admits-starlight-cruises-are-not-new.

Wolfe, Patrick. "Settler Colonialism and the Elimination of the Native." *Journal of Genocide Research* 8, no. 4 (2006): 387–409. https://doi.org/10.1080/14623520601056240.

Wright, David. "Report of the Commission of Inquiry into Matters Relating to the Death of Neil Stonechild." 2004. https://acrobat.adobe.com/link/review?uri=urn:aaid:scds:US:689381b9-c67e-3b8d-a55c-bb2379dbf0c9.

# Claiming the Lives and Stories of My People[1]

## *Displacement, Settlement, and Identity*

Fazeela Jiwa

### Thinking About Displacement and Movement

SOME DAYS I LOOK AROUND LONELY, MY MEMORY A SHALLOW well. This alienation I pin partly on colonial machinations that have twice displaced my ancestors over the last four generations. I cherish Mama's stories, but who were the ones before? Because of these displacements—their quick succession and mortality's innate brevity—the lives and stories of my people are wholly obscured to me.

I often wonder about those ancestors, the ones compelled to leave their homes to settle someone else's. It wasn't that long ago; probably around 1920. When my rickety house was being built in Kjipuktuk (colonially known as Halifax, Nova Scotia), my kin could have been leaving India for Uganda or Tanzania or Kenya. After the abolition of slavery, in the early 1900s the British faced a labour shortage in their colonies and embarked on the project of indentureship, discussed by others in this volume. I don't know if my people were indentured, but I know the Brits moved Indians they had already colonized to East Africa as settlers: railroad workers, labourers in resource-extraction projects, language and religion teachers, and a Brown managerial class installed as a buffer between Black and white. I have heard some vague passed-down stories about long-lost relatives leaving India with nothing, on a ship to who-knows-where.

The stories from Uganda are clearer because my living relatives were children then; those stories feature giant coffee bushes on dusty plantations. Then, in the 1970s my relatives came to Canada as refugees—during the Black nationalist independence movements in Africa, Uganda's Idi Amin and others understood them to be part of the British colonial apparatus. We don't fall on a clean or clear "side" of colonizer or colonized: we were displaced from India, settlers in East Africa, refugees from Uganda, and settlers in Canada. That's a complicated lineage.

I have no available grounding story older than the one of movement. Yet, living in the era of state-sponsored, essentializing multiculturalism, I am variously asked to explain my identity. Cue eye-roll.

Kim TallBear (Sisseton-Wahpeton Oyate) has said when she uses the word "identity" she puts it in scare quotes because it "is a poor substitute for relations": "It leans toward the individual and choice more than the collective, and it implies a property interest in said identity rather than necessarily requiring relations to exist."[2] This moves me to think about my own ancestry; I am hardly ever asked to explain my relations. Maybe a good thing? The identity question has always been hard to answer, but the relations one even harder.

I thought the other day, maybe displacement is my identity. It's what I think of first, estranged from the other common aspects of "culture." I don't really have language, as the Gujarati we speak at home has been broken and poetically mended with Swahili and English. My digestion can't handle the traditional foods Mama cooks; each sushi roll I bring home earns me a swat. I'm estranged from religion, so I have no occasion for the music, dance, and clothing so inextricably linked with it. The elders hold on longer to the bits they have so painstakingly gathered even while moving with nothing, the young'uns try to straddle what they've left and where they're going, and everyone who's here deals with some sort of estrangement from all the locations that have marked their bones.

Aside from these bits, I have no other hints about my ancestors who lived in India. Colonization erases collective memory; its project is to disrupt lineages, and sometimes I feel like it has succeeded in my family. And yet my melanated skin certainly feels the absence of the abundant sun my ancestors could claim; I often wonder if this absence is related to my multiple sclerosis, a disease for which vitamin D deficiency is mysteriously a major factor. Displacement—what I am missing and what I don't know I am missing—is built into my system.

Are my ancestors built in, too?

Their story—and my identity—is importantly not only one of displacement. It is also one of settlement. Both of these processes connect me to my kin. For this story, displacement and settlement need to be considered together.

## Settlement and Displacement

"Displacement" feels easier to claim than settlement because the colonizers are to blame for the movement of people that bereft us of our lands and cultures. It's an ongoing global atrocity that so many people are prey to border imperialism, a term organizer Harsha Walia defines as "the processes 'by which the violences and precarities of displacement and migration are structurally created as well as maintained,' including through imperial subjugation, criminalization of migration, racialized hierarchy of citizenship, and state-mediated exploitation of labour."[3] That kind of structured, global, forced displacement seems to leave little room for agency, which I understand as exercising power through choice. But that power is crucial to look for, especially when the available choices don't seem in any way related to freedom, because it humanizes those vast numbers of the dispossessed. They are not rendered powerless even while they are exploited; agency has always been practised by the oppressed, even up against the wall. It can be as monumental as running away; it can be as everyday as not speaking. It all matters, because agency is an exercise of inherent power. So, I am sure my ancestors practised agency in the process of displacement even under constrained choices.

However, there seems to be more agency connoted through "settlement" with its implication of an ongoing, purposeful violence.

Forced migration complicates the term "settler" for many folks because it can eschew the important nuances of how people got t/here. I can easily imagine the defensive bristle of my living kin if they were to read this—what agency would they readily claim in the process of their displacement from East Africa? That bristling is self-protection, understandable when there is so much hurt and loss in the recent past. Movement often continues, and is continuous, for so many migrants. But it's worth thinking through how to encompass the nuances of movement in words; for example, Métis scholar Chelsea Vowel uses "non-Black people of colour" because "non-European migrants do not have the power to bring with them their laws and customs, which they then apply to the rest of the peoples living in Canada."[4] She uses "settler" as shorthand for "settler colonials," while acknowledging Black descendants of kidnapped and enslaved Africans fall outside of this categorization. Similarly, Unangax̂ scholar Eve Tuck uses "immigrant" because only settlers can "implement their own laws and understandings of the world onto stolen land."[5] Métis scholar Emma LaRocque uses this language in a very different way: "Native peoples were the original settlers, in the sense of being a deeply rooted and settled Indigenous presence on this land we now call Canada" and as such, she refers to everyone else as "immigrant 're-settlers.'"[6] A Palestinian friend told me when she identified as a settler in Cree-Métis law professor Tracey Lindberg's class, she was asked to consider the language of "treaty beneficiary" to describe herself because Palestine is also currently under settler occupation.

What does that mean for those of us with no available grounding story other than the one of movement?

To hold the intricacies of displacement and settlement together, perhaps the right term for us would be "non-Black im/migrant-settlers." The migrant pays tribute to the centrality of movement. And I'll still keep *settler* centrally in there because Cherokee political scientist Daniel Heath Justice's discussion of why he uses the term "settler," despite its numerous complications, is compelling: "regardless of reason" or legitimate alliances and relationships built over time, groups of settlers "very often displaced Indigenous peoples and, in many cases, laid claim to the land and took its resources for their own."[7]

So, I understand *settler* as descriptive of where we collectively are now, regardless of how we came or where we will go. For my family, I think that applies to both Uganda and Canada. Simply by living t/here, my family and I participate in settler colonial systems even if they do not serve us, even if they oppress us, and even as we work in various ways to dismantle them and rebuild alongside Indigenous Peoples.

## Complicity

I'm careful of claiming displacement as the sole identity, because I don't want it to support a move to innocence[8]—alleviating my own sense of complicity in settler colonialism does nothing to meaningfully mitigate ongoing harm to Indigenous communities. I am descended from victims of colonial processes with which we are also complicit, which continue to oppress us in various ways, and from which we continue to benefit on stolen lands. After a thoughtful engagement with the terminology of settler, social work professor Elizabeth Carlson-Manathara and Muskego Inniniw scholar Gladys Rowe observe that "it is true that we exist in multiple matrices of privilege and oppression. It is also true that being oppressed in one area does not necessarily exempt one from experiencing colonial privilege and benefiting from Indigenous dispossession."[9] I think this is doubly applicable for my lineage, displaced twice but also participating in the same British imperial project in Africa and Turtle Island. Their movement was not their fault and probably would not have been their choice given other options, but when displacement is connected so intimately with settlement for us, it gets complicated.

My position as a refugee settler's child is fraught. How can I work against a sense of entitlement to someone else's lands and cultures just because I can't know mine? After all, I have lost them due to the same processes that brought me here.

My people came from Gujarat, I think, the Indian state infamous for anti-Muslim violence. What was it like to be there then? The British colonizers strategically deployed divide-and-rule tactics, and this is how I understand their moving my kin from already-occupied Gujarat to East Africa, which they were newly attempting to colonize. My ancestors were moved in as scaffolding to the racial structure of imperialism and capitalism. When I say racial capitalism, I'm referring to the thinking of Black Marxists like C.L.R James, Eric Williams, and Cedric J. Robinson, who documented the exploitation and colonization of racialized people as the foundation of industrial capitalism. Robinson makes a point that's directly pertinent to our displacement from India: "British imperialism required the organization of colonial subjects for their own subjugation and that of others."[10] Scaffolding, then—we helped prop up the tenuous project of British imperialism. This is how tension between Browns and Blacks was purposefully sown. And even years later, anti-Black racism is rampant in South Asian diasporic communities, especially those once installed on African or Caribbean lands.

## Racial Capitalism and Kin

What were the conditions of colonial rule under which my kin lived in India? Were any of them happy to move, was movement liberating? Did they believe they were better than those only just browner than we are in East Africa, informed by possibly pre-existing hierarchies of caste and shadeism? Did they believe the lies about the "Red Indian" being uncivilized, so Turtle Island was indeed terra nullius for the Europeans? Were there stories of when the same colonizers came to their own land in India? Did they resent the whites? Did they want to be white?

This last question is one I have struggled with in my own lifetime. Shadeism is a raging issue that blends patriarchy, colonialism, and poverty around the world and most certainly in India, but in Canada it lands a bit differently because of official multiculturalism. Wanting to be white, or at least emphasizing being less Brown, is a condition through which South Asians become a "model minority" under multicultural policy in Canada, which is to me at once completely understandable and palpably scab behaviour. Their working hard to survive and succeed in racial capitalism is both the reason for my existence and, at the same time, can work to thwart solidarity among non-whites. It's a well-understood joke these days how postcolonial or immigrant parents wanted us to be lawyers and not artists, but it's not really funny; it demonstrates in a nutshell how colonially informed ideologies of "progress" and "civilization" have been deeply ingrained over generations as the only way to succeed. Sometimes it feels like my ancestors have been pawns co-opted into the occupier's project, historic and contemporary, imperialism outright or the same in the form of official multiculturalism. One requires a managerial class; the other, a model minority. Indian historian Vijay Prashad has questioned this complicity in *Karma of Brown Folk* when, in response to W.E.B Du Bois's question "how does it feel to be a problem?" he asks Asians "how does it feel to be the solution?" in the context of being used as a "weapon" against Black liberation struggles in the United States.[11]

But Prashad's book also spends much time celebrating Black and Asian alliances throughout history. I know from the few stories available to me that some Indians resisted colonial oppression alongside their Black neighbours in Uganda, as some South Asians have resisted alongside Indigenous Peoples on Turtle Island. And while often mired in precarious low-wage labour under racial capitalism, migrants and refugees globally are some of the most prominent voices calling out the overlapping injustices of border imperialism while seeking emancipation from these oppressive structures. I might also choose to draw kinship from these tangible histories of deep solidarity between racialized peoples.

When these multiplicities fill my brain, and with obscured access to embodied answers, I get stuck on the central, troubling question: Were my ancestors complicit with settler colonialism, or did they resist and practise solidarity?

An awareness of complicity can be a generative condition if one can move past the paralyzing performance of it, often expressed as guilt. An old mentor once told me, "guilt is not a feeling; it is a judgment," and I often return to this observation. While guilt as a feeling reveals no path forward, guilt as a judgment is something I can work with. It's useful in determining my position and my next actions. In this way, as poet and scholar Smaro Kamboureli theorizes, "Identifying complicity is not about moralizing, but about the possibility of creating productive sites."[12] What can I *do* with all of these considerations? Here in Mi'kma'ki, I'm far away from my living kin. Complicity with the colonial condition looks different here than it does where they live now, on Coast Salish land; or where we were brought to, on African land; or where we came from, which is complex in its own myriad ways. There's complicity in all of these conditions because colonialism and racial capitalism has structured everything about how we live for at least five hundred years—even something as simple as feeding myself is caught up in this web of oppression. I'm not sure that my awareness of this makes me any less complicit than my kin, even if I support the Grassroots Grandmothers defending the Sipekne'katik River[13] while my relatives buy investment property.

Feminist philosopher Alexis Shotwell talks about the importance of "claiming bad kin" as a way of owning the uncomfortable but generative space of complicity. She asks, "What could it mean for those who benefit from oppression—white people, and settlers more generally—to claim kin with oppressors? If we are complicit in the pain of this suffering world, how might we take responsibility for our bad kin?"[14] While she speaks specifically to white people as beneficiaries of white supremacy and colonial displacement, her question moves me to think about the nuances of who benefits and supports this structure. I don't know if my ancestors or my living kin are "bad," but I do know that racial capitalism and settler colonialism draw every kind of person into their net, and some of us fall for its false promises of comfort at the expense of a multitude of other beings and, in the end, our own collective survival.

I have to remind myself constantly and against my Eurocentric training: while binaries may initially be a useful way to trace the contours of a complex thought, they are a very limited way of understanding the depth of the problem. So, the most useful way to answer that central troubling question is with a "both-and"—my ancestors were likely *both* desperate due to colonial conditions *and* complicit within colonial conditions. While desperation breeds complicity sometimes, perhaps desperation breeds resistance too.

## The Problems and Opportunities of Not Knowing

While ruminating on the connections between displacement and settlement and incessantly repeating so many tender, unanswerable questions, I have begun experimenting with a thought that feels okay: maybe I don't really need to know the answers to these questions to know what to do now.

In not knowing, I can own complicity in the "bad" and solidarity with the resistance that must make up the "good." I can focus on white supremacy as the central problem, rather than judging with incomplete information the limited choices dispossessed people of colour might make.

Maybe it's enough to just ask those questions about my ancestors, not necessarily seeking the answers, because asking those questions creates the condition for being a non-Black im/migrant-settler here on Turtle Island, both complicit and resistant. Yet again, at least a second time, living on someone else's land, again conscripted into racial capitalism, and probably again trying to find a way out of it through relationship. Relating—that's central to how complicity can be generative; it can inform my responsibilities in many different kinds of relationships. It stays as a principle even with the possibility of further movement.

Not knowing but claiming in my kin the probability of shitheads *and* revolutionaries, and probably everything in between, is a condition from which I can seek answers to a more present question—not what is my heritage, or what is my identity, but how am I relating, now? To this land I find myself on, these peoples, and the descendants of all those who were and continue to be dispossessed, displaced, stolen, and settled here through imperial movements. To my child, my future ancestors. To our future movements.

## Notes

1 A version of this chapter was previously published as "On Shitheads and Revolutionaries" in *Atlantis: Critical Studies in Gender, Culture, and Social Justice*, Volume 46 (2025).

2 Tallbear. "We Are Not Your Dead Ancestors."
3 Walia, *Border and Rule*, 2.
4 Vowel, *Indigenous Writes*, 16–17.
5 Tuck, "Settler Colonialism, an Overview."
6 LaRocque, *When the Other Is Me*, 7.
7 Justice, *Why Indigenous Literatures Matter*, 11.
8 Tuck and Yang, "Decolonization Is Not."
9 Carlson-Manathara with Rowe, *Living in Indigenous Sovereignty*, 36.
10 Robinson, *On Racial Capitalism*, 30.
11 Prashad, *Karma of Brown Folk*.
12 Kamboureli, "The Politics of the Beyond," 31–48.
13 Waldron, *There's Something in the Water*.
14 Shotwell, "Claiming Bad Kin."

## Sources


Carlson-Manathara, Elizabeth, with Gladys Rowe. *Living in Indigenous Sovereignty*. Fernwood Publishing, 2021.

Justice, Daniel Heath. *Why Indigenous Literatures Matter*. Wilfrid Laurier University Press, 2018.

Kamboureli, Smaro. "The Politics of the Beyond: 43 Theses on Autoethnography and Complicity." In *Asian Canadian Writing Beyond Autoethnography*, edited by Eleanor Ty and Christl Verduyn. Wilfrid Laurier University Press, 2008.

LaRocque, Emma. *When the Other Is Me: Native Resistance Discourse, 1850–1990*. University of Manitoba Press, 2010.

Prashad, Vijay. *Karma of Brown Folk*. University of Minnesota Press, 2001.

Robinson, Cedric J. *On Racial Capitalism, Black Internationalism, and Cultures of Resistance*. Edited by H.L.T. Quan. Pluto Press, 2019.

Shotwell, Alexis. "Claiming Bad Kin: Solidarity from Complicit Locations." *Bearing: The Society for the Diffusion of Useful Knowledge* 3 (2019): 8–11.

TallBear, Kim. "We Are Not Your Dead Ancestors: Playing Indian and White Possession." *Unsettle* (Substack) , June 14, 2021. https://kimtallbear.substack.com/p/we-are-not-your-dead-ancestors.

Tuck, Eve. "Settler Colonialism, an Overview." Prezi slideshow, last updated April 12, 2013. https://prezi.com/_3ldicckpppa/settler-colonialism-an-overview/?frame=51264d85536db62df9f694935f7ee75e8d99a8ed.

Tuck, Eve, and K. Wayne Yang. "Decolonization Is Not a Metaphor." *Decolonization: Indigeneity, Education & Society* 1, no. 1 (2012): 1–40.

Vowel, Chelsea. *Indigenous Writes: A Guide to First Nations, Métis & Inuit Issues in Canada*. Highwater Press, 2016.

Waldron, Ingrid R.G. *There's Something in the Water: Environmental Racism in Indigenous and Black Communities*. Fernwood Publishing, 2018.

Walia, Harsha. *Border and Rule: Global Migration, Capitalism, and the Rise of Racist Nationalism*. Fernwood Publishing, 2021.

# Relying Upon the Colonial Project

## *Francophone Communities in Minority Settings Within the Bilingual Settler Colonial State*

Jérôme Melançon

IN THIS CHAPTER, I TRY TO TELL A STORY, DRAWING ON MY memory. This is a story told to French speakers in Canada. It is shared in schools, in the media, in songs, through countless historical novels, in popular accounts of history, in political speeches, and in much of the academic record. I will share a specific variant of this story as it is told on the Prairies: Alberta, Saskatchewan, and Manitoba. This is not my story, nor is it the story we ought to be telling. It is a story that glorifies and justifies settler colonialism.

After telling the story, I will turn to the lessons it carries and the functions it fulfills, focusing on the deformations in history that make it possible to turn the idea of "francisation" into a positive, praiseworthy endeavour. I then turn to undermine the story's foundations, creating a roadmap for a conceptual analysis of the settler colonialism at play in francophone spaces in Canada. On this basis, I then offer a new story, the story I believe we need to tell if we are to work towards anything like (re)conciliation or, better yet, decolonization, engaging in what Paulette Regan calls "restorying,"[1] to move away from myths to listen and learn from the older stories that these myths were created to replace. Stories, and histories, are not neutral: they are not told for their own sake—but to serve the communities who tell them.

The analytical elements I share in the last section are meant to situate French speakers and Indigenous Peoples in each other's histories and to allow our gaze to turn to the systems that continued to keep them in a colonial relation that remained similar to what had been put in place in New France. They also put forward the idea that the Catholic Church did not merely allow for the survival of a French-Canadian nation within Canada but, in fact, allowed French Canadians to benefit from and participate in settler colonialism.

In doing this work, I focus on a central political problem at the heart of claims concerning the old story of the French presence in North America, that is, these claims attenuate or obfuscate the participation of French speakers in colonialism. Here we must be careful to lay neither collective guilt nor collective innocence on francophones, but to carefully analyze their active and ongoing participation in colonialism. I will also focus on francophone communities in minority settings in the Prairies: these are communities that were established in the first moments of colonization and who are now supported through the *Official Languages Act*, which provides funding for French and English as official languages and to French- and English-language communities in minority settings, to ensure the capacity for these communities to maintain their presence and their vitality.

## L'histoire qu'on nous raconte: The Story That Is Told to Us

New France was a great endeavour that stretched from Acadie, in what is now Nova Scotia, along the Mississippi down to Louisiana and the Gulf of Mexico, and as far as the Red River in what is now Manitoba. The territorial divisions within New France and the different political histories that followed meant that Acadians would never see themselves as French Canadians. The governments of New France did the best they could with the limited resources France committed to its colonies. It was chiefly an extraction economy, with the fur trade weighing heavily on social and political decisions. The Catholic Church functioned as the main institution, providing basic education and health care through its religious orders. The government played a major role in "pacifying" the First Nations that continue to be depicted as inclined towards war, for instance, in the Great Peace of Montreal treaty signed in 1701.

Permanent settlement was not the main goal in New France, although adventurers came in large enough numbers to begin a new life. Many were drawn to Indigenous communities, and some even joined them. The Church wanted to create the kind of gender balance that would allow French Catholic society to retain French men and attract Indigenous Peoples, so they convinced the King to bring women to New France. They are the "Filles du Roy": about eight hundred unmarried and widowed women who arrived between 1663 and 1673, many orphans from French-speaking urban areas in France. Many French-Canadian families can be traced back to these first families. Many other families, it is said, were founded through marriages between French men and Indigenous women. As a result, it is claimed that most descendants of early French settlers (that is, white Quebecers) have Indigenous blood or are Indigenous.[2]

Beginning in the early seventeenth century, missionaries, chiefly Jesuits but also Récollets and Capuchins (both Franciscan) and Sulpicians, created missions and schools and set out to "save souls" and teach the rudiments of reading and writing. Like the oblates after them, they often preached in Indigenous languages. These missions, which expanded to the Great Lakes region, were hubs for the fur trade, where the voyageurs and the coureurs des bois gathered during and between trips. In the north-western Prairies, explorers like La Vérendrye and his sons established contacts with Indigenous nations and created forts that would later become trading posts and settlements.

Throughout this history, conflicts between France and England had echoes in their colonies. Each could count on their Indigenous allies, which often comprised a great part of their military forces. And so the growth of the French Empire was limited, and then stopped, by England's desire for conquest.

In 1713, Britain took control of the Acadian territory. In 1755, Acadians refused to pledge unconditional allegiance to the British Crown. In an attempt to gain control over the territory and prevent resistance, Britain broke up communities and families, burned down some churches, deported many Acadians to Louisiana (some would come back; others settled there and became Cajuns) and to other parts of the French world, and forced many others to move, notably to New Brunswick and Québec, as did my ancestors, the Melançons.

At the end of the Seven Years' War—no, wait, that was in 1763, and this war is known as the *Guerre de la conquête*. Before that, in 1759, France lost its colony at the Battle of the Plains of Abraham; Montreal capitulated the following year. The Treaty of Paris that ended the war followed France's decision to keep its colonies in the Caribbean rather than in New France. Britain followed up with the *Royal Proclamation of 1763*—a constitutional document imposed on the peoples who lived on the territories Britain had gained. In the present time, I am told other stories that focus on the significance of this proclamation to Indigenous Peoples, but this is not part of the earlier story I am recounting. In this story, the *Royal Proclamation* is fundamentally negative for French Canada. It means that the Church is no longer part of the government; British criminal and civil law are imposed; land to be farmed is given out according to a new system and given to as many British soldiers as possible; Catholics have to renounce their religion and pledge allegiance to the British monarchy to serve in the public service. With the *Quebec Act* in 1774 the anti-Catholic part of the Test Oath was removed.[3] This moment is known as "La Conquête": the Conquest. It is the reason why, even today, many non-Indigenous French speakers refer to themselves as having been colonized by Britain.

The French-speaking elite fled in great numbers; the Church began advocating a nativist social policy, encouraging French-speaking Catholics (who called themselves *Canadiens*) to have as many children as possible, what would become known later on as "the revenge of the cribs." The Church fostered a society that assembled around agriculture, faith, and language; created an elite that could administer the civil law that once again replaced British common law; and denounced profit and capitalism as foreign and sinful ideas. This society resisted attempts at assimilation, like those contained in the *Durham Report* (1837) and the subsequent *Act of Union* in 1840.

The forts and settlements of the Prairies remained, and the large contingent of voyageurs and coureurs des bois continued to serve the fur trade, now led by Britain. In what was then called Rupert's Land, the North West Company operated west of the Hudson's Bay Company and adopted French as a language of work. When the companies merged, the balance was affected, but bilingualism continued to prevail.

The Dominion of Canada was created in 1867; the federation almost immediately signed treaties with First Nations and purchased Rupert's Land from the Hudson's Bay Company. Settlement began beyond the Red River Colony, and the Catholic Church worked hard to attract French-speaking Catholics from the United States and Québec to the Prairies, as well as immigrants from France and Belgium. While the Church favoured centralized communities, the government spread out the French-speaking population as much as possible to increase the chances of assimilating them into British society. As conflicts with First Nations and Métis peoples took place, *it is told* that French Canadians remained neutral or helped the French-speaking Catholic Métis. The Church advocated for Métis rights, for instance, working with Louis Riel and then on his behalf to negotiate the creation of Manitoba. Teaching in French was forbidden, and children who spoke French in school were sometimes met with violence. Teachers resisted and secretly taught in French. As English-speaking British subjects in Canada started calling themselves Canadians, French speakers began calling themselves French Canadians, Canadiens français.[4]

In the early twentieth century, the Church created associations for the rights of Catholics, who were generally French-speaking; these associations are today the central organizations structuring francophones' cultural lives. These organizations lobbied for the rights of French speakers and for the extension of the *Official Languages Act* to protect not only the French language itself but also francophone communities in minority contexts. They also created a shift within communities, such that they defined themselves through their language first and foremost, as francophones, and often through their provincial belonging (fransaskois·es in Saskatchewan, Franco-Albertain·es in Alberta, for example).[5]

Through lobbying and resistance, French speakers in Canada, be they Canadiens, French Canadians, francophones, or Acadiens, have managed to survive and, in some cases, thrive. They have received the possibility of governing their own school divisions, which are distinct from the public and separate school boards and divisions and their immersion schools (and often remain unofficially Catholic). Today, francophones face a different kind of disappearance: while their numbers continue to grow, few French-speaking immigrants make their way to communities outside Québec. As a result, the demographic weight of minority francophone communities outside Québec is quickly shrinking.

## What the Story Is Meant to Teach

This story above is the one I have been told many times. Much of it erases what Indigenous Peoples did by themselves, what was done to them by settlers, and the history that is proper to each people and community. I share this story briefly to contribute to a three-way dialogue where understanding must come first. Without this old story, the new story I hope to offer would not make much sense. Instead, I'm concerned about what the story tells French speakers in Canada about themselves, how it informs their individual and collective behaviour, and how it has helped bring English speakers to either feel sympathy and solidarity for French speakers or to negotiate seriously around official languages.

This old story conveys a myth disguised as a lesson: France's colonialism was gentle and inclusive. It aimed at a mixing of European and Indigenous Peoples, a métissage, but without the pejorative meaning of being *métissé*, or "badly woven." The same relationship without borders or distinctions between French Canadians and Indigenous Peoples continued under British rule. This relationship continues today to be presented as one of cousins, of two colonized peoples having much in common with one another, a relationship marked by the generosity of French Canadians towards Indigenous Peoples.

The old story also serves many functions in support of settler colonialism, demonstrating a French-Canadian settler move to innocence.[6] As Tuck and Yang explain, "moves to innocence" are ways to fashion a settler identity and a social, economic, and political position that counteract feelings of guilt for the appropriation of land and for the living conditions of Indigenous Peoples, but also as ways to respond to criticisms and demands for decolonization. In short, moves to innocence are the denial of historical and current responsibility. Family, community, and national narratives play a central role in these moves to innocence by presenting French stories of exclusion and even domination as equivalent to those of Indigenous Peoples.[7] French-speaking and Indigenous Peoples are thus presented as occupying a similar position within the British colonial order.

Franco-Canadians cannot possibly oppress other peoples within the story I shared—of having been oppressed and still being oppressed through their own ongoing colonization. In fact, they present themselves either as having done the most for Indigenous Peoples (in the case of the province of Québec) or as offering an example to follow in cultural and political survival (in the case of other francophone communities). And, of course, both versions of this white saviour narrative present Indigenous Peoples as needing help.

In parallel to this idea of francisation, the old story is also a source of self-Indigenization. Darryl Leroux has explored in depth the strategies Franco-descendants employ to claim an Indigenous identity and thus claim Indigenous Rights (be it for hunting and fishing or for rights to consultation and even land claims). These strategies all work around genealogy and lineage and include the reference to a root ancestor in New France who was Indigenous; a woman ancestor who is made to be, but was not, Indigenous; and a lateral ancestry, using descent from a relative by marriage of an Indigenous person (for instance, a non-Indigenous cousin of Louis Riel).[8]

As Métis scholar Chelsea Vowel explains in her criticisms of the documentary *L'empreinte*, which openly argues for the Indigeneity of all Quebecers, these strategies are another move to innocence.[9] The film presents the argument that French-Canadian culture comes from the mixing of French and Indigenous cultures and develops a version of Québécois attitudes and values that it says are inherited from Indigenous nations. This intense métissage would result from cultural intermixing, as well as intermarriage. French Canadians would thus *be* Indigenous *and* be the heirs of Indigenous heritage. And the move to innocence has clear implications: after all, if French Canadians are Indigenous, then they cannot colonize Indigenous nations or be responsible for colonialism. Tuck and Yang also describe self-Indigenization as a settler move to innocence in that it continues settler privileges and access to land and property within the Canadian system. Indeed, it makes it easier to enjoy them without feeling any guilt—but it also allows those who self-Indigenize to place themselves in the position of the oppressed rather than the oppressors, making Indigenous Peoples disappear from the conversation.[10]

In addition to these settler moves to innocence, the old story is a continuation of the early colonial strategy employed by France, which it called *francisation*. That word is still used today to describe the work that is done in francophone school divisions to bring children's linguistic competence to the level that is necessary to attend class with other students—and to teach them about (white, Canadian) francophone culture. In New France, francisation was an attempt to make French culture and economic life, as well as Catholicism, attractive to Indigenous Peoples. This served several goals: ensure the stability of trade, allow for control over the territory and its resources through control of the people who knew them best and could lay claim to them, and cement the participation of the Catholic Church in the colonial venture so that it would continue to provide missionaries. From 1611 on to 1763, from the area surrounding Québec City to the areas west of the Great Lakes, missions provided fur trading corporations with posts along trade routes and the government with agents who could spread messages, propaganda, and relay information. Society in New France submitted to the king, as Bouveresse argues, and "thus the Church teaches respect for political authority and submission to the king."[11]

In parallel to the francisation of Indigenous Peoples, from the thirteenth century until at least 1769, the French monarchy slowly brought under its rule the territories that now constitute the European part of France. Each had its own history, sense of belonging, and language. In other words, part of the colonization of Turtle Island is linked with the establishment of French hegemony over the territory claimed by the French Crown in Europe, another kind of colonization. When New France officially passed to Great Britain in 1763, Lorraine and Corsica were still not part of France.[12] A few decades later, the French revolutionary government would tend to see regional languages such as Basque and Breton as counter-revolutionary and French, the language spoken around Paris and Orléans, the regions originally controlled by what would become the French monarchy, as an Enlightenment language more able to carry revolutionary ideas. Yet in many French departments (or provinces), only clerics were bilingual. As a result of the desire for linguistic unification, in year II of the French Revolution (1793–1794), education in local languages was forbidden. And indeed, even up to the twentieth century, standard French was not spoken in many regions of France.[13]

Francisation is a central component of the French, Canadien, French Canadian, and francophone strategy to make French-speaking communities more attractive, either so that more people join them or so that they can receive further support from various publics and orders of governments. It is part of the establishment of cultural and political hegemony—an imperial strategy.

Against the idea that France desired a mixed colony, Leroux cites historical documents to show the centrality of francisation to French colonization.[14] In fact, Leroux shows that the myth of Quebecers being mixed—this claim of métissage—goes back to New France and is based on an invention. Following a thread in the arguments presented by both Leroux and Ruggiu, what is generally called métissage or mixity in fact only refers to a racialist understanding of relations between European and Indigenous Peoples. Francisation was the central policy, ensuring that the women who would bear the children of French men would already be assimilated and converted (francisées) and so that the children of mixed couples would be raised in French culture and as Catholics. And as Ruggiu argues, France saw a continuity and a fluidity between the populations on its European and North American territories, without a strict distinction, until the eighteenth century when colonies began to be seen not as provinces but as simple economic outposts of France, which acted as a colonial metropole.[15] This shift appears to take place only around the end of the Seven Years' War (1756–1763).



## A Conceptual Roadmap for Analysis

While the story I told above, as it was told to me, tends to exculpate francophones from any of the wrongs of colonialism, it is no better to blame institutions as if they were external to francophone communities.

These two exculpations must be kept in mind since francophones tend to see the federal and provincial governments as external to them, as "the institutions of the majority," meaning the English-speaking majority. Further, during the period of state-building and nation-building, Quebecers built their provincial state in competition with the federal state.

In order to account for the participation of francophones in Canadian colonialism, I have proposed the concept of *contradictory colonial locations*.[16] I draw on the ideas of Erik Olin Wright, who put forward the concept of contradictory class locations, and of Frantz Fanon, who described how different classes are created within colonies in order for colonizers to maintain their control over the colonized. The idea I propose is relatively simple: there are people who are colonizers and there are others who are colonized. The former have all the power over the institutions that allow for the control of land and peoples, the latter have none. But such positions of extreme domination are rare. There are also those among them and between them who at once are controlled and control others, who benefit and also suffer from colonialism. As Fanon highlights, there are also those who, in spite of their relatively privileged location within colonialism, decide to join the colonized in their struggle against colonialism.[17] Culture and access to material resources are as important as the actions undertaken to defend and extend colonialism or limit and undermine it.

I am also proposing that we think not only about colonialism historically but also about ongoing colonization and racialization, as well as recolonization, as theorized and applied by Joyce Green and Himani Bannerji. This orientation notably begins with the ownership of the land by groups who define themselves through agriculture, as well as the ties that unite different parts of the francophone population, such that there are relations between the members of religious orders who managed residential schools and other colonial institutions and community members.[18]

There exists a long-lasting animosity between French and English peoples and their descendants. However, this animosity between white descendants of the French and British settlers in no way resembles the racism that targets Indigenous Peoples and other racialized groups. Finally, we must pay attention to the strategies employed by the federal and provincial governments to regain control where political compromise and legal decisions allow for decentralization or decolonization. And we must keep in mind that this recolonization also affects new immigrants, who come from countries that have been previously colonized and are dominated and exploited through neo-colonialism.

A last conceptual element has to do with *claims to settler priority*, a concept I will develop briefly here. An important function of the story told by and about French-speaking Canadians is to provide legitimacy for their claims to sovereignty and, where it cannot be achieved, for political autonomy. Together with moves to settler innocence, which provide social legitimacy, claims to settler priority provide legal and political legitimacy to the development of institutions proper to French speakers. Through these institutions, Québec competes for jurisdiction against the "rest of Canada" (which it presents as a bloc rather than including two orders of government), or competes for resources and relative autonomy on cultural and educational matters. By claiming that they were here first, prior to the establishment of English-speaking settlements, for instance, *and* by claiming kinship with Indigenous Peoples or Indigeneity, elements within French-speaking communities are presenting Canada as built on no one's land (terra nullius) and free for the taking. They, thus, establish their legitimacy through a version of the doctrine of discovery, having settled first or simultaneously and so having a claim on the land and corresponding rights. Thus francophone politics can oscillate between reliance upon the "two founding peoples" story and the prior settlement story.

## L'histoire qu'on doit raconter: The Story We Must Tell

So what would a history of French-speaking communities in Canada look like if it were based on these concepts of claims to settler priority, contradictory colonial locations, as well as settler moves to innocence? Here is the story I believe we must tell.

Having launched itself in a contest over the conquest of the extra-European world, France built an empire that included, at first, a mode of colonization focused on the exploitation of resources with a minimal physical presence. In what it called New France, the fur trade steered the development of the colony. Explorers like Samuel de Champlain and La Vérendrye were given a royal monopoly over the fur trade in the areas they claimed for France. France's empire grew as it claimed territories based on its relations with Indigenous nations. Explorers brought missionaries with them, especially as forts and trading posts were created, in order to offer some basic services and spiritual and ideological coherence to the European communities they created, but also to help create an allegiance to France through conversion to Catholicism and through francisation. Major settlements were created at first along the Saint Lawrence River, and a system of itinerant workers—that is, the officially employed voyageurs and the independent coureurs des bois—linked French settlements with Indigenous communities. These settlements were either not the subject of express agreements with the Indigenous Peoples on whose land they were created or would quickly expand beyond the limits that had been agreed upon.[19]

As the Chartered Companies, beginning with the Compagnie de la Nouvelle-France in 1627, were given a monopoly over trade, they were tasked with establishing settlers in order to establish the physical presence that would be the basis for French sovereignty. The seigneurie system rewarded military officers. Land was parcelled out, given. Overlaying the agricultural grid, parishes were created. Beyond these settled lands, missionaries were sent for evangelization but also to prepare the way for closer trade ties and for settlement. In the North West, missions would often be created within trading posts.[20]

This system was partly dismantled after the Seven Years' War. However, it continued to exist, especially as Britain looked to appease its new subjects. Britain found a somewhat unlikely ally in the Catholic Church. Since Britain (then the United Kingdom, then Canada) hoped to retain control over the territory outside the borders of the expanding United States, settlement seemed inevitable. The Church then held up the dream of a French-speaking Catholic continent that had been at the heart of New France. The creation of the North West Company in Montreal in 1779, which led to its reliance on French-Canadian itinerant workers, brought a French-speaking Catholic population to the Great Plains. While English was the language of administration, French was the language of work on its territory, even after the merger with the Hudson's Bay Company in 1821.[21]

Looking back to La Vérendrye and at the operation of the North-West Territories, French Canadians have been claiming their precedence over English speakers, claiming linguistic rights not only as a matter of constitutional agreement but as a matter of historical priority over the land. While this strategy ultimately failed, it shows how French speakers continue to seek legitimacy through their history of settlement. Outside of Québec, French speakers and Catholics are claiming rights not over a territory but rather within a territory on the basis of being the first settlers and of having put in place the first settler institutions.

After the creation of Canada, settlement began in the North-West Territories—that is, the Great Plains as divided by the Jay Treaty of 1794. Through the purchase of Rupert's Land and the signing of the Numbered Treaties, Canada established its presence through legal means—that is, by creating the laws and constitutional agreements that would retroactively justify its presence on the territory. Working within the framework provided by the Canadian government, the Catholic Church fought for resources to establish residential schools, evangelized within Indigenous communities, which it did not see as nations, and recruited French-speaking settlers from Québec, Acadie, and Ontario, as well as from the Northeastern states, where many French Canadians had migrated looking for work in industrial areas. Using its vast networks, it also sought out immigrants in France, Belgium, and Switzerland—and even in Ukraine.[22]

An order founded in 1816 first to evangelize the poor within France, and Indigenous nations beginning in 1841, the Missionary Oblates of Mary Immaculate played a central role in at least three aspects regarding French-Canadian colonization and establishment of a settler state. They encouraged French-Canadian immigration; they supported French-Canadian communities once they were established; they controlled Indigenous communities through residential schools. Sister orders, such as the Grey Nuns or the Sisters of Saint Joseph of Saint-Hyacinthe, were brought into the systems they created to teach and to provide health care—although we must question how much teaching and how much care was provided.[23] Through these networks of schools, hospitals, and community supports, the Catholic Church established a state within a state, which remained in place more or less until the 1960s, as it was absorbed into the provincial welfare state. This state within a state allowed the Church to lead its own colonial project, establishing a mostly French-Canadian elite to govern the lives of French Canadians. As André Lalonde writes, "Convinced that 'language is the guardian of the faith,' clerics in the west took for granted that they had the duty to dominate the political, economic, and social life of their French language flock in order to ensure their salvation."[24]

The idea that a consociational state developed in Canada with power-sharing and spheres of influence divided between French and English Canadians is not new.[25] In such a state, political elites overcome fragmentation due to differences in cultures and political goals through negotiation and compromise. While the democratic majority may not approve of the resulting agreements, these remain sufficient approval for local elites to secure the participation of the minority culture within the wider state by maintaining the trust of the local population in them, and thus a limited attachment to the common political structures. In other words, it allows for the goals of both sets of elites to converge. The relevance of this concept is greater when speaking of the extra-constitutional arrangements between the Canadian state and the Catholic Church west of Québec than when addressing the reality in the federated province.

It must also be seen as a *settler* consociational arrangement and project with its own set of policies and practices. Participation in the British and Canadian settler colonial project was not merely a survival strategy but a colonial strategy, putting in place the means to allow Catholic French Canadians to benefit from the settler state and gain a measure of power and autonomy within it through the creation of separate institutions within the larger system. This is even as they were generally limited in the positions they could usually reach in the economic and political spheres, as their religion was often targeted (notably as a result of a strong presence of the British Protestant Orange Order) and as provincial legislation made linguistic transmission difficult.

Similarly, today, the *Official Languages Act* and its provisions providing support to francophone communities in minority settings are the foundation for funding community organizations across the country. These organizations support cultural, artistic, and economic life; they provide news and entertainment media; they take part in newcomer settlement; they provide political representation and cohesion. They work with the francophone school boards that are an extension of the constitutional right for those who attended French schools to have their children be educated in French and with francophone post-secondary institutions that give them the possibility to continue their studies in French. They make it possible to live at least in part in French. While these organizations are legally not for profit, they often present themselves not only as lobby groups and cultural groups but as a set of political institutions. They are theorized under the concept of institutional completeness,[26] which is said ought to be the goal of francophone communities.

Anecdotally, through my interactions with francophone community associations in the Prairies, I can report that they generally see their part in reconciliation as sharing with Indigenous Peoples their knowledge and expertise, while presenting a model for linguistic growth and a measure of political autonomy. However, understanding that the arrangements that have led to the rights and privileges recognized and granted to francophones in Canada are *colonial* arrangements demonstrates that the francophone model cannot simply be transferred or applied to Indigenous Peoples.

## Conclusion

A better understanding of the contradictory location of francophones within the Canadian settler state can contribute to reimagining possible relationships between francophone and Indigenous communities renouncing settler moves to innocence and claims to settler priority. One such possibility consists in participating in the translation of oblates' archives to support Indigenous communities' efforts to discover their history and the stories of the children who died and went missing in the residential schools that helped clear the land for French-speaking communities.

Another possibility begins with restorying the relationship between French-Canadian and Métis communities to foreground the stories told by Métis. This restorying should abandon the narratives created by a French-Canadian clergy who attempted to establish its settler priority through its connection with Métis "cousins," focusing on their common language and religion to create a false identity between the two peoples. As Lalonde notes, beyond the Red River settlement, Métis settlements such as Saint-Paul-des-Métis, Duck Lake, and Willow Bunch were used as bases for French-speaking Catholic settlers,[27] who essentially pushed the Métis out of these regions or cohabited with them.

More broadly, a new historiography is already under way, notably in the work of the Groupe d'étude sur le colonialisme québécois, led by Catherine Larochelle and Ollivier Hubert, or the Groupe de recherche sur les ordres coloniaux in France. While the focus is often placed on colonial states—or a federated province—there is a need to study the institutions that allow a variety of social and economic groups to benefit from colonialism.

But there are also limits to a historiography that is focused on chronology and on narrative. The story I present here only conveys elements of the relationships of French Canadians and their political descendants to the land, to the state, to the means of social reproduction, and to traditions and practices. All of these themes could be developed much further by historians, to enable a better understanding of the origins of the current political structures of the Canadian settler state. As a philosopher, I have chosen to limit my contribution to providing concepts and suggesting ways to mobilize them to help us review how French Canadians fit within this settler colonial system.



## Notes

1 Regan, *Unsettling the Settler.*
2 See, for instance, Bouchard, "Le faux 'sang indien.'"
3 Ghislain Otis lays out this story as well as a newer interpretation of the historical moment. Otis, "The Impact of the *Royal Proclamation*," 69–80.
4 Frenette, *Brève histoire.*
5 Hébert, *La révolution tranquille.*
6 Tuck and Yang, "Decolonization Is Not."
7 Tuck and Yang, "Decolonization Is Not," 9–10.
8 Leroux, *Distorted Descent.*
9 Vowel, "The Mythology of Métissage."
10 Tuck and Yang, "Decolonization Is Not," 9–11.
11 Bouveresse, "Le règne de Louis XIV."
12 Bagard, "Histoire."
13 Houdebine, "Le centralisme linguistique."
14 Leroux, "Le révisionnisme historique."
15 Ruggiu, "Des nouvelles France."
16 Melançon, "Contradictory Colonial Locations," 237–258.
17 Fanon, *A Dying Colonialism*, 150.
18 All the previous references are addressed in Melançon, "Colonisation, racialisation, recolonisation."
19 Harris, *A Bounded Land.*
20 Larochelle and Hubert, "Culture coloniale euroquébécoise."

21 Boily and Léonard, "Statut de la francophonie."
22 Painchaud, *Un rêve français*.
23 Truth and Reconciliation Commission of Canada, *Canada's Residential Schools*.
24 Lalonde, "L'Église catholique," 485.
25 See, for instance, Noel, "Consociational Democracy," in which Lijphart's formulation of the consociational state is extended to Canada.
26 Cardinal and Léger, "La complétude institutionnelle."
27 Lalonde, "L'Église catholique", 493.

## Sources


Bagard, Guillaume. "Histoire: comment Louis XV a réussi à intégrer en douceur la Lorraine au royaume de France." *Conversation*, April 20, 2022. https://theconversation.com/histoire-comment-louis-xv-a-reussi-a-integrer-en-douceur-la-lorraine-au-royaume-de-france-175704.

Boily, Frédéric, and Carol Léonard. "Statut de la francophonie de l'Ouest canadien: D'une francopétie avortée à une francopétie contrariée." *Bulletin d'histoire politique* 26, no. 1 (2017): 205–228. https://doi.org/10.7202/1041440ar.

Bouchard, Gérard. " Le faux 'sang indien' des Québécois." *La Presse*, February 7, 2015. https://www.lapresse.ca/debats/nos-collaborateurs/gerard-bouchard/201502/06/01-4841971-le-faux-sang-indien-des-quebecois.php.

Bouveresse, Jacques. "Le règne de Louis XIV, ou la rupture définitive entre la société française et la monarchie." *Les Annales de droit* 10 (2016): 77–96. https://doi.org/10.4000/add.332.

Cardinal, Linda, and Rémi Léger. "La complétude institutionnelle en perspective." *Politique et Sociétés* 36, no. 3 (2017): 3–14. https://doi.org/10.7202/1042233ar.

Fanon, Frantz. *A Dying Colonialism*. Grove Press, 1965.

Frenette, Yves. *Brève histoire des Canadiens français*. Les Éditions du Boréal, 1998.

Harris, Cole. *A Bounded Land: Reflections on Settler Colonialism in Canada*. University of British Columbia Press, 2020.

Hébert, Raymond-M. *La révolution tranquille au Manitoba français*. Éditions du Blé, 2012.

Houdebine, Anne-Marie. "Le centralisme linguistique. Brève histoire d'une norme prescriptive." *La linguistique* 52, no. 1 (2016): 35–54. https://www.cairn.info/revue-la-linguistique-2016-1-page-35.htm.

Lalonde, André. "L'Église catholique et les francophones de l'Ouest, 1818–1930." *Sessions d'étude—Société canadienne d'histoire de l'Église catholique* 50, no. 2 (1983): 485–497. https://doi.org/10.7202/1007218ar.

Larochelle, Catherine, and Ollivier Hubert. "Culture coloniale euroquébécoise et missions catholiques dans l'Ouest canadien au XIXe siècle." *Études d'histoire religieuse* 85 (2019): 5–21.

Leroux, Darryl. *Distorted Descent: White Claims to Indigenous Identity*. University of Manitoba Press, 2019.

Leroux, Darryl. "Le révisionnisme historique et la création des métis de l'est: La mythologie du métissage au Québec et en Nouvelle-Écosse." *Politique et Sociétés* 38, no. 3 (2019): 3–25. http://dx.doi.org/10.7202/1064728ar.

Melançon, Jérôme. "Colonisation, racialisation, recolonisation: Sur quelques dynamiques autour des communautés francophones des Prairies." *Cahiers franco-canadiens de l'Ouest* 35, nos. 1–2 (2023): 162–195. https://doi.org/10.7202/1107480ar.

Melançon, Jérôme. "Contradictory Colonial Locations: An Outline for a Theory Through Marxism and Phenomenology." In *Marxism and Phenomenology: The Dialectical Horizons of Critique*, edited by Bryan Smyth and Richard Westerman. Rowman & Littlefield, 2021.

Noel, S.J.R. "Consociational Democracy and Canadian Federalism." *Canadian Journal of Political Science* 4, no. 1 (1971): 15–18. https://doi.org/10.1017/S0008423900026251.

Otis, Ghislain. "The Impact of the *Royal Proclamation of 1763* on Quebec: Then and Now." In *Keeping Promises: The Royal Proclamation of 1763, Aboriginal Rights, and Treaties in Canada*, edited by Terry Fenge and Jim Aldridge. McGill-Queen's University Press, 2015.

Painchaud, Robert. *Un rêve français dans le peuplement de la prairie*. Éditions des Plaines, 1987.

Regan, Paulette. *Unsettling the Settler Within: Indian Residential Schools, Truth Telling, and Reconciliation in Canada*. University of British Columbia Press, 2010.

Ruggiu, François-Joseph. "Des nouvelles France aux colonies—Une approche comparée de l'histoire impériale de la France de l'époque moderne." *Nuevo Mundo Mundos Nuevos*, June 14, 2018. http://dx.doi.org/10.4000/nuevomundo.72123.

Truth and Reconciliation Commission of Canada. *Canada's Residential Schools: The History*. 2 vols. McGill-Queen's University Press, 2015.

Tuck, Eve, and K. Wayne Yang. "Decolonization Is Not a Metaphor." *Decolonization: Indigeneity, Education & Society* 1, no. 1 (2012): 1–40.

Vowel, Chelsea. "The Mythology of Métissage: Settler Moves to Innocence." âpihtawikosisân. Law. Language. Culture (blog), March 11, 2015. https://apihtawikosisan.com/2015/03/the-mythology-of-metissage-settler-moves-to-innocence.

# Straddling Different Worlds

## *Growing Up Mixed Race in Saskatchewan*

Desmond McAllister

COMPLEX. I THINK THAT IS THE BEST WORD TO DESCRIBE me. Whenever someone is bold enough or able to muster the courage to ask me what my background is, there is no simple answer. My life has been a complex, contrasting, and even a conflicting experience at times that took quite some time to figure out for myself. In my contribution, I want to share with you my life's journey to find out who I am and share my experiences growing up as a mixed-race person in Saskatchewan.

My story starts in two places—My mother, Joan, hails from the agricultural village (now town) of Barrackpore, Trinidad, a descendant of indentured servants from India who were coerced to work the sugar plantations after the emancipation of enslaved Africans. Her great-grandfather, Jairam, at the age of eighteen journeyed from his small agricultural village of Deeha Asharfabad, Jaunpur, Uttar Pradesh, India, to the "Coolie Depot" in Kolkata. Upon his arrival in Kolkata, Jairam was medically examined, approved as medically fit, and, with a simple *x* and a thumbprint, he was contracted as a "bound coolie" (indentured servant). Jairam then embarked on the SS *Coachin* and after a treacherous three-month journey, he arrived in Trinidad on April 7, 1870, and was assigned to the Esperance Sugar Estate in the south of the island. Like his fellow indentured servants, he toiled for some years under horrible conditions—intense heat and humidity, maltreatment from his superiors, as well as poor sanitation and living conditions. Essentially, indentured servitude was Britain's way of reinventing slavery after formal slavery had been abolished.

On the other hand, my father, Raymond (or Ray), hails from Southeast Saskatchewan—a descendent of settlers who came from England, Ontario, and the United States (of Irish, Scottish, English, and German stock) to farm in Saskatchewan in the early 1900s.

My maternal grandparents came from Muslim and Hindu families. The Presbyterian Church in Canada sent missionaries to Trinidad to "work with the East Indians" in the 1890s. As a result, my maternal grandparents eventually converted to Presbyterianism in an effort to access education for their children to escape the harsh conditions of the sugar cane estate as well as to avoid colonial social stigmas that were primarily perpetrated against the Hindu community.

My paternal grandparents' religious background was a blend of Anglican, United Church of Canada, and Judaism. However, as time went on, the majority of the family settled with the United Church of Canada.

My mother arrived in Regina in 1969, sponsored by relatives who were invited to study in Saskatchewan by the Presbyterian/United Church missionaries. My parents met in 1971 and were married in 1973. My father, being a bit of a traditionalist, believed that the bride needs to be home when she gets married—so they were wed in Trinidad. Dad instantly fell in love with Trinidad and Tobago and easily developed a deep affection and appreciation of the culture, music, and people.

I was born on May 9, 1978, in Regina, Saskatchewan. My parents named me Desmond Paul McAllister. "Desmond" after South African anti-apartheid activist Archbishop Desmond Tutu, and "Paul" after the Apostle Paul of the Bible. My given names (though I was named after great people) would never allude to the fact that I was of Indian descent, partly due to the psychological impact colonialism would have had on my mother's upbringing. My mother was born a British subject as Trinidad and Tobago was a British colony. When my mother was fourteen years old, Trinidad and Tobago achieved independence on August 31, 1962—and all citizens of the then-colony assumed Trinidad and Tobago citizenship. Though independence brought great pride and joy to Trinbagonians, colonial mentalities persisted.

It is well documented and understood that the British utilized "divide and rule" tactics in order to maintain and assert power—and this was no different in colonial Trinidad. Upon African emancipation there was a serious shortage of labour on the estates, and when the newly emancipated servants called for a living wage to go back to the estates, the colonial authorities and British government contacted the East India Company to send workers from India—essentially making indentured servants (unknowingly to them) strike breakers. Upon their arrival, the African community confronted these workers, and the seeds of mistrust were sewn. Over time, this animosity between the Indian and African communities has eased.

British colonialism in Trinidad also taught that "white is right," and that the fairer complexion you had, the higher you tended to be located on the social ladder. This specific attitude was one of the grievances many Trinbagonians held against foreign-owned corporate entities as well as the then government. It was on this backdrop that the 1970s saw Trinidad and Tobago (TT) experience social upheavals and uprisings in what has come to be known as the "Black Power Revolution." After this time things began to change for people of darker complexions. Prior to 1970, TT's natural resources of oil and petroleum were being exploited by companies whose boards were made up exclusively of foreigners and local white people. This, too, was the case for financial institutions and other corporate entities. Even to get a job as a bank teller, you had to be light skinned.

I have heard many stories of my mother's and her relatives' childhoods, growing up in colonial Trinidad where they spoke of their amazement and awe when the American or British or Canadian people would visit the churches or the oilfields in Barrackpore, the pride they felt when these people would bring or send food hampers at Christmas time. Due to colonialism, the mentality of their generation (as well as previous generations) seemed to have upheld the ideal of white superiority.

My mother left Trinidad immediately prior to the events of 1970. Being an Indian of a darker complexion, she did not see a future in Trinidad. So, with encouragement from her brother and her cousins living in Regina, Saskatchewan, she moved. When she arrived in Regina, she stayed with them and was able to easily adjust to the Canadian way of life. I think it is safe to assume that she would have experienced racism in some form in Regina, but for some reason or other, she never spoke of it. I remember my mother would ensure we children were dressed and groomed well at all times. I think it is partly due to the fact that she was a hairdresser by profession, but I think it was mainly an effort to stave off any racist or degrading comments from being directed at us.

Because of my father's love for Trinidadian music—more specifically the steel pan—my own involvement with steel pan actually started with his encouragement. My mother's cousin was a leader of a steel band in South Trinidad, and Dad, being a drummer himself, bought two pans with the intention of learning how to play. Being a steelworker on shift work, Dad was never able to commit to a schedule. He did, however, become active with my mother in the local Caribbean community. This involvement continued until they were in their seventies.

Regina's Caribbean community was centred around the Saskatchewan Caribbean-Canadian Association (SCCA), which was founded in 1979. It was brought about to unite the then-small community of Caribbean families. The SCCA was active and well-known in Regina, making its biggest impression at Regina's annual multicultural festival, Mosaic, with the Caribbean Pavilion. This was, arguably, the most popular pavilion for many years.

Being in a house where steel pans were set up, I was always intrigued by them. My father had vinyl records of steel bands, which were used to sooth me as a baby. I loved to see the steel band that would perform at the Caribbean Pavilion during Mosaic, but my true love for pan would hit me at the age of five on the streets of San Fernando, Trinidad, during the 1984 Carnival. I was able to see a full hundred-member steel band inch its way through the streets surrounded by a mass of humanity jumping and dancing to the music. I was sold!

In 1986, at the age of eight, I joined the SCCA's Caribe Steel Orchestra in Regina. As per tradition, I was taught how to play pan by rote. No musical score sheets—you were taught to play by watching the instructor play it on your pan, then he would hand the sticks over and teach you to play what he played. While frowned upon by a lot of traditional musicians, playing by rote and by ear was excellent for my musical development.

Music has and always will be my refuge. My recollection of events through my life is based on a soundtrack of sorts. As my father was a lover of the culture of Trinidad and Tobago, I was brought up listening to calypso, soca, and chutney music—particularly the music of calypsonians Lord Kitchener, Mighty Sparrow, Calypso Rose, Penguin, Shadow, David Rudder, and Black Stalin, chutney singers Anand Yankaran and Drupatee Ramgoonai, and the music of my dad's good friend (and pumpkin-vine cousin) the legendary King of Chutney, Sundar Popo. Dad would get records and tapes from Trinidad every year, and they would be played day in, day out—until he was able to get more the following year.

I have always felt tremendous pride and enjoyment in my Trinidadian heritage—through music, language, foods, traditions, and a tightly knit family on my mother's side. These things shaped my identity and made me different from the others. That being said, there were times when this all left me feeling extremely isolated—especially when I was singled out and ostracized because of my interests and tastes.

When my family came here from Trinidad, a lot of them did all they could to assimilate into Canadian society. From my discussions with them over the years, they felt that it was the proper thing to do away with a lot of their culture. They kept certain traditions and language hidden from their Canadian counterparts out of fear of being discriminated against. They sought out the easiest way to survive and maintain a level of decorum and dignity within society. Many of them even refused to deny being racially discriminated against and in some cases even took the side of the perpetrators!

When I started elementary school, I was one of the few children of colour. It was definitely an adjustment for me. I didn't feel that I quite fit in until I was in grade 2. The rest of my elementary school experience was pretty uncomfortable. Isolation, victimization, being bullied (a teacher or two even took the side of the bully), the usage of racial slurs such as P*ki and n*gger by some of my classmates had me in survival mode for the most part—just to get through the day. Due to this, I did not excel academically. Yes, I did have friends who treated me really well, but they did not fully understand my experience.

I found refuge in my culture and involvement in the Caribbean community. Being actively involved in the steel band and able to associate with people of similar cultures with similar experiences of living in Canada as people of colour gave me a sense of comfort and belonging. I think it is worth stating that Caribbean culture is *far* from homogenous—though there are similarities, each island has its own language, foods, ethnocultural compositions, political systems, etc. Through it all, our community at the time found a strength in binding together as one.

I started to notice an erosion of this foundation when our Caribbean local youth group was going to join forces with an "Afro-Caribbean" group, and they were going to rebrand the group as "Afro-Caribbean." The parents strongly rejected this idea as the Caribbean is an ethnically diverse region—which is something the majority of the SCCA membership valued. Though we did not proceed, we maintained close ties. That same year, the steel band went to Edmonton, Alberta, to participate in a Caribbean Carnival and while backstage one person in our group remarked "they have a nice show but it have too many coolie people here" (*coolie* being a highly offensive ethnic slur towards people of Indian descent in the Trinidadian vernacular—the equivalent to the N-word to Indo-Trinis). I instantly went from feeling like a valuable member of the group to feeling I was a mere third wheel. I was *devastated.* An apology was offered immediately, which I accepted, and I took the offensive word as a one-off thing, and we still have a good relationship. However, coupled with the events with the youth group, it threw me into an identity crisis of sorts. It was evident that while my white friends couldn't understand me, now the very people with whom I thought I was part and parcel were making remarks like that, and it was extremely traumatic for me.

Luckily, I was able to regain a sense of belonging in high school, where I was able to foster great, long-lasting friendships. I belonged to two groups of friends. One was a group of people from a variety of backgrounds, but we all had one thing in common—a love for hip-hop. At school we were neither popular nor unpopular. We fit in a grey area—we associated with everyone who was decent to us. A lot of the parties were thrown by people who I grew up with in the Caribbean community. With this group I was able to hone my social skills and "make a name for myself."

The other group was comprised of Caribbean and Nigerian students. At lunchtime we would stick together in the cafeteria, play dominoes, listen to hip-hop and dancehall music, "shit talk," and relate our experiences of racism in school. Because of this, we were able to form a tight bond with one another—which remains intact today. This group tended to inadvertently attract some "heat" from other groups, and even school administration. I can't recall how many times I went to the vice principal's office to be interrogated about a small infraction one of my buddies did during class or lunch. Of course, I remained tight-lipped and denied that I saw anything (chuckle).

I referenced hip-hop as a galvanizing factor in high school—it also must be noted that in particular, Indigenous youths at the time tended to also identify with hip-hop culture. Our circle of friends included Indigenous Peoples and because of said long-standing friendships, it brought into focus the misconceptions and prejudices I had growing up in a very white neighbourhood and going to a predominantly white elementary school. Being a person of colour myself, I was able to quickly identify similarities and parallels of what they faced. But being a person who happened to have a very vocal white father, I think I was shielded from a lot—while they faced discrimination due to deep-seated racial ideologies and social stigmas.

From 1995 through 1999 came an array of game-changers for me. The year 1995 marked the 150th anniversary of Indian arrival to TT; my favourite Calypsonian of all time, Black Stalin, won his fifth Calypso Monarch title with his "Tribute to Sundar Popo," which displayed a unity between Afro and Indo Trinbagonians; I had my first Carnival-type fete experience in Toronto; and Basdeo Panday became the first Indo-Trinidadian to be elected prime minister of Trinidad and Tobago. It was also a time when the Internet was beginning to assert itself as a major communication tool, so information was readily available at your fingertips. I was able to access information somewhat quickly and effortlessly, and I was able to research and get answers to the many questions I had about myself.

It was during that summer that the steel band re-formed after it broke up due to an unfortunate power struggle. (I was simply a player in the band who decided to remain neutral.) As I was the most senior remaining member, I was appointed bandleader. I was mainly the drummer for the group, but I had the opportunity to better understand the "mechanics" of the different pans and their functions within the band. I then took it upon myself to teach myself how to play the tenor pan (lead pan). Once I understood how it worked, I was able to make my first attempt at arranging a tune. The older people took notice and encouraged me greatly in this.

The following year, there seemed to be a surge in the popularity of Indo-Caribbean culture for Trinidad Carnival—Sonny Mann's Chutney soca song "Lootayla" (1995) was a runaway hit, and when it was remixed with elements of soca and dancehall, it took off even further. Brother Marvin (Selwyn Demming) took a serious swipe for the Calypso Monarch title with his ode to his Indian ancestry singing "Jahaji Bhai" (1996), and Chris Garcia's Carnival anthem "Chutney Bacchanal" stirred a frenzy in fetes.

It was on this backdrop that my family and I went to Trinidad after a long hiatus. I was able to finally immerse myself in my Indo-Trinidadian culture. It was raw, unfiltered, and glorious. Two years later, in 1998, we repeated the same trip. It was at that time that I met Lystra, who would later become my wife.

Lystra, who hails from Penal, in South Trinidad, grew up in a home that espoused a deep and unwavering devotion to Hinduism; however, they maintained a high level of respect for all faiths. When I went to Trinidad to visit Lystra, I was able to observe this in action.

For me this was a new experience—and also very confusing. While I was growing up, the version of Hinduism that was described to me involved acts of blood sacrifice and spiritual possessions (what I later learned is referred to as "tamasic" or Shakti worship)—which is very different from the "Satvic" traditions of Ahimsa (non-violence) that my wife and most Hindus in TT adhere to. Still, some of my Christian relatives painted Hinduism with a broad brush and made disparaging remarks about it. Some actually held the colonial belief in the hierarchy of Indo-Trinis—Christians were at the top, Muslims held the middle ground, while Hindus occupied the bottom of the social ladder. What I saw was absolutely different from everything I have heard.

Luckily for me, Lystra's Guru, the late Pandit Keso Maharaj, was an absolute wealth of knowledge. I always felt comfortable enough to ask questions of him. He understood my genuine intentions—I could ask him any question that would have come to my mind, and we would discuss different ways to look at the subject and how it would relate to spirituality and the "real world."

Due to the misconceptions and prejudices that some of my family had of Hinduism, there was a bit of a struggle. In Trinidad, most Hindus who married into Christian families at that time assumed Christianity. Lystra was and still is steadfast and unapologetic in her beliefs. Her treatment by some of my family opened my eyes not only to the stress that she endured but also to the lasting effects of colonialism. Because of this, I have been able to shake off these shackles and see the world clearly.

Listening to testimonies from the Truth and Reconciliation Commissions that took place in both Canada and South Africa, as well as research into the evils of the transatlantic slave trade and Indian indentureship, I was able to see how colonials used brute force, subliminal messaging, and religion as weapons to control those under their "whip."

Through my research and experiences, I see distinct similarities between British colonial rule in Trinidad (specifically with regards to Indian indentureship), India, and Canada and the treatment of Indigenous Peoples here. The suppression of language and culture, religious conversion, separation of family, seizing of land and assets, and the dehumanization of people to maintain control are evident in their histories and have left scars difficult to heal. As time separates us from our colonial past, I am encouraged to know that some of us have begun to address these injustices. Some of us have spoken up, and some of us have made a conscious decision to learn about, reclaim, and celebrate our rich traditional cultures and beliefs.

In all of my life experiences, good and bad, I have released myself from this mental bondage. I can see the world unfiltered, and I now know exactly how I fit in. The birth of our son caused me to re-evaluate my long-held prejudices...and I let them go. Consciousness, pride, and love have made the foundation we want our son to build his life upon. It was and still is my prayer that he and all of his peers will learn from history and do what they can do to live in an equal, progressive, and inclusive world.

# B'Chol Dor v'Dor

## *In Each and Every Generation*

Bernie Farber and Len Rudner

*In the yearly recitation of the Passover Haggadah, Jews read the narration of the exodus from slavery in Egypt as a current event: In each and every generation, we are obligated to see ourselves as recipients, beneficiaries, and guardians of that divine emancipation. We have a responsibility to remember the past and to create a present that future generations will find worthy of both remembrance and honour.*

*That is the point of departure for this chapter on the genocide of Indigenous Peoples in Canada.*

*We approach this subject as Canadians, as settlers, and as Jews.*

### Introduction

IN THIS CONTRIBUTION WE SHARE OUR SEPARATE PATHS TO a still-limited recognition of the experiences of the Indigenous community in Canada. As Canadian Jews, we have been drawn to the research done on—and the debate over—the question of genocide. We explore the timeline of genocide in Canada as well as attempts to obscure or deny its reality. Finally, confronting a genocide that has not ended, we ask: Where do we go from here?

## Background Reflections:
## An Evolving Awareness of Indigenous Peoples

I (Len) am a second-generation Canadian, well-educated and well-read. So how is it possible that it was not until I was more than forty years old that I heard about the Indian residential schools? While today it may seem hard to understand, I shouldn't be surprised. I grew up in a Montreal neighbourhood where the predominant diversities were of language (English and French) and religion (Catholic, Protestant, and Jewish). If there were Indigenous Peoples, I didn't see them. In grade school in the 1960s, my history classes taught me about Pierre-Esprit Radisson, Médard des Groseilliers, and Samuel de Champlain. If "Indians" (as they were called then) were mentioned in our schoolbooks, they were depicted in minor roles as helpers, an exception being where they appeared as the villains, maligned for supposedly cruelly torturing and murdering the saintly Jesuit missionaries Jean de Brébeuf and Charles Lalemant.

Later, in high school, Canadian history added Paul de LaSalle, René-Robert de Maisonneuve, and the Fathers of Confederation. We also learned about Louis Riel, although he was presented as a "traitor" to the Canadian nation-building project. In university in the early and mid-'70s, I had some choice as to what subjects I pursued, but my areas of study (English literature and European history) led me in a direction different from Indigenous history and culture.

So, through years of education and then full-time work in the '80s and early '90s, Indigenous Peoples were not on my mind. When I started work in the area of employment equity, I learned a little, but it wasn't about Indigenous history; it was about their representation in the workplace. It was only after a number of years in that job that an Indigenous employee made a veiled reference to her experiences in "a residential school." I nodded, but she didn't tell me more, and I had no knowledge to which this new fact could connect. I realize, now, that she was hinting at things more terrible than mean teachers and detentions. I'm sorry, now, that I did not have ears to hear her.

It took more years for the stories of Canada's treatment of Indigenous Peoples to move to the forefront of my consciousness. For this I owe gratitude to the work of the Truth and Reconciliation Commission (TRC), the National Inquiry into Missing and Murdered Indigenous Women and

Girls, and the thousands of men and women who opened deep and painful wounds and offered their truth so that people like me could have ears to hear.



In Judaism, remembrance is important. I must remember when I was a stranger in a strange land. I must remember more recent tragic history, so that *never again* will there be a Holocaust. I must also preserve a recollection of my dead so that *their memory will be for a blessing.* With the demands of memory, there is also a cry for repair. Whether we call it conciliation or reconciliation, there is a need for apology. This has to be more than saying "I'm sorry."

I'm a settler. I am late to the game in terms of my awareness of this identity. I ran no schools and have not knowingly engaged in acts of violence or discrimination against Indigenous Peoples, but my life and comfort in Canada rest on just such terrible acts. What do I do about that? Where do we go from here?

• • •

My beginning is different. I (Bernie) grew up in Ottawa in the shadow of my late father's experience of genocide. He was the sole Jewish survivor of a Polish village (Bocki) that was made part of the Nazi kingdom of death. My understanding of this tragedy is deeply personal, and my response to those who ignore or deny the reality is visceral. As a child of a Holocaust survivor, I knew all too well what it meant to be part of a community that lost more than a generation of its people. I viscerally understood Jew-hatred: on the streets of my neighbourhood, antisemitism was as regular as the Ottawa streetcar service. Much of it was religiously based, arising from Christian teachings about Jews.

My conceptions of discrimination and hatred were moulded by the reality of being a young Jewish child more or less alone in a sea of white Anglo-Saxon Christianity in the late 1950s and '60s. Antisemitism—sometimes violent—was something I had to regularly confront. If there were Indigenous families in my sphere, I was unaware of them until perhaps my late high school years. Then, and through my studies in university, the matter of residential schools and their impact on Indigenous Peoples in Canada played no part. I wish I had known.

It was only during my decade as a social worker, beginning in the mid-1970s, first with the Youth Services Bureau of Ottawa-Carleton and then with the Ottawa-Carleton Children's Aid Society, that I had my first personal encounter with Indigenous families.

One case stood out: an Inuit child was moved from his traditional home in the Northwest Territories to live with an aunt in the suburbs of Ottawa. I now understand that his frustration and acting out, sometimes quite violently, were a direct result of the settler state moving him from his home to which he was acculturated—linguistically, historically, and geographically—to a place that was foreign and ugly to him. He was, at my insistence and following much advocacy, returned to his home in the North. I wish I could report that all ended well, but I simply do not know. What I do know is that this was a lesson of the soul for me, one I carried with me into my work with Canadian Jewish Congress (CJC).

It was during my years with CJC that I began a connection with First Nations people that has lasted to this day. However, my first interaction with Indigenous leaders was a troubling one. In 2002, a former National Chief of the Assembly of First Nations, David Ahenakew, made a number of virulent antisemitic statements, which led to him being charged under Canada's anti-hate laws.[1] He was convicted of the charges, although the decision was later overturned on appeal in 2006. The major impact of the case was that it pointed out to the Jewish and Indigenous communities—both of which suffered the effects of hatred and bigotry—the need for a closer relationship.

A second trial, held in 2008, resulted in an acquittal in 2009, but by this time, leadership within both communities felt that it was time to begin building bridges. So, in 2008, a meeting was arranged between the leadership of the Federation of Saskatchewan Indian Nations, led by then-Chiefs Perry Bellegarde and Lawrence Joseph, and the leadership of CJC, led by the late Rabbi Reuven Bulka. Held at the national offices of CJC in Ottawa, gifts of tobacco and blankets were exchanged. Though tense at first, leaders on all sides gradually relaxed, and a relationship was slowly built.

A few years later, a joint trip was undertaken to Israel with leadership of CJC and the Assembly of First Nations, led by then-CJC President Edward Morgan and AFN National Chief Phil Fontaine. The trip was planned as an opportunity to share best practices on language preservation, water purification, and agriculture. In 2009, as CEO of CJC, I was asked to accompany Jewish philanthropist and First Nations supporter Larry Tanenbaum and former Prime Minister Paul Martin on a visit to Wabaseemoong reserve (Whitedog) in Northern Ontario.

As we landed in Kenora, Ontario, the first thing that hit us was the unbearable cold, wind, and rain. I was thankful to get into the warm van that was to take us sixty-five kilometres farther north to the Whitedog reserve. Before we could enter the reserve, we needed to pass through a roadblock. It was explained that the band council needed to find a way to limit the importation of paint solvent into the reserve. Children as young as eight were sniffing it to momentarily escape the hardships they were experiencing. Some would die of an overdose or would, with fatal results, wander onto dark highways at night.

We were met by Wabaseemoong Chief Eric Fisher, who would be our host. We were taken first to visit the elementary school. We were told that the vast majority of the 240 students would leave school by grade 6. This left us stunned. The teachers were armed with passion and dedication, but with little else. With virtually no resources, they persevered. These young children were in an almost impossible situation with seemingly little chance of educational and career success due to the available education system. Later, we were taken to the school gym, where the children in the younger grades put on an inspiring presentation. Embracing the spirit of their people and hearing them sing of the love for their culture was deeply moving.

At the very end of our stay, Paul Martin asked our host to take us to a "lacquer house" located on the edge of the reserve. I thought this might be a safe place for the youth to come, away from the temptations of lacquer sniffing. I was wrong.

It was an old shack. It had an earthen floor and windows with wood shutters that covered the broken glass and shut out the sunlight. We entered to an overpowering scent of stale, putrid air. Broken glass, dirty coffee mugs, and urine-soaked mattresses were scattered about. Three young girls and a young boy, none older than fourteen, were lying semi-conscious on the mattresses. We were told this was a "safe place" for young people high on lacquer to crash. As a former social worker for the Children's Aid Society, I thought there was little that could shock me, but this took my breath away.

How was it possible that these young people—children really—were left to fend for themselves? Clearly no resources from the federal government (who were mandated as such to protect them) were present. In many ways, this was the very beginning of consciousness-raising for me in relation to how governments were simply not there for Indigenous

Peoples and, more sadly, how the children were specifically neglected by the state.

I was impressed to see how Paul Martin engaged with the youth on this visit. There, on his hands and knees, was our former prime minister talking to a young girl. He was gentle, kind, and sensitive to her surroundings. But the historical state-sponsored neglect that I witnessed that day won out and made me feel ashamed as a Canadian.

Looking back, it seems to me that the prime minister undertook his own journey over his years as a politician. In the end he was more aware of the oppression caused by colonialism, and he became a champion of Indigenous life. The Martin Aboriginal Education Initiative, which works towards literacy and teaching, is a prime example of his ongoing work.

It also made me reflect on the impact colonialism had on Indigenous Peoples. Taken from their territories and traditions and introduced to alcohol and drugs by colonizers, this tragically became part of the experience of genocide. Truth be told, I was still on my own personal journey, and I had a long road to travel before I came to understand how settler betrayal of Indigenous Peoples led to genocide.

As I have come to learn, First Nations faiths and cultures are imbued with a rich sense of tradition and an emphasis on teaching and sharing. For me there is much here akin to the Jewish faith, one of the tenets of which is "tikkun olam," a directive to repair the world and to help make it a better place. Following that trip, the CJC committed to work with First Nations, guided by their traditions to build a Canada that is more welcoming, more consistent with who we are, and should be, as a nation.

In 2011, I left CJC and joined the team of First Nations advocate Dr. Michael Dan as a senior vice president of Gemini Power Corporation. I worked in partnership with Indigenous Peoples towards economic development and community self-reliance in a way that respected both the environment and First Nations' traditional values. I spent much time on reserves working with Indigenous leadership on various projects, including the use of water on traditional territory for hydro power, lumber procurement, and much more. Mostly I learned from my experiences, and there was so much learning to do. I needed to understand different concepts of time, history stories, and traditions. I had to learn to listen more carefully, to rid myself of European teachings, and to be open to a revision of my understanding of history.

Like Len, I, too, wonder, where do we go from here?

## Recognizing Genocide in Canada

On certain Jewish holy days, the cantor offers a personal prayer, "Hineini." In it the cantor asks that his words be accepted as if they come from one who is wise, "pleasant of voice and loved by his fellow man." *Hineini* means "here I am." Hineini is the first step in any interaction between people and people or between people and ideas or between people and history. Here we are.

For Jews, the Holocaust can be a lens through which reality is perceived. In our community, every comparison to other atrocities can feel like an attempt to diminish its significance. With so many dead, and with so few graves to visit, the memory itself takes on the status of a cemetery. It becomes sacred ground that must be protected. We ask: Can it be any different with the Indigenous community in the face of the discovery of its own unmarked graves?

But understanding and recognizing Indigenous genocide took time for us, as it has for many other settlers. When we worked for the Canadian Jewish Congress, we pushed against comparisons. We recognized, of course, the reality of other genocides, yet we placed a fence around our own communal tragedy. The pain was too great to be endured, yet at the same time too great to be shared.

So, then, what were we to do with the assertion that Indigenous Peoples in Canada experienced a genocide at the hands of the Canadian government? There's no one way to get through this impasse. For us it was a combination of things. For one of us (Bernie), it was the opportunity to speak with Indigenous leaders and to hear their stories, sometimes offered as background to the issue on the table and at other times foregrounded as the main topic of discussion.

For another (Len), it was through an informal but dedicated study of genocide as a recurring element of human behaviour. When you study only the Holocaust, it feels unique, but when the scope of genocide study is broadened to include the horrific fates of the Armenians, Ukrainians, and Rwandan Tutsis (naming but a few other groups targeted with genocide), then it becomes impossible to ignore the commonalities. When you read the UN Genocide Convention (UNGC) in conjunction with what Raphaël Lemkin[2] wanted (and what he settled for), then it becomes harder to ignore the realization that the word *genocide* is not being used for dramatic purposes; that it is indeed an accurate descriptor for what happened in Canada.

This leads to a position that now seems commonplace but a decade ago was less so: the Holocaust was an *example* of genocide, but not its *definition*. Thus, the Holocaust may serve as a lens through which to see more clearly. As Métis historian Tricia Logan observed, "the prevailing assumption that the Holocaust is *the* example of genocide still blinds many observers to the fact that genocide occurred outside of Europe prior to the twentieth century."[3]

The definition of genocide remains contested decades after the passage of the UNGC in 1948. Lemkin's own view was that "genocide does not necessarily mean the immediate destruction of a nation.... It is intended rather to signify a coordinated plan of different actions aiming at the destruction of the essential foundations of the life of national groups, with the aim of annihilating the groups themselves." He went on to write in *Axis Rule in Occupied Europe* (1944) that the objectives of such a plan would be disintegration of the political and social institutions, of culture, language, national feelings, religion, and the economic existence of national groups, and the destruction of the personal security, liberty, health, dignity, and even the lives of the individuals belonging to such groups."[4]

The order of these objectives is instructive. Despite personal loss, Lemkin ranked murder as the last of the objectives of genocide. He understood the overlap of colonialism and genocide and realized that the destruction of the essential foundations of the life of national groups was both the inevitable and desired goal of a colonial project.[5]

Even with this limited definition, there is space to implicate Canada's historic treatment of Indigenous Peoples. In a *Toronto Star* opinion piece that I (Bernie) wrote with Phil Fontaine and Michael Dan, we noted that "the recently exposed nutrition experiments carried out in the residential schools meets the criteria under point (b).... The decision by the government in the 1900s to allow native children to die of tuberculosis meet the criteria under point (c).... The residential school system itself, and the practice of forcibly removing First Nations children from Reserves and placing them with adoptive non-aboriginal families, common in the 1960s, and referred to as Sixties Scoop, meet the criteria under point (e)."[6] This article was prominently displayed at the Canadian Museum for Human Rights in Winnipeg, designed to provoke discussion into this topic.

But why was the definition of genocide so sharply limited in the first place? Given the correlation—if not the causative connection—between colonialism and genocide, our studying suggests that when the matter came before the UN General Assembly in 1948 those countries with a colonial past (or present, for that matter) were aware that the broader definition opened them up to accusations of being perpetrators.

It was expedient, then, to define genocide through the Holocaust. Genocide could then be reserved for the worst of the worst crimes because the deed was done with intent (think of the 1942 Wannsee Conference[7]), with a wide scope (Europe), and with an articulated goal of physical annihilation. This focus, as Tony Barta has argued, "while giving the word it's terrible leading edge," has succeeded "in devaluing all other concepts of less planned destruction, even if the effects are the same."[8]

The 2015 final report of the Truth and Reconciliation Commission was clear: "For over a century, the central goals of Canada's Aboriginal policy were to eliminate Aboriginal governments; ignore Aboriginal rights; terminate the treaties; and, through a process of assimilation, cause Aboriginal peoples to cease to exist as distinct legal, social, cultural, religious, and racial entities in Canada. The establishment and operation of residential schools were a central element of this policy, which can best be described as 'cultural genocide.'"[9] The qualifier was required as the mandate of the TRC did not permit the Commission to "hold formal hearings, nor act as a public inquiry, nor conduct a formal legal process"[10] into the matter of genocide.

But those who experienced the schools from the inside had little doubt. As the late Sagkeeng First Nation, Manitoba, Chief Theodore Fontaine (a survivor of the Fort Alexander Indian Residential School) noted, "the government and its agents, the churches, had in fact been intent on killing me as an Indian person. Their aim was to destroy the Indigenous Nations by taking away the children, using the tools of racism, indoctrination, removal, and institutionalization."[11]

Indigenous Peoples in Canada were treated more as objects than as people. The TRC found that "an estimated 6,000 children perished while held within Canadian Indian Residential Schools (IRS). From the mid nineteenth century until 1996, when the last school closed, about 150,000 First Nations, Inuit and Metis children were forcibly removed from their families and placed in institutions fundamentally designed to destroy their Indigenous identities."[12]

It's difficult not to see the qualifier—*cultural*—as a means of providing cover to the government and to those institutions that acted as its agents.

But if cultural genocide is seen as an unhelpful term, an unnecessary provocation, or as a "ghost of a crime,"[13] perhaps the easiest solution is to simplify matters: to state that what Indigenous Peoples experienced at the hands of successive governments of Canada was genocide as defined under the UN Genocide Convention. The Parliament of Canada recognized this in a unanimous vote in October 2022.[14]

This assertion has been made less controversial as a result of the important work done by the TRC. For us, it represented a growing realization that we had to overcome our own communal reflexes and spend more time in reflection with our books, friends, and teachers.

## Timelines of Genocide in Canada: What If It Never Stopped?

Every now and again, we encounter a question that forces us to think in a different way. Authors Roland Chrisjohn and Sherri Young offered just such a moment: "What if the Holocaust had never stopped. What if no liberating armies invaded the territory, stormed over by the draconian state? No compassionate throng broke down the doors to dungeons to free those imprisoned within? No collective outcry of humanity arose as stories of the state's abuses were recounted.... What if the Holocaust had never stopped, so that, for the State's victims, there was no vindication, no validation, no justice, but instead the dawning realization that this was how things were going to be?"[15]

It's difficult for us to wrap our heads around that idea. The Holocaust *did* end. There was a point at which the camps and ghettos were empty and the ovens were cold. There was a point at which the torture ended—though the agony persevered; where small measures of solace might be found and where the healing of broken bodies and souls could at least—imperfectly—begin. But what if for Indigenous Peoples in Canada, their genocide has not ended? *What if it never stopped?*

The solution to the "Indian problem" came in many forms, including the progressive dispossession of Indigenous Peoples from their lands, their movement to reserves (often using hunger as a means of coercion), and taking advantage of epidemics that followed the vector of settler expansion. Woolford notes that "at least half the Indigenous population of between 200,000 and 300,000 people was killed by disease between the beginning of the seventeenth century and the end of the nineteenth. This devastating death toll opened vast areas of land to European settlement and exploitation."[16]

It is difficult not to agree with Lemkin's view that colonialism and genocide are inextricably linked. Disease and hunger (caused in large measure by the deliberate decimation of the bison herds) made Indigenous Peoples less able to resist what was to come. As historian James Daschuk puts it, "by the turn of the 1880s, dominion officials tailored their response to the famine to further their own agenda of development in the west by subjugating the malnourished and increasingly sick Indigenous population."[17] By the 1890s, Daschuk again notes, "tuberculosis was increasingly seen as a hereditary disease by government officials," allowing settlers to downplay the suffering as "nature taking its course."[18]

We have come to realize that the residential schools were not the "First Solution" to the "Indian Problem," as Duncan Campbell Scott, deputy superintendent of the Department of Indian Affairs, stated in 1910.[19] They would, instead, be only "one more solution" to the seemingly persistent and frustrating problem posed by Indigenous Peoples to the expansion of the settler state. Indeed, we see a risk in using specific quotations from one politician or another, no matter how disturbing they may be, to reduce the time period of the genocide. By providing a specific beginning and an ending far enough in the past, we only maintain our present comfort and distance from genocide.

The truth, however, may be more complicated since there is not a clear beginning or endpoint, given that settler colonial practices continue and the intergenerational impacts of the residential schools and other genocidal crimes continue.[20] The raison d'être of the residential school system was to break the connection between Indigenous children and their parents and to impede in every way possible any opportunity for Indigenous cultures to be transmitted from one generation to another.[21] Many of the schools offered a regime of harsh discipline as well as both physical and sexual abuse. In addition, there is evidence to support the charge that the students were subjected to nutritional experiments, where food was withheld in order to study the impact of malnutrition.[22] Recent studies reflect early observations on the nature of the residential schools. As early as 1907, a report by Dr. Peter Bryce, Canada's first medical officer of health, showed that the Canadian government knowingly allowed thousands of Indigenous children to die of tuberculosis.[23]

## Denying Genocide

Settlers have shown an ability to focus on "positive aspects of Indigenous-settler relations in order to make history more digestible. Political scientist David MacDonald refers to this as "settler amnesia," which allows us to "choose the order in which we will consume our history, while also ignoring less palatable dishes."[24] Positive experiences of individual students, or schools where the students were not abused,[25] are held up as examples of the good work that was done in the residential schools, or are at least presented in the spirit of mitigation.

Gregory Stanton, president of the International Association of Genocide Scholars, asserts that "denial is the final stage of genocide."[26] I (Bernie) noted at the time of the TRC *Interim Report*: "Having battled Holocaust denial in all its evil forms, I know the pain it can cause survivors and their descendants. Surely, it's time to face our history and accept the undeniable truth. Failure to do so blocks the needed road to reconciliation."[27]

Today, no less than in 2015, it is unconscionable that the memory of those who had been abused and who had suffered such tremendous loss could be subject to attempts at erasure. I (Bernie) recall my father's pain, and the agony of other survivors who felt forced to relive their trauma and defend their mourned-for families against disinterment and interrogation. There is no doubt that some Canadians would prefer to ignore these issues. According to a 2018 Angus Reid survey, 53 percent of Canadians believe that "Canada spends too much time apologizing for residential schools—it's time to move on."[28] This sounds and feels very much like what we have heard ourselves: that Jews talk too much about the Holocaust, and it's time to move on.

Perhaps there is a time when the burden of the past—with its attendant responsibilities of memory and memorialization—can be laid to rest, but the decision of when to do that cannot be made by anyone but the wounded community. For others, that past, that memory, can be inconvenient and uncomfortable. That is, perhaps, as it must be.

But if we can honestly look at the effect of the residential schools on Indigenous Peoples in Canada,[29] we as settlers can perhaps finally understand that it is not necessary for the schools to be presented or understood as concentration camps for us to see them as genocidal.[30] Equally, it is not necessary for Sir John A. Macdonald to be Hitler or for his ministers (and those who followed) to be Nazis for us to recognize that genocide has taken place. However, it is certainly the case that genocide occurs when we do not value Indigenous cultures and when we try to coerce and manipulate people through hunger and spreading disease.

We support the conclusions of Chrisjohn and Young from 1997 when they observed that "residential Schools were one of the many attempts at the genocide of the Aboriginal Peoples inhabiting the area now commonly called Canada."[31] It is a discussion that is long overdue. To paraphrase words from the final report of the Inquiry on Missing and Murdered Indigenous Women and Girls, "the fact that this discussion is happening now doesn't mean that Indigenous people waited this long to speak up; it means it took this long for Canada to listen."[32]

And there is so much that we need to hear and to learn. We need to hear how the destructive behaviours demonstrated during the era of the residential school system manifested themselves in the Sixties Scoop, in which thousands of Indigenous children were removed from their homes. The problem persists. In Canada, 53.8 percent of children in foster care are Indigenous though they account for only 7.7 percent of the child population according to Census 2021.[33]

The effects of such destructive behaviour are devastating. According to Anishinaabe journalist Tanya Talaga, the rate of suicide in some Indigenous communities is so high that it starts to feel 'normal'...it becomes part of your normal everyday life."[34] Through our studies, we learned that the suicide rate among First Nations people in Saskatchewan is four times higher than the rate for the non-Indigenous population, and that teens make up a quarter of all First Nations suicide victims in Saskatchewan, while the rate among non–First Nations teens in the province is a much lower 6 percent.[35] What does it mean that, nationally, "the suicide rate for Indigenous people is three times the national average? And for young Indigenous men aged 15–24, it's five times higher than it is for those who aren't Indigenous."[36]

## Concluding Reflections: So Where Do We Go from Here?

One potential avenue is pursuing reconciliation, although the definition is contested.[37] From our perspective, the word suggests a return to a harmonious relationship between Indigenous Peoples and settlers. Was that in the eighteenth century, while imperial wars raged and fur trading was profitable, or was it in the early nineteenth century, before the land became more valuable than the relationship with its stewards? Certainly, as we see it, there is no time, post-Confederation, that can offer a checkpoint to which the damaged relationship can be reset. It's hard to make amends for past injuries when injuries are still being done. Commenting on a massive development that was taking place (in 2016) on the Ottawa River behind Parliament Hill, Algonquin Elder Albert Dumont wrote, "We are told over and over again in recent times that a 'new relationship of honour and mutual respect is at hand.' If Canadians are okay with a sacred site such as Asinabka being violated in the most despicable manner by the construction of high-rise buildings upon it, then their warped definition of 'reconciliation' is very different than mine."[38]

We like to think that Jewish tradition and Jewish experience has something useful to add to the settler discussion of how the journey to healing and reconciliation can be continued. Of course, we recognize that this is within the context that Indigenous Peoples must for themselves decide their own ways of knowing concerning the healing of their own communities. In Judaism, repentance first requires an apology that is complete and sincere. Second, there must be an effort to repair the damage that has been done. Finally, the behaviours that caused the injury must be utterly rejected and repudiated. Too often, and recently, we've read about governments who delayed on matters of compensation for Indigenous children caught up in the child welfare labyrinth; or we've read about pipeline construction that has continued in the face of protests led by hereditary Chiefs.

If we believe, as noted elsewhere in this chapter, that the genocide against Indigenous Peoples in Canada has not yet come to an end, then as settlers we have a responsibility to be *upstanders* rather than perpetrators or bystanders. We must stand up and stop genocide from continuing, we must refuse to act as passive bystanders when violence occurs.[39] The Holocaust taught Jews how easy it was to be abandoned. And that abandonment made the presence of rescuers shine all the more brightly. We need to find ways to be the righteous among *this* nation. It may require a certain amount of public courage to call out a friend or a colleague or a stranger for a thoughtless or racist comment, or to use our settler privilege for constructive purposes, but it's a courage that Jews, especially—because of our history—need to model. It requires that we listen to the voices of our better angels and, in the words of the prophet Isaiah: *Learn to do good. Seek Justice. Correct what is cruel. Rule justice for orphans. Fight the widow's cause.*

In so doing, as we help to heal others, we also heal ourselves.



## Notes

1 Smith, "Ahenakew Acquitted."
2 Raphaël Lemkin coined the word *genocide* and championed the creation of the United Nations Genocide Convention in 1948. Lemkin's interest was informed through his study of the mass murder of Armenians ordered by the leaders of the Ottoman Turks. His own family suffered grievously under the Nazis, with only his brother's family surviving the Holocaust. United States Holocaust Memorial Museum, "Coining a Word."
3 Logan, "Memory, Erasure, and National Myth," 149–165.
4 Powell and Peristerakis, "Genocide in Canada," 70–92.
5 Powell and Peristerakis, "Genocide in Canada," 72.
6 Fontaine, Dan, and Farber, "A Canadian Genocide."
7 United States Holocaust Memorial Museum, "January 20, 1942: Wannsee Conference."
8 Barta, "'They Appear.'"
9 Truth and Reconciliation Commission of Canada [TRC], *Honouring the Truth.*
10 Government of Canada, "Truth and Reconciliation Commission of Canada."
11 Fontaine, "Foreword," viii.
12 Woolford and Benvenuto, eds., *Canada and Colonial Genocide*, 373–390.
13 Brean, "'Cultural Genocide.'"
14 Raycraft, "MPs Back Motion."
15 Chrisjohn, Young, and Maraun, *The Circle Game.*
16 Woolford, "Ontological Destruction," 83.
17 Daschuk, *Clearing the Plains.*
18 Daschuk, *Clearing the Plains.*
19 Rheault, "Solving the 'Indian Problem.'"
20 Woolford and Benvenuto, eds., *Canada and Colonial Genocide*, 373–390.
21 Woolford, "Nodal Repair."
22 Mosby, "Administering Colonial Science."
23 Wattam, "Dr. Peter Henderson Bryce."
24 MacDonald, "Canada's History Wars."
25 Survivors of the Assiniboia Indian Residential School, *Did You See Us?.*
26 Stanton, "10 Stages of Genocide."
27 Farber, "Canada Must Stop."
28 Angus Reid Institute, "Truths of Reconciliation."
29 TRC, *They Came for the Children*
30 Woolford, *This Benevolent Experiment.*
31 Chrisjohn, Young, and Maraun, *The Circle Game*, 21.

32 National Inquiry into Missing and Murdered Indigenous Women and Girls, *Reclaiming Power and Place.*
33 Government of Canada, "Reducing the Number of Indigenous Children in Care."
34 CBC Radio, "Suicide Shouldn't Be 'Normal.'"
35 Stefanovich, "'We Don't Want Any More Tears.'"
36 Bird, "Report Makes 13 Calls."
37 Garneau, "Imaginary Spaces," 30.
38 Rousseau, "Selling Off."
39 Enough Project, "What Are Upstanders?"

## Sources

Angus Reid Institute. "Truths of Reconciliation: Canadians Are Deeply Divided on How Best to Address Indigenous Issues." June 7, 2018. https://angusreid.org/indigenous-canada/.

Barta, Tony. "'They Appear Actually to Vanish from the Face of the Earth': Aborigines and European Project in Australia Felix." *Journal of Genocide Research* 10, no. 4 (2008): 519–539. https://doi.org/10.1080/14623520802447768.

Bird, Lauren. "Report Makes 13 Calls to Action to Support Indigenous Youth Mental Health." CBC News, September 14, 2021. https://www.cbc.ca/news/canada/new-brunswick/indigenous-mental-health-youth-1.6175512.

Brean, Joseph. "'Cultural Genocide' of Canada's Indigenous Peoples Is a 'Mourning Label,' Former War Crimes Prosecutor Says." *National Post*, January 15, 2016. https://nationalpost.com/news/canada/cultural-genocide-of-canadas-indigenous-people-is-a-mourning-label-former-war-crimes-prosecutor-says.

CBC Radio. "Suicide Shouldn't Be 'Normal' in Indigenous Communities, Says 2018 Massey Lecturer Tanya Talaga." *The Current*, November 12, 2018. https://www.cbc.ca/radio/thecurrent/the-current-for-november-12-2018-1.4901727/suicide-shouldn-t-be-normal-in-indigenous-communities-says-2018-massey-lecturer-tanya-talaga-1.4902181.

Chrisjohn, Roland D., Sherri Young, and Michael Maraun. *The Circle Game: Shadows and Substance in the Indian Residential School Experience in Canada*. Theytus Books, 2006.

Daschuk, James. *Clearing the Plains: Disease, Politics of Starvation, and the Loss of Indigenous Life*. University of Regina Press, 2013.

Enough Project. "What Are Upstanders?" 2017. https://enoughproject.org/upstanders#.

Farber, Bernie. "Canada Must Stop Denying Its Genocide." *Ottawa Citizen*, June 19, 2015. https://ottawacitizen.com/news/national/bernie-farber-canada-must-stop-denying-its-genocide.

Fontaine, Phil, Michael Dan, and Bernie M. Farber. "A Canadian Genocide in Search of a Name." *Toronto Star*, July 19, 2013. https://www.thestar.com/opinion/commentary/2013/07/19/a_canadian_genocide_in_search_of_a_name.html.

Fontaine, Theodore. "Foreword." In *Colonial Genocide in Indigenous North America*, edited by Andrew Woolford, Jeff Benvenuto, and Alexander Laban Hinton. Duke University Press, 2014.

Garneau, David. "Imaginary Spaces of Conciliation and Reconciliation: Art, Curation, and Healing." In *Arts of Engagement: Taking Aesthetic Action In and Beyond the Truth and Reconciliation Commission of Canada*, edited by Dylan Robertson and Keavy Martin. Wilfrid Laurier University Press, 2016.

Government of Canada. "Reducing the Number of Indigenous Children in Care." May 24, 2024. https://www.sac-isc.gc.ca/eng/1541187352297/1541187392851.

Government of Canada. "Truth and Reconciliation Commission of Canada." Last modified May 28, 2024. https://www.rcaanc-cirnac.gc.ca/eng/1450124405592/1529106060525#chp2.

Logan, Tricia E. "Memory, Erasure, and National Myth." In *Colonial Genocide in Indigenous North America*, edited by Andrew Woolford, Jeff Benvenuto, and Alexander Laban Hinton. Duke University Press, 2014.

MacDonald, David B. A. "Canada's History Wars: Indigenous Genocide and Public Memory in the United States, Australia and Canada." *Journal of Genocide Research* 17, no. 4 (2015): 411–431. https://doi.org/10.1080/14623528.2015.1096583.

Mosby, Ian. "Administering Colonial Science: Nutrition Research and Human Biomedical Experimentation in Aboriginal Communities and Residential Schools, 1942–1952." *Histoire sociale / Social History* 46, no. 91 (2013): 145–172. https://doi.org/10.1353/his.2013.0015.

National Inquiry into Missing and Murdered Indigenous Women and Girls. *Reclaiming Power and Place: The Final Report of the National Inquiry on Missing and Murdered Indigenous Women and Girls*. Volume 1a. National Inquiry on Missing and Murdered Indigenous Women and Girls, 2019. https://www.mmiwg-ffada.ca/final-report/.

Powell, Christopher, and Julia Peristerakis. "Genocide in Canada: A Relational View." In *Colonial Genocide in Indigenous North America*, edited by Andrew Woolford, Jeff Benvenuto, and Alexander Laban Hinton. Duke University Press, 2014.

Raycraft, Richard. "MPs Back Motion Calling on Government to Recognize Residential Schools Program as Genocide." CBC News, October 27, 2022. https://www.cbc.ca/news/politics/house-motion-recognize-genocide-1.6632450.

Rheault, D'arcy. "Solving the 'Indian Problem': Assimilation Laws, Practices & Indian Residential Schools." 2011. https://www.omfrc.org/wp-content/uploads/2016/06/specialedition8.pdf.

Rousseau, Larry. "Selling Off Sacred Algonquin Land for Condos Not 'Reconciliation.'" *Huffington Post*, June 16, 2016. https://www.huffpost.com/archive/ca/entry/selling-off-sacred-algonquin-land-for-condos-not-reconciliation_b_10511760.

Smith, Joanna "Ahenakew Acquitted in Hate Case." *Toronto Star*, February 24, 2009. https://www.thestar.com/news/canada/ahenakew-acquitted-in-hate-case/article_3cc35d25-81c6-5e99-9351-051f7ef1aadf.html.

Stanton, Gregory. "10 Stages of Genocide." 2014. https://www.genocidewatch.com/tenstages.

Stefanovich, Olivia. "'We Don't Want Any More Tears': First Nations Urge Ottawa to Boost Mental Health Spending." CBC News, April 17, 2021. https://www.cbc.ca/news/politics/indigenous-mental-health-resources-federal-budget-2021-1.5989070.

Survivors of the Assiniboia Indian Residential School. *Did You See Us?: Reunion, Remembrance, and Reclamation at an Urban Indian Residential School.* Edited by Andrew Woolford. University of Manitoba Press, 2021.

Truth and Reconciliation Commission of Canada. "Honouring the Truth, Reconciling for the Future: Summary of the *Final Report of the Truth and Reconciliation Commission of Canada*." 2015. https://ehprnh2mwo3.exactdn.com/wp-content/uploads/2021/01/Executive_Summary_English_Web.pdf.

Truth and Reconciliation Commission of Canada. *They Came for the Children: Canada, Aboriginal Peoples, and the Residential Schools*. 2012. https://publications.gc.ca/collections/collection_2012/cvrc-trcc/ir4-4-2012-eng.pdf.

United States Holocaust Memorial Museum. "Coining a Word and Championing a Cause: The Story of Raphael Lemkin." https://encyclopedia.ushmm.org/content/en/article/coining-a-word-and-championing-a-cause-the-story-of-raphael-lemkin.

United States Holocaust Memorial Museum. "January 20, 1942: Wannsee Conference." https://encyclopedia.ushmm.org/content/en/timeline-event/holocaust/1942-1945/wannsee-conference.

Wattam, Jocelyn. "Dr. Peter Henderson Bryce: A Story of Courage." First Nations Child & Family Caring Society of Canada, 2016. https://fncaringsociety.com/sites/default/files/dr._peter_henderson_bryce_information_sheet.pdf.

Woolford, Andrew. "Nodal Repair and Networks of Destruction: Residential Schools, Colonial Genocide, and Redress in Canada." *Settler Colonial Studies* 3, no. 1 (2013): 65–81. http://dx.doi.org/10.1080/18380743.2013.761936.

Woolford, Andrew. "Ontological Destruction: Genocide and Canadian Aboriginal Peoples." *Genocide Studies and Prevention* 4, no. 1 (2009): 81–97. https://doi.org/10.3138/gsp.4.1.81.

Woolford, Andrew. *This Benevolent Experiment: Indigenous Boarding Schools, Genocide, and Redress in Canada and the United States*. University of Manitoba Press, 2017.

Woolford, Andrew, and Jeff Benvenuto, eds. *Canada and Colonial Genocide.* Routledge, 2018.

PART FOUR

# Asserting Indigenous Knowledges in Settler Colonial Canada

# asastîwa—They pile up

Solomon Ratt

ay-asastîwa kithâskiwin
ispî awasimî awâsisak
î-miskawihcik wâtihkânihk
oskaniwâwa î-asastîthiki.

ᐊᔭᓴᐢᑏᐘ ᑭᖭᐢᑭᐏᐣ
ᐃᐢᐲ ᐊᐘᓯᒦ ᐊᐚᓯᓴᐠ
ᐄ ᒥᐢᑲᐏᐦᒋᐠ ᐚᑎᐦᑳᓂᕽ
ᐅᐢᑲᓂᐚᐘ ᐄ ᐊᓴᐢᑏᖨᑭ᙮

Lies pile up
as more children
are found in graves
their bones in piles on top of each other

# Stolen Childhood

Solomon Ratt

cikôci:
î-awâsisîwiyan, î-papâmi-mîtawîyan,
î-papâmi-kwâskohtiyan, î-iskwâtawiyan mistikwak,
poko kîkway î-mâmaskâtaman
î-kihcinâhoyan î-sâkihikawiyan
...kîtahtawî ayamihikimâwak kâ-pî-kwâsihiskwâw.

ᒋᑰᒋ:
ᐄ ᐊᐚᓯᓰᐏᔭᐣ, ᐄ ᐸᐹᒥ ᒦᑕᐑᔭᐣ,
ᐄ ᐸᐹᒥ ᒁᐢᑯᐦᑎᔭᐣ, ᐄ ᐃᐢᒁᑕᐏᔭᐣ ᒥᐢᑎᑿᐠ,
ᐳᑯ ᑮᑿᐩ ᐄ ᒫᒪᐢᑳᑕᒪᐣ
ᐄ ᑭᐦᒋᓈᐦᐅᔭᐣ ᐄ ᓵᑭᐦᐃᑲᐏᔭᐣ
...ᑮᑕᐦᑕᐑ ᐊᔭᒥᐦᐃᑭᒫᐘᐠ ᑳ ᐱ ᒁᓯᐦᐃᐢᒁᐤ᙮

Imagine:
you are a child, playing about,
jumping, climbing trees,
marvelling at everything in the world,
secure in the love you feel from others
...then the priests came to kidnap

# Being and Knowing Home

Joyce Green

THESE DAYS, IN WINTER DARKNESS AND IN SUMMER light I arise early and watch dawn advance over the Rockies—the remains of Naɬmuq¢in. Naɬmuq¢in is central to the ancient Ktunaxa creation story and is a grandfatherly figure to Ktunaxa.[1] When he knew he was to leave this world (to die), he travelled throughout ʔamakʔis Ktunaxa and named many places, as a gift for Ktunaxa, his children, who he knew would soon arrive. He was preparing this place for us. And then he died, and his remains became the Rocky Mountains, the largest mountain range in the North American part of Turtle Island. The Rockies are on the eastern side of ʔamakʔis Ktunaxa, which extends out onto the eastern slopes and foothills. Naɬmuq¢in's remains extend from yakɬiki ("where one's feet are," in this case referring to Naɬmuq¢in's feet[2]) near Yellowhead Pass in the north, to south of Tuhuɬnana, which means little bull trout, at contemporary Missoula; and down into the Yellowstone area, to the place Naɬmuq¢in called Ear; and to the west of Ktunwakanmituk Mi¢qaqas, which means chickadee (Revelstoke); ¢aɬnunʔiḱ (Nakusp); ʔaqiyamɬup, which means clear water (Nelson); Kiksiɬuk (Castlegar); and Spukin (Spokane).[3] With these names, I am telling you some of the parameters of Ktunaxa territory so that, should you live here or visit, you will know where you are. I am also telling you these things so that wherever you are, if you make a land acknowledgement, you will undertake to do so with attention to where you are and whose land you are on.

I want you to think about the significance of this. ʔamakʔis Ktunaxa, Ktunaxa territory, the unceded, ancestral, stolen, and occupied home of the Ktunaxa people, is defined in large part by the story of which Naɫmuqȼin is a part. The places on this territory were named by Naɫmuqȼin in the Ktunaxa language, an ancient isolate unrelated to other languages. The story, the language, and the people predate Canada by millennia. This is how we know the extent of our territory. These kinds of stories and ancient accounts are how Indigenous Peoples know and demonstrate where their specific land is. They are an iteration of Indigenous law.[4]

My tiny plot of land is on the outskirts of Cranbrook—named after the British home of one of the earliest land thieves and oppressors of Ktunaxa. Its Ktunaxa name is ʔa·kiskaqɫiʔit—"where two trails meet on the prairie." To the southeast, ʔa·kin̓mi (pile of arrows) looms, which the locals call Mount Baker, named for the one who named Cranbrook. Its summit is adorned with communications towers that quite unintentionally prove the point of an ancient Ktunaxa story about that mountain, one that teaches about disobedience, jealousy, and consequences.[5] Which name is more authentic to this place? Pay attention to the politics of naming: they tell you where and who you *are* or *are not*.

I see the English names as an historical progression of white men pissing on Ktunaxa territory and others' territories, pissing on ancient names with venerable stories drawn from these lands and replacing them with their names, or names tied to anywhere but here. This served their purpose of replacing Indigenous Peoples with themselves. It fuelled their myth of terra nullius, the discredited legal doctrine that framed Turtle Island as an unknown and empty land awaiting white European settlement and white European names. As though Indigenous Peoples weren't here, had no rights and nothing of value, offered no knowledge, held no standing in the colonizers' pantheon of law and religion.

When I use Ktunaxa names, I am making it clear to you that we *are* here. This is our territory, and our names are the original, most authentic ones. If you make land acknowledgements *here, anywhere* in ʔamakʔis Ktunaxa, you must acknowledge that you are on the *unceded, stolen* territory of the Ktunaxa Nation, and you may not acknowledge any other nation. I encourage you to learn where you are, and to use the Ktunaxa names.[6] And I encourage you to think about what it means to be on, to benefit from, the *unceded, stolen* territory of the Ktunaxa Nation. Do you think you have responsibilities arising from this?

Much of the Ktunaxa language has been erased by the genocidal work of residential schools and the racist repression from settler governments and communities.[7] I am a very junior student of Ktunaxa. My maternal grandmother was raised as a speaker. The language was spoken, along with English, in her childhood home. "You go forward, you don't go back," she said, and no more, when I asked her why she would not teach us a word of it. In her experience, being Indigenous meant being excluded, ignored, and unsafe. I only recently learned that she and her sister were sent to residential school as "day students"—who were there all week, for they could not be brought back and forth from their distant home. She never spoke of this, except once, to my mother. *I didn't like it*, she said. She did what she thought best for her and for us, but it did not save any of us from the intergenerational consequences of her own experiences and her life decisions.

Those losses are why I, in my sixties, must struggle to learn something about Ktunaxa culture, language, and history. Both the losses and the reconnections are hard. Those of us who have been away, or have never been home, are not welcomed by everyone. We search for connection, avoid connection, fear rejection. We try to find spaces where we might be accepted. In the words of Amanda Buffalo, writing about intergenerational cultural alienation, "The pain is intense. It is real. It is raw. It is why I write".[8] Me too.

Ka titi ma qakłik Bessie (my late maternal grandmother whose name was Bessie) and I did not have a good relationship. She suffered from an emotional condition I call "clamshell heart"—she could not accept affection, she rarely gave it to her children, and she gave it to only some of her grandchildren. I was not one of them. Clamshell heart is often a consequence of childhood trauma. I wonder if the residential school was part of that—and what the other parts of her life were like. She was a woman of few words, silent or monosyllabic in most spaces. She was without the power to define her own life, accustomed to her interests and her wishes being ignored by those she lived with and depended on. As an adult she lived with abuse in her marriage. Because my grandmother was a woman who did not—perhaps could not—speak of her own life, I do not know how she experienced these things.

Once, when I returned from university wearing a beaded barrette in my hair, she said to me in a soft voice laden with disapproval, "Boy, you're going Indian." I did not attend her funeral, angry at her harshness and rejection over the years. But some years after her death I had a dream about her. For all my life she had worn her straight grey hair short, held back by two plastic combs. In my dream she had long dark hair, she was young, and she spoke to me in Ktunaxa. "Grandma, I can't understand you," I said, but she answered "yes you can" and continued to speak Ktunaxa. I awoke and understood she had given me permission, the permission she had never given any of us, withheld during her lifetime but granted to me after her death. And I understood that she was finally comfortable being who she was.

It took many more years before I was in a position to proceed, though; years before I was on disability leave and returned home, before I was around Ktunaxa speakers, before I learned of the magnificent Ktunaxa language initiatives that have offered me so much. I think of Bessie very often as I learn a word, a phrase, a story... an insight into who we are.

So, I want you to think about that: the colonial practices and the racism that stripped Indigenous Peoples of their languages, making it harder to recount the stories that prove specific Indigenous title. To know the stories that remind Ktunaxa of the love that Naɬmuqǂin expressed for us when he named our territory *for us*. Think, too, about the shame and fear that people felt for *being* Indigenous and that produced clamshell heart; the loss of language, stories, and practices that make us fully who we are and demonstrate our title to our territories. That title is to unceded stolen land and to sovereignty and jurisdiction over it. In the words of the late great Nisga'a leader Joe Gosnell, we own it "lock, stock and barrel."[9]

Indigenous title is practised by the specific relationships we have with our land. For Ktunaxa, that relationship is framed by the principle of ʔa·kxamis q̓api qapsin—our responsibility to all living things. This is a relationship mandated by Nupik̓a, the Creator. When I tell you that I watch dawn advance, I'm inviting you to think about this ancient order, the pre-eminent claim on this territory, and the relationships to the land invoked by that claim. I want you to think about the colonial and capitalist conditions that contest Ktunaxa reality and the realities of other Indigenous nations in the context of Canada's claim to sovereignty. This is framed by *the truth of that little land theft matter*.[10]

Corporate activity authorized by the state has served the purpose of supporting the sovereignty claims of Canada: think of the Hudson's Bay Company (HBC) and its monopoly charter granted by the crown of a state on the other side of the Atlantic Ocean. As the HBC extended its territorial reach, it was extending the reach of British law and the

Crown's sovereignty claim through the alchemy of a Crown grant of the authority to do this. There is a plethora of corporate examples of extending colonialism, extending the state's domination of Indigenous Peoples, in tandem with the pursuit of corporate profitability. Perhaps a certain pipeline rammed through unceded Wet'suwet'en lands and through səlilwətaɬ lands (the Tsleil-Waututh Nation) without consent, with the protection of the King's Cowboys, and completed in 2024 at enormous taxpayer expense,[11] comes to mind. Colonialism is not merely historic. I digress.

Corporate interests, not adventure, saving souls, or philanthropy, is what always motivates colonialism. Now, corporate interests are fused with democratic government interests and are presented as essential for a newer god: "the economy." Corporate interests continue to be a preoccupation of Canadian governments—especially important to the policies of land theft and in support of extractivist capitalism. Furs and fish, bison meat and hides. Railways, highways, hydro dams. Clearcut and old growth logging. Coal and mineral mining. Pipelines, ski hills, and golf courses. That's colonialism. In ʔamakʔis Ktunaxa and in the territories of other Indigenous nations, all of these things and more produce wealth *from our lands* for settler communities, corporations, and governments, while violating the principle by which Ktunaxa are supposed to live, ʔa·kxamis q̓api qapsin—responsibility to all living things.

They also violate our title without respect for the fundamental Indigenous right to give or withhold our *free, prior, and informed consent*[12] and impose destruction on our territories and all living things. Here in ʔamakʔis Ktunaxa there is a long list of extinctions and extirpations—a list that includes swaq̓mu (salmon), naxni (mountain cariboo), naɬmiť (badgers), and certain frogs, birds, fish, bats, and insects, particularly bees. The large predators and the ungulates are hunted by those who do not have a responsibility to all living things—who do not know these creatures are our relatives. The waterways have been dammed and used as sewers and conduits for everything from pulp mill effluent to toxic levels of selenium.[13] Settlers intent on "recreating" quad and drive into the back country, further stressing those creatures that remain there. They descend on parts of the territory like locusts, stripping the huckleberries and the morels, sometimes for profit and without regard for the creatures that depend on them or our interest in these things. Our ancestral home has become a source of wealth and an amusement park for those who have no concept of responsibilities to all living things, or of our pre-eminent claim to this land.

At its core, colonialism is about profit acquired by stealing someone else's land and resources while denying the sovereignty and humanity of those who are oppressed. It is legitimated by racism and by belief in the inferiority of those who are being replaced, who *need* to be replaced. The process and the belief system are bureaucratized into public policy, enforced and administered by apparently good people in the name of us all, on behalf of governments that continue to deny our rights. The process and belief system are distilled into the dominant culture. That's Canada.

As the late great Elijah Harper[14] said, "With your democratic state, you oppressed us, democratically."[15] And still do.

Structural racism is embedded into Canadian politics, institutions, and cultures, invisible especially to the privileged white male cadre that benefits from them. "White privilege" is a relatively new term to many. It refers precisely to the unearned benefits of whiteness, sustained by state and private institutions and by narratives in popular culture.[16] Many consider the state-wide affirmative action opportunities that benefit white folks as "merit"; those who don't succeed in this paradigm are considered to lack merit. Most white people consider themselves to be good people, in no way implicated in past and continuing colonialism and its oppression of Indigenous Peoples.[17] They do not recognize their privilege: the state, built on white privilege, capitalist interests, and against Indigenous Peoples, was designed for them at Indigenous expense. It still is.

Because of settler state propaganda in our education systems, most white folks don't know the Canadian history of colonialism: don't know its processes and its consequences, don't understand their privilege and culpability because of it, and in respect of the land, don't actually know where they are. Here, they are in "Cranbrook," "British Columbia," where they look at "Mount Baker" and "Fisher Peak"; where (until 2023, when the name was changed to "Spirit of the Rockies" while some "locals" ranted about the insult to "our" history[18]) they celebrated "Sam Steele Days," named after another early oppressor of Ktunaxa, with some dressing up as caricatures of paramilitary scouts and privileged white ladies—demonstrating colonial ignorance and enacting white supremacy in their entertainments.[19] Sam Steele Days, like similar festivals across Turtle Island, re-enact settler mythologies, even when organizers invite a few "Indians" to ride horses or a float in their parade.

But they still hold and abuse our land.

My birth, childhood, and youth were shaped by this territory, as my family moved from ʔaqiyamɬup (Nelson) to ʔaqanɬiqat ("something that has no tail," or Perry Creek), to ʔa·kiskaqɬiʔit (Cranbrook), to Kamanusuk̓pun, meaning *pine forest with no low branches—one could see a long way* (Canal Flats, lying between Columbia Lake and the Kootenay River), to Nicholson, a hamlet with no Ktunaxa name because there was no need for one, and then to our farm up the Blaeberry north of ʔaknuqɬuk (which means *muddy water making it look white*, describing the Kicking Horse River at Golden). I graduated from Mount Baker Secondary School in Cranbrook (named for Colonel Baker, memorialized on schools, hotels, and streets in Cranbrook and in Nelson) a very long time ago, part of a cohort of nearly entirely white students. No one noticed the missing Ktunaxa students, and no one noticed me either. I have never been notified of a class reunion. It is as though I was never there.

Thanks to Canada Student Loans and encouragement from an unsuccessful NDP electoral candidate, I left to go to university, to learn interesting things, to stretch my wings and find a means to support myself rather than rely on a patriarchal oppressor for my well-being. I cannot overstate the gratitude I have to that woman, whose name I cannot recall, for her encouragement to the class she came to speak to, in which I heard that message. In my family, there was not much value placed on school, and there were no expectations that I would get a university education and a career. We were rural people, and women were expected to marry, procreate, and carry on servicing the needs of others. *I didn't wanna live like that.* And once I left, life took over, and the larger chunk of it passed before I returned.

Well into my fifties, teaching at the University of Regina and married, I became incapacitated from a disability resulting from a spinal injury, surgery, and related complications. It was a blessing. Because of my disability I was able to return to this territory and spend time with my elderly and frail mother. I've become a student again, of my Ktunaxa heritage, the Nation and language, and the complicated politics of the Nation in the context of twenty-first-century colonialism. I have come home, as much as one can when home is ultimately a place in time.

Identity is complicated for most of us. My heritage is English on my dad's side, and English, Ktunaxa, and Cree-Scots Métis (or half-breeds, as we would have called it) on my mom's side. I am all of these things. It doesn't always fit together easily. Coming to terms with the problematics in the context of people I love and relationships that define me has been essential to accepting myself. My adored British grandmother was a most loving presence in my life—and utterly confident in the righteousness of the British Empire and its activities. My mother acquired "Indian Status" from the Canadian government and membership in our ancestral community, Yaq̓it ʔa·knuqⱡiʔit (Tobacco Plains), at the age of eighty-five. That latter event invokes a conceit of colonialism: the suggestion she *became* something through an incantation of government recognition. Yet she has been who she is all of her life, despite not being recognized as "Indian" by the state or by our band. I, too, am recognized by Yaq̓it ʔa·knuqⱡiʔit as a band member, with more family members expected to join as their applications work their way through the daunting and lengthy federal and band processes. This represents a form of homecoming for us, members of our ancestral family that never had "status" and were largely segregated from our Ktunaxa kin and community by the decisions of others.

Living as an authentic person in the conditions of political and personal contradiction and complexity is, for me, a life work still in progress. Perhaps that is a life work for all of us. I have a political analysis of Canada, and I pursue the political objective of contributing to revisioning the state and repositioning Indigenous Peoples as the rightful owners of our territories. I am a product of and an advocate for ʔamakʔis Ktunaxa, where I drew my first breath. When I draw my last, I shall return to the earth here.

Relationship to place is fundamental to Indigenous identities. We are deeply connected to particular geographies, to territory that has framed and sustained our nations for millennia, recounted by ancient stories and practices. Here, I know where our families ranched, hunted, logged, lived, loved, suffered, survived, and died. Ka ma qaklik Shirley (my mother, Shirley) was born in her great-aunt's farmhouse in the South Country, at Flagstone, now long gone. I have graves to visit, sites that contain the remains of many of my ancestors and include my brothers, father, grandparents, great-grandparents, great-great-grandparents, great-great-great-grandparents, and extended family. Before them, graves were more ephemeral, but our ancestors' bones form the soil here. We do not so much claim this land as we are claimed by it and return to it. It is a sacred space.

Ktunaxa have always had visitors from other nations, and some stayed with us with our permission, but it was not until 1884 that visitors arrived who claimed our land. That year, the Ktunaxa community in the Tobacco

Plains area was visited by Major Peter O'Reilly, superintendent of Indian reserves for the province of British Columbia. He spoke to Chief David, a respected Ktunaxa Nasuʔkin (leader) and ka ʔa·kniǩnamu ma qaklik Nasuʔkin Kanuhusłi/Tawit (my relative; my kin—specifically, my great-great-great-grandfather). David's name (Tawit, in Ktunaxa pronunciation) is remembered by some as Red Horn—Kanuhuskɨi—but only his English baptismal name given by a priest is recorded in the historical document to which I refer here. Think about that too—how we are known, and who decides.

Some years later, one Mr. Galbraith, then the Indian agent for the Tobacco Plains Indian Reserve, took depositions about this meeting from people who knew of it or were at it. This was because Ktunaxa people at Tobacco Plains challenged what had happened, which is not what was supposed to happen and not what Chief David agreed to, in the matter of the reserve. In what follows I draw on two versions of the Galbraith notes. You will bear in mind that David was almost certainly speaking Ktunaxa, and O'Reilly, English. The interpreter is not identified.

O'Reilly insisted on speaking with David: "I should like to speak with the principal man" (and do think about the patriarchal and governance assumptions in that). When David arrived, there was some discussion between them about their individual authority for the meeting: David was selected by his community and was a noted warrior and leader; O'Reilly was a government apparatchik. David noted that he did not speak for all Ktunaxa and that Isadore and the Chiefs from Ktunaxa on the Saint Marys River should participate, but O'Reilly, the visitor, would not accommodate that request. O'Reilly claimed he had been sent by the queen to "give" the "Indians" lands for reserves. He claimed that the Crown owned the land; David said he owned his lands. David noted that he was a Chief, had earned his status as a warrior, and his words "could not be thrown away." He noted he was afraid of white men's promises because he had seen they did not keep them: he referred to the case of the Blackfoot people who had signed Treaty 7 in 1877. He said Ktunaxa did not want and had not asked for reserves but would take their land where they wanted. He asked how O'Reilly imagined he could give us lands, which were already our lands. He said he would take all of Turtle Island for the native people of Turtle Island.

O'Reilly told this senior Nasuʔkin, "Don't talk like a child. Talk sensible and choose your land."

David outlined the extent of ʔamakʔis Ktunaxa far more precisely than I have done for you, from north to south and east to west, as Naƚmuqȼin named it *as a gift to Ktunaxa*, and said that was the land he wanted for Ktunaxa.

O'Reilly again dismissed the Chief's words, telling him to stop talking "nonsense," that settlers were coming, and David must choose a reserve. He refused to accept that David's lands were on both sides of the Medicine Line—the international boundary that never took into account the Indigenous Peoples it divided, that still divides Ktunaxa (known as Ksanka or Kootenai, south of the border) people and territory, and many other nations too. The majority of David's community and family lived to the south of it. David said, "Who are you to run a line through my house and divide my children?"

David made one more effort to identify Ktunaxa territory on the Canadian side of the Medicine Line and said, "This I want, and that is my last word." Further discussion made it evident there was no agreement, and O'Reilly terminated the meeting, saying he would come see David the following day at noon to continue the discussion. But when David and his advisors arrived, O'Reilly had packed up and moved on. He had arbitrarily identified Tobacco Plains—the reserve—and an Indian agent, Michael Phillipps (Ka ma ʔaȼmiƚukpukam, my great-great-grandfather, who married David's daughter Rowena), was appointed to manage it. Ktunaxa were forced onto four tiny reserves, policed by Indian agents and cops, separated from each other by force and the *Indian Act* and separated from Ksanka in the so-called USA, and subjected to the oppressive and genocidal practices of the church and the Canadian government. And yes, there was a residential school in that set of policies, the one where my grandmother Bessie and many others went and learned to be silent, to forget, to hide feelings, to deny *themselves*.

And the rest of this story is our collective history—yours and mine. That is the history you need to acknowledge, unpack, and remedy if there is to be anything worthy of the notion of "reconciliation."[20] Most settlers do not know this history, and settler governments continue to inflict policies on Indigenous Peoples that make a lie of their blandishments about "reconciliation." Colonialism begins with land theft and imposition of alien and racist priorities, laws, and policies. Here on Turtle Island, and on ʔamakʔis Ktunaxa, colonialism has never ended.

Dawn advances, just the same. Some things are immutable. The constellations wheel across the firmament with the seasons, each with a Ktunaxa story that teaches us something. Many of you, too, watch and marvel at these things. The moon—¢iłmitił natanik̓ (night sun)—rises over ʔa·kiňmi, a mountain with the ancient Ktunaxa story about deceit, jealousy, and consequences. Nałmuq¢in marks the eastern part of ʔamakʔis Ktunaxa, black against early dawn and the last place lit by natanik̓ at dusk. In this place, days are fragrant with juniper, fir, and pine, and sweet with the sound of the wind in the trees. Many of you, too, know and love this place.

Some of you perform land acknowledgements to show your respect for Indigenous Peoples. Be careful in matters like this, because some of you do not know what you are doing. Remember this: in Canada, you are on Indigenous Land wherever you are. In ʔamakʔis Ktunaxa, some of you acknowledge nations that are not from here, who contest our claim to our territory.[21] You may not choose who you recognize: this is not a popularity contest for settlers to decide. All Indigenous nations have their own laws for resolving such matters, but you may not participate in that. You must recognize what *we* say our lands are, not what others say they are. Do not thank us: we have not invited you or given you permission. Nałmuq¢in named this land as a gift to us. He died, and we were placed here. Kanuhuskłi / nasuʔkin Tawit (Chief David) claimed ʔamakʔis Ktunaxa for us *because it is ours*. When you are on the territory framed in the Ktunaxa creation story, that great expanse of land that includes the East and West Kootenay, the eastern slopes of the Rockies, into the Columbia, and down into Montana, Idaho, and Washington, you are on ʔamakʔis Ktunaxa, the unceded and stolen territory of the Ktunaxa Nation. Say it with respect.



## Notes

1 My account of this part of the Creation Story is informed by my Ktunaxa language class, taught by Vi Birdstone, Elise McKay, Terrance Gatchalian, and Mara Nelson.

2 Vi Birdstone, personal communication with author, February 2, 2024.

3 I am only a beginning student of Ktunaxa language. My thanks to Sophie Pierre, Vi Birdstone, and ka nana qak̓łik Mara Nelson for their help with Ktunaxa. For those who would like to know what the Ktunaxa language sounds like, consult First Voices online (https://www.firstvoices.com/explore/FV/sections/Data/Ktunaxa/Ktunaxa/Ktunaxa). The Ktunaxa language uses some letters that English speakers will not recognize, but

when you hear them, you will recognize the sounds as ones that are easy to make.

4 Indigenous law and Indigenous title may be seen in the suites of culturally specific practices of particular Indigenous Peoples, which are transferred intergenerationally. While not unproblematic, even the Supreme Court of Canada has had to begin thinking of the embodiment of Indigenous law and title in intergenerational practices and in ancient stories: See *Delgamuukw v. British Columbia* and *Tsilhqot'in Nation v. British Columbia.*

5 I am grateful to Sophie Pierre and Alfred Joseph for clarifying the meaning of *The War in the Sky*. Personal communication with Sophie Pierre, March 31, 2023.

6 The Columbia Basin Environmental Education Network offers introductory classes in Ktunaxa from time to time. See online, for example, "Ktunaxa Language Course" and "Contact Us."

7 Many in the settler population understand the fact of genocide in Canada's treatment of Indigenous Peoples, but for those who are still struggling to understand this, consult Canadian Political Science Association, "CPSA Reconciliation Committee's Statement."

8 Buffalo, *Kēdzéntēdé Kedzedį̄*, 32–33.

9 See Nisga'a Lisims Government online; Kerr-Lazenby, "Planned Completion ."

10 Green, "Enacting Reconciliation."

11 Initially budgeted at $7.3 billion, the cost of the project exceeded $34 billion. Bakx, "For Its Next Trick."

12 United Nations, "Declaration on the Rights of Indigenous Peoples," sections 10, 19, and 29. See also United Nations, "Free, Prior and Informed Consent."

13 Cruickshank, "$1.2B Later."

14 De Bruin, "Elijah Harper."

15 Green, ed., *Indivisible*, 20.

16 For contextualized discussions about how white privilege functions and its negative impact, see Gebhard, McLean, and St. Denis, eds., *White Benevolence*. For a thoughtful white-friendly and blessedly brief consideration of racism and white privilege intended to facilitate understanding of these matters, see Parasram and Khasnabish, *Frequently Asked White Questions*.

17 Humphreys, "Even those Saying Indigenous Land Acknowledgments." According to Humphreys, "a solid majority of Canadians accept that injustice to Indigenous people in Canada amounts to genocide, but few think they have personal responsibility, even for injustices continuing today; few even blame the government.... A solid majority of Canadians—60 per cent of respondents—accept that Indigenous peoples were the target of some form of genocide in Canada, the poll says; 29 per cent strongly agreed and 31 per cent agreed somewhat. A quarter of respondents rejected the genocide label and 15 per cent didn't provide an answer. Most Canadians reject personal responsibility for past and current injustices targeting Indigenous peoples, according to the poll. Almost 80 per cent of

respondents across the country said they strongly disagree with the notion they bear personal responsibility for past injustice."

18 As of 2023 Sam Steele Days is renamed Spirit of the Rockies, to the disapproval of some. Warner, "Name Change" and "Support Sam Steele Days." These submissions demonstrate how invisible Ktunaxa are and how little certain settlers think or know about Ktunaxa and Canadian history and realities.

19 Those wishing to explore the concept of whiteness in relation to power and privilege may want to consult Dua, "'Our Canadian Culture.'" 196–244.

20 Green, "Enacting Reconciliation."

21 See the land acknowledgement of the East Kootenay SPCA online for an example of this (BCSPCA, "East Kootenay"). The SPCA is squarely in exclusive Ktunaxa territory; evidently, the SPCA doesn't know where it is.



## Sources

Bakx, Kyle. "For Its Next Trick, Ottawa Must Unload the $34B Trans Mountain Pipeline. It Won't Be Easy." CBC News, April 14, 2024. https://www.cbc.ca/news/canada/calgary/tmx-trans-mountain-sale-freeland-1.7176629.

BCSPCA. "East Kootenay." https://spca.bc.ca/locations/east-kootenay/.

Buffalo, Amanda. *Kēdzēntēdé Kedzedį: Aunties, Disestablishment, and the Making of Communiversitea*. PhD diss., Department of Social Justice Education, University of Toronto, 2022.

Canadian Political Science Association. "CPSA Reconciliation Committee's Statement and Briefing Note on Genocide on the Anniversary of the December 15, 2015 Release of the TRC's *Final Report*." December 15, 2021. https://cpsa-acsp.ca/wp-content/uploads/2021/12/CPSA-Genocide-Statement_Briefing-Note-11-12-2021_E.pdf.

Columbia Basin Environmental Education Network. "Contact Us." https://cbeen.ca/contact-cbeen/.

Columbia Basin Environmental Education Network. "Ktunaxa Language Course." https://cbeen.ca/ktunaxa-language-course/.

Cruickshank, Ainslie. "$1.2B later, Teck Resources Has Barely Put a Dent in Its Pollution Problems, Documents Show." *Narwhal*, April 6, 2023. https://thenarwhal.ca/bc-teck-selenium-water-treatment/.

de Bruin, Tabitha. "Elijah Harper." *Canadian Encyclopedia*, last edited May 30, 2024. https://www.thecanadianencyclopedia.ca/en/article/elijah-harper.

*Delgamuukw v. British Columbia* [1997] 3 SCR 1010. https://scc-csc.lexum.com/scc-csc/scc-csc/en/item/1569/index.do.

Dua, Enakshi. "'Our Canadian Culture Has Been Squeamish About Gathering Race-Based Statistics': The Circulation of Discourses of Race and Whiteness Among Canadian Universities, Newspapers, and Alt-Right Groups." In *Coloniality and Racial (In)Justice in the University: Counting for Nothing?*, edited by Sunera Thobani. University of Toronto Press, 2022.

Gebhard, Amanda, Sheelah McLean, and Verna St. Denis, eds. *White Benevolence: Racism and Colonial Violence in the Helping Professions*. Fernwood Publishing, 2022.

Green, Joyce. "Enacting Reconciliation." Canadian Political Science Association, 2016. https://cpsa-acsp.ca/documents/conference/2016/Green.pdf.

Green, Joyce, ed. *Indivisible: Indigenous Human Rights*. Fernwood Publishing, 2014.

Humphreys, Adrian. "Even Those Saying Indigenous Land Acknowledgments Don't Feel Personal Responsibility for Injustices: Poll." *National Post*, July 1, 2023. https://nationalpost.com/news/canada/canada-indigenous-poll.

Kerr-Lazenby, Mina. "Planned Completion for Trans Mountain Pipeline Another Blow for Tsleil-Waututh Nation." *North Shore News*, April 8, 2024. https://www.nsnews.com/local-news/trans-mountain-pipeline-project-tsleil-waututh-nation-8565677.

Nisga'a Lisims Government. https://thestarphoenix.com/opinion/columnists/doug-cuthand-first-nations-are-fighting-the-sask-first-act.

Parasram, Ajay, and Alex Khasnabish. *Frequently Asked White Questions*. Fernwood Publishing, 2022.

*Tsilhqot'in Nation v. British Columbia* [2014] 2 SCR 257. https://scc-csc.lexum.com/scc-csc/scc-csc/en/item/14246/index.do.

United Nations. "Free, Prior and Informed Consent of Indigenous Peoples." Human Rights Office of the High Commissioner, 2013. https://www.ohchr.org/sites/default/files/Documents/Issues/IPeoples/FreePriorandInformedConsent.pdf.

United Nations. "United Nations Declaration on the Rights of Indigenous Peoples." September 13, 2007. https://www.un.org/esa/socdev/unpfii/documents/drips_en.pdf.

Warner, Gerry. "Name Change to Spirit of the Rockies a Bad Decision." *East Kootenay News*, January 29, 2023. https://www.e-know.ca/regions/cranbrook/name-change-to-spirit-of-the-rockies-a-bad-decision/.

Warner, Gerry. "Support Sam Steele Days Over Spirit of the Rockies." *East Kootenay News*, March 6, 2023. https://www.e-know.ca/regions/cranbrook/support-sam-steele-days-over-spirit-of-the-rockies/?fbclid=IwAR3dvWD5INRO7vuMLDfAXciNHJrnsbYs6VNHoyOIH85tZeu2s2rEjpafpJs.

# Surviving Institutions in Canada's Polite Society

Rebecca Major

When thinking of Canada, there is an association with politeness, which can easily be found in casual conversation, on the Internet, and in publications. Tropes of politeness, however, can hide another side: the experience of those marginalized by colonial society and its government institutions and the service delivery agencies they operate. Indigenous-settler relations are grounded in settler colonialism and are part of the daily experiences of Indigenous Peoples (First Nations, Métis, and Inuit) living in Canada. Over the years and well into the twenty-first century, many politicians have denied that racism or a colonial history and its ongoing legacies exist.[1] Unfortunately, the behaviour of settler Canadian "polite society" remains detrimental, as the denials of institutional racism and other negative daily experiences sometimes result in the loss of life. Service agencies, while generally thought to be neutral public goods, are actually structures that can and do imperil the lives of Indigenous Peoples. These institutions include health-care settings such as hospitals, social services, and the criminal justice system.

"Polite society's" institutions are, at minimum, exhausting and can be, at maximum, deadly for Indigenous Peoples. This chapter begins by comparing examples of Canadian settler leaders denying colonial history, contributing to entrenched institutional denialism that impacts Indigenous lives. Denialism ensures settler social privilege; it functions at the expense of Indigenous Peoples' differences and seeks to erase their lived experience and history. As Canadian leadership shifts to acknowledge these institutional problems, those administering the institutions must also be active agents of change. The problem is that those who make the decisions often deny problems exist, which creates an additional problem: no one can address a problem that is not acknowledged. How Indigenous Peoples survive and—in far too many instances—do not survive the Canadian public service institutions are the conversations we are not supposed to have.

## Denialism

Denialism is complex but can be broadly construed as stories of renunciation by "people, organizations, governments or whole societies" when a mass atrocity or genocide occurs that is morally unsettling.[2] In the colonial context, such denialism take several forms, including literal and interpretive denial.[3] Literal forms of denial can include refusing to acknowledge something happened or denying historical events. Interpretive forms can include changing or distorting the meaning of an event, such as telling someone that a lived experience is perspective and not necessarily truth.[4]

Some examples in Canada include national myth-making to maintain the collective ideas of events or history[5] and denialism with Indian residential schools.[6] In these kinds of scenarios, we can pinpoint an exercise of the interpretive denialism that can include telling someone events were simply their interpreted understanding and not fact, which is a form of violence.[7] In some cases, interpretive denialism leads to behaviour involved in a refusal of equitable or respectful service, and this can determine whether someone will survive their interaction with a public service, such as a hospital visit.[8] When government employees and service delivery people practise interpretive denialism, the violence is more personal because there is a direct impact on someone's individual experience. In this way, "polite society" maintains and regulates social space through forms of denialism, which informs service delivery institutions.

## Denial of Institutional Discrimination Against Indigenous Peoples

The Canadian settler state has a history of discrimination through policies such as the *Indian Act*, but also a history of denying that its policies and positions are discriminatory: this is interpretive denialism.

The NIMMIWG *Final Report*, released in 2019, attributes the problem of violence towards Indigenous women and girls to colonization (as a structure and a mechanism) and its ongoing effects.[9] One might expect a denial of institutional racism or discrimination by someone in the Conservative Party of Canada, as the party has a history of minimizing the significance of race in its political approaches. As an example, during the 2021 federal election, the Conservative Party of Canada exercised literal denialism through a lack of policy or political platform in dealing with racism.[10] This narrative—the denial of racism—continued after changes in leadership when Andrew Scheer (2017) and then Erin O'Toole (2020) took over.[11]

Liberal Prime Minister Justin Trudeau also started his time in office with denialism. While talking at New York University, Trudeau stated that Canada did not have some of the baggage other Western nations have, such as a colonial past.[12] Former MP Romeo Saganash explained to reporters how he found these statements similar to those of Stephen Harper in the past.[13] Following Trudeau's statement in New York, his position did change around denials of colonial history when confronted, but that did not necessarily translate to other offices of leadership within the federal bureaucracy.

## Engaging Institutions

Health care and the Canadian judicial systems are government public institutions that exist through physical spaces such as hospitals, courthouses, and correctional institutions, to name just a few. The racism embedded in institutions is the result of colonial history in Canada. The general settler population in Canada turn to these institutions when they need help or support. However, these institutions are neither helpful nor supportive of Indigenous Peoples.[14] The rates of violence and racism towards Indigenous Peoples are disproportionate to other Canadians when interacting with these public agencies.[15] In recent years, several inquests took place investigating the deaths of Indigenous Peoples after they engaged with institutions designed to provide assistance.[16] These investigations include deaths in hospital settings and at the hands of police, such as inquests into the death of Joyce Echaquan in a Joliette, Québec, hospital in 2023, and Chantel Moore, who died during a police wellness check in 2020.[17]

The inquests and inquiries reveal institutional racism in hospital visits and police checks, as well as forced sterilization, and, while tangible government responses indicate acknowledgement of these detrimental experiences, the state's responses to help combat racism and institutional inequities are lacking.[18] The federal government attempts to make changes and report progress, but it took horrendous circumstances for the federal government to get involved and work on improvement strategies.[19]

The Truth and Reconciliation Commission's *Final Report* (2015) highlights systemic racism within many institutions, as does the National Inquiry into Missing and Murdered Indigenous Women and Girls' *Final Report* (2019).[20] In their overall findings, the NIMMIWG *Final Report* notes, "designed to displace Indigenous Peoples... colonialism, discrimination, and genocide explains the high rates of violence against Indigenous women, girls, and 2SLGBTQQIA people."[21] Findings from such reports are not surprising, especially when considering the scope of the commission's investigation.[22] Many settler colonial institutions meant to help or service the general population are spaces of violence for Indigenous Peoples.

## Health and Wellness Checks

Indigenous Peoples sometimes encounter police due to health or wellness checks. These occur when police attend a location, often a residence, to establish the state of someone's mental health and wellness. There exists an over-reliance on Canadian police services to perform these "wellness checks." Additionally, there is an institutional distrust of police services towards Indigenous Peoples and a track record of over-policing in Canada.[23] In 2020, the federal government released committee notes on procedure and training after a *Hill Times* article and the Canadian Mental Health Association released a statement. The CMHA requested changes to how police engage in wellness checks and other mental health encounters.[24]

As the Covid pandemic sent much of the world into isolation, reports started coming out about the circumstances of people who lost their lives while engaging with police for health-related matters. In June 2020, four cases of people losing their lives in health or welfare checks by police garnered national attention: Regis Korchinski-Paquet, Chantel Moore, Rodney Levi, and D'Andre Campbell.[25] While certainly not all those who engaged with police and lost their lives were Indigenous, all victims were people regarded as racialized. Indigenous and Black individuals are over-represented in deaths, as identified in a CBC study of data from 2000 to 2017.[26] In 2020, two Indigenous women lost their lives while having encounters with police: Korchinski-Paquet died from a balcony fall in Ontario, followed by Moore the next week in New Brunswick.[27] The summer of 2020 was an avalanche of exposure of institutional police failings and calls to action and change as more incidents emerged in the media.[28]

One clear observation from these wellness checks is that if someone, in crisis or otherwise, needs help, they should not end up deceased. However, death is a risk when Indigenous Peoples in Canada rely on colonial government institutions for support. Calls for change are grounded in the understanding that racism embedded in institutions is responsible for the tragedies discussed above.[29]

## Forced Sterilization and Tubal Ligations—Institutional Acts of Genocide

Settler colonial governments marginalized Indigenous women through the *Indian Act* of 1876 and associated policies like the *1979 Indian Health Policy*.[30] Indigenous women must survive health-care institutions in spaces beyond emergency care. Until recent years, conversations about forced sterilization largely revolved around the policies and legislation historically in place in British Columbia, Alberta, and Saskatchewan.[31] In Alberta, legislation was used disproportionately against Indigenous women.[32] Few public conversations discuss this ongoing practice in Canada, a lived experience for many Indigenous women.[33] When complaints arose in Saskatoon regarding the forced sterilization of Indigenous women, the Saskatoon Health Region (now the Saskatoon Health Authority) responded with an internal review to move forward.[34] A 2017 report highlighted the history of forced sterilization and tubal ligation in Canada and among Indigenous populations.[35]

Thanks to advocacy work, forced sterilization is gaining attention as more individuals come forward to share stories.[36] The ongoing forced sterilization of Indigenous women in Canada illustrates two issues: first, continuing institutional racism in the Canadian health-care system as it is reserved for Indigenous Peoples; and second, how the experiences of surviving institutions exist in the shadows of Canadian society. The practice targeting Indigenous women indicates embedded racism in health institutions.[37] What deepens this problematic practice is that it is an act of genocide. According to the United Nations' 1948 Convention on the Prevention and Punishment of the Crime of Genocide, sterilization is one of the five ways of committing genocide: "imposing measures intended to prevent births within the group."[38] The use of the word *genocide* routinely creates extreme discomfort in mainstream Canada, as observed in public reaction to the NIMMIWG's use of the term in its findings; many were more focused on the language used rather than the content of the report.[39]

Despite public attention, practices of forced sterilization and tubal ligations continued, as documented in the 2021 Senate of Canada report *Forced and Coerced Sterilization of Persons in Canada*.[40] This continued practice sends a message to Indigenous Peoples that identifying a genocidal practice publicly is still not enough to stop the activity.[41] This example demonstrates how hard it is to effect change when Canadian society prefers to debate definitions of genocide rather than admit to the ongoing practise of it.

## Conclusion

In settler colonial Canada, the state uses institutions such as government agencies, services, and policies to perpetuate the discrimination and marginalization of Indigenous Peoples. Denialism stems from settler colonial history and continues in government institutions, becoming a pattern of behaviour in government and administrative leadership. Even when political denialism wanes, it does not mean those carrying out government duties have a change in attitude or perspective. The challenge related to this denialism is that one cannot address issues that profoundly affect people until one genuinely acknowledges the problem. While Trudeau acknowledged genocide against Indigenous women and girls in 2019, and the House of Commons recognized genocide in 2022, what has truly changed in Canada's polite society? Grassroots groups and those who provided testimony to various inquiries and inquests over the decades know that ignoring colonial history has dramatic effects on Indigenous Peoples and their lived experiences in Canada.

As noted in the NIMMIWG *Final Report*, health care, welfare, justice, and police are all institutions where Indigenous Peoples, especially women, experience violence and discrimination.[42] Today, the systemic racism in institutions continuing these violent acts dismisses the human experiences and the ongoing acts of genocide in Canada. This cursory overview of the lived experiences of Indigenous Peoples, whether surviving these institutions or not, is a clear result of the denial of colonially derived problems.

Education and training are ways to acknowledge the past and how colonial history continues to contribute to the experience of Indigenous Peoples in Canada. Institutions must make solid commitments to learning and applying the TRC's calls to action and implement practices alongside Indigenous Peoples. Part of settler colonial discourse involves reproducing systemic marginalization, and denialism supports this reproduction at the expense of Indigenous Peoples' livelihood, with the traumas and abuses at the hands of institutions remaining a daily reality. Creating space for Indigenous Peoples in decision-making is the beginning of the disruption of colonial reproduction.

## Notes

1 See Stephen Harper's remarks at a G20 press conference in Ljunggren, "Every G20 Nation"; CBC News, "Full Text "; Fontaine, "What Did Justin Trudeau Say?"
2 Cohen, *States of Denial*, 1.
3 Cohen, *States of Denial.*
4 Cohen, *States of Denial.*
5 Cohen, *States of Denial.*
6 Joseph, "A Jade Door," 61.
7 Major and Stirbys, "Blurred Lines."
8 White, "Discourse, Denial and Dehumanisation," 8; Welch, "Trampling Human Rights," 11.
9 Buller, Audette, Robinson, and Eyolfson, *Reclaiming Power and Place*, 3.
10 Patel, "The Word 'Racism.'"
11 Kwak, "Problematizing Canadian Exceptionalism," 1186.
12 Barrera, "NDP Pounces."
13 Fontaine, "What Did Justin Trudeau Say?"
14 Buller, Audette, Robinson, and Eyolfson, *Reclaiming Power and Place*, 114, 414.
15 McLane et al., "First Nations Emergency Care."
16 Razack, *Dying from Improvement*. See also Ministry of the Solicitor General Ontario, "2022 Coroner's Inquests' Verdicts."
17 New Brunswick Justice and Public Safety, "Coroner's Inquest."
18 Public Safety Canada, "Tabling of the Government Response."
19 Indigenous Services Canada, "Government of Canada Actions."
20 Truth and Reconciliation Commission of Canada, *Canada's Residential Schools*; Buller, Audette, Robinson, and Eyolfson, *Reclaiming Power and Place.*
21 Buller, Audette, Robinson, and Eyolfson, *Reclaiming Power and Place*, vol. 1b, 174.
22 "[It is] the mandate of the National Inquiry to include issues such as family violence, institutional racism in health care, child welfare, policing and

the justice system, and other forms of violence that stem from the same structures of colonization." Buller, Audette, Robinson, and Eyolfson, 58.

23 Government of Canada, "Overrepresentation of Indigenous People."

24 Public Safety Canada, "Police Intervention and Wellness Checks"; Canadian Mental Health Association, "Mental Illness Is Not a Crime."

25 Cooke, "Recent Deaths."

26 Cooke, "Recent Deaths."

27 Cooke, "Recent Deaths."

28 Canadian Press, "Lac La Ronge"; Independent Investigations Office of BC, "IIO Is Investigating"; McLachlan, "Advocates Question RCMP's Role."

29 Britneff, "Police Wellness Checks."

30 Allan and Smylie, *First Peoples, Second Class Treatment*, 10, 15; Lavoie et al., *The Aboriginal Health Legislation*, 3.

31 Stote, *An Act of Genocide*, 46; *The Sexual Sterilization Act*, SA 1928, c 37.

32 Stote, *An Act of Genocide*, 46–47.

33 Ward, "Forced Sterilization."

34 Boyer and Bartlett, *External Review*, 3.

35 Boyer and Bartlett, *External Review*, 39–42.

36 International Society of Female Professionals, "The International Society."

37 Boyer and Bartlett, *External Review*, 31.

38 Boyer, "Forced Sterilizations."

39 At the time, many people did not focus on the calls to action; rather they spent their time debating the use of the word *genocide*, which the media's headlines in the first week of June 2019 demonstrates. Abedi, "Why 'Genocide' Was Used."

40 Canada and Standing Senate Committee, *Forced and Coerced Sterilizations*, 8, 26, 27.

41 Bell, "Quebec Indigenous Groups."

42 Buller, Audette, Robinson, and Eyolfson, *Reclaiming Power and Place*, 625.

## Sources

Abedi, Maham. "Why 'Genocide' Was Used in the MMIWG Report." Global News, June 4, 2019. https://globalnews.ca/news/5350772/genocide-canada-mmiw.

Allan, Billie, and Janet Smylie. *First Peoples, Second Class Treatment: The Role of Racism in the Health and Well-Being of Indigenous Peoples in Canada*. Canadian Electronic Library, 2015.

Barrera, Jorge. "NDP Pounces on PM Trudeau Over Muddled Comments on Canada's 'Colonial Past.'" *APTN National News*, April 22, 2016. https://www.aptnnews.ca/national-news/ndp-pounces-on-pm-trudeau-over-muddled-comments-on-canadas-colonial-past/.

Bell, Susan. "Quebec Indigenous Groups Collecting Stories of Forced Sterilization." CBC News, September 24, 2021. https://www.cbc.ca/news/canada/north/indigenous-forced-sterilization-quebec-study-cree-1.6186212.

Boyer, Yvonne. "Forced Sterilizations of Indigenous Women: One More Act of Genocide." *Conversation*, March 4, 2019. https://theconversation.com/forced-sterilizations-of-indigenous-women-one-more-act-of-genocide-109603.

Boyer, Yvonne, and Judith Bartlett. *External Review: Tubal Ligation in the Saskatoon Health Region: The Lived Experience of Aboriginal Women*. July 22, 2017. https://senatorboyer.ca/wp-content/uploads/2021/09/Tubal-Ligation-in-the-Saskatoon-Health-Region-the-Lived-Experience-of-Aboriginal-Women-Boyer-and-Bartlett-July-11-2017.pdf.

Britneff, Beatrice. "Police Wellness Checks: Why They're Ending Violently and What Experts Say Needs to Change." Global News, June 24, 2020. https://globalnews.ca/news/7092621/police-wellness-checks-experts-change/.

Buller, Marion, Michèle Audette, Qajaq Robinson, and Brian Eyolfson. *Reclaiming Power and Place: The Final Inquiry into Missing and Murdered Indigenous Women and Girls*. National Inquiry into Missing and Murdered Indigenous Women and Girls, 2019.

Canada and Standing Senate Committee on Human Rights. *Forced and Coerced Sterilizations of Persons in Canada*. June 2021. https://sencanada.ca/content/sen/committee/432/RIDR/reports/ForcedSterilization_Report_final_e.pdf.

Canadian Mental Health Association. "Mental Illness Is Not a Crime." August 25, 2020. https://cmha.ca/brochure/statement-on-police-and-wellness-checks/.

Canadian Press. "Lac La Ronge Indian Band Calls for Removal of RCMP Officer After Video Published Showing Mountie Entering Home with Axe." *Saskatoon StarPheonix*, August 28, 2020. https://thestarphoenix.com/news/local-news/lac-la-ronge-indian-band-calls-for-removal-of-rcmp-officer-after-video-published-showing-mountie-entering-home-with-axe.

CBC News. "Full Text of Peter Mansbridge's Interview with Stephen Harper." December 17, 2014. https://www.cbc.ca/news/politics/full-text-of-peter-mansbridge-s-interview-with-stephen-harper-1.2876934.

Cohen, Stanley. *States of Denial: Knowing About Atrocities and Suffering*. Blackwell, 2001.

Cooke, Alex. "Recent Deaths Prompt Questions About Police Wellness Checks." CBC News, June 23, 2020. https://www.cbc.ca/news/canada/nova-scotia/police-wellness-checks-deaths-indigenous-black-1.5622320.

Fontaine, Tim. "What Did Justin Trudeau Say About Canada's History of Colonialism?" CBC News, April 22, 2016. https://www.cbc.ca/news/indigenous/trudeau-colonialism-comments-1.3549405.

Government of Canada. "Overrepresentation of Indigenous People in the Canadian Criminal Justice System: Causes and Responses." Department of Justice: Reports and Publications, April 4, 2020. https://www.justice.gc.ca/eng/rp-pr/jr/oip-cjs/p4.html.

Independent Investigations Office of BC. "IIO Is Investigating an Incident in Williams Lake (2022-167)." July 10, 2022. https://iiobc.ca/media/iio-is-investigating-an-incident-in-williams-lake-2022-167/.

Indigenous Services Canada. "Government of Canada Actions to Address Anti-Indigenous Racism in Health Systems." Government of Canada: Indigenous

Health, August 6, 2021. https://www.sac-isc.gc.ca/eng/1611863352025/1611863375715.

International Society of Female Professionals. "The International Society of Professionals Recognizes Alisa Lombard." July 8, 2021. https://www.theisfp.com/the-international-society-of-female-professionals-recognizes-alisa-lombard-b-s-sc-ll-l-l-l-b/.

Joseph, Rob. "A Jade Door: Reconciliatory Justice as a Way Forward." In *Te Tatau Pounamu: The Greenstone Door—Traditional Knowledge and Gateways to Balanced Relationships*. Nga Pae o te Maramatanga, 2008.

Kwak, Laura J. "Problematizing Canadian Exceptionalism: A Study of Right-Populism, White Nationalism and Conservative Political Parties." *Oñati Socio-Legal Series* 10, no. 6 (2020): 1166–1192. http://dx.doi.org/10.35295/osls.iisl/0000-0000-0000-1127.

Lavoie, Josee, Laverne Gervais, Jessica Toner, Odile Bergeron, and Ginette Thomas. *The Aboriginal Health Legislation and Policy Framework in Canada*, Vol. 35. National Collaborating Centre for Aboriginal Health, 2011.

Ljunggren, David. "Every G20 Nation Wants to Be Canada, Insists PM." Reuters, September 25, 2009. https://www.reuters.com/article/columns-us-g20-canada-advantages-idUSTRE58P05Z20090926.

Major, Rebecca, and Cynthia Stirbys. "Blurred Lines: Boundaries and Consequences for Indigenous Women in Politics in the Era of #MeToo." In *Gender-Based Violence in Canadian Politics in the #MeToo Era*, edited by Tracey Raney and Cheryl N. Collier. University of Toronto Press, 2023.

McLachlan, Philip. "Advocates Question RCMP's Role in Death of WLFN Man, Demand Public Inquiry." *IndigiNews*, July 20, 2022. https://indiginews.com/okanagan/advocates-question-rcmps-role-in-death-of-wlfn-man-demand-public-inquiry.

McLane, Patrick, Cheryl Barnabe, Brian R. Holroyd, Amy Colquhoun, Lea Bill, Kayla M. Fitzpatrick, Katherine Rittenbach, Chyloe Healy, Bonnie Healy, and Rhonda J. Rosychuk. "First Nations Emergency Care in Alberta: Descriptive Results of a Retrospective Cohort Study." *BMC Health Services Research* 21, article 423 (2021).

Ministry of the Solicitor General Ontario. "2022 Coroner's Inquests' Verdicts and Recommendations." Government of Ontario, last modified April 17, 2023. https://www.ontario.ca/page/2022-coroners-inquests-verdicts-and-recommendations.https://doi.org/10.1186/s12913-021-06415-2.

New Brunswick Justice and Public Safety. "Coroner's Inquest Makes Recommendations Regarding Police Interventions, Training and Equipment." Government of New Brunswick, May 20, 2022. https://www2.gnb.ca/content/gnb/en/departments/public-safety/news/news_release.2022.05.0255.html.

Patel, Raisa. "The Word 'Racism' Doesn't Appear Anywhere in the Conservative Party's Campaign Platform." *Toronto Star*, August 17, 2021. https://www.thestar.com/politics/federal-election/2021/08/17/the-word-racism-doesnt-appear-anywhere-in-the-conservative-partys-campaign-platform.html.

Public Safety Canada. "Police Intervention and Wellness Checks." July 22, 2020. https://www.publicsafety.gc.ca/cnt/trnsprnc/brfng-mtrls/prlmntry-bndrs/20201119/025/index-en.aspx

Public Safety Canada. "Tabling of the Government Response to the Standing Committee Report on Systemic Racism in Policing in Canada." June 2, 2022. https://www.canada.ca/en/public-safety-canada/news/2022/06/tabling-of-the-government-response-to-the-standing-committee-report-on-systemic-racism-in-policing-in-canada.html.

Razack, Sherene. *Dying from Improvement: Inquests and Inquiries into Indigenous Deaths in Custody*. University of Toronto Press, 2015.

*Sexual Sterilization Act*, SA 1928, c 37. https://www.canlii.org/en/ab/laws/astat/sa-1928-c-37/latest/sa-1928-c-37.html.

Stote, Karen. *An Act of Genocide: Colonialism and the Sterilization of Aboriginal Women*. Fernwood Publishing, 2015.

Truth and Reconciliation Commission of Canada. *Canada's Residential Schools: The Final Report of the Truth and Reconciliation Commission of Canada*. Vol. 1. McGill-Queen's University Press, 2015.

Ward, Dennis. "Forced Sterilization a Symptom of 'Colonial Hangover' Says Lawyer." *APTN News*, April 7, 2020. https://www.aptnnews.ca/facetoface/forced-sterilization-a-symptom-of-colonial-hangover-says-lawyer/.

Welch, Michael. "Trampling Human Rights in the War on Terror: Implications to the Sociology of Denial." *Critical Criminology* 12, no. 1 (2004): 1–20. http://dx.doi.org/10.1023/b:crit.0000024444.09103.d4.

White, Lisa. "Discourse, Denial and Dehumanisation: Former Detainees' Experiences of Narrating State Violence in Northern Ireland." *Papers from the British Criminology Conference* 10, no. 3 (2010): 3–10. http://dx.doi.org/10.13140/RG.2.1.2209.2642.

# On the Illegitimacy of the Canadian Constitutional Order[1]

Paul Simard Smith

THE CENTRAL ISSUE OF THIS CHAPTER CONCERNS THE Canadian constitutional order. It asks whether Canada's constitutional order is legitimate. A direct answer to this question would require answering the more abstract question "What makes any constitutional order legitimate?" However, my approach will be to take a more concrete, yet indirect, approach to this issue. I do so by addressing the question "Does Canada's constitutional order satisfy its own standards of legitimacy?" This chapter develops a negative answer to that question; it makes the case that Canada does not satisfy its own standards of legitimacy.

The core idea is that for Canada's constitutional order to be legitimate according to Canada's own standards, it is necessary for Canada's fundamental laws, policies, and institutions (or *fundamentals*, for shorthand) to be justified from the perspective of Indigenous legal traditions. However, this is not the case. Hence, the Canadian constitutional order fails to satisfy a necessary condition for the satisfaction of its own standards of legitimacy. Insofar as it is plausible to think that a constitutional order is illegitimate when it fails to satisfy its own standards of legitimacy, then, to that extent, it would be plausible to conclude that the Canadian constitutional order is illegitimate.

The following section ("Methodology and Key Concepts") provides a brief note on methodology. "Canada Fails to Satisfy the Liberal Principle of Legitimacy" then presents the *basic argument* that Canada fails to satisfy the so-called liberal principle of legitimacy (or just *liberal legitimacy*, for short). This section contains several subsections that expand on some of the core concepts deployed within the basic argument. The section has two primary goals. One goal is to make the case for the truth of each premise of the basic argument, and hence of the argument's overall cogency. The other goal is to make the case that the Supreme Court's theory of Canada's constitutional legitimacy relies on the so-called liberal principle of legitimacy. First, drawing on the Supreme Court of Canada's discussion of constitutional legitimacy in *Reference re Secession of Quebec*, I argue that the Court's theory of legitimacy relies on a principle akin to liberal legitimacy. If (i) the Court's account of constitutional legitimacy is a plausible basis for thinking that liberal legitimacy is a standard of legitimacy underlying the Canadian constitutional order, and if (ii) the *basic argument* is sound, then it follows that Canada does not satisfy its own standards for the legitimate exercise of authority under Canada's Constitution. Accordingly, I proceed to make a case that the basic argument that Canada fails to satisfy liberal legitimacy is sound, identifying several examples of fundamentals that are not justified from the perspective of Indigenous legal traditions.

## Methodology and Key Concepts

What is a constitutional order? Broadly speaking, I employ the expression *constitutional order* to refer to the constitutional aspects of a legal order. The International Council on Human Rights Policy characterizes a *legal order* as a collection of "norms, rules and institutions formed by a society or a group of people to ensure social stability. They usually describe what is right and how to act, and what is wrong and how not to act; and the remedies and consequences of such actions."[2] Val Napoleon states that a legal order is "a system of authority for regulating disputes and making decisions."[3] What David Dyzenhaus calls "the question of constitutionality" asks what it is "that all legal orders share in having a constitution."[4] This problem is vexed, partly because the notions of a constitution and of a legal order are themselves difficult to pin down.[5] Consequently, rather than attempt a complete account of the notion of a constitutional order here, I simply highlight some of its key features.

Broadly speaking, I employ the term *constitutional order* to refer to those norms and rules within a legal order that are *constitutional in nature*, as well as to the institutions and social practices involved in the administration and regulation of such constitutional norms and rules. I regard norms and rules to be "constitutional in nature" when they have the following features. First, they provide the ultimate source for the validity of the rules and norms of the entire legal order.[6] For example, the validity of some piece of legislation depends on its accordance with constitutional norms and rules, and as such constitutional norms and rules could identify bodies and persons that have the authority to pass legislation of a certain kind. Second, constitutional norms and rules are *entrenched*. That is to say that the process for revising them is substantially more onerous—in the sense that it requires substantially broader public support—than the process for making other collective decisions. Third, constitutional norms and rules are *constitutive* in the sense that they create, structure, and define "the limits of government power or authority."[7] For example, they may define legislative, judicial, and executive branches of government and the limits of their powers. Alternatively, Aaron Mills contends that the constitutional logic of Anishinaabe variants of constitutionalism is mutual aid.[8] Mutual aid is a kind of "mechanism that justifies the community."[9] The structure "through which the mechanism is realized, sustained and practiced" is, as Mills explains, family.[10] In both examples, norms and standards provide a constitutive logic for the community and define the structures through which those norms are implemented.

Having clarified the key features of the notion of a constitutional order, the next point to note is that constitutional orders possess conceptual foundations. Just as concepts such as knowledge, truth, time, causation, spirit, or Creator play a role in the conceptual foundations of overarching frameworks for making sense of reality, the roots of the Canadian constitutional order consists of several liberal legal and political ideals. These include ideals such as the rule of law, democracy, sovereignty, individual and collective rights, constitutionalism, freedom, equality, and—of specific importance to the argument of this chapter—legitimacy.

This investigation will draw on tools found within theoretical philosophy to carefully untangle conceptual inconsistencies, absurdities, and other defects in the philosophical foundations of Canadian constitutional order. Specifically, its focus is how the standard of legitimacy endorsed within the Canadian constitutional order goes unsatisfied by Canada in its relations with Indigenous Peoples. However, in addition to contemporary theoretical social and political philosophy, this essay also draws inspiration from rhetorical approaches employed by Louis Riel, an important and inspirational leader of the Métis Nation during the Red River and North West Resistances. Specifically, I draw on a rhetorical strategy used by Riel during his trial speeches. One of Riel's criticisms of the Canadian government during his address to the jury, during his trial for treason, of July 31, 1885, uses an underlying logic that is shared with the critical strategy I employ here. Riel argues

> that the House of Commons, Senate, and Ministers of the Dominion and [those] who make laws for this land and govern it, are no representation whatever of the people of the North-West.... [And] that the North-West Council generated by the Federal Government has the great defect of its parent.... The number of members elected for the council by the people make it only a sham representative legislature and no representative government at all.[11]

Herein, Riel criticizes the Canadian government by pointing out that Canada upholds a standard of good governance—in this case, the standard in question is that of so-called responsible government—that it, in practice, fails to satisfy. Similarly, the point of the critique I develop here is, as mentioned, that Canada does not satisfy its own standard of legitimacy. As was the case in Riel's speech, the foundations of the Constitution of Canada are the target upon which the critical lens of this investigation is directed. Like Riel, I claim that principles endorsed by Canada are not satisfied by Canada. And, as noted, using the techniques of contemporary analytical philosophy, I carefully untangle inconsistencies, absurdities, and defects of the target.

As a proud citizen of the Métis Nation, with ties to my Métis community and my Métis kin and a good sense of my family's history, as well as being an analytically trained philosopher, drawing on one of these approaches to the exclusion of the other would be not only epistemically incomplete but also lacking in authenticity. However, it is important to note that in drawing on thinkers and approaches from incongruent intellectual perspectives and worldviews, it does not entail, nor should it be regarded as suggesting, that these perspectives stand in agreement on all, or even most, points.

## Canada Fails to Satisfy the Liberal Principle of Legitimacy

The *basic argument* that Canada fails to satisfy liberal legitimacy is straightforward. However, some work is required to unpack the concepts used within the argument and to make the case that the argument's premises are relevant to the overall issue of the legitimacy of the Canadian constitutional order. Thus, I proceed by stating the basic argument. I continue with a discussion of the concepts within the argument and of the relevance of the premises to the matter at hand.

The basic argument goes as follows:

1. A constitutional order satisfies the liberal principle of legitimacy if and only if its fundamental laws, public policies, and institutions are justifiable to all reasonable citizens.
2. In the Canadian constitutional order some fundamentals are not justifiable from the perspective of Indigenous legal traditions.
3. Therefore, the Canadian constitutional order fails to satisfy the liberal principle of legitimacy.

First, it should be noted that this argument is logically valid. This means that if the argument's premises are true, the conclusion is true too. So, if one can convince themselves that premises one and two are true, then one's beliefs would be inconsistent if they also rejected the truth of premise three. Therefore, a case can be made that this argument is cogent by explaining why the first and second premise ought to be regarded as true. In the following subsection, I proceed to make that case for premise one through an explanation of why liberal legitimacy is relevant to evaluating the overall legitimacy of the Canadian constitutional order. I then make the case for the truth of premise two.

### *Premise One: The Truth of the Basic Argument*

Premise one is true in virtue of the definition of liberal legitimacy. This principle requires that "fundamental political principles, laws and institutions, to be legitimate, must be justifiable from the point of view of all reasonable citizens."[12] Thus, a constitutional order that satisfies the condition of being justifiable from the point of view of reasonable citizens is, by definition, one that satisfies liberal legitimacy. I make no commitment to the claim that liberal legitimacy is the correct account of legitimacy in general. However, as will be explained, I contend that liberal legitimacy underlies Canada's constitutional order. Thus, if Canada can be shown to fail to satisfy liberal legitimacy, then that would entail that Canada does not satisfy a standard that it regards as justifying its exercise of authority under the Constitution of Canada.

Liberal legitimacy, as introduced in John Rawls's *Political Liberalism*, assumes that the exercise of political authority must be justified to be legitimate.[13] Within the context of a society characterized by irreconcilable pluralism and composed of citizens who are supposed to be treated as free and equal, Rawls argues that any justification of political authority must be acceptable to all reasonable citizens.[14] Rawls holds that under such conditions an exercise of political power could be legitimate "only when it is exercised in accordance with a constitution the essentials of which all citizens as free and equal may reasonably be expected to endorse in light of principles and ideals acceptable to their common human reason."[15]

The rational grounds for liberal legitimacy is a moral principle of respect.[16] If a law, policy, or institution is imposed for some end without appropriate regard to the reasonable concerns of those upon whom it is imposed, then that fails to treat those persons with due respect. Any such rule is not based on good faith social cooperation and reciprocity. Instead, such a rule is an act of imposition.[17] Contrarily, liberal legitimacy is grounded on respect. It requires genuine social cooperation and reciprocity in the formation of a society's fundamentals. For a society to satisfy this principle would mean that its "constitutional essentials" are based upon this kind of mutual respect, cooperation, and reciprocity. The idea is that amid irreconcilable comprehensive religious, cultural, moral, and philosophical perspectives, legitimate laws, policies, and institutions must provide a stable and predictable framework that is acceptable from the diversity of reasonable perspectives.

*Premise One: The Relevance of the Basic Argument*

What evidence is there that liberal legitimacy is endorsed by Canada? One line of supportive evidence can be found within the Supreme Court of Canada's discussions of the general legitimacy of the Constitution of Canada in the *Reference re Secession of Quebec*. Here, the Court regards the elements of constitutional legitimacy as involving more than just popular democracy or majority rule. Rather, the Court identifies several additional principles that are jointly supposed to ensure that democracy occurs within a stable legal framework that can reasonably be expected to acquire broad acceptance among a diverse citizenry. These principles include constitutionalism and the rule of law, and the protection of minority rights. The Court explains that

> democracy in any real sense of the word cannot exist without the rule of law. It is the law that creates the framework within which the "sovereign will" is to be ascertained and implemented. To be accorded legitimacy, democratic institutions must rest, ultimately, on a legal foundation.... The system must be capable of reflecting the aspirations of the people. But there is more. Our law's claim to legitimacy also rests on an appeal to moral values.
>
> ... It would be a grave mistake to equate legitimacy with ... majority rule alone, to the exclusion of the other constitutional values.[18]

Other values, such as the predictable and fair application of law, protection of the rights of minorities, and a constitution that reflects, entrenches, and protects common aspirations and moral values are also important elements of constitutional legitimacy. Popular democracy, without the other constitutional principles, could generate a constitutional regime that is erratic, arbitrary, and alienating to minority groups.

One intended effect of this package of constitutional principles is to secure acceptance from a more diverse array of citizens than could reasonably be expected of a constitutional order based on the principle of popular democracy alone. The underlying idea is that the principles of respect for minority rights, protection of widely shared moral values, and predictability and fairness in the application of laws prevent a so-called "tyranny of the majority." If the only constitutional principle were popular democracy, then the majority could freely violate the rights of minorities.

Further, this package of constitutional principles is compatible with majority groups dominating the legislative and policy agenda. While perhaps falling short of a tyranny of the majority, such a constitutional arrangement is also unlikely to be acceptable to minority groups. One attempt at mitigating this problem is an additional constitutional principle that the Court emphasizes in the *Secession Reference*—that principle being *federalism*.

As the Court explains, "In a federal system of government such as ours, political power is shared by two orders of government: the federal government on the one hand, and the provinces on the other. Each is assigned respective spheres of jurisdiction."[19] According to the Court,

> the principle of federalism recognizes the diversity of the component parts of Confederation, and the autonomy of provincial governments to develop their societies within their respective spheres of jurisdiction. The federal structure also facilitates democratic participation by distributing power to the government thought to be most suited to achieving the particular societal objective having regard to this diversity.[20]

Thus, federalism is supposed to involve a recognition that there is diversity of groups, some that make up majorities in dispersed geographic regions but are not part of the overall federal majority. For example, the Quebecois make up a majority in the province of Québec, but not within the totality of Canada. To prevent minority groups from being swamped by the overarching Canadian majority, significant jurisdiction of the provinces enables diverse geographically concentrated groups to "develop their societies within their respective spheres of jurisdiction" and pursue "particular societal objectives" that are distinctive to their people.

If one only employed the principle of popular democracy, as we have discussed, one could not reasonably expect people outside of majority groups to accept such a constitutional order. Even without the federalism principle, one could not reasonably hold such expectations. However, if one instead believed that groups outside the majority ought to have reasonable basis to find the constitutional fundamentals acceptable—that is, if one believed liberal legitimacy—then that would provide a compelling reason to go beyond the principle of popular democracy in a theory of constitutional legitimacy.[21] Thus, the claim here is that the Court's underlying belief in liberal legitimacy offers the best explanation for why the Court goes beyond simple popular democracy and endorses the full package of constitutional principles that it does in the *Secession Reference*.

Unfortunately, while the *Secession Reference* does discuss the legitimacy of the Canadian constitutional order, it does not speak to the Crown's relationship with Indigenous Peoples and the problems of legitimacy that are raised through a consideration of that troubled relationship. Some, however, may argue such an omission is appropriate and claim that the language of legitimacy is not an adequate framework for assessing the relationship between Indigenous nations and the Crown. The language of constitutional legitimacy developed in the *Secession Reference* is only appropriate in characterizing the constitutional relationship among the provinces and the federal government. With respect to Indigenous Peoples, such a perspective would hold, the language of Aboriginal and Treaty Rights, recognized and affirmed in subsection 35(1), is the appropriate framework. On this view, the legitimacy of Indigenous-Crown relationships would then turn on respecting Aboriginal and Treaty Rights *as opposed to* constitutional legitimacy as outlined in the *Secession Reference.*

In response, I note that respecting Aboriginal and Treaty Rights is clearly an important constitutional principle, one that is essential to any legitimate and just relationship between the Crown and Indigenous Peoples. However, respecting these rights does not preclude a consideration of constitutional legitimacy. It is far from clear that the language of constitutional legitimacy, detailed in the *Secession Reference*, can be consistently withheld from a comprehensive evaluation of the relationship between the Crown and Indigenous Peoples while simultaneously being applied to the relationship between the provinces and the federal government.[22] The inherent rights to self-government and self-determination of Indigenous Peoples are part of the package of rights that are recognized and affirmed by subsection 35(1). For example, chapter 5.02(b) of the *Métis Nation Within Saskatchewan Self-Government Recognition and Implementation Agreement*, signed by Canada and the Métis Nation–Saskatchewan in February of 2023, explains that "the Métis Nation within Saskatchewan has the inherent right to self-determination that is recognized in [UNDRIP] and the inherent right of self-government recognized and affirmed in common law by section 35 of the *Constitution Act, 1982*."[23] Arguably, associated with these section 35 rights is a requirement that the relationship between Indigenous governments and the Crown align with standards of legitimacy in addition to respect for Aboriginal and Treaty Rights.

In light of these considerations, even though the Court does not apply its conception of legitimacy to evaluating the relationship between Indigenous nations and the Crown in the *Secession Reference*, it is, I submit, worthwhile to consider whether the Court's own conception of general constitutional legitimacy would be satisfied with respect to the Crown's relationship with Indigenous Peoples. Whether the Court has directly posed this question to itself or not, from a philosophical, moral, and justice-based point of view—if not from a legal one—it is natural to ask whether the Crown's overarching conception of constitutional legitimacy is satisfied in the Crown's "nation-to-nation" relationship with Indigenous Peoples.

If the Court's general conception of constitutional legitimacy developed in the *Secession Reference* can be understood as offering a statement of Canada's conception of legitimacy, then Canada's conception of legitimacy can be regarded as involving a commitment to liberal legitimacy. However, the basic argument makes a case that Canada does not satisfy this conception of legitimacy with respect to its relationship with Indigenous Peoples. If so, it would follow that Canada doesn't satisfy the very standard it regards as licensing exercises of authority under the Constitution of Canada. However, we have yet to establish the truth of premise two, that Canada's constitutional fundamentals are not justifiable from the perspective of some Indigenous Peoples' legal traditions.

*Premise Two: The Case that the Canadian Constitutional Order Is Not Justifiable from the Perspective of Indigenous Legal Traditions*

The goal of this section is to present the case for the truth of premise two of the basic argument. The argument in support of this claim involves three cases of fundamental laws, policies, and institutions within the Canadian constitutional order that involve justifications that may be cogent from the point of view of some interpretations of Euro-derived legal traditions but are not cogent from the perspective of, at least some, Indigenous legal traditions.

By way of explaining the first case, it will help to begin by reflecting on some points made by Val Napoleon and Hadley Friedland in their essay "Indigenous Legal Traditions: From Roots to Renaissance."[24] Napoleon and Friedland ask their readers to consider what would occur if Canadians, and the contemporary Canadian legal order, were subjected to the same kind of colonialism that Indigenous Peoples have been subjected to as the Canadian state came to enforce a monopoly on coercive force.

> Imagine then, if one day, another society's legal actors took the Canadian judge, the police officer, or the prison guard into custody, tried and found them guilty of an offence, say, of kidnapping or forcible confinement, and then imprisoned or otherwise punished them for their actions. What then if it were announced to the community

> at large, through word of mouth, official notices, and through social media, that these respected people—the judges, police officers, and prison guards—were backwards, superstitious, and had to be stopped from doing what they had always done?
>
> As a Canadian people, for our protection, we would now have to rely entirely on the outside legal actors who had criminalized, ridiculed and debilitated our laws and justice system....
>
> Our current legal actors would be placed in an untenable position.... Even if other aspects of our legal traditions were not disintegrating around us, the gutting of these core elements related to human violence and vulnerability would shatter the foundation of the entire legal order. This is what happened, everywhere, with Indigenous societies.[25]

The institutions employed to implement a monopolization of coercive force by the state are fundamental and not, I submit, social institutions grounded on cogent legal arguments from the perspective of Indigenous legal traditions. Rather, a means of maintaining public safety that is in line with legal concepts and processes of Indigenous Peoples, and one that has substantive and effective mechanisms for judicial and regulatory influence, control, and oversight from diverse Indigenous communities, is more likely to be cogent from such perspectives.

John Borrows illustrates how various flawed ideologies about Indigenous Peoples and Indigenous Lands underlie much of the legal reasoning that invokes legal principles such as *discovery*, *occupation*, *prescription*, and *conquest*. Legal arguments employing these principles, in these fashions, are not likely to find much currency internal to Indigenous legal traditions.[26] Nevertheless, they have carried influence in the development of significant aspects of Canadian Aboriginal law.[27] They also tend to provide populist arguments among some settler commentators in support of elevating European laws over Indigenous laws.[28] This point, I think, provides a second case, this time one involving a package of fundamental legal principles that, while justified by arguments that might be regarded as cogent from the perspective of certain understandings of the common law legal tradition, are not justified from the perspective of Indigenous legal traditions.

Finally, the third case consist of the policy of so-called "thick" state sovereignty.[29] One of the most infamous expressions of the notion of thick sovereignty in Canadian law is found in the Supreme Court's *Sparrow* decision, quoted earlier. In that decision, the Court said, "there was from the outset never any doubt that sovereignty and legislative power, and indeed the underlying title, to such lands vested in the Crown."[30] The grounds for this "thick" sovereignty is supposed to be an "historic and ongoing assertion of British and Canadian sovereignty."[31] In considering this argument for thick sovereignty from the internal perspectives of Indigenous legal traditions, however, Borrows says, "an important question is whether authority of an imposed, obstructionist and unrepresentative government should be recognized as infringing or extinguishing any jurisdiction of Indigenous peoples."[32]

Collectively, I think these three cases offer support for the second premise within the context of the political arrangement currently found within Canada. They highlight that several fundamentals of the Canadian constitutional order are not based on reasons that would render those fundamentals acceptable from the perspective of some Indigenous legal traditions. However, if premise two is true, then basic conditions for the satisfaction of the liberal principle of legitimacy are unmet by the Canadian constitutional order.

## Concluding Remarks

This completes the case for the cogency of the basic argument. If sound, this argument would establish that the constitutional order of Canada is not legitimate according to its own conception of constitutional legitimacy—that at the base of the Constitution of Canada lurks a deep inconsistency whereby the principle that authorizes legitimate exercises of authority under the Constitution of Canada is unsatisfied by Canada itself.

The requirement that fundamental laws, policies, and institutions must be justified by arguments that are cogent from the internal perspective of Indigenous legal traditions is an inversion of the way the Court has often framed discussions surrounding Aboriginal law. Dale Turner notes that while the Court has been open to making space for forms of evidence employed within Indigenous legal traditions, it was also "dictating the language within which the evidence was to be articulated and understood."[33] According to the Court, while forms of evidence arising from Indigenous worldviews, legal traditions, ways of knowing, and ways of being must be considered by the courts when adjudicating claims to Aboriginal rights, the perspectives of Aboriginal people "must be framed in terms cognizable to the Canadian legal and constitutional structure."[34]

As Turner puts the Court's point, "if Indigenous philosophies, embedded in Indigenous languages, are to play a normative role in determining the scope of rights protected in section 35(1), they must be articulated in the legal and political discourses of the state."[35] However, while this may characterize the realities of the Court's conception of Aboriginal rights, this conception is incompatible with liberal legitimacy that, as was argued, conceptually underlies the Court's own reasoning in the *Secession Reference* and is part of the broad liberal framework that underlies fundamental aspects of the Court's legal-philosophical worldview. The requirements of this principle would necessitate that the content, policies, and nature of Aboriginal law is justifiable by argumentation that is cogent from the perspective of the variety of Indigenous legal traditions. Thus, rather than requiring that normative discourses be cognizable within the Canadian legal and constitutional structure, this principle, in fact, would also require that modes of evidence, and the laws more generally speaking, are cognizable to Indigenous legal perspectives too.

A major point of this chapter is to highlight that this one-way lens through which the Court considers the matter of Aboriginal rights, while perhaps reflecting present-day realities of the Canadian legal landscape, flies in the face of the Court's own broadly liberal conception of legitimacy. As Turner argues, "our survival as Indigenous peoples demands . . . that we must engage the discourses of the state more effectively."[36] However, while Turner is correct that our practical needs of survival amid settler colonial realities necessitate effectively engaging the state's political discourses, there is something important left out of this picture. Specifically, what is left out is the, at least statements of aspiration from the Court, and from some segments of Canadian leadership more generally, to be on a sounder and more ethical footing with respect to its relationship with Indigenous Peoples. Thus, while our survival may require effective engagement of the state's political discourses, to the extent that Canada aspires to genuinely rest on moral foundations, a significantly more profound and transformational shift is required by the Court, one in which the current perspective on the forms of normative discourse the Court understands as meaningful must be significantly expanded. In particular, for such aspirations to materialize, the fundamental legal and political structures and norms underlying the Canadian legal order must be cognizable not only to the ways of knowing and being of dominant legal traditions, but also to those of the variety of Indigenous legal traditions. To make a long story short: while it may be correct that our survival depends on effectively engaging the normative discourses of the Canadian state, the moral legitimacy of Canada depends on it effectively engaging the norms and principles of our peoples and governments.

## Notes

1 I would like to take this opportunity to express my gratitude to Professor Hans V. Hansen of the University of Windsor, editor of *Riel's Defense: Perspectives on His Speeches*. Professor Hansen was an important mentor as my MA supervisor at the University of Windsor and as Department Head on my first limited term appointment as an Assistant Professor at the University of Windsor. I am greatly indebted to his support over the years.

2 International Council on Human Rights Policy, "When Legal Worlds Overlap."

3 Napoleon et al., *Mikomosis and the Wetiko*.

4 Dyzenhaus, "The Idea of a Constitution," 10.

5 Dyzenhaus, "The Idea of a Constitution"; Tamanaha, *Legal Pluralism Explained*, 1–3.

6 Thanks to Michael Guidice and Xavier Scott for helping with this conception of constitutional norms.

7 Waluchow and Kyritsis, "Constitutionalism," §10.

8 Mills, "A Preliminary Sketch," 3.

9 Mills, "A Preliminary Sketch", 3.

10 Mills, "A Preliminary Sketch", 3–4.

11 Riel, "Address to the Jury, 31 July 1885," 38–39.

12 Jønch-Clausen and Kappel, "Social Epistemic Liberalism," 371.

13 Mandle and Roberts-Cady, eds., *John Rawls*, 15.

14 For discussion of the nature of the conception of freedom invoked within the Métis community during the Red River Resistance of 1869 to 1870, see O'Toole, *The Red River Resistance*.

15 Rawls, *Political Liberalism*, 137

16 Larmore, *What Is Political Philosophy?*, 148.

17 Larmore, *What Is Political Philosophy?*, 153.

18 Supreme Court of Canada, *Reference re Secession of Quebec*, para 32, 217.

19 Supreme Court of Canada, *Reference re Secession of Quebec*, para 56.

20 Supreme Court of Canada, *Reference re Secession of Quebec*, para 58.

21 The best explanation of the Court's full package of constitutional principles outlined in the *Secession Reference* would be its underlying endorsement of the liberal principle of legitimacy. This is not put forward as a "knock down" argument, but as a plausible theory of the political philosophy motivating the Court's discussion of legitimacy in the *Secession Reference*.

22 Indigenous Peoples are, after all, peoples with distinctive languages, histories, interests, structures of political governance, legal traditions, land bases, and cultures. They existed as distinctive nations prior to the effective control of the Crown over territories currently called Canada. The Crown has entered into a variety of agreements with different Indigenous Peoples that it has itself characterized as "nation-to-nation" and "government-to-government" agreements. See Government of Canada, "Highlights from the Report of the Royal Commission on Aboriginal Peoples." If the Court employs the notion of constitutional legitimacy in their discussion of the relationship between the Quebecois and the Crown, they should do so in their discussion of the relationship between Indigenous Peoples and the Crown. If the democratic will of the Quebecois can trigger a crisis of constitutional legitimacy that is to be addressed through an equal and reciprocal process of negotiation, why would the democratic will of Indigenous Peoples not be able to trigger similar obligations from the Crown? See Whitecap Dakota Nation, *A Self-Government Treaty*, agreed to by Whitecap Dakota First Nation and the Crown. In "Canada's Collaborative Modern Treaty Implementation Policy," the Government of Canada states its "commitment to meet its obligations under modern treaties and to fully embody true nation-to-nation, government-to-government and Inuit-Crown relationships with Indigenous Modern Treaty Partners." Government of Canada, "Canada's Collaborative Modern Treaty Implementation Policy."

23 Chapter 5.02(b) (p. 14) of the *Métis Nation Within Saskatchewan Self-Government Recognition and Implementation Agreement*, signed by Canada and the Métis Nation–Saskatchewan in February of 2023. Accessible online at https://metisnationsk.com/wp-content/uploads/2021/12/Metis-Government-Recognition-and-Self-Government-Agreement-.pdf.

24 Napoleon and Friedland, "Indigenous Legal Traditions."

25 Napoleon and Friedland, "Indigenous Legal Traditions," 7–8.

26 Borrows, *Canada's Indigenous Constitution*, 12–22.

27 For further discussion, see Hamilton and Nichols, "Reconciliation and the Straightjacket," 229–231.

28 See Borrows, *Canada's Indigenous Constitution*, 12.

29 The term *thick sovereignty* comes from Hamilton and Nichols, "Reconciliation and the Straightjacket."

30 Supreme Court of Canada, *R. v. Sparrow* [1990] 1 S.C.R. 1075, para 14.

31 Borrows, "Sovereignty's Alchemy," 546.

32 Borrows, "Sovereignty's Alchemy," 547.

33 Turner, *This Is Not a Peace Pipe*, 83.

34 Supreme Court of Canada, *R. v. Van der Peet*, [1996] 2 S.C.R. 507

35 Turner, *This Is Not a Peace Pipe*, 83.

36 Turner, *This Is Not a Peace Pipe*, 8.

## Sources

Borrows, John. *Canada's Indigenous Constitution*. University of Toronto Press, 2010.

Borrows, John. "Sovereignty's Alchemy: An Analysis of *Delgamuukw v. British Columbia*." *Osgoode Hall Law Journal* 37, no. 3 (1999): 537–596. https://doi.org/10.60082/2817-5069.1522.

Dyzenhaus, David. "The Idea of a Constitution: A Plea for *Staatsrechtslehre*." In *Philosophical Foundations of Constitutional Law*, edited by David Dyzenhaus and Malcolm Thorburn. Oxford University Press, 2019.

Government of Canada. "Canada's Collaborative Modern Treaty Implementation Policy." May 23, 2023. https://www.rcaanc-cirnac.gc.ca/eng/1672771319009/1672771475448.

Government of Canada. "Highlights from the Report of the Royal Commission on Aboriginal Peoples.." September 15, 2010. https://www.rcaanc-cirnac.gc.ca/eng/1100100014597/1572547985018.

Hamilton, Robert, and Joshua Nichols. "Reconciliation and the Straightjacket: A Comparative Analysis of the Secession Reference and *R v Sparrow*." *Ottawa Law Review* 52, no. 2 (2021): 205–255. https://canlii.ca/t/tb1l.

International Council on Human Rights Policy. "When Legal Worlds Overlap Human Rights, State and Non-State Law." 2009. https://ssrn.com/abstract=1551229.

Jønch-Clausen, Karin, and Klemens Kappel. "Social Epistemic Liberalism and the Problem of Deep Epistemic Disagreements." *Ethical Theory and Moral Practice*, 18, no. 2 (2015): 371–384. https://doi.org/10.1007/s10677-014-9523-y.

Larmore, Charles. *What Is Political Philosophy?* Princeton University Press, 2020.

Mandle, Jon, and Sarah Roberts-Cady, eds. *John Rawls: Debating the Major Questions*. Oxford University Press, 2020.

Mills, Aaron. "A Preliminary Sketch of Anishinaabe (a Species of Rooted) Constitutionalism." *Rooted* 1, no. 1 (2021), 2–7. https://indigenous-law-association-at-mcgill.com/wp-content/uploads/2021/06/rooted-vol-1-issue-1-full-pdf-final-2.pdf.

Napoleon, Val, et al. *Mikomosis and the Wetiko: Teaching Guide*. Indigenous Law Research Unit: 39, 2014. https://www.indigenousbar.ca/indigenouslaw/wp-content/uploads/2013/04/Mikomosis-and-the-Wetiko-Teaching-Guide-Web.pdf.

Napoleon, Val, and Hadley Friedland. "Indigenous Legal Traditions: Roots to Renaissance." In *The Oxford Handbook of Criminal Law*, edited by Markus D. Dubber and Tatjana Hornle. Oxford University Press, 2014.

O'Toole, Darren. "The Red River Resistance of 1869–1870: The Machiavellian Moment of the Métis of Manitoba." PhD diss. University of Ottawa, 2011.

Rawls, John. *Political Liberalism*. Columbia University Press, 2005.

Riel, Louis. "Louis Riel's Address to the Jury, 31 July 1885." In *Riel's Defence: Perspectives on His Speeches*, edited by Hans V. Hansen. McGill-Queen's University Press, 2014.

Self-Government Recognition and Implementation Agreement Between Métis Nation–Saskatchewan and His Majesty the King in Right of Canada as Represented by the Minister of Crown-Indigenous Relations.

Snyder, Emily, Lindsay Borrows, and Val Napoleon. *Mikomosis and the Wetiko: A Teaching Guide for Youth, Community, and Post-Secondary Educators.* Indigenous Law Unit, 2014.

Supreme Court of Canada. *Reference re Secession of Quebec.* [1998] 2 S.C.R. 217. https://decisions.scc-csc.ca/scc-csc/scc-csc/en/item/1643/index.do.

Supreme Court of Canada. *R. v. Sparrow* [1990] 1 S.C.R. 1075. https://decisions.scc-csc.ca/scc-csc/scc-csc/en/item/609/index.do.

Supreme Court of Canada. *R. v. Van der Peet* [1996] 2 S.C.R. 507. https://decisions.scc-csc.ca/scc-csc/scc-csc/en/item/1407/index.do.

Tamanaha, Brian. *Legal Pluralism Explained: History, Theory, Consequences.* Oxford University Press, 2021.

Turner, Dale. *This Is Not a Peace Pipe: Towards a Critical Indigenous Philosophy.* University of Toronto Press, 2006.

Waluchow, Wil, and Dimitrios Kyritsis. "Constitutionalism." In *The Stanford Encyclopedia of Philosophy* , edited by Edward N. Zalta. 2022. https://plato.stanford.edu/entries/constitutionalism/.

Whitecap Dakota Nation. *A Self-Government Treaty: Recognizing The Whitecap Dakota Nation/Wapaha SKA Dakota Oyate.* https://www.whitecapdakota.com/pdf-documents/230501-final---A-Self-Government-Treaty-Recognizing-the-Whitecap-Dakota-Nation-Wapaha-Ska-Dakota-Oyate---May-1-2023.pdf.

# Resistance and Resurgence

## *Asserting Indigenous Peoples' Rights in Settler Colonial Canada*

Emily Grafton

IN SETTLER COLONIAL CANADA, INDIGENOUS PEOPLES, rights exist on a spectrum that includes inherent rights, Treaty Rights, Aboriginal rights, Indigenous human rights, and international Indigenous Rights, in addition to those rights held as Canadian citizens. These rights can conflict, complement, and overlap in their component makeup, origin, and codification source. These rights exist while the settler state, throughout Canada's history, also attempts to assimilate Indigenous Peoples and circumvent or erode their rights. In Canada, therefore, those Indigenous Rights that are recognized and codified by the state ought to be understood within the settler state model of erasure to ensure benefit to the settler project. The result of this recognition and erasure is a complex spectrum of rights that are ever-changing through the long-standing practices of Indigenous Peoples' inherent rights. Many of these complexities are due to changes in Canadian case law and legislation, Indigenous-led resurgence movements, and developing articulations of Indigenous Rights in the international sphere.

As a citizen of the Métis Nation who grew up in Treaty 1 territory and now lives as a guest in Treaty 4, I have come to understand a few key elements of Indigenous Peoples' rights in Canada. The various rights that Indigenous Peoples hold are complex, and in many ways I am summarizing these to offer conceptual understanding of this vast rights-based terrain: there are details and nuance that a short chapter will not be able to sufficiently capture. This chapter is informed by the scholarship noted and my own lived experiences learning alongside Indigenous Knowledge Sharers and thought leaders.

## Settler State Recognition and Erosion of Indigenous Peoples' Rights

The settler Canadian state attempts to erode Indigenous Peoples' rights as part of its erasure efforts, or the logics of elimination,[1] to benefit the settler project. Yet, in contradictory political practices, the state also recognizes the distinct rights of Indigenous Peoples. There is a dichotomy at work here: settler colonial rights erasure and recognition. This dichotomy can be illustrated by American Indian scholar Jodi Byrd's development of the cacophony, a concept that blurs the distinction between Indigenous dispossession and settler benefit.[2] Byrd details the dichotomy of Amerindian absence/presence that occurs when states establish and erode Indigenous Peoples' nationhood, rights, and history at the same time.[3] I see this in Canada when the state "absences" (erases) and "presences" (recognizes) the rights or nationhood of Indigenous Peoples.[4]

Settler scholar Lorenzo Veracini expands Bird's discussion on cacophony to "contradictory cacophony."[5] This conceptualizes the dichotomy (absencing/presencing) that both contributes to eliminatory efforts while also justifying the erasure of Indigenous Peoples' presence. This chapter argues that the spectrum of existing Indigenous Peoples' rights in Canada is a contradictory cacophony that eliminates and recognizes Indigenous Peoples' rights.

The state's rights recognition can, also, be understood in the conceptual terms of Glen Coulthard's politics of recognition,[6] which argues that while the Canadian state has shifted its political approach to Indigenous Peoples from assimilation to rights recognition, these relations remain fundamentally colonial with the intention of assimilation and oppression. As Coulthard writes, "instead of ushering in an era of peaceful coexistence grounded on the ideal of reciprocity or mutual recognition, the politics of recognition in its contemporary liberal form promises to reproduce the very configurations of colonialist, racist, patriarchal state power that Indigenous Peoples' demands for recognition have historically sought to transcend."[7] These politics of recognition, that of erasure and assimilative intent, surface in the long history of the Canadian state[8] and its intent to dismantle Indigenous Peoples' inherent rights in the effort to support settler colonial benefit.

The process of "absencing" or the erasure of Indigenous Peoples' rights and their inherent sovereignty[9] began long ago. Much like other settler colonial states, Canada was founded through the reign of imperial colonial expansion that relied upon the doctrine of discovery and terra nullius, which is Latin for "vacant lands." These international doctrines asserted foreign powers could justifiably exert authority or sovereignty over these lands, effectively eroding Indigenous title and nationhood.[10] Imperial colonial expansion was further founded on religion, specifically Christianity, and the international imposition of foreign powers in these territories was based on religious expansion as well as accessing lands and resources.[11]

Though this approach of "might makes right" prevailed in North America, so, too, did "presencing." The *Royal Proclamation of 1763*, a legal doctrine integral to the settlement of North America, did codify European imperial powers' acknowledgement of Indigenous Peoples' sovereignty.[12] The *Royal Proclamation* was endorsed by Great Britain, France, and several Indigenous nations. Many view this document as evidence of diplomacy among equal, sovereign nations[13] and argue that these bilateral diplomatic relations were fostered on a nation-to-nation level between Indigenous nations and the British Crown.[14] Many Indigenous Peoples understand that the *Royal Proclamation* upholds their nations' rights to sovereignty and refer to it as the "Indian Magna Carta."[15]

Over time, the application of the *Royal Proclamation* shifted away from being a document that was used to alleviate conflict over lands, curb settler land theft, and assure Indigenous Peoples that settlement would not come at the expense of Indigenous Peoples' lands to a tool that could foster land dispossession.[16] For example, when the *British North America (BNA) Act, 1867*, the constitutional document that established the Canadian federation, was created, the nature of federal authority over Indigenous Peoples was established in its section 91(24).[17] As Arthur Manuel (Secwepemc Nation) and Grand Chief Ronald Derrickson (Westbank First Nation) write, "it is most clear that the BNA Act was a white supremacist document designed for a white supremacist country."[18] Here, the nation-to-nation balance became diluted,[19] a process akin to "absencing."

From this brief history, we can perhaps see how "absencing" (erosion) and "presencing" (recognition) are deeply entrenched in Indigenous-Canadian state relations. On the one hand, the *Royal Proclamation* is the

"Indian Magna Carta." It recognizes in the law the nation-to-nation diplomacy among Indigenous nations and the Crown. On the other hand, the *Royal Proclamation* was used by the Crown and later the federal and provincial governments to circumvent Indigenous nations' sovereignty.[20] To further complicate the contradictory cacophony, consider that it is these inherent rights of Indigenous Peoples that constitute an integral component to Indigenous-centred resistance to settler colonial erasure: they frame resurgence movements centred on exercising sovereignty, which are antithetical to settler colonial projects of Indigenous assimilation.

## Understanding Indigenous Peoples' Rights in Canada

Around the world, Indigenous Peoples have distinct or inherent rights that have been practised for many millennia, and as a result of colonial denial, these rights are increasingly recognized in countries shaped by colonization.[21] Indigenous Peoples' rights are both long-standing inherent rights that predate colonial occupation as well as a "consequence" of colonization and, therefore, a mechanism of decolonization. In many ways, contemporary Indigenous Peoples' rights are fought for in resistance to the long history of state-imposed rights erosion. Importantly, these rights are not stagnant[22] and they continue to evolve.[23]

Indigenous Peoples' rights exist on a spectrum of differing rights in Canada; yet, there is significant overlap in codification, practice, and interpretation of these rights. In Canada there is, as Kulchyski writes, "no clear, evolutionary logic" to Indigenous Peoples' rights, and, what's more, "the rights were sometimes recognized and more often than not ignored outright."[24] Importantly, in Canada, these rights ought to be understood according to Coulthard's politics of recognition, which argue that such recognition of state rights continues to support colonial motives (or the assimilation of Indigenous Peoples to benefit settler society).

### *Indigenous Peoples' Inherent Rights*

Indigenous Peoples' inherent rights are those rights that are "self-originating" and are not derived from the Canadian state but predate European contact and colonial oppression.[25] It would be impossible to define Indigenous Peoples' inherent rights due to the wide-sweeping variation of Indigenous nationhood throughout Canada because these rights are specific to distinct Indigenous nations. As a citizen of the Métis Nation with lived experiences in Treaty 1 and Treaty 4 territories, I have come to understand a few key elements that set Indigenous inherent rights apart from other rights.

Indigenous inherent rights are sui generis,[26] or unique, and self-originating. I was taught that they are sourced from the Creator and codified in lands, languages, relationships, and cultural expressions.[27] These cultural rights–based connections to lands are inherent rights that predate colonial occupation and continue to exist. These inherent rights are an essential foundation for Indigenous resurgence movements or reasserting sovereignty.[28]

As discussed, these inherent rights are acknowledged by the Canadian state through the *Royal Proclamation* and, as will be discussed, the *Constitution Act, 1982*. This process of acknowledgement has long been and continues to be fought for by Indigenous Peoples for two significant reasons. First, Indigenous Peoples' inherent rights stand in the way of colonial settlement, which is premised on extractive processes of resource industries, namely for capitalist profits.[29] The state has interest in eroding the relations of Indigenous Peoples to lands, held in part through inherent rights, to enable the settler colonial project's success. Extractive resource use conflicts with Indigenous practices of taking care of lands and resources through kinship relations, creating settler colonial settlement.[30] As such, Indigenous Peoples' rights hold decolonial potential in that they can and are used to govern in ways alternative to the mechanics of colonial-informed governance.

Second, Indigenous Peoples have struggled to resist forms of colonial state recognition that bring Indigenous Peoples further into the colonial project through assimilation, much as Coulthard has critiqued as the state's operation of rights recognition to further enable assimilation. Indigenous Peoples, therefore, want state recognition that these rights exist prior to the formation of the settler state and are not granted by the Crown.[31] Indigenous Peoples have never ceased advocating that their rights exist prior to European colonial contact and occupation, and separate from settler colonial legal sources. Today, however, the settler state commonly frames this relationship not through nation-to-nation relations but as those akin to sovereign-subject or state-citizen, as demonstrated by Canada's centuries-long colonial history.

Another tension for settler states is that these states struggle to understand and accommodate these inherent rights in the existing Westphalian system of organization that places sovereignty with the state. Deviation from this model is often interpreted as jeopardizing state sovereignty.[32] This has been the experience in Canada, where, as one example, the state conceived of Indigenous Peoples' self-determination as rights that could be codified in the *Indian Act* and exercised constitutionally as though First Nations were municipalities.[33] While this example is specific to First Nations peoples and not applicable to all Indigenous Peoples, it should be clear that this approach circumvents the kinds of rights discussed above as inherent (or self-originating) and, furthermore, is based not on a model of nation-to-nation relations but on a continuation of colonial imposition of federal authority that Indigenous Peoples attempt to dismantle through rights expression. Through determination and perseverance, Indigenous Peoples fought against these colonizing tactics to have their existing inherent rights and Treaty Rights encoded through the process of constitutional patriation in section 53 of the *Constitution Act, 1982*, which will be discussed below.

### *Treaty Rights*

From an Indigenous perspective, treaty is a "relationship"[34] or a "shared common approach to alliance-building."[35] Being in treaty is exercising or living according to a set of ongoing (not certain or final) dynamic responsibilities. Treaties are long-standing, as are the related traditional practices of Indigenous Peoples across differing nations.[36] You may have heard from Knowledge Keepers, as I have, that treaty is held in relationships with lands, waterways, skies, more-than-human beings, and neighbours. Métis scholar Zoe Todd explains that the philosophical underpinnings of treaties rests upon reciprocal responsibilities with more-than-human beings, lands, and waterways; these are complex environmental kin relations and relational responsibilities of care.[37]

Typically, treaties signed with the Crown and later the Canadian government are understood according to their historical development, including the Peace and Friendship Treaties (signed during the eighteenth century in what became Eastern Canada), pre-Confederation/historical treaties (signed during the eighteenth and nineteenth centuries), Numbered Treaties (Treaties 1 through 11, signed between 1871 and 1921), and modern-day treaties (since 1975). [38] The treaties contain many guarantees to Indigenous treaty-holders such as access to education and health care, annual annuities, or designated lands and rights to land use such as harvesting, hunting, or fishing; the specific components differ across the many treaty agreements.

Treaties are complex in settler colonial contexts because, in addition to acknowledging the inherent rights of Indigenous nations, they are also a tool that allows European settlement. Treaties were, in fact, a common requirement at the time of European contact for settlement, alongside military conquest.[39] Given the colonial context of treaty-making in Canada, the treaties have been used to secure lands for the Crown to expedite settlement and are assumed by the state to extinguish Aboriginal title.[40] Aboriginal title refers to the rights of Indigenous Peoples to their traditional lands and is recognized as sui generis in Canadian law.[41] This process of extinguishment through treaty might be described as a land "grab" or theft.[42] Today, modern-day treaties can include comprehensive treaties, such as self-government and land claims agreements, and specific treaties, which include resolving unfulfilled treaty promises and scrip.[43] These modern-day treaties are often understood to benefit Indigenous communities by promoting Indigenous nationhood, though others do argue that they bring Indigenous nations further under the model of the settler state.

In settler colonial society, treaties are routinely understood as a benefit to Indigenous Peoples, which ignores the very evident benefit that they provide to the Canadian state and settler society.[44] Some treaty commissions promote the slogan "we are all treaty people" to encourage Canadians to see how treaties provide benefit to all Canadians and do not provide differential benefits only in favour of Indigenous Peoples.[45] Some argue that treaties have hurt Indigenous Peoples by circumventing nationhood to benefit the settler project.[46] This circumvention is assumed because the Canadian state and much of society have come to interpret treaty as an extinguishment of Indigenous Peoples' rights to traditional territories.[47] This is a false interpretation that has been disproven through the oral testimonies of Elders and Knowledge Sharers, who speak of the "spirit and intent" of the treaties,[48] and the courts, which uphold ongoing Aboriginal title through treaty.[49] In fact, I've heard many Elders describe treaty as representing Indigenous Peoples' inherent rights to the lands and others, such as Kulchyski, discuss treaty as the heart of the Canadian Constitution.[50]

### *Aboriginal Rights*

Kulchyski writes, "Aboriginal rights themselves have been oriented as another tool of totalization, but also still contain the hidden promise of something else."[51] He goes on to explain that the "totalizing" social nature of settler colonial projects, including the political and economic premises of liberal democracy and capitalism, is in conflict with Indigenous societies, and this suggests evidence of the "impossibility of defining Aboriginal rights."[52] For Kulchyski, that Aboriginal rights are defined by the settler state and, specifically, the Canadian justice system is evidence of "unjust relations" structured to ensure Indigenous Peoples' rights are restricted and oppressed.[53] And yet, they also contain the "promise of something else."

Let's consider how the state has come to define these rights. Aboriginal rights are codified in section 35 of the *Constitution Act, 1982*.[54] This constitutional arrangement results from decades of the political struggles of Indigenous Peoples—First Nations, Inuit, and Métis people—against the state for recognition in the Constitution. At the time of constitutional patriation, these rights were left to be defined at subsequent first ministers' meetings attended by premiers and Indigenous political leaders.[55] After three such meetings and two national referendums, these Aboriginal rights remain largely undefined and left to the courts to determine. The history of Aboriginal rights claims and settlements in the courts is colossal and, therefore, is not summarized in this single chapter.

Section 35 does acknowledge the pre-existing nature of Indigenous inherent rights and protects these rights,[56] which it characterizes as "sui generis," or originating outside of the Canadian legal system.[57] The government determines that Aboriginal rights include: 1) Aboriginal title (ownership rights to land); 2) rights to occupy and use lands and resources, such as hunting and fishing rights; 3) self-government rights; and 4) cultural and social rights.[58] There is significant conflict, however, between Indigenous Peoples and the federal and sub-national orders of government when interpreting these rights, with the latter placing "caveats on the interpretation."[59] These caveats are intended to circumscribe Indigenous Peoples' rights or, as Green describes, have a "sanitizing effect" on the assimilative intentions of the state.[60] Thus, we see how settler colonialism's "totalizing" effect arises to minimize what is "undefinable." Perhaps we also see the "promise of something else" evident in these four areas of Aboriginal rights, which can be evidenced through numerous asserted rights claims in the courts.

### *International Indigenous Rights*

The United Nations Declaration on the Rights of Indigenous Peoples (UNDRIP) was adopted by the United Nations in 2007, though it was not endorsed by Canada until 2016, which we might assess as a measure of continued colonial assimilative erasure through Canadian state-sanctioned rights suppression or "absencing." Though UNDRIP is a non-legally binding declaration,[61] it sets out and upholds numerous rights. Importantly, as Manuel and Derrickson write, this is a "virtual declaration of independence for Indigenous Peoples."[62] UNDRIP states: "Recognizing and reaffirming that... Indigenous Peoples possess collective rights which are indispensable for their existence, well-being and integral development as peoples."[63] These rights are legal entitlements held collectively to ensure the existence and well-being of Indigenous Peoples.[64] These include, as examples, UNDRIP's provision of a number of rights specific to the promotion and protection of Indigenous Peoples' education, culture, and traditional expressions of cultures, identity, nationhood, and self-determination (Article 3) and self-government (Article 4), as well as protections against assimilation (Article 8) and forced removal from lands (Article 10).

The culmination and ratification of UNDRIP are due to Indigenous Peoples' resistance and efforts to effect transformative politics spanning several decades. Its passage is often understood as a testament to Indigenous Peoples' agency and fortitude in the face of colonial political processes.[65] As Sheryl Lightfoot explains, when Indigenous Peoples' previous efforts of resistance to colonization did not succeed in recognition of Indigenous Peoples' rights to nationhood, many chose to work within the structure of the international arena to fundamentally change the colonial system from within.[66] Specifically, those previous decolonization movements resulting from the Declaration on the Granting of Independence to Colonial Countries and Peoples (United Nations, 1960) largely ignored Indigenous Peoples' decolonization and assertions of nationhood in many settler states.[67]

Much like s.35 of Canada's *Constitution Act*, UNDRIP can be understood as a significant structural change from within the colonial system; however, understood from a perspective of rights recognition, one could conclude that these rights within the colonial system maintain and extend colonial relations among settler states and society and Indigenous Peoples. For this, and other reasons, the UNDRIP can be controversial. For some, it is not implemented as fully as desired.[68] For example, globally Indigenous Peoples' right to self-determination remains underdeveloped while the right to free, prior, and informed consent (FPIC) has advanced as an accepted norm.[69]

Interestingly, in Canada the Aboriginal right to self-government is affirmed in s.35 of the *Constitution Act, 1982*, yet FPIC remains undefined as a regulatory mechanism. In some ways, FPIC might be similar to the duty to consult already established in Canadian law or an extension of the current industry practice of impact and benefit agreements.[70] Some might argue an obligation to consult is far less meaningful than the legal requirement to gain consent (FPIC). Others, however, point out the limitations to these mechanisms' ability to ensure Indigenous Peoples' agency at the decision-making table.[71] The *Act* (Bill C-15, *An Act Respecting the United Nations Declaration on the Rights of Indigenous Peoples*) states that implementation of UNDRIP will occur through an action plan developed over three years; this does not ensure, however, that this process will result in a clear road map for government or industry regarding the vast complexities of FPIC.[72]

Additional controversy arises from the "fragile" nature of UNDRIP.[73] The fragility is due to a tension discussed earlier: the Westphalian system of international organization that interprets Indigenous Peoples' rights as endangering states' sovereignty.[74] This fragility is also in relation to the liberal model and international scope of these rights frameworks, as the next section will address. Lightfoot argues that UNDRIP gives a framework to guide Indigenous-state relations as a plural sovereignty and power-sharing framework that recognizes nation-to-nation understandings of self-government.[75]

### *Indigenous Human Rights*

Many argue that Indigenous Peoples' fundamental human rights are unmet.[76] That Indigenous Peoples in Canada are routinely subjected to deplorable living conditions in urban, rural, and reserve communities that lack potable drinking water, safe housing, and adequate health and education services, as just some examples, encourages many to argue that Indigenous Rights are human rights. As Clapham writes, "The language of human rights is deployed to criticize, defend, and reform all sorts of behaviour."[77] It is, thus, an accurate assessment, when considering the disproportionate rates of Indigenous Peoples' incarceration or child apprehension and those intersections of abject poverty, and impetus to call for Canada to meet the fundamental human rights of Indigenous Peoples across the country. These conditions are, in fact, intentional colonial practices that push Indigenous Peoples further into the settler population.[78] Yet, Indigenous human rights are anything but straightforward. Some settlers see Indigenous Rights as primarily an elimination of these disparities; equality, however, is not akin to Indigenous Rights, which, as will be discussed, is ensuring the recognition and restoration of inherent rights, self-determination, and lands.

Indigenous Peoples' rights have been eroded as a tactic of assimilation to benefit the colonial project, and, therefore, Indigenous Peoples have had to use international human rights frameworks to effect and exercise their distinct rights within settler nations,[79] specifically the Universal Declaration of Human Rights.[80] However, these individually framed human rights regimes are simply insufficient to support Indigenous Peoples' rights struggles, which are premised on collective rights;[81] instead, Indigenous Peoples need collective-based Indigenous human rights protections to combat the fundamental human rights violations that are commonplace in settler colonial societies (hence the work of UNDRIP). These connections between human rights and Indigenous Peoples' rights are integral to Indigenous Peoples' ability to secure rights at the international level and, as a result, to varying degrees, at the domestic level.[82] Many have argued that there is an inherent interconnection between Indigenous Rights and human rights.[83] Fan explains that "Indigenous Peoples' rights have emerged as a specialized category of human rights,"[84] and Green states that "Indigenous or Aboriginal rights are a species of human rights."[85] Indigenous Peoples have contributed to the evolution of human rights frameworks by developing the domain of collective rights within human rights frameworks.[86] Thus, we might conclude, a symbiotic relationship between Indigenous Peoples' rights and human rights has emerged over the last few decades concerning rights advancements (and protections) in the international arena.

There are, however, various oppositional arguments that maintain Indigenous Peoples' rights are not akin to human rights. Human rights are developed according to Western-conceived understandings of rights within the Westphalian system and are ideologically liberal. Human rights are, for example, premised on the rights of the individual, which presents a significant contradictory tension with the principles of Indigenous Rights, which are of a collective nature.[87] For some critics, this ideological tension jeopardizes the ability of Indigenous Peoples to exercise their inherent rights and, instead, brings Indigenous Rights into a closer alignment with the Western state.[88] In fact, Coulthard argues that it is the explicit intent of liberally framed rights discourse to separate Indigenous Peoples from their traditional lands and sources of inherent rights to benefit the expansion of the settler colonial project.[89]

Indeed, there is much evidence that human rights are Western-oriented constructs, but does this necessarily mean that Indigenous Peoples' rights conflict with human rights? Certainly, human rights have a long history shaped by liberal theory,[90] they protect individual rights,[91] and are entrenched within democratic political systems.[92] The philosophical conflict between liberalism and Indigenous ways of knowing is deep and, thus, difficult to overcome. A related conflict, as Green clarifies, are those measures of equality that Indigenous Peoples seek: to evade the assimilative forces of settler society and, also, to escape the colonial legacies of poverty.[93]

A secondary concern includes the application of Indigenous inherent rights that are specific to particular relationships to lands, animals, waterways, and other non-human beings through a global mechanism: What tensions might arise when the protections of these specific inherent rights emerge from broadly scoped and wide-sweeping international rights frameworks? Fan explains that Western approaches to law "compartmentalize rights into different categories," and these categories "do not reflect Indigenous Peoples' aspirations, or cannot accommodate the web of connections embodied by their IK [Indigenous knowledge]."[94] Thus, liberal systems conceive of rights in ways that do not correspond to Indigenous-centred conceptions of rights. In a sense, UNDRIP was developed as a different framework from that of the Universal Declaration of Human Rights to overcome this and to better accommodate Indigenous-centred human rights. In addition to this explanation, Green clarifies that human rights are abstract and neither identical nor homogenous: they *are* applied with difference to specific circumstances.[95] In this way, Indigenous human rights exist somewhere between the universal and specific or, perhaps, take up both universal and specific to be that unique "species" described by Fan and Green earlier. These debates certainly demonstrate that Indigenous inherent rights require continued and renewed conceptual framing to transcend both liberal conformities and assimilative tactics that reinforce the politics of recognition.

## Conclusion

Coulthard argues that contemporary relations between the Canadian state and Indigenous Peoples, including rights frameworks, are characterized by the continuation of colonizing factors. These politics of recognition support the continued project of assimilation or, as Patrick Wolfe describes, the logic of elimination: colonial states are premised on eroding Indigenous difference through rights loss to assume Indigenous identity into the project of settlement. This chapter demonstrates this premise through the history of Indigenous Peoples' rights recognition—"presencing"—and erosion—"absencing"—by the Crown and the Canadian state for settler benefit.

This chapter has looked at Indigenous People's inherent rights and the Canadian state's varying approaches to Indigenous Peoples' rights recognition—Treaty Rights, Aboriginal rights, Indigenous human rights, and international Indigenous Rights. What began as nation-to-nation relations, recognized by the *Royal Proclamation* and treaty-making, gave way to imposed imperial colonial and, later, settler colonial forms of rights dispossession and socio-economic realities that are akin to abject human rights violations. These early recognitions of Indigenous sovereignty continue to give form to expressions of Indigenous Peoples' rights within the Canadian state, and more recently the international arena has been an effective place for Indigenous Peoples to assert agency and establish the development and protection of rights. However, both settler state rights recognition and transferring the internationally scoped rights to the domestic sphere present tensions, including the long-standing practices of using liberal rights frameworks to erode the collective nature of Indigenous inherent rights and tactics that assimilate Indigenous Peoples into the settler state. The result is a complex spectrum of Indigenous Peoples' rights that are in regular and continual flux. As Indigenous Peoples continue to exercise agency to effect and exercise their distinct rights, we will see continued change in the domain of Indigenous Peoples' rights in Canada.

## Notes

1 Wolfe, "Settler Colonialism."
2 Byrd, "Colonialism's Cacophony.
3 Byrd, *Transit of Empire.*
4 Byrd, *Transit of Empire.*
5 Veracini, "Introducing Settler Colonial Studies."
6 Coulthard, *Red Skin, White Masks.*
7 Coulthard, *Red Skin, White Masks*, 3. An additional note is that liberalism is a political philosophy that shapes liberal democracies such as Canada. Some

of its basic tenets include the importance of promoting and protecting the rights of the individual and equality of opportunity.

8 The Canadian state is understood as the stable governing institutional order of Canada that operates in the international order and includes the ongoing operations of the domestic government, including the branches of government (executive, legislative, and judicial) that create and implement laws and provide social services to the citizenry.

9 There are various ways to understand Indigenous sovereignty. From my time spent with Indigenous Old Ones, community leaders, and political leaders, as well as my career working in politics, I have developed an understanding of Indigenous sovereignty. The concept of sovereignty has long been tethered to the Westphalian state system, which shapes the contemporary international order. In this way, Indigenous sovereignty positions Indigenous nations as sovereign and equitable to the state. This understanding is not without deep theoretical practical tensions, and Audra Simpson (Haudenosaunee Nation) has neatly articulated these fraught logics of Indigenous sovereignty. Simpson describes sovereignty as tethered to the international state system being the mechanism responsible for the centuries of forcible detachment and displacement of Indigenous Peoples from their lands and their long-standing inherent connections and rights to these lands (Simpson, "The Sovereignty of Critique," 686–687). The force behind this dispossession is imperial colonialism and capitalist extraction: the plight for sovereign recognition does not stifle colonial dispossession and genocide, but instead further promotes it (688–691).

10 Venne, "Understanding Treaty 6"; Borrows, "The Durability of Terra Nullius."

11 Dickason, *The Myth of the Savage*, 273–275.

12 *Royal Proclamation, 1763*, R.S.C., 1985, App. II, No. 1.

13 Borrows, "Wampum at Niagara," 156; Kulchyski, *The Red Indians*, 29.

14 Tidridge, *The Queen at the Council Fire*.

15 Magna Carta is a document that generated a set of legal rights for many, but not all, subjects of the English Crown in Runnymede, England, in 1215, with several subsequent documents developed over the next century (Breay, *Magna Carta*). While the intent, importance, and continued impact of Magna Carta is contested, many have argued that Magna Carta led to numerous rights-based causes such as the American and French Revolutions, modern-day parliamentary democracy, and the United Nations Declaration of Human Rights (Breay, *Magna Carta*). From such a standpoint, Magna Carta is argued to be an important symbolic or actual bearer of rights.

16 Borrows, *Aboriginal Legal Issues*, 159; Hall. *The American Empire*.

17 The *British North America Act*'s s.91(24) states that "Indians, and lands reserved for the Indians," are the responsibility of the federal government. See *Constitution Act, 1867*. 30 & 31 Vict, c 3.

18 Manuel and Grand Chief Derrickson, *Unsettling Canada*, 63.

19 Lightfoot, "Indigenous Mobilization," 256.

20 Tidridge, *The Queen at the Council Fire*, 53.

21 Patton, "Philosophical Justifications," 13.

22 As John Borrows evidences, "Aboriginal ideologies, like Aboriginal practices, are not frozen." Borrows, "Frozen Rights in Canada," 64.

23 Heather Exner-Pirot and Martin Ignasiak write on this evolution that "we are witnessing an evolution of Indigenous rights from a *shield* for proponents... towards Indigenous rights as a *sword* for proponents." Exner-Pirot and Ignasiak, "From Shield to Sword," 9–10.

24 Kulchyski, ed., *Unjust Relations*, 9.

25 Frideres, *First Nations in the Twenty-First Century*, 153.

26 Henderson, "Sui Generis and Treaty Citizenship."

27 Grafton and Peristerakis, "Decolonizing Museological Practices," 236–237.

28 Simpson, *As We Have Always Done*.

29 Kuokkanen, "Self-Determination."

30 Barelli, "Development Projects," 69.

31 Frideres, *First Nations in the Twenty-First Century*, 151; Kulchyski, ed., *Unjust Relations*, 8.

32 Lightfoot, "Indigenous Mobilization," 254.

33 Frideres, *First Nations in the Twenty-First Century*, 151.

34 Office of the Treaty Commissioner [OTC], *Statement of Treaty Issues*, 12.

35 OTC, *Statement of Treaty Issues*, 14.

36 Henderson, "Sui Generis and Treaty Citizenship," 428.

37 Todd, "Fish, Kin and Hope," 103–107.

38 University of Victoria, "Indigenous Law/Indigenous Legal Traditions." Typically, treaty is thought to be held by Inuit and First Nations peoples, though, many Métis people did enter into treaty with the Crown through a process of scrip, which are monetary and land titles transferred between the Crown to Métis people. Treaties do not cover all of Canada, but they do extend to many (but not all) Indigenous Peoples.

39 Culhane, *The Pleasure of the Crown*, 47–48.

40 Frideres and Gadacz, *Aboriginal Peoples in Canada*, 208.

41 Borrows and Rotman, "The Sui Generis Nation."

42 Daschuk, *Clearing the Plains*, 79.

43 Frideres and Gadacz, *Aboriginal Peoples in Canada*, 210–230.

44 Frideres and Gadacz, *Aboriginal Peoples in Canada*, 199.

45 Lowman and Barker, *Settler*, 66.

46 Lowman and Barker, *Settler*, 67.

47 Kulchyski, ed., *Unjust Relations*, 9.

48 Kulchyski, ed., *Unjust Relations*, 9.

49 Treaty and Aboriginal Rights Research Centre, *A Debt to Be Paid*, 11.

50 Kulchyski, ed., *The Red Indians*, 7.

51 Kulchyski, ed., *Unjust Relations*, 1.

52 Kulchyski, ed., *Unjust Relations*, 1–4.

53 Kulchyski, ed., *Unjust Relations*, 4–5.

54 It is important to distinguish that non-Status Indians are not included here. Non-Status Indians or non-Status First Nations peoples include those who have lost status, according to the *Indian Act*, due to the state

enfranchisement practices intended to eliminate Indigenous Peoples. For many, this lack of specific inclusion is an additional measure of assimilation by the state.

55 Frideres, *First Nations in the Twenty-First Century*, 151.
56 Frideres, *First Nations in the Twenty-First Century*, 153.
57 Ladner, "Gendering Decolonisation," 62.
58 Government of Canada, "INAN."
59 Frideres, *First Nations in the Twenty-First Century*, 157.
60 Green, "From Colonialism to Reconciliation," 37.
61 Lennox and Short, "Introduction,", 5.
62 Manuel and Grand Chief Derrickson, *Unsettling Canada*, 53.
63 United Nations, "United Nations Declaration on the Rights of Indigenous Peoples," 7.
64 Odello, "The United Nations Declaration," 56.
65 Lightfoot, "Indigenous Mobilization," 254; Fan, "Evolution of Indigenous Peoples' Rights," 239.
66 Lightfoot, "Indigenous Mobilization," 254.
67 Lightfoot, "Indigenous Mobilization," 255.
68 Lennox and Short, "Introduction," 1.
69 Lennox and Short, "Introduction," 1.
70 Gogal, "A New Era."
71 Gogal, "A New Era."
72 Gogal, "A New Era."
73 Lennox and Short, "Introduction," 1.
74 Lightfoot, "Indigenous Mobilization," 254.
75 Lightfoot, "Indigenous Mobilization," 254–256.
76 Lennox and Short, "Introduction," 1–2.
77 Clapham, *Human Rights*, 1.
78 Frideres and Gadacz, *Aboriginal Peoples in Canada*, 4–9.
79 Odello, "The United Nations Declaration."
80 Lightfoot, "Indigenous Mobilization".
81 Lightfoot, "Indigenous Mobilization," 255.
82 Lennox and Short, "Introduction," 4.
83 Odello, "The United Nations Declaration," 58.
84 Fan, "Evolution of Indigenous Peoples' Rights," 237.
85 Green, "From Colonialism to Reconciliation," 26.
86 Lennox and Short, "Introduction," 4.
87 Odello, "The United Nations Declaration," 54–56.
88 Kulchyski, *Aboriginal Rights*; Patton, "Philosophical Justifications," 13.
89 Coulthard, *Red Skin, White Masks*.
90 Patton, "Philosophical Justifications," 18; Clapham, *Human Rights*, 5.
91 Odello, "The United Nations Declaration," 54.
92 Green, "Introduction," 1.
93 Green, "From Colonialism to Reconciliation," 27.
94 Fan, "Evolution of Indigenous Peoples' Rights," 237.
95 Green, "From Colonialism to Reconciliation," 23.

## Sources

Barelli, Mauro. "Development Projects and Indigenous Peoples' Land: Defining the Scope of Free, Prior and Informed Consent." In *Handbook of Indigenous Peoples' Rights*, edited by Corrine Lennox and Damien Short. Routledge, 2016.

Borrows, John. *Aboriginal Legal Issues: Cases, Materials & Commentary*. LexisNexis Canada, 2007.

Borrows, John. "The Durability of Terra Nullius: Tsilhqot'in Nation v British Columbia." *University of British Columbia Law Review* 48, no. 3 (2015): 701–742.

Borrows, John. "Frozen Rights in Canada: Constitutional Interpretation and the Trickster." *American Indian Law Review* 37, no. 1 (1997): 37–64. https://digitalcommons.law.ou.edu/cgi/viewcontent.cgi?article=1275&context=ailr.

Borrows, John. "Wampum at Niagara: The *Royal Proclamation*, Canadian Legal History, and Self-government." In *Aboriginal and Treaty Rights in Canada: Essays on Law, Equality and Respect for Difference*, edited by Michael Asch. University of British Columbia Press, 1997.

Borrows, John, and Leonard I. Rotman. "The Sui Generis Nation of Aboriginal Rights: Does It Make a Difference?" *Alberta Law Review* 36, no. 1 (1997): 9–46.

Breay, Claire. *Magna Carta: Manuscripts and Myths*. British Library, 2002.

Byrd, Jodi A. "Colonialism's Cacophony: Natives and Arrivants at the Limits of Postcolonial Theory." PhD diss., University of Iowa, 2002.

Byrd, Jodi A. *The Transit of Empire: Indigenous Critiques of Colonialism*. University of Minnesota Press: 2011.

*Constitution Act, 1867*, 30 & 31 Vict, c 3. https://canlii.ca/t/ldsw.

Clapham, Andrew. *Human Rights: A Very Short Introduction*. 2nd ed. Oxford University Press, 2015.

Coulthard, Glen. *Red Skin, White Masks: Rejecting the Colonial Politics of Recognition*. University of Minnesota Press, 2014.

Culhane, Dara. *The Pleasure of the Crown: Anthropology, Law and First Nations*. Talon Books, 1998.

Daschuk, James. *Clearing the Plains: Disease, Politics of Starvation, and the Loss of Indigenous Life*. University of Regina Press, 2013.

Dickason, Olive P. *The Myth of the Savage and the Beginnings of French Colonialism in the Americas*. University of Alberta Press, 1997.

Exner-Pirot, Heather, and Martin Ignasiak. "From Shield to Sword: The Evolution of Indigenous Economic Rights in Canada." Macdonald-Laurier Institute, February 15, 2023. https://macdonaldlaurier.ca/from-shield-to-sword-the-evolution-of-indigenous-economic-rights-in-canada/.

Fan, Rebecca C. "Evolution of Indigenous Peoples' Rights and Indigenous Knowledge Debate." In *Handbook of Indigenous Peoples' Rights*, edited by Corrine Lennox and Damien Short. Routledge, 2016.

Frideres, James. *First Nations in the Twenty-First Century*. Oxford University Press, 2016.

Frideres, James S., and René R. Gadacz. *Aboriginal Peoples in Canada*. 9th ed. Pearson Canada, 2011.

Gogal, Sandra A. "A New Era: Free Prior and Informed Consent." Miller Thomson, August 12, 2023. https://www.millerthomson.com/en/insights/aboriginal/free-prior-and-informed-consent/.

Government of Canada. "INAN - Section 35 of the *Constitution Act 1982* - Background - Jan 28, 2021." https://www.canada.ca/en/immigration-refugees-citizenship/corporate/transparency/committees/inan-jan-28-2021/inan-section-35-consitution-act-1982-background-jan-28-2021.html.

Grafton, Emily, and Julia Peristerakis. "Decolonizing Museological Practices at the Canadian Museum for Human Rights." In *Indigenous Notions of Ownership and Libraries, Archives and Museums*, edited by Camille Callison, Loriene Roy, and Gretchen Alice Lecheminant. International Federation of Library Associations, 2016.

Green, Joyce. "From Colonialism to Reconciliation Through Indigenous Human Rights." In *Indivisible: Indigenous Human Rights*, edited by Joyce Green. Fernwood Publishing, 2014.

Green, Joyce. "Introduction: Honoured in Their Absence: Indigenous Human Rights." In *Indivisible: Indigenous Human Rights*, edited by Joyce Green. Fernwood Publishing, 2014.

Hall, Anthony. *The American Empire and the Fourth World: The Bowl with One Spoon, Part One*. McGill-Queen's University Press, 2003.

Henderson, James Sákéj Youngblood. "Sui Generis and Treaty Citizenship." *Citizenship Studies* 6, no. 4 (2002): 415–440. https://doi.org/10.1080/1362102022000041259.

Kulchyski, Peter. *Aboriginal Rights Are Not Human Rights: In Defence of Indigenous Struggles*. Arbiter Ring Publishing, 2013.

Kulchyski, Peter. *The Red Indians: An Episodic, Informal Collection of Tales from the History of Aboriginal People's Struggles in Canada*. Arbeiter Ring Publishing, 2007.

Kulchyski, Peter, ed. *Unjust Relations: Aboriginal Rights in Canadian Courts*. Oxford University Press, 1994.

Kuokkanen, Rauna. "Self-Determination and Indigenous Women—'Whose Voice Is It We Hear in the Sámi Parliament?'" *International Journal on Minority and Group Rights* 18, no. 1 (2011): 39–62. https://doi.org/10.1163/157181111x550978.

Ladner, Kiera L. "Gendering Decolonisation, Decolonising Gender." *Australian Indigenous Law Review* 13, no. 1 (2009): 62–77.

Lennox, Corinne, and Damien Short. "Introduction." In *Handbook of Indigenous Peoples' Rights*, edited by Corrine Lennox and Damien Short. Routledge, 2016.

Lightfoot, Sheryl R. "Indigenous Mobilization and Activism in the UN System." In *Handbook of Indigenous Peoples' Rights*, edited by Corrine Lennox and Damien Short. Routledge, 2016.

Lowman, Emma Battell, and Adam J. Barker. *Settler: Identity and Colonialism in 21st Century Canada*. Fernwood Publishing, 2015.

Manuel, Arthur, and Grand Chief Ronald M. Derrickson. *Unsettling Canada: A National Wake-Up Call*. 2nd ed. Between the Lines Books, 2021.
Odello, Marco. "The United Nations Declaration on the Rights of Indigenous Peoples." In *Handbook of Indigenous Peoples' Rights*, edited by Corrine Lennox and Damien Short. Routledge, 2016.
Office of the Treaty Commissioner. *Statement of Treaty Issues: Treaties as a Bridge to the Future*. Office of the Treaty Commissioner, 1998.
Patton, Paul. "Philosophical Justifications for Indigenous Rights." In *Handbook of Indigenous Peoples' Rights*, edited by Corrine Lennox and Damien Short. Routledge, 2016.
*Royal Proclamation, 1763*, R.S.C., 1985, App. II, No. 1.
Simpson, Audra. "The Sovereignty of Critique." *South Atlantic Quarterly* 119, no. 4 (2020): 685–699. https://doi.org/10.1215/00382876-8663591.
Simpson, Leanne Betasamosake. *As We Have Always Done: Indigenous Freedom Through Radical Resistance*. University of Minnesota Press, 2017.
Tidridge, Nathan. *The Queen at the Council Fire: The Treaty of Niagara, Reconciliation, and the Dignified Crown in Canada*. Dundurn Press, 2015.
Todd, Zoe. "Fish, Kin and Hope: Tending to Water Violations in *amiskwaciwâskahikan* and Treaty Six Territory." *Afterall: A Journal of Art, Context and Enquiry* 43 (2017): 102–107. https://doi.org/10.1086/692559.
Treaty and Aboriginal Rights Research Centre, *A Debt to Be Paid: Treaty Land Entitlement in Manitoba*. Treaty and Aboriginal Rights Research Centre, 1994.
United Nations. "United Nations Declaration on the Rights of Indigenous Peoples." September 13, 2007. https://www.un.org/esa/socdev/unpfii/documents/drips_en.pdf.
University of Victoria. "Indigenous Law/Indigenous Legal Traditions." https://libguides.uvic.ca/iluvic/treaties.
Venne, Sharon. "Understanding Treaty 6: An Indigenous Perspective." In *Aboriginal and Treaty Rights in Canada: Essays on Law, Equality and Respect for Difference*, edited by Michael Asch. University of British Columbia Press, 1997.
Veracini, Lorenzo. "Introducing Settler Colonial Studies." *Settler Colonial Studies* 1, no. 1 (2011): 1–12. https://doi.org/10.1080/2201473X.2011.10648799.
Wolfe, Patrick. "Settler Colonialism and the Elimination of the Native." *Journal of Genocide Research* 8, no. 4 (2006): 387–409. https://doi.org/10.1080/14623520601056240.

# Afterword

Jeremy Patzer

There was a period some years ago—and I am getting to the age where I find myself offering intentionally vague chronologies such as "some years ago"—when a younger Jeremy was exploring the tools offered by different disciplinary and theoretical traditions. There is a bit more of a backstory to that moment, but it has been related a number of times over the years, by me and others, such that I do fear making it somewhat of a tired "origin story." To put it as briefly as possible, a brush with the law in my youth would later pique my interest in Indigenous Rights. Namely, my younger cousin and I were charged with hunting a single duck, out of season, next to our farm in the Interlake Region of Manitoba. I could offer all sorts of extenuations here, including that it was one of those odd years in which the duck season nonsensically opened two days *after* the goose season, instead of on the same day, or that the law knows little about measuring and apportioning justice in cases involving *two* Indigenous boys and *one* duck.[1]

Of course, although it may have been lost on the conservation officer and the rural magistrate who embodied the force of the law in this situation, there was a larger question of law, justice, and colonialism that backgrounded and transcended our individual historical anecdote. To encapsulate it as tersely as possible, after the Red River Resistance and the Métis leadership's negotiation of the entry of Manitoba into Confederation in 1870,[2] federal and provincial governments ignored the existence of the Métis for over a century and recognized no Indigenous Rights for them. They even continued with this policy framework—charging Métis harvesters and their cousins—for more than two decades after the passage of the *Constitution Act, 1982*, which recognizes and affirms the inherent and Treaty Rights of Canada's Indigenous Peoples and specifically includes Métis within the ambit of this recognition.[3]

Then, a handful of years after our incident with the duck, the Supreme Court of Canada delivered the 2003 decision for *R. v. Powley*.[4] For the first time, the highest court in the country recognized an inherent Aboriginal right to hunt for two Métis claimants in Northern Ontario. Of course, Indigenous Rights advocates know all too well the pace at which the law and settler governments typically bring change for Indigenous Peoples: not only did it take more than two decades to give any sort of effect to the recognition of the Métis in the *Constitution Act, 1982*, but Métis have had to spend the more than two decades since *Powley* attempting to use the precedent, region by region, in their efforts to have their section 35 Aboriginal rights recognized across the Homeland.[5]

Nevertheless, my scholarly origin story is not the essential point in this case—my search for an intellectual mooring is. With these significant developments at the turn of the millennium, Indigenous Rights and Indigenous resistance became a source of keen interest for me, as well as a source of inspiration to pursue graduate studies. Within my search for a theoretical home field, I came across *postcolonialism*.

As Peter Kulchyski notes in his contribution to this volume, postcolonialism is one of several theoretical movements that developed in a somewhat shared era of "posts": postmodernism, poststructuralism, postcolonialism, etc. Interpreting the work being done by this *post-* prefix, Ali Rattansi describes postcolonialism and postmodernism as both possessing the peculiarity of marking out "a supposed historical period as well as a distinctive form of theorization and analysis."[6] While some within the field draw longer histories of postcolonialism that include the varied strains of Marxist thought that accompanied national struggles for independence through the twentieth century,[7] Rattansi's view of postcolonialist studies is decidedly poststructuralist, describing it as "the investigation of the mutually constitutive role played by colonizer and colonized, centre and periphery, the metropolitan and the 'native,' in forming, in part, the identities of both the dominant power and the subalterns involved in the imperial and colonial projects of the 'West.'"[8] Citing Stuart Hall's famous invocation of "the West and the Rest,"[9] Rattansi emphasizes the *mutual imbrication* of such binary identities—the colonizer and the colonized, or the civilized and the savage—in the sense that each side of the binary depends on the other for its meaning, through a process of being defined "in opposition to." According to Rattansi, "it was in constructing the 'natives' as black, pagan, irrational, uncivilized, pre-modern, libidinous, licentious, effeminate and childlike that the self-conception of the European as superior, and as not only fit to govern but as having the positive *duty* to govern and 'civilize' came into being."[10] Similarly, Gayatri Chakravorty Spivak deploys the philosopher Jacques Derrida's concept of *trace*,[11] or the notion that there is the mark or spectre of the Other, as an always-already absent presence, within either side of the binary. This relationship of meaning-through-difference is, of course, both reflective of and productive of asymmetrical relations of power and violence.[12]

While it is certainly beyond the scope of a short afterword to explore the richness of an entire scholarly movement such as postcolonialism, one can see how its concepts and matters of concern doubtless offer fertile ground for the counter-colonial pursuits of Indigenous scholars and their allies. And yet, perhaps not surprisingly in the world of critical scholarship, controversies abound. The extent to which the colonial experiences of Indigenous Peoples in North America figure into the literature is itself a source of debate.[13] Louis Owens does not mince words, arguing that "it would not take much time spent browsing through contemporary critical/theoretical texts—including especially those we call postcolonial—to discover an even more complete erasure of Native American voices."[14] In my initial foray into the field, however, what struck me most were those moments when the words of postcolonial theorists themselves made Owens's case for him. Robert Young, in his comprehensive historical introduction to postcolonialism, posits in the first few pages that "postcolonialism might well be better named 'tricontinentalism'"—in direct reference to Latin America, Africa, and Asia.[15] Rattansi, shifting away from his theoretical-analytical definition of postcolonialism and towards the historical, argues that

> the concept of the "postcolonial" should, in terms of historical periodization, be restricted to time-spaces inaugurated by the formal independence of former colonies of Western powers.
>
> This implies that specifically "postcolonialist" writing may properly be said to emerge after the end of formal colonialism. Before that formal severance, what we have are forms of *anti*-colonial

> writing, which obviously cannot reflect upon the structures and events unleashed in the aftermath of independence.[16]

While many non-Indigenous Peoples in settler colonial states might associate Rattansi's mention of formal independence with their celebrated national stories of pulling out from under the thumb of the British Empire, this is not his intention. (Indeed, from the perspective of many Indigenous Peoples in settler colonial states, contemporary "Independence Day" celebrations do not represent the same shaking off of the yoke of subjection that they do for non-Indigenous citizens.) Rattansi subsequently writes that "the legitimacy of the term 'postcolonial' can still be seriously doubted when viewed from the perspective of the aboriginal populations of North and South America and Australia and New Zealand which are still fighting what they might see as *anti-colonial* struggles."[17]

None of this, to be clear, is to question the worth of postcolonialism as a scholarly endeavour. Without question, I still find much of value in postcolonial studies. (However, this very value suggests to me that we should be wary of enforcing categorical lines of exclusion between colonized peoples based upon questions like "formal" independence. Postcolonial theory itself offers so many foundational guideposts that complicate unreflective celebrations of sovereignty and formal independence.[18]) Nevertheless, the rich and extensive collection offered by the editors and contributors within this volume has brought me to reflect anew on these complex questions of canon, disciplinarity, and boundaries. Namely, this volume accentuates for me the stunning productivity of Indigenous scholars and their allies, *within settler colonial contexts*, over the past several decades. They stand with tricontinental scholars, to be sure, but they also stand on their own merits. This is why such a volume is particularly gratifying to see: the richness of it is testament to the richness of the contemporary critical scholarly engagement with settler colonialism, be this through the burgeoning fields of Indigenous studies and settler colonial studies or from scholars in traditional disciplines who share space and common cause with these.

Some of the key themes broached by contributors, and reflective of the distinctive scholarly work concerning Indigenous Peoples and settler colonialism, are those of violence, resistance, and relationality. Because, yes, a core lesson still being learned by many Canadians is that violence, in the settler colonial context, is both *historical* (Daschuk and

Kulchyski, respectively, in this volume) and *ongoing* (Duhamel, Lindgren and Stewart, and Major—among all the other contributors in this volume). As mentioned by multiple authors in this volume, the paradigmatic expression of the ongoing nature of settler colonial violence is found in Patrick Wolfe's clarification that settler colonialism is a *structure* and not an *event*.[19] In short, although the modalities and methods of settler colonialism may change with time, the underlying objective of colonial dispossession—that the settler enjoy the spoils of dispossession—does not change. In addition, scholars in the social sciences and humanities emphasize that violence is experienced and transmitted via a plurality of modalities. It can be physical or non-physical,[20] sourced in a variety of levels of awareness, intentionality, action, *and* policy, and affect a variety of groups, categories, or markers of identity. These intricacies concerning violence, often overlooked in broader societal and political discourses, relate closely to Duhamel's critique of conventional frameworks for understanding violence against missing and murdered Indigenous women, girls, and 2SLGBTQQIA+ people. Relatedly, contemporary scholarly work recognizes the above-mentioned variabilities within the scope of genocide as well[21]—key advancements within genocide studies that underlie the chapters offered by MacDonald, Woolford, and Farber and Rudner.

The prospect of resistance to the violences of settler colonialism is indelibly entwined with the issue of relationality. And herein lies a contentious set of moral complexities for our times. In many instances, the work that we do is not necessarily a matter of having all the answers but of at the very least asking the right questions. What does it mean to be non-Indigenous in the settler colonial context? All the more complex, what does it mean to be *newly arrived* into this dynamic, especially for those who themselves descend from the displacements of slavery, colonization, and empire? This is where the critical engagement in *On Settler Colonialism in Canada* shines, bringing the reader to consider complex questions—pertinent to a country in which 44 percent of the population are either first-generation or second-generation Canadians[22]—related to displacement, implicatedness, complicity, identity, and solidarity with Indigenous Peoples (see Jiwa, Midzain-Gobin, Parasram, McAllister, and Bryan in this volume). Questions concerning the varied positionalities of peoples within the settler colonial context are not purely of recent vintage, however, as evidenced by Wong's discussion of the deeply racialized exploitation of Chinese labour from the nineteenth century onward, and by Melançon's incisive analysis of French-Canadian narratives of conquest as a settler move to innocence.[23]

Lastly, with the benefit of Indigenous knowledges, relationality truly comes to the fore. Within the Canadian context, one of the earliest manifestations of this was likely in Indigenous conceptions of the treaty relationship itself, with the forging of sacred and reciprocal bonds, mutual responsibilities, and an enduring kinship between the treaty parties. Though Canada often forgets the nature of this relationship, the lesson continues to be taught time and again, most recently with the modern adage of "we are all treaty people." Canada would do well to continue to learn from Indigenous knowledges when it comes to relationships. With the convergence of Indigenous ontologies and post-humanist/new materialist approaches in the social sciences,[24] Woolford's chapter reveals that the new lesson finally coming to be recognized within critical scholarship is our undeniable and essential relationship to the more-than-human: be this with non-human animals[25] or something as essential as water itself.[26]

If *one duck* tells me anything, it is that we all find our way into critical scholarship along distinct paths. What this makes for, within a diverse and changing settler colonial context, however, is a depth and breadth of critical engagements with settler colonialism that make for a positively flourishing area of scholarship. There is much work done, and much work to do. Having a collection that brings this into frame can put wind in one's sails.

## Notes

1 For a deconstructive critique of the law's logic of exchange or equivalence, see Valverde, "Deconstructive Marxism," 339.

2 *An Act to amend and continue the Act 32–33 Victoria, chapter 3; and to establish and provide for the Government of the Province of Manitoba*, 33 Vict, c 3 (Canada) [*Manitoba Act*].

3 *Constitution Act, 1982*, s. 35, being Schedule B to the *Canada Act 1982* (UK), 1982, c. 11.

4 *R v Powley*, 2003 SCC 43, [2003] 2 S.C.R. 207 [*Powley*].

5 See Patzer, "Even When We're Winning."

6 Rattansi, "Postcolonialism," 481. Italics removed from original.

7 See, for example, Young, *Postcolonialism*.

8 Rattansi, "Postcolonialism," 481. Italics removed from original.

9 Hall, "The West and the Rest," 184–227.

10 Rattansi, "Postcolonialism," 482. Emphasis in original.

11 See Derrida, *Speech and Phenomena*, 156.
12 Spivak, "Can the Subaltern Speak?," 66–111. See, in particular, page 76.
13 See Stoler, "Tense and Tender Ties"; Shackleton, "Native North American Writing"; Nagy, "Native North America."
14 Owens, "As If an Indian Were Really an Indian," 13.
15 Young, *Postcolonialism*, 5.
16 Rattansi, "Postcolonialism," 490–491. Emphasis in original.
17 Rattansi, "Postcolonialism," 492. Emphasis in original.
18 For his influential concept of neo-colonialism, which persists after political independence, see Nkrumah, *Neo-Colonialism*; on national sovereignty's inability to address internal divisions and fragmentation, see Chatterjee, *The Nation and Its Fragments*; on cultural hybridity challenging the idea of cohesive national identities, see Bhabha, *The Location of Culture*; on the challenges wrought by globalization, see Appadurai, *Modernity at Large*; for a critique of the persistence of colonial modes of governance in postcolonial African states, see Mbembe, *On the Postcolony*.
19 Wolfe, "Nation and MiscegeNation," 96; Wolfe, *Settler Colonialism*, 2; Wolfe, "Settler Colonialism," 388.
20 See, for example, Bourdieu's concept of *symbolic violence* in Bourdieu and Wacquant, *An Invitation*.
21 Moses, "Conceptual Blockages"; Powell, "What Do Genocides Kill?"
22 Statistics Canada (Table), "Census Profile, 2021 Census of Population," Statistics Canada Catalogue no. 98-316-X2021001, Ottawa. Last Updated November 15, 2023, https://www12.statcan.gc.ca/census-recensement/2021/dp-pd/prof/index.cfm?lang=e (accessed July 2, 2024).
23 For the concept of the *settler move to innocence*, see Tuck and Yang, "Decolonization Is Not."
24 Rosiek, Snyder, and Pratt, "The New Materialisms."
25 For Indigenous scholarly engagements in this area, see Hubbard, "Buffalo Genocide," 292–305; Todd, "Fish Pluralities."
26 For a similar issue in New Zealand, see O'Bryan, "Giving a Voice to the River."

## Sources

Appadurai, Arjun. *Modernity at Large: Cultural Dimensions of Globalization*. University of Minnesota Press, 1996.

Bhabha, Homi K. *The Location of Culture*. Routledge, 1994.

Bourdieu, Pierre, and Loïc J.D. Wacquant. *An Invitation to Reflexive Sociology*. University of Chicago Press, 1992.

Chatterjee, Partha. *The Nation and Its Fragments: Colonial and Postcolonial Histories*. Princeton University Press, 1993.

Derrida, Jacques. *Speech and Phenomena, and Other Essays on Husserl's Theory of Signs*. Translated by David B. Allison. Northwestern University Press, 1973.

Hall, Stuart. "The West and the Rest: Discourse and Power." In *Formations of Modernity: Understanding Modern Society, an Introduction*, edited by Bram Gieben and Stuart Hall. Polity Press, 1992.

Hubbard, Tasha. "Buffalo Genocide in Nineteenth-Century North America: 'Kill, Skin, and Sell.'" In *Colonial Genocide in Indigenous North America*, edited by Andrew Woolford, Jeff Benvenuto, and Alexander Laban Hinton. Duke University Press, 2014. https://doi.org/10.1515/9780822376149-015.

Mbembe, Achille. *On the Postcolony*. University of California Press, 2001.

Moses, A. Dirk. "Conceptual Blockages and Definitional Dilemmas in the 'Racial Century': Genocides of Indigenous Peoples and the Holocaust." *Patterns of Prejudice* 36, no. 4 (2010): 7–36. https://doi.org/10.1080/003132202128811538.

Nagy, Katalin Bíróné. "Native North America as Reflected in Theories of Colonialism and Postcolonialism: An Overview." *Eger Journal of American Studies* 9 (2005): 75–91.

Nkrumah, Kwame. *Neo-Colonialism: The Last Stage of Imperialism*. Thomas Nelson & Sons, 1965.

O'Bryan, Katie. "Giving a Voice to the River and the Role of Indigenous People: The Whanganui River Settlement and River Management in Victoria." *Australian Indigenous Law Review* 20 (2017): 48–77.

Owens, Louis. "As If an Indian Were Really an Indian: Native American Voices and Postcolonial Theory." In *Native American Representations: First Encounters, Distorted Images, and Literary Appropriations*, edited by Gretchen M. Bataille. University of Nebraska Press, 2001.

Patzer, Jeremy. "Even When We're Winning, Are We Losing? Métis Rights in Canadian Courts." In *Métis in Canada: History, Identity, Law and Politics*, edited by Chris Adams, Gregg Dahl, and Ian Peach. University of Alberta Press, 2013.

Powell, Christopher. "What Do Genocides Kill? A Relational Conception of Genocide." *Journal of Genocide Research* 9, no. 4 (2007): 527–547. https://doi.org/10.1080/14623520701643285.

Rattansi, Ali. "Postcolonialism and Its Discontents." *Economy and Society* 26, no. 4 (1997): 480–500. https://doi.org/10.1080/03085149700000025.

Rosiek, Jerry Lee, Jimmy Snyder, and Scott L. Pratt. "The New Materialisms and Indigenous Theories of Non-Human Agency: Making the Case for Respectful Anti-Colonial Engagement." *Qualitative Inquiry* 26, nos. 3–4 (2019): 331–346. https://doi.org/10.1177/1077800419830135.

Shackleton, Mark. "Native North American Writing and Postcolonialism." *Hungarian Journal of English and American Studies* 7, no. 2 (2001): 69–84.

Spivak, Gayatri Chakravorty. "Can the Subaltern Speak?" In *Colonial Discourse and Post-Colonial Theory: A Reader*, edited by Patrick Williams and Laura Chrisman. Routledge, 2015.

Stoler, Ann Laura. "Tense and Tender Ties: The Politics of Comparison in North American History and (Post) Colonial Studies." *Journal of American History* 88, no. 3 (2001): 829–865. https://doi.org/10.2307/2700385.

Todd, Zoe. "Fish Pluralities: Human-Animal Relations and Sites of Engagement in Paulatuuq, Arctic Canada," *Études/Inuit/Studies* 38, nos. 1–2 (2014): 217–238. https://doi.org/10.7202/1028861ar.

Tuck, Eve, and K. Wayne Yang. "Decolonization Is Not a Metaphor." *Decolonization: Indigeneity, Education & Society* 1, no. 1 (2012): 1–40.

Valverde, Mariana. "Deconstructive Marxism." *Labour/Le Travail* 36 (1995): 329–340.
Wolfe, Patrick. "Nation and MiscegeNation: Discursive Continuity in the Post-Mabo Era." *Social Analysis* 36 (1994): 93–152.
Wolfe, Patrick. "Settler Colonialism and the Elimination of the Native." *Journal of Genocide Research* 8, no. 4 (2006): 387–409. https://doi.org/10.1080/14623520601056240.
Wolfe, Patrick. *Settler Colonialism and the Transformation of Anthropology: The Politics and Poetics of an Ethnographic Event*. Cassell, 1999.
Young, Robert. *Postcolonialism: An Historical Introduction*. Blackwell, 2001.

# Index

C

U